THE AESTHETIC CONTRACT

THE AESTHETIC CONTRACT

Statutes of Art and Intellectual Work in Modernity

HENRY SUSSMAN

STANFORD UNIVERSITY PRESS

Stanford, California

1997

Stanford University Press
Stanford, California
© 1997 by the Board of Trustees
of the Leland Stanford Junior University
Printed in the United States of America

CIP data appear at the end of the book

For Gregor S., Ahab, Moby, Emma B.,
Raskolnikov, René Cardillac, Hop-Frog, Maldoror,
Tamdoror, Minkie, Pookie, Deena,
and Father Al

ACKNOWLEDGMENTS

This is the introduction to a book that would presume one of its primary achievements to be a map. Introductions traditionally incorporate a map or guide to the intellectual and personal inspirations prompting the written responses that follow. Mine will be no exception. J. Hillis Miller, Richard Macksey, and Jacques Derrida continue to be models of intellectual and ethical achievement and sources of guidance and support that I try to emulate. Carol Jacobs, Rodolphe Gasché, Samuel Weber, Werner Hamacher, Jill Robbins, Joan Copjec, Raymond Federman, Susan Eilenberg, Richard Feldstein, Joseph Kronick, Gary Stonum, and Brian McHale are colleagues whose evolving work has been of enormous consequence to my own, and whose support has had tremendous interpersonal consequences. Professor Macksey, in his longstanding role of friendly editor, brought Chapter 7 to any writerly elegance it can claim; Professor Gasché offered valuable criticism of the same chapter and its immediate predecessor. Professor John O'Neill and the students of the Program in Social and Political Thought at York University near Toronto provided me an indispensable first occasion to air the theoretical sections of this book. The astute and constructive comments made by York graduate students John Caruana and Scott Schaffer were particularly helpful.

Helen Tartar, Carola Sautter, Eric Halpern, William Sisler, and Carl Lovitt are editors who have graciously offered their encouragement, good offices, and material support through the inordinately pleasurable collaboration of creating books. Pamela MacFarland Holway and Ann Klefstad of Stanford University Press brought my text to its present level of polish and consistency with wit, patience, and considerable ingenuity.

A substantial portion of this project was completed between February and July of 1994, when I was a senior lecturer in comparative literature at the Hebrew University in Jerusalem. The leave was generously supported by the Fulbright Commission, while the book took shape amid the amazing hospitality and consideration accorded me by students and colleagues in English and comparative literature. My sincere gratitude and happy memories extend, among others, to Shimon Sandbank, Moshe Ron, Zvi Jagendorf, Shuli Barzilai, Ruth Ginzburg, Elizabeth Freund, Baruch Hochman, Lawrence Besserman, Judy Levy, Leona Toker, and Gavriel Ben-Ephraim. Work done at the Camargo Foundation, Cassis, France, in 1985–86 and again in 1990 stands behind this and any of my future work. The foundation and its director, Michael Pretina, have my ongoing appreciation.

Even at a time when comparative literature is a hybrid discipline functioning alongside departments grounded in national languages and literatures and shouldering substantial undergraduate teaching loads, Dean Kerry Grant has demonstrated consistent support and encouragement at SUNY/Buffalo, where the Lockwood Library continues to be an efficacious and affirmative storehouse of resources. Ms. Leslie Walker of the SUNY/Buffalo slide library has been a most cheerful source of visual materials both for the World Civilization course I regularly teach and for the pictorial examples in this volume. Peter Gold, of the Undergraduate College at the same university, has rendered inestimable support to World Civilization faculty and has done much to realize the goal of multicultural general education on campus.

In writing books, I have found one of my fondest fulfillments. The above-named people and institutions, and others, have furnished generous encouragement and support, for which I am and always will be deeply grateful.

CONTENTS

ILLUSTRATIONS

THE AESTHETIC CONTRACT

Criticism and Cartography

What lies ahead of you, in very rough and broad strokes, is a literary map of the broader modernity. Only as I conclude this study do I arrive at the notion of the map as the format of the criticism I have produced here. The modes of criticism are as multitudinous as the types of artifacts that criticism addresses: surely not every critical treatment of a body of texts and paintings results in a map. As is well known, criticism may constitute paraphrase; discursive or generic translation; elucidation; thematic rearrangement; formal analysis; historical or biographical account; the assembly of historical, literary, and extraliterary precedents and sources; the minute analysis of the proliferation and rearrangement of telling sememes; the "application" of certain critical operating systems to the artifact; and even the theoretical reconsideration of critical operating systems, whether as applied to the work in question or in general.

And, I am arguing, one possible product of a critical voyage of discovery is a map, an enunciation of the territory and coordinates within whose parameters certain orders of knowledge and writing hold sway. The unannounced ports of call I visited during my latest critical adventure included Plato, da Vinci, Dürer, Holbein, Luther, Calvin, Shakespeare, Donne, Locke, Berkeley, Hume, Rousseau, Kant, Kleist, Melville, Wittgenstein, Benjamin, and Schiele, Mondrian, and Rothko. Only at journey's end do I recognize the project's ultimate result to be the map of its own possibility. I mean "map" not only in the Foucauldian sense of a somewhat structured, stable compendium of knowledge but in a more dynamic way as well: as the lineaments, outlines, tracings of an invariably provisional, imperfect, and inconclusive assay at knowledge.

At a certain point, my attention shifts away from the singular play of signifiers and codes constitutive of every artifact and toward the wider outlines and patterns traced by the ferment of writers whose fundamental questions achieve a certain degree of satisfaction, and only a certain degree—*only* in script. Writing is the sole significant liberty over the much too vast period I am attempting to characterize. Yet its play is not merely an encompassing whimsy—or an enabling statute—but rather a margin of possibility existing in dynamic relation to overall conditions of knowledge. Partly out of skepticism toward the succession of ages that have been imposed on official knowledge—including the Renaissance, the sixteenth through eighteenth centuries, Romanticism, and modernism—I am attempting to register some of the wider patterns that emerge, in the West, from the script that supplements a tormented individuality, an aggravated need for self-regulation, polarized moral alternatives, and hitherto unprecedented possibilities for privacy, secrecy, and the transgression of inherited values.

A map is by nature a generalization. Even at the largest scale, a map suppresses the local nuances of terrain, geological feature, and configuration that have so much to say concerning the experience of a place. In a sense, the map is insensitive to the very characteristic features we confront as we occupy any single place encompassed by it. The map destroys the very places it is intended to locate. But it does—in large—indicate certain important relations between areas and sites.

What would a map of a distinctive script or writing be? It would be an outline extrapolated from an endless set of squiggles. The map that I am depositing with you, surely for worse as well as for better, is a composite drawing of the traces that emerge from a common predicament underlying conditions of *thought* and *intellectual work* over an age beginning with such phenomena—always in the "West"—as a conflictual relation between ecclesiastical and "national" political organizations; an increasing importance of market economies that subverts the hegemonies of Church and feudalism; and the development of towns and cities toward their modern forms, as seats of markets, homes for secular culture, and sites of privacy and individualistic behavior as well as all the conflicts, "experienced subjectively," that such relative autonomy brings.

I am arguing that over the period in question there is a vague and problematic, but nonetheless pervasive parallelism between the vicissitudes of "subjectivity" and experience, on the one hand, and linguistic possibility and articulation. A double tale demands to be told. The story of subjectivity over the period makes little sense in the absence of its language-oriented supplement, and vice versa. And the parallelism between accounts is not a simple adequation. As *external* constraints on behavior and the ideology that predicates it become effaced, confused, impractical, impossible, an alternate set of controls—ideologically sanctioned, but experienced as human-oriented, "homemade," *internal,* implicit, immanent, take their place. Writing—as characterized by a Borgesian "secret society" of authors, including Shakespeare, Sterne, Nietzsche, Baudelaire, Mallarmé, Kafka, Benjamin, Blanchot, Derrida, and Borges himself—becomes the single dimension for the exercise of a liberty arising in the aftermath of an immanent repression that is itself a response to crude political and ecclesiastical control. The dynamics of writing, and certain elements of the history of aesthetics that it carries with it, becomes the counterrevolution to the Enightenment liberal revolution that initiated the end of the French monarchy, the beginning of the U.S. state, and the adjustments to liberal ideology orchestrated by the Napoleonic adventure, the uprisings of 1848, and subsequent implicated events. The emergent ideology of writing, itself an oxymoron and an antinomy, does not oppose itself to such liberal ideas as universal enfranchisement, but it does, supremely in the case of writers as diverse as Nietzsche and Freud, register the possibility that "homegrown," human-originated controls are more repressive (or debilitating) than ones "experienced externally."

Subjectivity may itself be nothing more than a delusion entrenched through its commonality. It is the sense of individuality, autonomy, discretion, and agency held by the person. The locus of subjectivity is more polymorphous than the delusion itself: how and where do we "experience" our subjectivity? As a mental space, a scene of cognition or thinking? An interpersonal slot, the unique location extrapolable from the sum of our presumably unique map of interpersonal interactions? An ethical position, from which we negotiate the decisions that our social setting and historical moment allow?

Subjectivity may be described from "within" the purported subject; extrinsically, from the perspective of the prevailing ideology in which the subject "operates"; or in some combination of the two. Those who are drawn to characterize subjectivity immanently must invariably address its status as an intuition, whether this intuition is ascribed to timeless and universal aspects of the human condition, as in Kant's *Critique of Pure Reason,* or whether the intuition of being a subject transpires under specific historical and sociopolitical conditions. There are already textual entities who bear the basic traits of modern subjects, from whenever we date their origin, in the literatures of the Egyptian Old and Middle Kingdoms.

Our only record of subjectivity is in language, yet there is a point, in the West, where the spiritual constraints upon subjectivity demand the expulsion of those aspects of language that would limit the purity, ideality, immanence, and intuitiveness of subjective activity. Jacques Derrida powerfully situates this ur-ambivalence in Plato's *Phaedrus* and in the Egyptian mythological and literary sources that the *Phaedrus* appropriates. At least since ancient Egypt there has been a sense of the disruption of idealism (both as a sociopolitical ideology and as a format for personal "experience" and expression) posed by language (whose disruptive functions Derrida links under the umbrella of "writing"). Within the specifically modern rendition of the ongoing cultural struggle between idealism's purity, exclusiveness, self-sacrifice, and self-perfection and language's play, proliferation of possibilities, and confusion of clarity that is the occasion of the following book, the modern "subject" in the West has been cut an unprecedented degree of slack, to which linguistic play furnishes an uncannily available simulacrum. If the following set of texts devolves upon any central "event" in the cultural history of modernity, it is the emergence of the artist as the figure who exercises a certain prerogative in relation to the ideal, but who also indulges, in a privileged fashion, in the linguistic disfiguration that traditionally constitutes the degradation and perversion of the ideal. Within the history that I am tracing, the artist emerges as an inescapable character, situated on both sides of the watershed delineated by the regulative structure of antinomy itself. Since the consolidation of this idealized/degraded position of the artist roughly in the years between 1780 and 1840, it has more than once happened that the statutes of Original Genius and inspired creativity have prevailed in artifacts and productions despite producers' extreme skepticism toward this ideology. Indeed, one of the primary paradoxes conditioning intellectual work at the present moment of activity is the degree to which statutes of originality, "brilliance," and paradigmatic superiority continue to operate in spite of the availability of rhetorical and deconstructive modes of exegesis that are fundamentally inimical to these assertions.

I posit the notion of the aesthetic contract developed over the following pages in part as an alternate paradigm for artistic and intellectual production over the broader modernity, one less invested in presuppositions regarding intuition, inspiration, faculties, and powers. There is surely a strongly sociological dimension to the notion of the aesthetic contract, one that may be indicative of my desire to restore social thought to some of its prominence as an arena receptive to theoretical issues and the theoretical elaboration of culture and artifacts. It was, for example, in theoretically oriented departments of sociology and anthropology that the contributions of Barthes,

Lévi-Strauss, Adorno, and Benjamin first became known to audiences in the United States and Canada.

The notion of the aesthetic contract is a compelling one for me because it is implicitly endowed with an allegorical dimension. As an alternative to scenarios of originality and inspiration, I am arguing that modes of production (that is, French symbolist poetry, cubist painting, Elizabethan sonnets, deconstructive exegeses) arise, and then fall into disfavor, less in keeping with essential transcendental qualities, and far more in conformity with sociological principles having to do with recognition, mutual affirmation, and promotion. The notion of the aesthetic contract is allegorical to the core, because the same principles (substantively) defining the artist are at play in the dynamics between schools of thought, production, and style. The very set of concepts evident in the construction of the artist is in question as various contracts and their corollaries go in and out of effect. I believe that the notion of the aesthetic contract of the broader modernity elaborated above all in this Introduction and in Chapters 1 through 6, functions both on constative and performative levels.[1] The first arena in which I was able to discern the operation of this contract was the interplay between interpretative models in the contemporary intellectual marketplace. There is, in other words, an important extension of the aesthetic contract within the purview of the critical contract. (Indeed, it may be the latter that structures the former.) The intellectual and cultural histories of artifacts and their modes and styles may well be illuminated more compellingly by notions of contracts that fluctuate in validity than by scenarios of unique and inspired artists, each with a privileged relation to "reality" or "the truth."

The exasperatingly complex and difficult interplay between writing and subjectivity is thus implicated in the emergence of a modernity that can account, in however specific and differentiated a way, for certain pivotal conditions of knowledge in the West over the past several hundred years. It is not by accident that precisely the same problem—the conflict between language and subjectivity-driven models of thought—bedevils the enterprise of cultural exegesis in the West and beyond as I write. The extreme positions of this tension—wholesale dismissal of the subjective and psychological by rhetorically "driven" modes of thinking, with a parallel rejection of the focus on language on the part of interest-oriented and area-studies approaches (including *some* New Historicism and cultural studies) because of the former's purported insensitivity to considerations of history, class, race, gender, and related subjective conditions—the extreme possibilities in this conflict are only too attractive, because they resolve it and allow the business of concept-model-application to go on as usual. Everything that my own compulsive writing-habit has taught me, including my own early exposure to "the subjective experience of emptiness" at play in the West since the beginning of the broader modernity, militates for an allowance of understandings conditioned by *both* the dynamics of the linguistic medium *and* considerations of subjectivity. We should *entertain*—humor, tolerate, allow, nurture, know— illuminations emanating from both these (at times antithetical) frameworks, because *at times, under different circumstances,* we have need of their contrary illuminations.

Writing and subjectivity exist at best, in relation to each other, askew. This is a condition that antedates modernity, in the historical, epistemological, and writerly senses with which "modernity" will be endowed in the following study. It is not a question whether writing and subjectivity falsify each other—they are too coincident while disengaged for that. Kant erred in positing a unified intuition by which the Transcendental would make itself known, to those *in the know* and those not. Writing and subjectivity speak to two sets of issues and two modes of knowledge. Each is predicated by its own set of "takes." Each explains its own set of situations. Alas, both are made known to us by language. The distinctive modern tragedy is the futile effort to resolve the registers of writing and subjectivity. (This may be a thumbnail definition of the tragic genre itself.) Because the knowledges of writing and experience are transmitted via the same linguistic medium, we are fated to attempt to resolve the two domains. But alas, as in tragedy, what is so intimate, so close, is only too far. We could learn an enormous amount, and transform our interdisciplinary squabbles into profound questioning, if we could only *allow* for both the inquiries and the results of models oriented to language and those oriented to subjectivity. A frank acknowledgment of the differences and values of these two domains would obviate the need for much interdisciplinary axe-grinding.

A map is an "inert image"[2] of a near-infinitude of squiggles, each of which arises in its moment and predicament, each of which points to *something*. The contours on a map, however large the scale, hopelessly generalize the features—natural and political boundaries, differences in density and fundament, elevations and declivities—on which it is based. The compression of particular details and extrapolation of overarching contours involved in mapmaking is gross, *immense*. Why make maps? Why foist them upon the public, as if there were a need for them? If their distortion is so unconscionable, why not simply call for their demise and discontinuation?

There is an answer, in writing, to this question at the end of *Du côté de chez Swann*, the initial segment of Marcel Proust's grand survey of culture, writing, society, and subjectivity under conditions of modernity, in *A la re-*

cherche du temps perdu. The narrator compares reminiscence to two different ways of "experiencing" space, one reading its stabilized representation on a map and one being subjected to its anomalies by passing through it. The passage I have in mind recounts the very origin of the writer's vocation, his reminiscence of his earliest problematization of how writing could preserve and annotate his beloved impressions as well as his disappointments. The "mature" narrator recounts his youthful concern that the evanescence of his impressions would distract him from his task of perceiving "what lay beneath them" (*SW*, 195).[3] It is precisely this penetration to the depths of a rich phenomenal surface that defines, for the narrator of the *Recherche,* the crux of the writer's vocation.

> It was certainly not impressions of this sort that could restore the hope I had lost of succeeding one day in becoming an author and poet, for each of them was associated with some material [*particulier*] object devoid of intellectual value and suggesting no abstract truth. But at least they gave me an unreasoning [*irraisonné*] pleasure, the illusion of a sort of fecundity, and thereby distracted me from the tedium, from the sense of my own impotence which I had felt whenever I had sought a philosophic theme [*sujet*] for some great literary work. But so arduous was the task [*le devoir*] imposed on my conscience by these impressions of form or scent or colour—to try to perceive what lay hidden, beneath [*derrière*] them—that I was not long in seeking an excuse which would allow me to relax so strenuous an effort and to spare myself the fatigue that it involved. As good luck would have it, my parents would call me; I felt that I did not, for the moment, enjoy the tranquillity necessary for the successful pursuit of my researches. (*SW*, 195)

A passage in a monumental work entitled *A la recherche du temps perdu,* an epigenetic passage both returning in time to the source of the writer's vocation and defining that work in terms of an empirical-aesthetic *research*—such a "moment" in the text can only be pivotal. Proust's major work has for many reasons been typecast as marginal and eccentric: its length, the equality of the credence it lends to homosexual and heterosexual lifestyles, its stylistic excesses, and its sociological breadth. Yet despite these extremities, the young artist's understanding of his writerly vocation places him well within the range of the statutes for creative and intellectual work prevailing over what will be called below "the broader modernity," or simply "modernity": there is the possibility that his "impressions," the reactions of a discrete individual to his environment, could be both unique and worthy of public attention; there is the desire to imbue these observations with some "scientific" objectivity, scientificity being less a matter of protocols and equipment than the implicit belief that human beings alone could generate implicit criteria for the truth and value of human observations; finally, there is the awareness of the fragile interface between empirical experience and representation (in writing), the only way that the writer's sensibility will be transferred to some public. The youthful narrator (Proust coyly holds out to us, near the very end of the monumental text, the possibility of addressing him as "Marcel") is quite "aware" of his vocation within a culture and history in which human individuality could be the source of something precious to the community; he realizes that the mining of this value, under the rubric of the enterprise of Art, requires special faculties and skills that will be deployed in a confrontation with obstacles of exasperating difficulty, such as the deferred translation of unique impressions into public language. It requires, for example, both special vision and ingenuity to perceive and write "what lay hidden beneath" the impressions emanating from the phenomenal field. It may be a striking insight on the part of the "youthful" Marcel that he is already an artist, but his definition of this special vocation is already in keeping with the history of individuality in modernity and with the designation of the artist as the gifted individual who will, with both credit and risk as rewards, negotiate the "higher" powers, whether these emanate from the sublime heights or the ineffable depths (it is the latter case that prevails throughout Proust).

The backward-looking narrative of the *Recherche* is here remembering both the epigenesis of writing and the writer's special proclivities for this endeavor. It is not surprising, then, that the narrative, having set this framework for the artistic vocation, should proceed to what might be called a *demonstration* of the artist-in-question's early indications of his gifts. There are two primary examples of these gifts that unfold in the sentences immediately following those cited above: one involves a special sensitivity to the perceptual field and what lies behind it; the other requires a unique awareness of spatial relations both on immediate and grand (environmental) levels and the ability to maintain consciousness of changes in both registers of scale at the same time. One of Proust's illustrations of the special skills required of the artist, in other words, is facility at mapping: conceptualizing the broader map (or narrative framework, in the case of a novel, even a long one) on which a plethora of discrete events and changes transpire. The *Recherche*'s emphasis on place names, shifts of location to special sites of vision and creativity (Venice, for example), and the local differences of the regions of France (and the nobility who embody these regions) is in keeping with this selection of mapping, vision, and sensibility at the widest scale, as a basic aesthetic facility. (Please note, in keeping with these sentences, that in offering you "a map of the broader modernity" as my ultimate finding in this study, I am betraying my own claim to achievement on an artistic scale.)

And so I would concern myself no longer with the mystery [*chose inconnue*]
that lay hidden in a shape or a perfume, quite at ease in my mind since I was
taking it home with me, protected by its visible covering which I had imprinted on my mind and beneath which I should find it still alive, like the fish
which, on days when I had been allowed to go out fishing, I used to carry
back in my basket, covered by a layer of grass which kept them cool and
fresh. Having reached home I would begin to think of something else, and so
my mind would become littered (as my room was with the flowers that I had
gathered on my walks, or the odds and ends that people had given me) with
a mass of disparate images [*images différentes*]—the play of sunlight on a stone,
a roof, the sound of a bell, the smell of fallen leaves—beneath which the reality I once sensed, but never had the will-power to discover and bring to
light, has long since perished. (*SW,* 195–96)

The Proustian artist as a young man in this passage serves as a special pro-
tector of the particular, in whose details, prefiguring Borges's Funes, he discerns a special significance. The young narrator preserves the "odds and
ends" of sensation and perception that other individuals discard by reflex; he
keeps these impressions "cool and fresh," like the bounty of a fishing trip,
even while lacking a pragmatic sense of their utility. The poignancy of the
particular details to which he is sensitive and that he retains, such as the evanescent toll of a bell, the perfume of decaying leaves, extends to the enterprise
of appreciating and remembering that which is otherwise ignored and
lost. Yet there is another model for the artist in these pages, distinct from
the servant of the minute, the memory of the evanescent, and the infuser of
the precious into the public sensibility. This other artist is a geometer, not
unlike the land-surveyor of Kafka's *The Castle,* who scrutinizes a panorama with Cartesian features that nonetheless incorporates the anomalous
and the incommensurable. I am arguing here that one function that can be
served by a critical discourse that has allowed itself to be informed by the
specifications of the modern aesthetic contract is the presentation of a map
within whose parameters certain bounded games and experiments in art and
culture transpire. Seated beside Dr. Percepied (a reference, perhaps, to
Charles Bovary, who ill-advisedly mangles Hyppolite's clubfoot in Flaubert's
novel) in the latter's carriage, the youthful "Marcel" observes the shifting
silhouettes of church spires on the horizon as the vehicle moves between the
local villages:

At a bend in the road I experienced, suddenly, that special pleasure which
was unlike any other, on catching sight of the twin steeples of Martinville,
bathed in the setting sun and constantly changing their position with the
movement of the carriage and the windings of the road, and then of a third

steeple, that of Vieuxvicq, which, although separated from them by a hill and
a valley, and rising from rather higher ground in the distance, appeared none
the less to be standing by their side.

In noticing and registering [*constantant*] the shape of their spires [*flèche*],
their shifting lines, the sunny warmth of their surfaces, I felt that I was not
penetrating to the core of my impression, that something more lay behind
that mobility, that luminosity, something which they seemed at once to contain and to conceal.

The steeples appeared so distant, and we seemed to be getting so little
nearer them, that I was astonished when, a few minutes later, we drew up
outside the church of Martinville. I did not know the reason for the pleasure
I had felt on seeing them upon the horizon, and the business [*l'obligation*] of
trying to discover that reason seemed to me irksome; I wanted to store away
in my mind those shifting, sunlit planes [*ces lignes remuantes*] and, for the time
being, to think of them no more. (*SW*, 196−97)

The youthful writer here registers, takes note of, a contrast in the concrete
experience of space, in its shifts of terrain and perspective, an experience that
must sometimes allow for anomalies (near-far shifts, unexpected juxtapositions); he notes the striking difference between this dynamic space and its
stabilized counterpart as represented in maps and charts. As in the above passage that notes the artist's sensitivity to singular and fleeting impressions, the
translation of the narrator's spatial intuitions into writing is a process shrouded
in uncertainty. Yet even in the empirical field, the narrator, while fascinated
by space's destabilizing possibilities, betrays the sensibility of a mapmaker, of
one who wishes to inscribe and register movements and impressions first
appearing *in fine* within the parameters of an encompassing framework, even
if this larger scale is replete with its own distortions. (This is the fictive equivalent of relativity's account of anomalies in the relation between matter and
energy and in the impact of the scientific observer that can be discerned only
at the extremes of universal scale and the speed of light.) [4]

The modern artist, according to Proust's rendition, is a mapmaker at the
same time she or he is a privileged ally of the singular, the evanescent, and
the minor. It is important, within the Proustian sensibility, to maintain some
fragile hold upon the wider patterns in which events, impressions, and representations maintain themselves, as well as upon the minute particulars. The
scene of the youthful narrator's ride through the Combray neighborhood
with Dr. Percepied incorporates not only "Marcel's" liquid impressions but
the preserved, *Aufgehoben* text in which, while still a child, he set down these
impressions in writing. The carriage-ride episode is thus epigenetic of writing in the full sense of the word: it presents the evolution of the sensibility
that could generate something worthy to write; and it cites the writing

that the youthful artist was able to compose in response to his narrated "experience."

The narrative, in reaching in this episode toward an account of art in the broader modernity, encompasses several simultaneous functions: it remembers a moment in the surrogate artist's "life" when sensations and impressions were particularly vibrant; it registers certain aptitudes conducive to artistic creativity and production. Among these latter must be numbered sensitivities (for example, to colors, sounds, and spatiotemporal conditions) and faculties (in the areas of narrative and mapmaking, for instance). The passage reenacts a peak early moment in the young artist's career, when he succeeded in a task that has repeatedly been characterized as excruciatingly difficult and elusive: retaining quintessentially fleeting impressions long enough to deploy them in a written composition that is successful from a representational point of view, that manages to convey the vividness and singularity that made them notable in the first place.

This episode, in which mapmaking plays a significant role, thus *demonstrates* at the same time that it *remembers*. It demonstrates the skills and proclivities that the youthful artist needed to have, and it demonstrates the rising of the remembered artist in question to those particular demands. The narrative incorporates a youthful piece of writing by the exemplary modern artist. Whether or not it was composed by the young Marcel Proust is not terribly important. In terms of the present discussion, what is important about this graft is twofold: the aesthetic sensibility that predicates the incorporated fragment is in keeping with the modern personification of the artist and the characteristics of the artist formulated in the chapters below; and a significant product of the artistic process is a map of the territory within which the distinctively modern freedom of inscription takes place.

> The minutes passed, we were travelling fast, and yet the three steeples were always a long way ahead of us, like three birds perched [*posés*] upon the plain, motionless and conspicuous in the sunlight. Then the steeple of Vieuxvicq drew aside, took its proper distance, and the steeples of Martinville remained alone, gilded by the light of the setting sun which, even at that distance, I could see playing and smiling upon their sloping sides. We had been so long in approaching that I was thinking of the time that must still elapse before we could reach them when, all of a sudden, the carriage turned a corner and set us down at their feet; and they had flung themselves so abruptly in our path that we had barely time to stop before being dashed [*ne pas se heurter*] against the porch. (*SW*, 198)

This passage substantively repeats what the backward-looking narrator has told us, but in this iteration, only a few lines down from the initial account,

we are to believe that the current piece of writing is an "old" one, composed
shortly after the spatial and perspectival experience itself, when the youthful
narrator still spent his summers at Combray. Proust is not known for being
compact in his writing style; even so, the cited "youthful" extract entails a
degree of repetitiveness unusual for its author, at whatever age it was written.
The utility of the repetition doesn't consist in hammering home the point
that seemingly inert space can play tricks when observed (or "experienced")
from the perspective of two registers simultaneously; the "mature" narrator
established that only too well. The repetitiveness of the relevant points arises
in the joy of grafting; in the certitude that certain "experiences," "phrases,"
and modes of expression remain constant despite the vicissitudes of circumstances and age. And indeed, those inclinations and faculties whose constancy
the narrative is emphasizing through the mechanism of its extended citation
are, *au fond,* aesthetic ones. The "young Marcel" receives an opportunity to
shine here, to shine through the advanced age and "maturity" of his older
emanation. Even as a child, the narrator is able to add allegorical flourishes
to phenomenologically vivid and aesthetically coded descriptions.

> We resumed our journey. We had left Martinville some little time, and the
> village, after accompanying us for a few seconds, had already disappeared,
> when, lingering alone on the horizon to watch our flight, its steeples and that
> of Vieuxvicq waved once again their sun-bathed pinnacles in token of fare-
> well. Sometimes one would withdraw, so that the other two might watch us
> for a moment still; then the road changed direction, they veered in the eve-
> ning light like three golden pivots, and vanished from my sight. . . . They
> made me think, too, of three maidens in a legend, abandoned in a lonely
> place over which night [*l'obscurité*] had begun to fall; and as we drew away
> from them at a gallop, I could see them timidly seeking their way, and after
> some awkward, stumbling movements [*gauches trébuchements*] of their noble
> silhouettes, drawing close to one another . . . forming now against the still
> rosy sky no more than a single dusky shape [*ne plus . . . qu'une seule forme noir*].
> (*SW,* 198)

Proust's *Recherche,* one of the towering early twentieth-century works of
gay literature, is no more a place to visit in search of phallic towers than it is
a showcase for macho heroes. (Robert Saint-Loup is both the rule and the
exception.) In the end, the steeples withdraw any rigidity in their location
and their particularity. They become timid maidens instead of transcendental
pricks. This is an *early* fancy on the part of the narrator. And yet the entire
steeple passage, the narrative "surround" as well as the "graft," with its multiple (directional, temporal, and citational) indices, implicates mapmaking,
and the sensibility that mapmaking entails, among the irreducible compo-

nents of artistry as the intensification of freedom and individuality during the broader modernity. In its fascination with topography, Proust's text joins a body of work whose privileged sites include Swift, Kleist, Dickens, Tennyson, Hardy, Faulkner, Kafka, Borges, and Calvino. It so happens that several of these writers have figured prominently on the map of J. Hillis Miller's reading, and are deployed in his recent *Topographies,* a splendid exploration of the topographical contours of texts at the same time that it is a chart of key sites that have inspired his particular literary imagination and critical acuity. Miller incorporates into his study many of the inevitable ports of call in an exploration of literary topography: Hardy, Dickens, Tennyson, Nietzsche, and Faulkner, to name a few. Kleist, Kafka, and Proust are writers who appear prominently both in Miller's excursus and in the one that follows. Where Miller holds true to a tropic *space* of representation, with its corresponding theater of allegory and hermeneutics, readers will find that the present study offers itself as a map of a historical epoch, what I am calling the broader modernity, and therefore assumes the paradoxical status of a *map of time.*[5]

<hr>

The following readings of a wide range of artifacts are connected by a common argument concerning the nature of subjectivity and the status of art and writing over several hundred years. Such coherence, or attempted coherence, in an extended study is a first for me. There is an implicit position regarding historical and cultural periodization in this argument, and before writing further, I should render it explicit.

Having agonized in earlier work about the parameters of modernism and postmodernism, attempting to satisfy both the improvisational radicality and historical specificity of these categories, how is it that I am now willing to lump productions spanning a megaperiod at least from the Renaissance to modernism together? By the constellation assembled in this study, the mega- (or is it meta?) period would roughly extend 400 years, from 1545, when the Complete Edition to Luther's Latin writings appeared, to 1945, the end of all but the purely formal Modern. I do so presupposing some correlation, although a problematic and interesting one, between conditions of subjectivity and thought and the aesthetic enterprise that, in different attitudes, supplements, embellishes, exemplifies, figures, and allegorizes these conditions. I am implicitly arguing that "base conditions" of thought and subjectivity, somewhat akin to Foucauldian *épistème,* are a more meaningful way of identifying an age than matters of technology, warfare, ruling dynasties, and other time-specific criteria, although these can be terribly important, as will be indicated in Chapters 8 and 9.

From the perspective of the conditions under which (at least urbanized) Europeans and U.S. inhabitants have lived, the histories of art and intellectual production require only a single mega-period from the epoch of the Dürer painting that is the insignia of this project at least through modernism. This is because the freedoms, repressions, and defenses that furnish the most meaningful context for creative production and thinking remain fairly constant over this period. Even writing, which brackets the delusions of subjectivity with such finesse and finitude, has a location on the map of the aesthetic enterprise and its aspirations. At a certain point in the interplay between writing and sanctioned modern Western aesthetics, the latter disavows the former in the name of situating art at the interstice between the transcendental and the empirical. Even so, there is a degree to which the promise of freedom and systematic liminality formulated in Enlightenment-Romantic aesthetics infiltrates writing on the far side of modernity.

Writing is the only meaningful Other and liberty of a Western subject who has remained more or less intact since the days of Dürer, Luther, Calvin, Cervantes, Shakespeare, and Descartes. It is in the context of the perdurance of this subject, and the writing that both does and undoes "it," that the assertion of an essential difference between the productions of the eighteenth and nineteenth centuries stretches credibility. A more convenient hypothesis in terms of the present project (and a book is seldom more than a working hypothesis) projects the scope and persistence of the broader modernity, the arena in which Western people coped with unprecedented possibilities for discretion emerging from a range of tangible and intangible conditions. Within this modernity, events do occur in sequence: there are reasons why the Thirty Years' War and the French Revolution take place when they do. But the notion of the broader modernity makes it possible, for however fleeting a moment, to understand a wide range of phenomena and artifacts in terms of an ongoing progression of emancipations, self-regulations, and phantasmatic displacements and allegorizations of these eventualities within the sphere of aesthetic production.

Under the purview of the broader modernity, the modernism and postmodernism (c. 1890–) whose artifacts, so dear to me, have been the starting point for my own cultivation constitute both the culmination of and the departure from this implied system. One way of talking about modernism's "characteristic" works would be to say that they displace a liberty that has accrued to people onto the perceptual field and the elements of language. Subjective metaphysics goes; a vibrant play of structures, dimensions, shapes, literary characters, and modes remains. Art analyzes at least as much as it asserts, espouses. Unities, harmonies, and resolutions go; affect, mood, coloration, sexual desire remain. Yet already implicit in modernism is the atonality, the discoloration—what I have elsewhere called indifference—that for me captures the mood-change of postmodernism. Does the postmodern persistently marshal itself toward an exit from the epoch defined by the broader modernity and its remarkable perdurance? Quite possibly.

To a certain extent, conceptualizing literary and cultural histories as a series of prevailing aesthetic contracts that go into and out of effect also addresses the question of periodization that I am raising here. The unprecedented liberty and discretion of the modern subject may figure in a broad range of different aesthetic contracts, including eighteenth-century novels and the conceptual platforms of empiricist philosophy. But this drama of freedom, enquiry, self-imposed restraint, and social collaboration or isolation does not extend to all contracts. As will be formulated in Chapter 6, one definition of postmodernism is a series of aesthetic contracts from which clauses concerning conventional desire, identity, and representability have been largely suspended.

~

On a map of my own writing, the last port of call on my journey and experiment was a study of contemporary object-relations theory in psychoanalysis and its implications for critical theory: *Psyche and Text: The Sublime and the Grandiose in Literature, Psychopathology, and Culture.*[6] Object-relations theory furnishes an indispensable interpersonal supplement both to the Freudian field, which is ultimately oriented to the vicissitudes of the drive, and to the Lacanian revision, which pursues the linguistic constitution of the psyche and its manifestations. In extrapolating the interpersonal dimensions and implications that get lost amid the foci of the Freudian and Lacanian worlds, object-relations theory performs an indispensable service. Precisely by virtue of its vocation, this model does not always aspire to the same conceptual rigor as its Freudian and Lacanian counterparts. It is hazy, for example, in its scenario of "introjection." Writers such as Roy Schaefer have only begun the analysis of what can be rigorously meant by "incorporation," "internalization," "projection," and the like.[7] Object-relations theory hinges on the boundaries that presumably separate one psyche from another, but it has not yet explored the implications of such spatial metaphors on their own terms. This psychoanalytical model, by the same token, has not reached a definitive point of departure from its Freudian precedents. In keeping with

Margaret Mahler's "separation-individuation subphase,"[8] it declares its autonomy from what Greenberg and Mitchell term the Freudian "drive-structure model"[9] while still depending on Freudian formats in strange ways—for example, in Kohut's invocation of the "reality ego" in contrast to the excesses of the grandiose,[10] or in Kernberg's explanation of borderline bipolarity as one effect of a vicious superego.[11]

In spite of such theoretical issues yet to be brought to a higher level of polish, the psychoanalytical theory of object relations does furnish a compelling scenario for psychological conditions in an age of demographic stress, sociological isolation, and what Kernberg terms "the subjective experience of emptiness."[12] Its account of the day-to-day conditions of psychological life hinges on jarring fluctuations between moderation, modesty, existence in what Hartmann has described as the "nonconflictual sphere,"[13] and grandiosity, a state denoted by expansiveness, whether in terms of awe, contempt toward others, or living "on the edge." Although there are some affinities between the grandiose and the extreme conditions of both the id and superego, object-relations theory focuses on the "origin" and impact of this psychological roller-coasting in interpersonal relations rather than as an effect of fulfilled or unrealized drives. As I suggested in my earlier study, this model does open up certain exciting avenues of speculation from a linguistic point of view, above all concerning the crucial notion of introjections, which comprise a "primitive" register of private expressions, many of which are absorbed at the pre-Oedipal stage, before they can be moderated by logic or interpersonal nurturing. According to object-relations theory, the basic "language of our selves" is a palimpsest of "primitive" and modulated expressions, much as our psychological experience fluctuates between grandiose and moderate states. Yet this parallel account of the impact of interpersonal relations upon language does not take linguistic—and related conceptual, cognitive, and visual—phenomena "at their word" to the same degree as Lacanian psychology insists upon.

The most dramatic effect of the pronounced fragmentation of subject-conditions instituted if not invented by modernity may well be "splitting," the condition chronicled by object-relations theorists in which clients readily pass between radically different and in some cases antithetical states (of emotion, ethical awareness, and behavior) with little marking of the disparities or concern for them.[14] "Splitting" belies the dialectical nature of the fissures the term summons up. It is an overall rubric that characterizes a broad range of lapses, whether described as parataxes, caesuras, or vacancies that take place. Object-relations theorists stress a number of tendencies on the part of their pathologically narcissistic and/or borderline clients. These include dividing the world into "all good" and "all bad" people and entities, with little middle ground between them; alternately idealizing and devaluing one's fellow human beings, treating them only with a combination of exaggerated admiration and contempt; maintaining an often bewildering combination of destructive and constructive spheres and behaviors alongside each other, in a violent metonymy, and passing with impunity between them.

Though tempered considerably by the history and dynamics of dialectics, the notion of splitting extends far beyond a simple structure of binary opposition. The characterization of consciousness during an age of proliferating authorities and obligations, extreme individuation, and sensory and informational overload requires a motif of differential heterogeneity as much as a structure of dualistic conflict. Although the splitting that pertains to the Kernbergian "subjective experience of emptiness" sometimes involves a division of the world into "all good" and "all evil" valences, this bifurcation is not the sole thrust of its activity or impact. The splitting that increasingly becomes a *general* condition of subjectivity during our age is also a *dissociative* environment allowing for a heterogeneous *coexistence* of moods, aspirations, and acts marked by their violent repudiation of each other. The splitting that characterizes the state of late capitalistic societies as well as the psyches of their citizens is as much a condition of differential heterogeneity as of polar conflict. The breathtaking uncanniness that fictive subjects such as Moosbrugger, a murderer in Robert Musil's *The Man Without Qualities,* or Thomas Harris's Hannibal Lecter—or actual people such as Susan Smith, a South Carolina woman who has confessed to drowning her young children— evoke in us consists as much in the *coexistence* of radically different emotive and cognitive states as in the logical conflict between them. It is the *variety* of the temperamental, ethical, and modal conditions that modern subjects, the descendents of Hamlet, can simultaneously sustain that is at times so awe-inspiring, at times so blood-curdling.

Whether the fundamental thrust of our inquiry is linguistic or subject-based, the notion of splitting has become a prominent and inevitable feature within the landscapes of epistemology and creative work during the broader modernity. Splitting is a paradigm not only for linguistic, psychological, and behavioral *heterogeneity;* it helps account for the *fragmentation* that has been such a major force in art at least since Romantic theory elevated it to an esthetic category. The notion of splitting is broad enough to encompass both the dialectics of bipolar logic and a fragmentation within the subjective sphere that amounts to the maintenance of diverse "self-fragments" alongside each other. One way of conceptualizing the uncanny trope of *parabasis,* for which Friedrich Schlegel is justly remembered, is as a scenario allowing for an endless proliferation of fragments, whether these are represented intra- or extrapsychically.[15] When its historical and cultural implications are extended, the object-relations conception of splitting can be deployed in accounting for a complex predicament prevailing throughout the broader modernity: the continuity of fragmentation within a dialectically structured subjective sphere. Even the work of so linguistically rigorous a philosopher as Jacques Derrida has registered the impact of splitting upon the broader modernity. While strenuously and successfully eschewing subjective constructs, Derrida, in *Glas,* whose bicolumnar architecture spans the Enlightenment and post-modern extremes of modernity, cannot avoid developing a massive rhetoric of cuts, castrations, splits, and divides in characterizing the metaphysics that Hegel assembles and that Genet both empties and brings to an extreme.[16]

In a historical sense, the notion of a borderline that object-relations theory crystallizes in order to characterize the least integrated subjects may be understood as an *extension* of a set of conditions that have been at play in the West since the beginning of the current modernity. Whatever conditions prompt the emergence of this era—and they include the decline of the medieval world order, the rise of towns as market-driven, trade-oriented free zones, and the ideological and epistemological adjustments to Western idealism made by Protestantism (and subsequently, by Catholic countermeasures)—the modern subject is sundered among more authority-sources than he or she can comply with, is faced with more freedom than he or she has been accustomed to, and hence fluctuates between expressions of relative autonomy and a need for self-imposed (defensive) mechanisms of regulation. In this context, it becomes possible to recognize in the psychoanalytical writings of Jacques Lacan an enormously subtle, linguistically oriented schematization of the defenses that the modern subject generates as a means of addressing such conditions as systematic splitting, the extreme proliferation of obligations and their authority-sources, and uncanny freedom. In the culturally oriented work of contemporary critics such as Joan Copjec and Slavoj Žižek,[17] Lacan is more urgently a chronicler and philosopher of modern defensive strategies than the caretaker of the linguistic dimension within the Freudian discourse.

A rather focused exercise on the applicability of the theory of object relations and personality disorders to literary studies led me, in other words, to the historical dawn of the conditions to which these psychosocial phenomena constitute a reaction. What Kernberg, Kohut, and other object-relations theorists mean by "splitting" is merely the extension—exacerbated by millennial demographics and living and working conditions under late capitalism—of the multiple allegiances and obligations (and their impossibility) achieving a recognizable form by the end of the Renaissance. The Romantics and those coming after have to contend not only with the vestiges of the medieval hierarchies that dominated politics, theology, and economics alike, but also with the repressive aspects of the countermeasures to medievalism: the need for a regulation and self-regulation so stringent that it anticipates such characters as Dr. Jekyll and Mr. Hyde, Norman Bates, and Hannibal Lecter, as well as the psychology that accounts for their behavior.

In different ways, the following essays trace out the effects of unprecedented freedom, individuality, privacy, and defensiveness upon culture and experience over the broader modernity. The book begins with Luther and Calvin and ends with Rousseau and Melville. Over this span, art and artistry emerge as a secular arena dramatizing both the capabilities and the dangers of human freedom and its correlative in behavior, creativity. In many ways, the pivot of this book is the enabling legislation for artists, as secular figures who both exemplify and bound human capability, that was drafted by Kant in his *Critique of Judgment*.

PART ONE

The Emergence of the Artist as Priest in a Secular Art Religion

CHAPTER I

Portraits of Modernity

Those bastions of canonical art known as museums overflow with framed faces whose arbitrary Being-there seems to preempt the disclosure of anything beyond the transitoriness of a lost moment or the absence of a certain subject. Yet a portrait-image occasionally trespasses the corridors of the collection in which it is housed or the binding of the book in which it has been reproduced. Such portraits seize us with a violence belying the solemnity prevailing in temples of art and become talismans of the epistemological conditions allowing for their own possibility.

Dürer's Portrait of Heironymus Holzschuher

The portrait—or rather its subject, a certain character—stares at us compellingly across the centuries. It exercises a certain hold on us that is both gripping and uncanny. A more recent rendition of this irresistible hold, one issuing not by chance from the age of Romantic irony, is the hold Coleridge's Ancient Mariner exerts upon the hearers of his compulsively repeated tale.

It may assure us, perhaps, to know that the individual represented in the portrait was named Hieronymus Holzschuher. The portrait was painted by Albrecht Dürer. It is dated 1526. Holzschuher stares out toward stage left at something that in turn exerts some pull on him. He appears to be a man of means and substance. His fur coat is both an account of wealth and an occasion for painterly virtuosity. On the basis of this costume, I suspect that the historian Fernand Braudel would place Holzschuher among a class of rising merchants during an age anticipatory of modern capitalism.[1] There is an ex-

Figure 1. Albrecht Dürer, *Portrait of Hieronymus Holzschuher,* 1526. Reproduced with the kind permission of the Gemäldegalerie, Staatlichen Museen zu Berlin— Preussicher Kulturbesitz.

pression of resolve and personal strength in his mouth, yet his eyes have seen something. Dürer incorporates the wrinkles and bagginess around Holzschuher's eyes into the painted text. Holzschuher, in all his corporeal and economic substantiality, has seen something, is perturbed and agitated. This master is at once a Hegelian bondsman, who has trembled to every fiber.

Holzschuher is a particularly modern subject who has had the audacity to be painted in 1526. He is individuated, tormented, suspicious, beautiful. Dürer has invested a considerable share of painterly love (or *Sorge*) into his subject's hair (scalp and facial) as well as into the fur coat. The hairs that cascade onto Holzschuher's forehead mark his *Angst* in a way even more powerful than the wrinkles.

Holzschuher is a fully individuated, tormented, modern subject, in 1526. His expression assumes an emotional authenticity and realism that simply puncture the intervening time. Holzschuher is painted, in fact, at a perfect distance for a photographic portrait, and the portrait's uncanny realism has a photographic dimension. In this portrait, at least, Dürer has anticipated a great deal, as Shakespeare will do, three quarters of a century later, in *Hamlet* and related dramas. The *Portrait of Hieronymus Holzschuher* is an artifact of intense and disconcerting Benjaminian aura. It resides at an extreme of uncanny modernity in Dürer's work. The artist also bequeathed to us engraved allegories that were steeped in symbolism deriving from remote epistemological epochs. Other of his portraits are similarly dated: none quite stares out at us with Holzschuher's uncanny contemporaneity. Dürer himself resides at an epistemological crossroads. We could invoke Benjamin's vision here: behind Dürer stand the piles of debris created by the already venerable traditions of Western idealism, with its radical mind/body split, its worship of deities (and values) bespeaking unattainable purity, its ethos of exclusivity and unbroken fidelity in religious affiliation and sexual bonding. These vast graveyards of cultural remains almost obscure the horizon. Ahead of Dürer stretches a modernity whose conditions he—along with the love poets of Provence; along with Cervantes, Holbein, and Shakespeare—uncannily anticipated. There is no consistent and coherent picture of this modernity yet: just a random "shot in the dark," an odd snapshot of an individuation and freedom, with their concomitant terror and need for internalized mechanisms of regulation, that become the stock-in-trade of the subject conditions prevailing throughout the broader modernity.

A *Holzschuher* is a maker of wooden shoes, a clog-maker. By what incredible coincidence does Heidegger make Van Gogh's *sabots* a talisman for a twentieth-century aesthetics powered by the disclosure of the linguistic dynamics contained (and released) within cultural codes?[2] Heidegger frames the aura and uncanniness of linguistic disclosure as an *image* for invention, for the play between World and Earth, much as Dürer frames, in his *Portrait of Hieronymus Holzschuher*, the image of a subjectivity constituted by terror, anxiety, indecision, and guilt.

Another Portrait: Holbein's The Ambassadors

Beneath the resplendent costume of the two subjects represented in the painting stands the fact of their remarkable similarity. It is almost as if Holbein squeezes two figures for his painting out of one persona. With a little imagination at the level of window-dressing, one pictorially represented identity can suffice for two figures.[3]

We seem to be universes away from Dürer's setting of unsettling individuation for Hieronymus Holzschuher. Yet whether the painterly world (and the frame) shrinks down to a single, intensely self-aware human surrogate, or whether it accommodates a multiplication of figures (here emulating Hindu sculpture), Holbein's canvas, also emanating from the founding epoch of modern subjectivity, raises a pivotal issue of identity. At the same moment when the individuated, guilt-ridden subject remains a novelty, the idea of doubles and shared identities presents an attractive image. These well-dressed emissaries are nothing if not attractive.

The painting thus issues out of the epoch of *The Return of Martin Guerre*,[4] a time when individuated people are on the way, but when it is possible for one man to usurp the identity of another, in the eyes of the community at least. Identity is the central issue, but it is none too sure.

This is a painting replete with experiments: the enterprise of empiricism has entered the space of painting. Several trappings of science are evident: globes, sextant, barometer. These human emissaries are at leisure to chart, measure, and colonize the world, but it is not terribly important if they are distinct from one another. The arts are at peace with the sciences in the painting as well. Lute, pipes, and psalter are displayed as additional instruments of knowledge just one shelf below the vessels of scientific knowledge.

Stylistically, the painting has its own empirical aspirations. There is the famous isomorphic experiment in the foreground. The painting not only depicts modern science, it *is* that science, at least when the questions concern light, perspective, and outline. The painting is a scientific experiment launched in the quest for knowledge of the order of the visible. In celebration of this quest, the scientific and musical instruments are rendered in exquisite detail; the rug at the top of the stand (*Gestell*)[5] is unflappably accurate despite its fold and buckle; and the floor on which the ambassadors stand is a map of geometric perfection.

Figure 2. Hans Holbein the Younger, *The Ambassadors*, 1533. Reproduced with the kind permission of the National Gallery, London.

There is so much to be known, and it is accessible, even if emissaries have to be sent to great distances. The known articulates itself on markedly different registers, but these are in wondrous communication with each other. The arts and sciences have positioned themselves perfectly to comprise a comprehensive science, a *Gesamtwissenschaft*.

All of this is dawning. An enormous amount of power and knowledge is accessible to modern European society. These ambassadors, by their facial expressions as well as their clothes, are formidable representatives.

But it is not crucial for them at this phase of history to be terribly different from each other. They stare outward not only toward the painter but also toward an unknown that they can still enter collectively. Yet the very unknown they contemplate will someday evolve into an abyss that is experienced, above all, in a most individual, solitary, and sometimes terrifying way.

More Images

The radicality of the portraiture of Dürer and Holbein, in terms of allowing for highly individuated subjects, receives an ample comfirmation when we peruse counterexamples subscribing to the contractual terms governing Renaissance aesthetics. What we find here, as we would expect in Italian examples by the likes of Botticelli or da Vinci, but also in a northern painter such as Hans Memling, is some difficulty in coming to terms with the seedier details of particularity in the depiction of human subjects. Renaissance portraiture, like Renaissance lyrical poetry, moves toward the discreteness of individuals, but insists upon representing them within a framework of high idealization. Renaissance painters remain within an aesthetic contract of exemplary models and geometrical proportions; and if in certain respects they undermine this ideology, they do so under the constraints of formalized idealism. The "early modern" painters we have begun to examine are comfortable with subjects who are simply beyond the pale of ideality in specimen; they are content to paint these very particular individuals—not always beautiful, or uplifted in gesture or expression—in lurid detail.

As my first example of a Renaissance portrait, I select one whose subject can hardly be described as beautiful, Ghirlandaio's *An Old Man and His Grandson* (c. 1480). The middle-aged gentleman on the left of the canvas who lovingly glances down toward his grandson does indeed come replete with warts. This is the famous Renaissance painting of "the man with the cauliflower nose." But the impasse of the portrait is precisely that, even in moving toward something not inspiringly or archetypically beautiful, the protuberances on the gentleman's nose are themselves perfectly regular and geometrical. Each wart is a perfect dome. The grandson is a cherub; the boy's locks flow down in geometrically parallel golden waves. In the background, through a window, we see the landscape that repeats the wave motions in the domestic scene outward toward the horizon (according to Leo Bronstein, a characteristic feature of Renaissance backgrounds).

The impasse of Renaissance portraiture (and I suspect lyrical poetry) is this: a *will* to pass outside the frame of idealization, but a *resolve* to remain within the parameters of a priori rules. These are precisely the rules that "early moderns" such as Dürer and Holbein violate; their primary loyalty is to the individuality and discreteness of their subject matter, not to the implicit operating system of perfect proportionality. Hence their subjects glower at us in a breathtakingly vivid, particular, modern way.

Figure 3. Ghirlandaio, *An Old Man and His Grandson,* 1480. Reproduced with the kind permission of the Musée du Louvre, Paris.

Renaissance painting expresses an impulse to challenge the a priori geometrical rules: it does this through innuendo insinuated within the frame of
ideality, not through a departure from the framework itself.

An example could be Da Vinci's *Mona Lisa* (c. 1505). What could be more
banal? One way of interpreting the famous smile is as the insinuation (lips are
sinuous, if not sensuous) of the nonideal within the representational framework of ideality. The smile is not all that does this: there are the slightly
glazed eyes, the overlarge hands. But the setting, the torso, the posture, the
background: purely "classical." *Mona Lisa* becomes an allegory of the im-
pregnation of utopia by the nonideal, within a painterly aesthetic that follows
classical protocols.

Botticelli's *Birth of Venus* (c. 1480) is another example. Classical rules can
produce an image of female beauty, though the central figure is no one *you*
know. The central figure is surrounded with the mummery of allegory: an
allegorical breath from the angel; an allegorical dress on the lady-in-waiting;
allegorical flowers floating in the air; allegorical sea-waves. The allegory is
supposed to import some discursive meaning to the exquisite central product
of the application of the "classical" rules of beauty. But does it, or is what we
have here again a portraiture whose particularity is restrained by a refusal to
exit the framework allowed by a priori representational rules? Do we not
have here, in other words, a portraiture whose individuation is held to the
same level as its enslavement to the formal equivalent of idealization in
painting?

Memling's portraiture is void even of the attempts to subvert the idealization. The *Portrait of Maarten van Nieuwenhove* and *Portrait of a Lady* are simply
out of this world. Memling adopts a particular *style* of idealization: there is a
contrast between the dark, almond-shaped eyes, with their fetchingly blank
expression, and the invariably ovoid shapes of the faces (at least in young
subjects). A Memling perfect human creature is different from one by Botticelli. But within the Memling style of idealized human representation,
there is Wittgensteinian "family resemblance" to a near-absurd degree.[6] The
Patroness Barbara van Vlaenderberch, in the right panel of a triptych com-
missioned by her husband, is surrounded by eleven of her daughters (and also
Saint Barbara).

"Family resemblance" gives Memling the opportunity to repeat (and
slightly vary) a single model of idealized beauty almost *ad infinitum*. Not one
of the van Vlaenderberch women is what we would call an individual: each
is a (close) variation upon an archetype, configured by idealized, abstract, a
priori proportions and principles. Memling paints in the North. His representations of people are closer to the archetypical representations by Cima-

Figure 4. Hans Memling, Barbara van Vlaenderberch with her daughters and St. Barbara, right wing, *The Triptych of St. Christopher (Moreel Triptych)*, ca. 1484. Reproduced with the kind permission of the Municipal Museum of Fine Arts, Bruges.

bue and Giotto than they are to the "subversive" examples we have examined
by Ghirlandaio and da Vinci.

There is a parallel predicament in the love poetry of the period. Eroticism
is invariably the primary cultural mark of individuation; in the medieval age
and the Renaissance, it is the primary arena in which individuality announces
itself and exists. Yet in the age of the portraits we are examining in this section, the erotic desire by one individual for another cannot exist long without being subsumed within a framework of ideation and ideology. This
tendency is distinct from the one we will observe in Donne's "The Canonization," in Chapter 3 below: by the time of Donne's erotic poetizing, the
poet has access to a full range of secular, pedestrian imagery (from commerce,
diplomacy, and so on) to qualify his yearnings and his arrangements with his
mistress. But in Petrarch's sonnets, there is a tangible tension between the
erotic, which at the time is the only sphere in which there is room for individuality and personal freedom, and the ideal, which in this case functions
as a public register of images and tropes exercising the sociological function
of sanction. As an example much in the spirit of Botticelli's "The Birth of
Venus," one of many examples in which this tension is evident, I select
Petrarch's Sonnet 90 to Laura, "She Used to Let Her Golden Hair Fly Free"
("Erano i capei d'oro l'aura sparsi"):

> She used to let her golden hair fly free
> For the wind to toy and tangle and molest;
> Her eyes were brighter than the radiant west.
> (Seldom they shine so now.) I used to see
>
> Pity look out of those deep eyes on me.
> ("It was false pity," you would now protest.)
> I had love's tinder heaped within my breast;
> What wonder that the flame burned furiously?
>
> She did not walk in any mortal way,
> But with angelic progress; when she spoke,
> Unearthly voices sang in unison.
>
> She seemed divine among the dreary folk
> Of earth. You say she is not so today
> Well, though the bow's unbent, the wound bleeds on.
>
> *Trans. Morris Bishop*[7]

This sonnet cannot broach the issue of Laura's erotic power without almost immediately referring it to two qualifying frameworks: divine transcendence and the temporality of Eternity. In terms of the poem's specific tem-

poral setting, Laura has *lost* the divinity with which she once peered, in pity, at her fellow mortals, including her lover. Yet from a rhetorical point of view, her not walking "in any mortal way," the "unearthly voices" in her speech, and her "seeming" divinity manage to bind, within the safety of the Derridean "guardrail,"[8] the erotic liaison to her lover tangibly described in the first two quatrains.

Eroticism is at play here. A space for the enunciation of very particular observations by very private and unique "individuals" is emerging, but for the nonce, this evolution can only be conveyed by tropological conventions asserting the timeworn human-divine split. Please note, nonetheless, that the divine and human, mortal and immortal spheres exist, in this text, in gentle cooperation and supplementarity. The highly conventional, idealized rhetoric to which Petrarch can yet refer the threats of eroticism and "free agency" is also a force of amelioration: sensuality in Petrarch is spared the violently bipolar attractive/repulsive values that become a necessary defensive posture in a world of direct responsibility to God, without the mediatory conventions. This violent bipolarity, as we shall see, becomes a staple of Western culture with the removal of mediatory institutions, rhetorics, and conventions of self-regulation by Luther, Calvin, and other authors of the Reformation and Counter-Reformation. Petrarch in effect *contains* the impact of an erotic liaison with Laura within a framework of tropes and conventions garnered from classical antiquity. In the post-Reformation modernity subsequent to Petrarch's age, Laura—and her eroticism—circulate free of this baggage. But at the same time, Laura becomes a potential Jezebel; her sensuality is potentially a very dangerous thing, capable of bringing down an entire system of social welfare.

CHAPTER 2

Framing Modernity:
Protestant and Critical Reformations

The more I practice the discipline of criticism, the more explicitly do I find that, in one dimension of my performance, I am telling a story: my discourse is intertwined with narrative. As I confront different hermeneutic problems in progressing from one project to another, I find that the stories I tell have increasingly simple plot structures. The story I began to tell one specific day, let's call it February 2, 1994, has for its "factual" basis the effacement of extrinsic regulatory institutions and structures during what we call the Renaissance; a hitherto unprecedented burden of individuality and liberty, whose delirious possibilities may be most memorably registered in the literature and fine arts of the late eighteenth century and Romanticism; a subjectivity defined by its failure to satisfy competing jurisdictions and by its radical splitting.

Here I at least momentarily follow Max Weber's footsteps in returning to the Protestant Reformation as an informing moment in the emergence of these sociological and subjective conditions:

The Reformation meant not the elimination of the Church's control over everyday life, but rather the substitution of a new form of control for the previous one. It meant the repudiation of a control which was very lax, at that time scarcely perceptible in practice, and hardly more than formal, in favor of a regulation of the whole of conduct which, penetrating to all the departments of private and public life, was infinitely burdensome and earnestly enforced. The rule of the Catholic Church, "punishing the heretic, but indulgent to the sinner," as it was in the past even more than to-day, is now tolerated by peoples of thoroughly modern economic character, and was

borne by the richest and economically most advanced peoples on the earth
about the turn of the fifteenth century. The rule of Calvinism, on the other
hand, as it was enforced in the sixteenth century . . . would be for us the most
absolutely unbearable form of ecclesiastical control of the individual which
could possibly exist. (*PESC,* 36–37)[1]

The development that Weber describes is akin to a pronounced double message regarding authority that prevails in certain nuclear families: the rise of
Protestantism signaled the end of a certain authority system that had been
perceived as corrupt, as interfering in certain crucial aspects of the human-
divine interaction, and as nevertheless, in a certain way, lax. As Weber specifies at the very outset of the concluding segment of his tripartite *Sociology of
Religion,* entitled *The Protestant Ethic and the Spirit of Capitalism,* Protestantism
may have liberated the subject from certain questionable regulations and mediations (inter)posed by the Catholic Church. But Protestantism's "liberation" initiated at the same time the imposition of controls of an even more
intrusive and severe nature.[2] We are uncannily familiar with this new order
of constraints, as we are with the features of Hieronymus Holzschuher's portrait; it speaks of some of the terrors, guilts, and discontinuous shifts between
contentment and anguish characterizing our most contemporary lifestyles.

The Protestant Reformation to which the following study will refer is less
a defining event in the development of a particular religion than a moment
of cultural history with repercussions for all theologies and cultures upon
which it had impact. The occurrences of history are too complex and multifaceted to be ascribed to any single theology or ideology with any degree of
assurance. Fernand Braudel gets this point just right as he dissociates the excruciatingly complicated development of economic forms toward modern
capitalism from any particular theological or ideological framework:

> The fact that Jewish merchants were to be found in all the key centres of cap-
> italism does not mean to say that they created them. There are outstanding
> Jewish scientists all over the world today; are we therefore to describe nuclear
> physics as a Jewish invention? In Amsterdam, they certainly *became* leading
> practitioners of speculation in the forward market of stocks and shares, but
> such manipulations had originated with non-Jewish speculators like Isaac Le
> Maire.
>
> As for Sombart's argument that the capitalist mentality coincides with the
> principle tenets of the Jewish religion, this is to re-echo Max Weber's theory
> about Protestantism, for which there are some good and bad arguments. One
> might just say the same of Islam; "it has been suggested that Islamic law and
> the Islamic ideal of society shaped themselves from the very first in accor-
> dance with the ideas and aims of a rising merchant class," but "this tendency
> [should not be] linked . . . specifically with the religion of Islam itself."[3]

Epistemological and cultural manifestations should not, by the same token, "be linked specifically with" the formulations of any theological or political formation.

The developments of the broader modernity are too intricate and complex to be ascribed to any nation, enterprise, or religion. Braudel's massive *Civilization and Capitalism: 15th–18th Century* is a testament to how many materials, sociopolitical organizations, and ideas were involved in the evolution from such conditions as feudalism, serfdom, and household-based manufacture to the world of high capitalism. The rise of Protestantism is a distinctive event on the temporal map that can be sketched from the period of Braudel's interest, but we need to understand Protestantism as a culture and compendium of certain hermeneutic gestures rather than as an empirical social institution or set of religious practices. In this sense, Protestantism, as a cultural ideology that emerged quite loosely and arbitrarily from certain canonical discourses by Luther, Calvin, Zwingli, and their historical *compères,* entered Catholicism (in its Counter-Reformation measures and tradition), and impacted significantly upon Judaism, Islam, and the emerging national organizations in and around Europe as well.

Only in this loose sense of Protestantism as a body of hermeneutic and cultural moves necessitated from within the history of Western idealism can we say that we are indebted to it for the Declaration of the Rights of Man as for the Holocaust, for the recognition and protection of individual rights, often at considerable social cost, and for the radical splitting depicted in *Psycho* and *The Silence of the Lambs* and prevailing at the psychological borderline. (All of the longstanding religions of the West maintain, in some sector of their field of operation, the sharply polarized moral values that prescribe the psychological borderline.) Protestantism is merely the most recent overall paradigm for what is to be most cherished in liberal, enlightened societies and for the repression that has become a transparent, because so pervasive, aspect of capitalism and late capitalism. Protestantism, in other words, becomes one way of naming the modern ideological framework in which an individual and collective subject is engulfed and tormented by a freedom that has either been won or foisted upon it. So pervasive has the modernity in part implicated by the culture of Protestantism become to the working of late-capitalist societies, that as an epoch and collective state of mind it is inherently self-contradictory. It legislates, at the same time, the acquisitiveness of multinational corporations, the ideology of democracy, the ethos of individual sexual expression, the curiosity of modern science, the vigilance of "opposition" and "activist" organizations, and the stringency of fundamentalist religious sects.

The modernity that emerges from the socioeconomic developments chronicled by Braudel and from the disputations of Western ontotheology over the period is one writ large, in capital (and capitalist) letters, MODER-NITY. (In this text, I do play on the difference between orders of conceptual generality that magiscule and miniscule letters allow. I hope readers will forgive me this.) The modernity that will be the framework for this book is a period over which operate remarkably contemporary conditions of freedom, discretion, and a direct and individualistic approach to authority, whose conditions are "internalized" within the subject. This unprecedented discretion, the effacement of a presumably once lucid and comprehensive medieval world order that once prevailed,[4] occasions internalized mechanisms of self-regulation and control also unprecedented in their severity. The Protestant Reformation emerges in this regard as the broadest and most prominent historical backdrop to these modern subject conditions. The philosophy of Descartes is often cited as the herald to objective as well as subjective conditions in modernity,[5] but I would argue that much of what is treated as most "modern" in Descartes is already conditioned by the arguments concerning freedom, mediation, and political and corporeal corruption in Luther, Calvin, and related theological thinkers of the sixteenth century.[6]

I would argue that the modern institution of the artist is a development in the aftermath of the arguments that were hashed out during and after the Protestant Reformation. By the end of the eighteenth century, it has become pressingly urgent to rethink questions of subjective liberty and social participation and control in secular, antiauthoritarian ways. In many significant ways in this regard, the figure of the artist was a direct descendent of those of the king and the priest. The immediate intuition and inconceivable omniscience with which this notion of "the artist" is endowed owe much to the issues of authority, mediation, individuality, and freedom that the major early Protestants felt compelled to dispute.

$\backsim$

There is a historically nonspecific platform for the following meditations as well. Over the modernity that is the period of this study, linguistic expression and improvisation constitute the text in which (subjective and nonsubjective) singularity and individuation are most sharply underscored. This is, of course, true of every epoch. Language is *always* the dimension of "subjectivity" that is most idiosyncratic and challenging to truisms and generalities enunciated by ideology. The interface between language and subjectivity gives the lie to all historical generalizations, including the ones that I am positing as an intellectual-architectural platform for the following readings and observations.

So the fact that inventive linguistic activity is the sphere in which modern subjects most experience the conditions of individuation and freedom first elaborated by Luther, Calvin, and others is a truism that applies to all historical arenas and periods. Yet illuminating comments can be made about the *particularity* of the subject-language interface over the span of an epistemological epoch. I am arguing not only that there are particular and peculiar conditions characterizing subjectivity and the subject-language interface over the broader modernity; but also that these considerations became crucial in the designation of the artist as the cultural agency for the mediation of affairs with the Transcendental and the Real, at least since the emancipatory struggles in Europe and North America in the late eighteenth century.

By the time of the systematic speculative efforts of Kant and Hegel, the figure of the artist is a paradigm of the possibilities for subjectivity and intellectual work in a European world operating in accordance with Enlightenment principles. The artist intensifies the subjective attributes of individuation and freedom initially negotiated in the documents of the Protestant Reformation and worked out in tangible detail in the exploratory discourse of empiricism. The figure of the artist that has been synthesized by the outset of the nineteenth century is endowed with extraordinary powers and privileges, but is also held to statutes of limitation. The artist may be a special person, but she also embodies, to some degree, liberties pertaining to every subject, or at least, in Kant's speculations, to every subject who can participate in culture's evaluation of beauty. The artist who emerges in part from Reformation and Counter-Reformation disputations about theology is both a paragon and a monster.

The aesthetic contract is my term both for the conditions defining and constraining the artist and for the memorable experiments—though the principles of inclusion and exclusion in this memory remain highly problematic—in the modern histories of literature and art. The aesthetic contract defines the artist's transcendence and degradation as well as the terms of the experiments, such as the Elizabethan sonnet, *décadence,* Imagiste poetry, cubism, and structuralism, in which, partly for their own recognition and protection, groups of artists and intellectuals agree to work, *for a time.*

The issue of the Protestant Reformation that plays a role in this study, then, is not so much the genesis of a new religious or ethnic category as it is the removal of a substantial system of mediation with the Transcendental. The system of social differentiation, stratification, delineation, and distribution was also eroded by the same forces. The Protestant Reformation is one example of what happens when a (cultural and conceptual) system hitherto offering definition, mediation, and protection withdraws (or is effaced). The withdrawal of structure is an event that takes place within sociopolitical and intellectual histories. While being specific about how the artist and the aesthetic contract of modernity emerge, at least in part, from conditions surrounding the Protestant Reformation, we can also extend these observations to other situations involving the effacement and withdrawal of structures. Two examples of this process coming immediately to my mind are the celebratory demolition by modernism (in its time-specific, "smaller" sense) of Victorian moral scruples and systematic pretensions; and postmodernism's emptying out of structures that, although explosive in a modernist context, were nonetheless specifically configured and repetitive.

~~

The question of questions obsessing the critical world as I write is the nature of the divide and interplay between language-based theoretical paradigms and their subject-based counterparts. One of the motivations underlying current interest-oriented critical research, in, say, cultural studies, is surely an impatience with the impersonality of poststructuralist approaches, which identify artifacts' ultimate import as their disclosure of and variation upon an ultimately impersonal and ahistorical system of language. There remains an enormous amount of misery, injustice, and disenfranchisement in the empirical world, in precincts beyond where such paradigmatic disputes are held. Some of the impatience with pure language-oriented critical models also stems from earnest concern regarding the continuance of the misery and the muting of marginalized and disenfranchised cultural voices. Advanced conceptual work in the West during the 1970's and 1980's drew a significant share of its inspiration from the fundamental modernist (in the narrow sense) apprehension of the priority of language in all artifacts of culture. Precisely because of concerns indicated immediately above, readers and thinkers who in the 1980's and 1990's have gravitated toward fields such as cultural studies and the New Historicism, are militating for a *linguistically aware* retelling of the story of modernity from a subjective point of view. It should be noted that interest-oriented impatience with such areas as twentieth-century phenomenology and deconstruction shares something with the original Christian repudiation of Judaism on the grounds of its abstraction and formalism, a development in the history of Western theology that was to play a significant role in the Protestant Reformation. I would not presume to render any definitive judgment regarding the complex mutual undermining and supplementation performed by language- and subject-based theoretical models except to underscore the issue itself and to militate for an informed working through of this interplay as opposed to choosing the ultimate superiority of one type of paradigm over the other. My own sense is that the ultimate intractability, duplicity, singularity, and supplementarity of language described so well by Derrida *do* ultimately place the findings of all conceptual, implicitly ideological work in reserve. At the same time, there are certain phenomena, artifacts, and conditions that simply respond better to subject-based theoretical paradigms, especially where the specific subjectivity deployed is qualified, than to language-driven (tropological, semiological, rhetorical) models. I believe that by now, we have struggled so hard for sophistication regarding subjective as well as linguistically oriented approaches that we should feel empowered, so long as we account for our positions, to work anywhere along the interstitial continuum. To the degree that the following story of the emergence of bipolarity, guilt, and extreme fluctuations between idealization and degradation occupies a historical dimension, it will need to deliberate at regular intervals on its *own* swings between language- and subject-based critical models.

Regarding the prominence of Western civilization, the commonplace has been for some time now, in sociology as well as history, that while the West did not invent idealism, it organized its disciplines and institutions around this mode of conceptualization with greater fervor and consistency than any other arena of civilization. Idealism involves at least these factors: deployment of transcendental values as orientation points for religion, morality, science, jurisprudence, and so on; a pervasive underlying ethos to the effect that human endeavors should result in the progressive realization or approximation of the ideal; a willingness to modify and even disregard received and present wisdom in the name of knowledge better approximating the ideal; and a conceptual framework or apparatus, or logic, that performs, in its organization of the materials of argument, the functions ascribed to the soul in its influence upon the body.

In the aftermath of the values established by Judaic theology and Greek philosophy (which prompted James Joyce to coin the terms "jewgreek" and "greekjew"),[7] Western civilization is set on a pronounced course of parallel (and sometimes mutually counterproductive) idealisms in religion, philosophy, science, law, art, and politics and social administration. Progress or development in each of these areas becomes tantamount to the successive revisions in prevalent modes of idealism. In theology, an area that will concern us, for example, the entire progression from Judaism and Greek philosophy through Christianity, Islam, Roman Catholicism, the Greek Orthodox Church, and Protestantism may be understood as a series of adjustments to ideal-based belief systems in the name of the interest of particular communities and cultures.

As Max Weber understood full well and elaborated in his *Sociology of Religion,* it is not that Chinese and central Asian cultures lacked idealism; they merely did not cling to it so exclusively or tenaciously as the single format for productive thinking and behavior.[8] Indeed, fidelity and exclusivity are two markedly Western values once God, in Exodus, declares that "Thou shalt have other no gods before Me" (Exodus 20:3).[9] For a grand portion of history, a Chinese person has been able to access the idealistic theology of Buddhism, the secular moral code of Confucianism, the worldly mysticism of Taoism, as well as local rites, some centering on the family, with impunity, without feeling disloyal to any particular segment of this heritage. In India as well, codes that question the mind/body split so prominent in the West through practices of meditation and meditative exercise function alongside a mythopoetic religion, Hinduism, and alongside Buddhism, in a society organized by professions and social strata as well as by religion.

The issue is not that idealism is lacking anywhere in the world, whether among Africans or Amerindians or Pacific Islanders, but that Western civilization, in part because of its mores of fidelity and exclusivity and its severe mind/body split, exaggerated its structuration according to this ideological modality, both in extent and in degree.

One way of understanding and appreciating deconstruction's contribution that in no way exhausts its purview is to regard it as an extended, structural, infrastructural, and local debunking and undermining of the claims and other manifestations of idealism. In its idealism-critiquing bearing, deconstruction achieves a historical purview, even where it is most suspicious toward historical claims and practices. Deconstruction facilitates a study of successive models of religion, philosophy, and science as revisionary adaptations of idealism. In this sense, there is a surprising affinity between deconstruction and the analysis of successive religions that Max Weber made in his *Sociology of Religion.* Deconstruction is certainly not alone among theoretical models of the past half-century in questioning and delimiting idealism's role in the determination of culture and epistemological protocols. Yet deconstruction is perhaps the most consistent critique of ideational assumptions and procedures, a theoretical model that takes writing quite seriously not only as a system of inscription but as an epistemological model. Deconstruction thus eventuates at a Proustian "joining of the ways" between idealism and writing that is as powerful as their divergence. Writing, which in one dimension constitutes a blot or stain upon idealistic purity, cannot go on without a grasp, a *visée* of its own. This is true whether writing is extrapolated in the highly singular expositions of Jacques Derrida or is allegorized in the works of the most "writerly" writers: for instance, Sterne, Rousseau, Kleist, the Schlegels, Wordsworth, Shelley, Flaubert, Hopkins, Baudelaire, Poe, Melville, Mallarmé, Nietzsche, Proust, Kafka, Joyce, Stein, Pound, Benjamin, Heidegger, Wittgenstein, Artaud, Beckett, Blanchot. Writing, in order to sustain itself, resides between a congenital besmirching of idealism's pretensions and a resolute persistence-in-spite-of that approaches the status of an inbuilt, locally calibrated idealism of its own. Writing dies where its service to extrinsic ideals, whether substantive, formal, or aesthetic, is too severe; and also where its intrinsic, local motive or raison d'être (if not ideal-orientation) withdraws. There has been a *something* to motivate, to pull along, even those singular texts, in Nietzsche, Mallarmé, Blanchot, and so on, that Derrida has flagged as instances of the most unencumbered, relatively "pure" textuality.

In the remarks that follow, I want to demonstrate that, radically different as were the contexts in which Plato and Luther and Calvin developed their formulations, there is an uncanny affinity between the Greek philosopher and the early modern theologians. The discursive continuity that could link the pivotal thinker in classical philosophy to the effective founders of Protestantism is precisely the attempt to perfect systematic concepts based on idealism.

No element of the Westernness whose fanaticism in certain matters struck Weber so powerfully is more prominent than the mind/body split serving as an ideological rationale in so many areas of theology, science, and social administration. In *Phaedo,* Plato makes death and the afterlife the proving grounds for the spiritual purity that corporeality is hell-bent upon corrupting:

> So as long as we keep to the body and our soul is contaminated with this
> imperfection, there is no chance of our ever obtaining satisfactorily to our
> object, which we assert to be truth. In the first place, the body provides us
> with innumerable distractions in the pursuit of our necessary sustenance, and
> any diseases which attack us hinder our quest for reality. Besides, the body
> fills us with loves and desires and fears and all sorts of fancies and a great deal
> of nonsense, with the result that we never literally get a chance to think at all
> about anything. Wars and revolutions and battles are due simply and solely to
> the body and its desires. All wars are undertaken for the acquisition of wealth,
> and the reason why we have to acquire wealth is the body, because we are

slaves in its service. That is why, on these accounts, we have so little time for philosophy. Worst of all, if we do obtain any leisure from the body's claims and turn to some line of inquiry, the body intrudes once more into our investigations, interrupting, disturbing, distracting, and preventing us from getting a glimpse of the truth. We are in fact convinced that if we are ever to have pure knowledge of anything, we must get rid of the body and contemplate things by themselves with the soul by itself. (*Phaedo,* 66b–d; *CD,* 49) [10]

We read above one of the most comprehensive Platonic diatribes regarding the problematical relationship between body and soul. In a paradox not lost later on Luther, we are both slaves and masters to the body: somatic impulses enslave, yet also compel us to undertake the conquests of warfare. Our corporeality binds us to a world far less essential than it seems, in part because it is devoid of essence, when this is identified with the ideal. This implicit teleology in Plato will not be lost on Luther and Calvin either. The function of philosophy, serving as classical Greek Sunday school, is to somehow uplift the subject from this corporeal morass. In the above passage alone, the body sickens us with disease, starves us of our true nourishment, deranges whatever small thinking that manages to take place in its presence, and leads us astray into our worst political fiascos. "The soul is most like that which is divine, immortal, intelligible, uniform, indissoluble, and ever self-consistent and invisible, whereas body is most like that which is human, mortal, multiform, unintelligible, dissoluble, and never self-consistent" (*Phaedo,* 80 b–c; *CD,* 63).

Even though Plato is writing before the dawn of European empiricism, that is, before Cartesian duality, itself forged by counterforces played out in the Protestant Reformation, and thus before that empiricism opened a register on which experience could evolve its own criteria for the evaluation of experience, he has Socrates subject these speculations to an empirical acid-test. The proof of the pudding, when it comes to spiritual purity and the corporeal corruption that threatens it at every turn, is what happens upon the *experience* of death:

The truth is much more like this. If at its release the soul is pure and carries with it no contamination of the body, because it has never willingly associated with it in life, but has shunned it and kept itself separate as its regular practice—in other words, if it has pursued philosophy in the right way and really practiced how to face death easily . . . if this is its condition, then it departs to that place which is, like itself, invisible, divine, immortal, and wise, where, on its arrival, happiness awaits it, and release from uncertainty and folly, from fears and uncontrolled desires, and all other human evils. (*Phaedo,* 80e–81a; *CD,* 64)

A marvelous afterlife awaits the well-tempered soul, the spirit that has restrained the immoderate demands of the body. The *vita contemplativa* involves less in the way of good deeds than purely spiritual (that is, ideational) exercise. This particular specification will be of importance to us below; it explains why the philosophical *psyche* will eventually attain a setting as ineffable and perfect and unconstrained by tangible qualities as it is itself.

The most striking quality of this dialogue may well be the intertwining of a pre-Christian teleology with the elaborate schematic distinction between spirituality and corporeality. In this melodramatic trial of the soul, philosophy appears as a quiet, self-effacing, and infinitely patient and forgiving teacher:

> And philosophy can see that the imprisonment is ingeniously effected by the prisoner's own active desire, which makes him first accessory to his own confinement. Well, philosophy takes over the soul in this condition and by gentle persuasion tries to set it free. She points out that observation by means of the eyes and ears and all the other senses is entirely deceptive, and she urges the soul to refrain from using them unless it is necessary to do so, and encourages it to collect and concentrate itself by itself, trusting nothing but its own independent judgment upon objects considered in themselves, and attributing no truth to anything which it views indirectly as being subject to variation. . . . Now the soul of the true philosopher feels that it must not reject this opportunity for release. (*Phaedo*, 82e–83c; *CD*, 66)

The deity of Philosophy is, like the one of Christianity will be, a teacher of near-infinite patience. What this feminine teacher has to offer at the end of a meticulous but gentle course of study is spiritual release. The persistent ideological value underlying this self-reflexive home-study course has been the deceptiveness and brutality of sensation and other empirical means of knowledge as opposed to immanent, intuitive certitudes, accruing from spiritual insight. Even in Plato, the immediacy of spiritual knowledge bespeaks a certain subjective liberty ("its own independent judgment").

The philosophical acuity that a subjectivity has either gained or not gained in the course of a worldly lifetime devolves in a most dramatic way upon a judgment scene uncannily anticipatory of Jewish liturgy, the New Testament, and the scenarios of calling and predestination in the Protestant revision of Judeo-Christian idealism:

> Those who are judged to have lived a neutral life set out for Acheron, and embarking in those vessels which await them, are conveyed in them to the lake, and there they dwell, and undergoing purification are both absolved by punishment from any sins they have committed, and rewarded for their good deeds, according to each man's just deserts. Those who on account of the

greatness of their sins are judged to be incurable, as having committed many gross acts of sacrilege or many wicked and lawless murders or any other such crimes—these are hurled by their appropriate destiny into Tartarus, from whence they emerge no more.

Others are judged to have been guilty of sins which, though great, are curable—if, for example, they have offered violence to father or mother in a fit of passion, but spent the rest of their lives in penitence, or if they have committed manslaughter after the same fashion. These too must be cast into Tartarus, but when this has been done and they have remained there for a year, the surge casts them out. (*Phaedo,* 113d–114b; *CD,* 94)

The spiritual Day of Judgment imaged by Plato is as severe as Philosophy the teacher was nurturing and gentle. The Platonic trial of the soul in these lines is cumulative and summative, sharing something of the metempsychosis possible in Indian religions, and closer to the Christian scenario of a final Judgment Day than the corresponding Jewish trial, which repeats itself on a yearly cycle and leaves nothing overly dramatic to be resolved at the end of life. Spiritual judgment, as elaborated by Plato, is a philosophical affair: the souls of the dead are sorted by logical process. As in Christianity, the categories are the unimpeachable, the savable, and the hopeless. Plato effects a superimposition between two idealism-determined dualities in his scenario of judgment: he piggybacks the metamorphosis that takes place with corporeal death onto a possibly more deeply ingrained split between the spiritual and bodily components of the human being. In the Platonic system, only the corporeal needs to perish at the time of death; spirituality is as much liberated by death as it is jeopardized. In a certain sense, in a system where the ultimate good is philosophical in nature, the death of corporeality has the virtue of eliminating a number of confusions, particularly those instigated by the appetites and what Freud would call the drives. Dying may make you a better philosopher; this is one consolation that Plato has to offer.

The Platonic texts may in fact comprise the most comprehensive overview and *précis* of the basic terms in which Western idealism articulates itself. It certainly is the best illustrated, by the metaphoric flights and elaborations making Plato one of the great poets in Western (and possibly non-Western) literature. The metaphor in Plato enunciates the soul's position. Plato has no difficulty incorporating a spiritual hypertext into disputations insisting on the soul's absolute division from and superiority over the body. The metaphor, whether the chariot in the *Phaedrus* or the many coats worn by the soul in the *Phaedo* (87b–e), exists alongside, supplements, the argument in Plato with an ease that belies the ideology of spiritual antagonism to the corporeal. This ease with the corporeality of metaphor is also in sharp contrast with many philosophers who follow in the speculative tradition initiated in the Platonic dialogues.

When we skip from Plato to the theological disputations in which Luther and Calvin were intensely engaged (a move of outrageous scale), what we see is that while the Renaissance Christian theologians address a context markedly different from Plato's arena of contention, they must still engage in a rather pure analysis of idealism as a basis for their polemics. The issues have remained quite similar. How can the soul purify itself? Can the relinquishing of a certain body—whether the corporeal body, or the body of the Church, or the body of Christ as symbolized in the sacrament of the eucharist—be tantamount to the attainment of a certain freedom? Does this freedom constitute progress in the life of the soul or is it a regression? Luther, in order to establish the conceptual legitimacy of the doctrinal and institutional changes he wishes to implement, must return to the grounding principles of Western idealism. The development of Protestantism constitutes as much a return to the basic issues of Western idealism as it does a return to a purer doctrine and a less encumbered theological institution.

One of Luther's major early pieces of conceptual work, "The Freedom of a Christian," explores the implications of a revised Christian idealism for the notion of freedom:

> I shall set down the following two propositions concerning the freedom and bondage of the spirit:
>   A Christian is a perfectly free lord of all, subject to none.
>   A Christian is a perfectly dutiful servant of all, subject to all.
>   These two theses seem to contradict each other. If, however, they should be found to fit together they would serve our purpose beautifully. Both are Paul's own statements, who says in I Cor. 9 [:19], "For though I am free from all men, I have made myself a slave to all," and in Rom. 13 [:8], "Owe no one anything, except to love one another." Love by its very nature is ready to serve and be subject to him who is loved. (*SW,* 53) [11]

There is every reason for the issue of spiritual freedom to come up early in a theology seeking a more direct address to the divinity and attempting to simplify existing theological institutions. And it is in keeping with the intervening centuries of Christian theology that the activity of spirit be identified as love. The idea that love for one's fellow human beings is a quintessential spiritual function continues in the tradition of Christianity's basic revision to Judaism. The very person of Jesus Christ amounted to a correction of an ideal-based and -structured theology gone wrong: gone astray through the development of a formalistic set of laws and observances that had overshadowed the possibility of a humanistic, empathic address to the deity. Christianity's initial raison d'être is the need for a godhead to humanize an idealism that has become abstract, distant, and formalistic. The pre-Christian Judaic system of idealism mediated an abstract (though philosophically rigorous, in Platonic terms) deity through a highly structured system of laws and commandments. In its earliest emanation, Christianity supplanted an abstract, remote, unitary deity with a dualistic God, in which, through personification, a vibrant and intimate interface between humanity and divinity was achieved. As the result of this newfound intimacy in the interaction between people and God, it was, at least for a time, possible to vastly trim and simplify the mediatory code of laws, commandments, and other religious obligations in Judaism. Through this process of idealistic restructuration, Christianity adjusts spiritual freedom and transcendence, which in the Platonic world is depicted as poetic creativity and emotional exuberance, into an ethos of brotherly love, sympathy, and empathy.

This overall revision of idealism, the very grounding principle of Christian theology, behind him, Luther contemplates the options for spirituality and religion in a *Christianity* that has been simplified. This drive to simplify was given force by opposition to a bureaucracy and practices, such as the selling of indulgences, that have intervened between people and the deity. Partially because Luther's meditations coincided historically with the formation of European sociopolitical structures that have continued to this day, the historical momentousness of the options he explored can hardly be overstated. Luther pondered the freedom of the Christian spirit at a time when the power of Europe's last functioning theocracy, the Holy Roman Empire, was succumbing to the inevitable limits occasioned by the rise of ideologically neutral economies and the cities that serviced these economies. As Luther thought and wrote, two longstanding models for sociopolitical organization were emerging: more or less centralized nationalities, such as France, Spain, and England, that would undergo evolution in matters of economy, technology, and governance on a societywide level; and urban center–based cultures, such as in Germany, Italy, and Eastern Europe, that would, for a considerable time in the future, function as loose confederations of political entities subscribing to more or less common national languages, histories, and traditions.[12]

The above passage bears certain of the distinctive features of Luther's thinking and prose. One is immediately aware of the vigor with which he wants to prove his points by citing letter and verse, in this case from Paul. And in a tradition that will continue at least until Kant specifies that emanations of the Transcendental filtering into the empirical world inevitably do so in the form of antinomies, Luther's logic bifurcates the inherent but rethought freedom of a Christian into two diametrically counterposed propositions: Christian freedom is both a universal lordship and a universal service.

Luther's rhetoric moves subtly: his propositions concerning freedom and servitude highlight the former by mentioning it first; by the time the passage
moves to the quotations from Paul, the proposition of universal servitude
(and service to God) has occupied center stage.

Luther's logic is bipolar.[13] He is a vigorous master of argumentation, and
his binary logic places him in a position where he has power to idealize what
falls on the salutary side of his logical dividers and to excoriate what falls on
the unfavorable side. From our brief Platonic reading, we can argue that all
Luther is doing is taking over binary structures from the history of philosophy, such as the mind/body split. But something is added to the power and
perdurance of this bipolarity when we factor in the pivotal historical moment
at which Luther offered these revisions, and when, with hindsight, we observe their profound historical and cultural impact. So on the one hand, it is
no news when Luther specifies, in the very next paragraph, that "Man has a
twofold nature"; but the aftermath of these conceptual moves will be far
longer-lasting than just another Plato lesson.

I'm going to quote this statement of Luther's regarding the duplicity
of human nature, but then continue with this passage from early in "The
Freedom of a Christian" to demonstrate its position within Luther's overall
rhetoric:

> Man has a twofold nature, a spiritual and a bodily one. According to this
> spiritual nature, which men refer to as the soul, he is called spiritual, inner,
> or new man. According to the bodily nature, which men refer to as flesh,
> he is called a carnal, outward, or old man, of whom the Apostle writes in
> II Cor. 4 [:16], "Though our outer nature is wasting away, our inner nature is
> being renewed every day." Because of the diversity of nature the Scriptures
> assert contradictory things concerning the same man, since these two men in
> the same man contradict each other, "for the desires of the flesh are against
> the Spirit, and the desires of the Spirit are against the flesh" according to
> Gal. 5 [:17].
>
>   First, let us consider the inner man to see how a righteous, free, and pious
> Christian, that is, a spiritual, new, and inner man, becomes what he is. It is
> evident that no external thing has any influence in producing Christian righ-
> teousness or freedom, or in producing unrighteousness or servitude. A simple
> argument will furnish the proof of this statement. What can it profit the soul
> if the body is well, free, and active, and eats, drinks, and does as it pleases?
> For in these respects even the most godless slaves of vice may prosper. On
> the other hand, how will poor health or imprisonment or hunger or thirst
> or any other external misfortune harm the soul? Even the most godly men,
> and those who are free because of clear consciences, are afflicted with these
> things. None of these things touch either the freedom or servitude of the
> soul. It does not help the soul if the body is adorned with the sacred robes of

priests or dwells in sacred places or is occupied with sacred duties or prays, fasts, abstains from certain kinds of food, or does any work that can be done by the body and in the body. The righteousness and the freedom of the soul require something far different since the things which have been mentioned could be done by any wicked person. Such works produce nothing but hypocrites. (*SW,* 53–54)

The tone of the first paragraph in this extended citation is set by the marvelous phrase, "since these two men in the same man contradict each other." The result of a predetermined twofold human nature is a kind of encapsulation of one sort of person, say spiritual, inside another, physical. Through this implicit metaphor of internal deadlock, or psychomachy, between two subjects who are at the same time one, Luther sets a tone of unresolvable conflict within the subjectivity of his age.

Yet Luther will resolve this tension in the next paragraph; he will resolve it into the platform statement of the Christian's true freedom, a freedom attainable through faith alone, from all acts and services corresponding to the corporeal side of the mind/body split. This second paragraph serves as a foundation in the essay for this basic element of Luther's ideology. The logical operation that Luther must perform in order to prove the inessentiality and even frivolousness of good works, rituals, sacramental garb, and so on, is to definitively *exacerbate* the mind/body split evident, but treated with a soft touch, in Plato. Luther *resolves* the mind/body split decisively in favor of the spirit. In the wake of this decision, nonetheless founded on a bipolar notion of subjectivity, faith alone, a spiritual activity, determines the prospects of the soul and the course of religion; anything tainted with corporeality, and the extensions of this notion such as acts, things, and places, are relegated to inessentiality and stained by Cain's mark of corruption and corruptibility.

And so the invention (or resurrection) of a pure faith-based religion amounts to a vehement repudiation of the physical. "Faith alone is the saving and efficacious use of the Word of God" (*SW,* 55). Not only is this faith of a different order than works; it must take place rigorously excluded from them. "This faith cannot exist in connection with works" (*SW,* 55); "faith alone, without works, justifies, frees, and saves" (*SW,* 57). Yet the Son of God "was made flesh, suffered, rose from the dead, and was glorified through the Spirit who sanctifies" (*SW,* 55).

~~~

In this last snatch of text, Luther is wandering into the position of Derrida's logocentrists, who, while they impugn and castigate writing, eventually re-

alize the need for some communication medium, which they then rehabili-
tate as "good writing." [14] In the present case, Luther must somehow resolve
the corporeality of the Son of God with the exclusively spiritual thrust of his
theological campaign. It is precisely when philosophers err into their own
aporias (and I am arguing here that we read Luther as a *philosopher*) that it
proves wise to examine their inevitable metaphorics. Luther is a more rigorous philosopher than Plato, if we take this predication to mean that he is
more sparing of his metaphors. One could argue, and I will do so on another
occasion, that the philosophy of writing is the history of rigorous discourse's
struggles with, resistances to, and inevitable seduction by figurative language,
at least within certain parameters. And so we will pursue the progress of
"The Freedom of a Christian" for a spell, wandering into the metaphors that
Luther offers us, wondering all the time whether metaphors are the spirit or
the body of language.

There is no question that Luther identifies as an unavoidable rhetorical specification the need to proceed logically. He devotes considerable energy to
logical exposition: "The following statements are therefore true: 'Good works
do not make a good man, but a good man does good works; evil works do
not make a wicked man, but a wicked man does evil works.' Consequently
it is always necessary . . . that good works follow and proceed from the good
person" (*SW,* 69). Luther elaborates a logic here according to which acts are
secondary and subordinate to qualities. In effect, he calls for a quality-based
theology. Luther's logical work is convincing. It runs into trouble only when
he attempts to implement it through extended metaphors, such as emerge in
the following passage:

> No good work can rely upon the Word of God or live in the soul, for faith
> alone and the Word of God rule in the soul. Just as the heated iron glows like
> fire because of the union of fire with it, so the Word imparts its qualities to
> the soul. It is clear, then, that a Christian has all that he needs in faith and
> needs no works to justify him; and if he has no need of works, he has no need
> of the law; and if he has no need of the law, surely he is free from the law. It
> is true that "the law is not laid down for the just" [I Tim. 1:9]. This is that
> Christian liberty, our faith, which does not induce us to live in idleness or
> wickedness but makes the law and works unnecessary for any man's righ-
> teousness and salvation. (*SW,* 58–59)

Luther's metaphors derive from deep in the histories of spirituality and the
mind/body split. On this we can rest assured. But once in play, the meta-

phors lead Luther astray by virtue of their internal logic, or alogic. In the above passage, the Spiritualized Word—that is, stabilized, sanctified language—impresses its qualities upon the soul like the iron heated up by the spirit of fire. In order for this metaphor to work, the essential entity, the spirit, must be forged and in a sense created by the secondary and corporeal characters of iron and the Word.

A second metaphor both sanctified by the history of Western metaphysics and problematical in its particular deployment is the marriage that is so similar to the bond of faith:

> The third incomparable benefit of faith is that it unites the soul with Christ as a bride is united with her bridegroom. By this mystery, as the Apostle teaches, Christ and the soul become one flesh [Eph. 5:31–32]. And if they are one flesh and if there is between them a true marriage . . . it follows that everything they have they hold in common, the good as well as the evil. Accordingly the believing soul can boast of and glory in whatever Christ has as though it were his own, and whatever the soul has Christ claims as his own. Let us compare these and we shall see inestimable benefits. Christ is full of grace, life, and salvation. The soul is full of sins, death, and damnation. Now let faith come between them and sins, death, and damnation will be Christ's, while grace, life, and salvation will be the soul's; for if Christ is a bridegroom, he must take upon himself the things which are his bride's and bestow upon her the things that are his. If he gives her his body and very self, how shall he not give her all that is his? And if he takes the body of the bride, how shall he not take all that is hers? (*SW*, 60)

This complex and interesting passage is structured by relations of substitution and horizontal/vertical displacement. The implicit theological ecstacy in the passage is the possibility that a marriage experienced horizontally—that is, with interpersonal reciprocity and intimacy, could all the time amount to a transcendental rise or elevation, since the spouse in the marriage of faith happens to be the human facet of the dualistic Christian deity.[15] The bridegroom is Christ, and human believers are the brides, they are women. This "true marriage," as opposed to nitty-gritty "human" ones, is itself double in nature. On the one hand it is described as mutual—"everything they have they hold in common"—but on the other, by virtue of the entrenched privileging of the male position, the divine bridegroom "takes upon himself" the negativity—frailty, moral blots, damnations—of his human/feminine partner. So there is a shifting back and forth, laterally, of sins and weaknesses in the marriage metaphor, and beyond that, another shift: the humanistic, fundamentally Christian idea of a horizontal intimacy between people and their God subtly metamorphoses itself into the terms of a vertical power relation.

In order for this metaphor to work, the soul, which earlier in the essay has to be the irreproachable foil to the body and its related works and deeds, is now "full of sins, death, and damnation." In order for Christ to save the soul, in a religion now metaphorically depicted as a union of pure faith, the soul must start out in an initial state of degradation. This runs counter to Luther's earlier appropriation of the venerable mind/body split in Western culture as the structuring platform of his faith, that is, transcendental religion. The metaphor of a wedding of faith to God is fundamentally polymorphous in nature: the marriage demonstrates both Christ's intimacy with people and his superiority and nobility. The placement of people in the feminine position, even though marriage is a ritual of sanctification, also connects them to an underlying cultural motif of staining and dirt: "So he takes to himself a glorious bride, 'without spot or wrinkle, cleansing her by the washing of water with the word' [Eph. 5:26–27] of life" (SW, 61). Metaphorically, here as well the ideological call for a theology of pure faith and a pruning away of the purported clutter and corruption in the Catholic Church may result in a certain salutary institutional simplification, but on a figurative level the complexities are only heaping up. This, in a nutshell, is the situation of Luther's theology: at the level of ideation, there is a mandate for a welcome directness in theological matters and a liberation from alienating, formalistic practices (one attributed to the Jews, for example); but underlying this ideation are all the possibilities for chaos and anomie, evidence for which we find here in the treacherously shifting metaphors it takes *to describe* a creed of faith. For now, let it suffice to point out that it will require extraordinary, internalized regulatory mechanisms in order to *control* the not-necessarily-Christian freedoms set into relief through the clearing away of arbitrary theological and cultural structures of mediation, whether to God or to the Real.

Before concluding this overview of Luther's "The Freedom of a Christian," let us shift our attention back from metaphoric displacements to ideological tenets. This is not in any way to minimize the impact of Luther's metaphoric elaboration upon the tradition that he initiated, but to round out the basic components of this system that he included in his pivotal essay:

> We must, however, realize that these works reduce the body to subjection and purify it of its evil lusts, and our whole purpose is to be directed only toward the driving out of lusts. Since by faith the soul is cleansed and made to love God, it desires that all things, and especially its own body, shall be purified so that all things may join with it in loving and praising God. Hence a man cannot be idle, for the need of his body drives him and he is compelled to do many good works to reduce it to subjection. Nevertheless the works

themselves do not justify him before God, but he does the works out of spontaneous love in obedience to God and considers nothing except the approval of God. . . . But those who presume to be justified by works do not regard the mortifying of the lusts, but only the works themselves, and think that if only they have done as many and as great works as are possible, they have done well and have become righteous. At times, they even addle their brains and destroy, or at least render useless, their natural strength with their works. This is the height of folly and utter ignorance of Christian life and faith. (*SW,* 68)

This passage highlights a certain disgust at corporeal drives and articulates a stigma with regard to idleness that, as Max Weber notes, becomes a fundament of Protestant ideology. It does so in the process of providing some small value for good works; they at least distract the mind from more corrupting thoughts and activities. But to discern any intrinsic value in the works themselves is to confuse their secondary nature with the primacy of faith as a fundamental spiritual quality.

To confuse works with faith is tantamount to confusing religion with the existing Catholic Church. This final passage from the "Freedom" essay highlights Luther's polemical gesture as establishing the space for a new religion by clearing away the mediatory clutter associated with the old. The freedom of a Christian amounts to release from a corpus of mediatory structures and rituals, yet, as we have already begun to see, the release is not one-sided or unambiguous:

This ignorance and suppression of liberty very many blind pastors take pains to encourage. They stir up and urge on their people in these practices by praising such works, puffing them up with their indulgences, and never teaching faith. If, however, you wish to pray, fast, or establish a foundation in the church, I advise you to be careful not to do it in order to obtain some benefit, whether temporal or eternal, for you would do injury to your faith which alone offers you all things. Your one care should be that faith may grow, whether it is trained by works or sufferings. Make your gifts freely and for no consideration, so that others may profit by them and fare well because of you and your goodness. In this way you shall be truly good and Christian. Of what benefit to you are the good works which you do not need for keeping your body under control? Your faith is sufficient for you, through which God has given you all things. (*SW,* 79)

The passage is very much in keeping with the received theological history in which Protestantism declared itself a counter to an excessive corruption that had built up in the Church. Once again, "free" works, ones performed with no expectation of their inherent good or essentiality, are acceptable.

But to accord them any intrinsic value is to concede that true religion can reside in the institutionality of the Church.

～

We associate the name John Calvin with the doctrine of predestination, which so much leaves the modern soul in the lurch, not knowing exactly whether its moral stringencies can secure ultimate assurance as to a favorable teleological outcome. Calvin does fill out the Lutheran disputations in terms of their temporal-teleological dimension. But his speculations in this regard rest solidly on the basis of the positions Luther had to concretize in articulating a counter-theology and in founding a "counter-Church." These fundamentals include a vivid soul/body distinction, inherited from Platonic philosophy, a rejection of the mediatory function in relation to the divinity played by the Catholic Church, and starkly bipolar moral values. In order to dramatize the individual's struggle for teleological assurance, Calvin must subordinate the events that transpire during mortal existence to the eternal temporality of the soul. Calvin legitimates the existence of *some* church to serve as a framework for theological activity at the same time that he excoriates *the* Church as a setting of untold corruption. Calvin supplements Luther's platform for a church of protest primarily in the attention he pays to *future* prospects for the soul, and to the role of this futurity in a theology that increasingly subordinates the outcomes of the mortal world to an existence that transpires in a vastly attenuated tempo. Like Luther, Calvin is a hermeneutically rigorous and rhetorically acute *reader*. Exegetical rigor becomes not only a way in which Protestant theology reinforces its positions: it becomes a vital element in the secular art-religion that, by Kant's day, becomes an available substitute for or supplement to theocracy in enlightened Western cultures.

Calvin's theology is founded in the same emphatic mind/body duality that we have found common to Plato and Luther. And as the soul approaches sublime purity and transcendence, the body becomes an ever more putrid source of corruption:

> For, because the organs of the body are directed by the faculties of the soul, they pretend the soul to be so united to the body as to be incapable of subsisting without it, and by their eulogies of nature do all they can to suppress the name of God. But the powers of the soul are far from being limited to functions in the body. For what concern has the body in measuring the heavens, counting the number of the stars, computing their several magnitudes,

and acquiring a knowledge of their respective distances. (*Institutes,* "On God the Creator," *OCF,* 16) [16]

Our perdition therefore proceeds from a sinfulness of our flesh, not from God, it being only a consequence of our degenerating from our primitive condition. And let no one murmur that God might have made a better provision for our safety by preventing the fall of Adam. For such an objection ought to be abominated, as too presumptuously curious, by all pious minds; and it also belongs to the mystery of predestination. . . . Wherefore let us remember that our ruin must be imputed to the corruption of our nature that we may not bring an accusation against God himself, the author of nature. That this fatal wound is inherent in our nature is indeed a truth; but it is an important question whether it was in it originally or was derived from any extraneous cause. ("On God the Redeemer," *OCF,* 45–46)

Calvin's dialectics on the mind/body split are a bit more involved than Luther's. Calvin will define original sin as follows: "Original sin, therefore, appears to be a heredity depravity and corruption of our nature, diffused through all the parts of the soul, rendering us obnoxious to the divine wrath and producing in us those works which the Scripture calls 'works of the flesh'" ("On God the Redeemer," *OCF,* 42). The passages immediately above indicate that Calvin's struggle of the soul is pitched as much in terms of radically charged countervalances as is Luther's. But in Calvin's account, the soul is as much to blame in human failure as the body. The soul is simply not coextensive with the body; this means that it can undergo an enlightenment and purification which the body cannot follow. In the first citation immediately above, Calvin characterizes the soul's extension beyond the body as a quest for knowledge. This is a wise move: it indicates that Protestantism contains a good tolerance for the empirical curiosity that is beginning to arise in European culture independently of theology. This is as opposed to the persecutions of Galileo and Copernicus mounted by the Catholic Church. The high value that Protestant theology places upon rigorous, "scientific" exegesis is another indication of this toleration and even fostering of empirical methodology. Calvin adds complexity to the dialectic of body and soul by attributing some responsibility for corporeal lust to the soul. He also at least considers whether some responsibility for the sorry state of human affairs should not be assessed to God the Creator. He is deliberating on this possibility in the second passage immediately above. "How could God," ponders Calvin a little bit below this passage, "who is pleased with all his meanest works, be angry with the noblest of all his creatures? But he is more angry with the corruption of his work than with his work itself. . . . Thus vanishes the foolish and nugatory system of the Manichaeans, who, having imagined in man a substantial wickedness, presumed to invent for him a new creator, that they might not appear to assign the cause and origin of evil to a righteous God" ("On God the Redeemer," *OCF,* 46). Calvin is not above considering the Manichaean solution, the invention of a God of Evil, in explanation of the "fatal wound" inherent in human nature. It is essential to his system to reinforce a *human* source of evil; and to provide for an "extra margin" of spirituality that will become the dimension in which the redemption of an inherently corrupt human condition can transpire. Yet with all these modifications to Lutheran formulations, Calvin's scenario for spiritual development is grounded in a stark mind/body split and a bipolar logic.

Calvin's subtlety is again evinced when we consider his attitude toward the Church—Catholic and "in general." While he can envision the Church, in the spirit of Luther, as a festering den of corruption, Calvin is also capable of appreciating an institutional rubric for Christian matters of the spirit. The passage below is surely reminiscent of Luther's strong skepticism toward the Church:

> The head of that cursed and abominable kingdom, in the Western Church, we affirm to be the Pope. When his seat is placed in the temple of God, it suggests that his kingdom will be such that he will not abolish the name of Christ or the Church. Hence it appears that we by no means deny that Churches may exist even under his tyranny; but he has profaned them by sacrilegious impiety, afflicted them by cruel despotism, corrupted and almost terminated their existence by false and pernicious doctrines, like poisonous potions; in such Churches, Christ lies half buried, the gospel is suppressed, piety exterminated, and the worship of God almost abolished; in a word, they are altogether in such a state of confusion that they exhibit a picture of Baby- lon rather than of the holy city of God. (*Institutes,* "On Communion with Christ," *OCF,* 104)

Calvin adopts an image of Luther's: under Catholicism, Christianity has entered a Babylonian captivity of the sort suffered in ancient times by the Jews. The Protestant ambivalence toward Judaism is truly bipolar, on the one hand espousing the more direct Judaic humanity-God relation, on the other hand treating it as utter blasphemy. The attitude toward the Church in the above passage is a bit more moderate: the Papal Church is an abomination; churches themselves are necessary communal and theological institutions. "We may even learn from the title 'mother' how useful and even necessary it is for us to know the Church," Calvin has written in the same passage, "since there is no other way of entrance into life unless we are conceived by her, born of her, nourished at her breast, and continually preserved under her care and government till we are divested of this mortal flesh and become 'like the angels'" ("On Communion with Christ," *OCF,* 103). The maternal image in this last passage is a useful one; Calvin too may have embarked on a path of alternate Christianity, may deploy a revised hermeneutic with which to interpret prior Judeo-Christianity and the classical heritage. But his relation to his resources, even those he rejects, is a filial one toward a past figured as a mother: a source we may outgrow, but whose nurturing must be prolonged. Like Luther, Calvin adopts a sharply polarized value system, although at moments he is prepared to accord some value to the negative elements in his comparisons.

Calvin went beyond Luther, and may have initiated new directions in Protestantism, in his careful consideration of Christian teleology and *its* implicit assertions regarding the relationship between the here and the hereafter, human existence and one ascribed to eternity. Among his central conceptions is the notion of predestination. In ascribing the ultimate determination of man's spiritual fate to God, Calvin is of course bolstering divine control of these matters. Yet curiously, the assertion that people have no direct say as to whether they will be among the elect or the damned can work both ways, as Max Weber has remarked.[17] The margin of Calvinist doubt can make people try to take the matter into their own hands, and live the industrious lives that Weber associates with the Protestant ethic. But it is possible under this system to feel a certain distance and alienation from the ethical wear-and-tear of everyday matters. Calvin's subordination of the temporal, empirical world to one of much greater weight and perdurance endows his discourse with a momentous sense of fate. This momentousness may underlie the tenor of events in Kleist's fiction, which we shall explore in Chapter 4; and it may color the aesthetic of melancholy, to which Benjamin ascribes the distinctive tone of Renaissance and baroque drama.

> With whatever kind of tribulation we may be afflicted, we should always keep this end in view: to habituate ourselves to a contempt of the present life, that we may thereby be excited to meditation on that which is to come. For the Lord, well knowing our strong natural inclination to a brutish love of the world, adopts a most excellent method to reclaim us and rouse us from our insensibility, that we may not be too tenaciously attached to that foolish affection. There is not one of us who is not desirous of appearing, through the whole course of his life, to aspire and strive after celestial immortality. . . . But if you examine the designs, pursuits, and actions of every individual, you will find nothing in them but what is terrestrial. . . . In a word, the whole soul, fascinated by carnal allurements, seeks its felicity on earth. To oppose this evil the Lord, by continual lessons of miseries, teaches his children the vanity of the present life. That they may not promise themselves profound

and secure peace in it, therefore he permits them to be frequently disquieted and infested with wars or tumults, with robberies or other injuries. That they may not aspire with too much avidity after transient and uncertain riches, or depend on those which they possess—sometimes by exile, sometimes by the sterility of the land, sometimes by a conflagration, sometimes by other means, he reduces them to indigence, or at least confines them within the limits of mediocrity. That they may not be too complacently delighted with conjugal blessings, he either causes them to be distressed with the wickedness of their wives, or humbles them with a wicked offspring, or afflicts them with want or loss of children. . . . We therefore truly derive advantage from the discipline of the cross only when we learn that this life, considered in itself, is unquiet, turbulent, miserable in numberless instances, and in no respect altogether happy. (*Institutes*, "On the Grace of Christ," *OCF*, 72–73)

Calvin enunciates here a credo of otherworldliness. We should not become attached to this world, both because the Lord booby-traps it with immeasurable disappointments and because it diverts us from the world to come, the true horizon of our strivings. This position rests on a performative foundation whose primary gestures are undervaluation and overvaluation. We should "habituate ourselves to a contempt of the present life" (*OCF*, 72). The present life is vain. "This life, considered in itself, is unquiet, turbulent, miserable in numberless instances" (*OCF*, 73). The miseries of human life are not by chance, but are part of a divine plan. In this world, our strivings in every major arena will fail, or will be confined "within the limits of mediocrity" (*OCF*, 73). This complete conviction in "the miserable condition of the present life" (*OCF*, 75) brings about a compensatory overvaluation: of everything divine and otherworldly. "*Hope of the enjoyment of God's presence makes this life bearable*" (*OCF*, 75). The inbuilt, predetermined misery of our world, and the unavoidable failure of human strivings, make it "a post at which the Lord has placed us, to be retained by us till he call us away" (*OCF*, 76).

Calvinist theology therefore demands a submission, an accession to a fate not in human hands. This is the famous doctrine of predestination.

Predestination, by which God adopts some to the hope of life and adjudges others to eternal death, no one, desirous of the credit of piety, dares absolutely to deny. . . . When we attribute foreknowledge to God, we mean that all things that have ever been, and perpetually remain, before his eyes, so that to his knowledge nothing is future or past, but all things are present; and present in such a manner that he does not merely conceive of them from ideas formed in his mind, as things remembered by us appear present to our minds, but really beholds and sees them as if actually placed before him. And this foreknowledge extends to the whole world and to all the creatures. Predestination we call the eternal decree of God by which he has determined in himself what he would have to become of every individual of mankind. For they are not all created with a similar destiny, but eternal life is foreordained for some and eternal damnation for others. Every man, therefore, being created for one or another of these ends, we say he is predestined either to life or death. This God has testified not only in particular persons, but has given a specimen of it in the whole posterity of Abraham, which should evidently show the future condition of every nation to depend on his decision. (*Institutes*, "On the Grace of Christ," *OCF,* 91–92)

Predestination is a very particular teleological model, but predicated, among other places, in the Platonic scenario of the trial of the soul cited above. As interesting as are the implications of predestination—both to strive in a last-ditch effort to influence election and to participate in one's own fate with a certain detachment—is the scenario in which God foresees the fate of every individual in a suspended eternal present. Divine spatial presence in the world slides over into a divinely eternal temporal present. In illustrating his hypothesis of divine foresight, Calvin actually depicts God as he "beholds and sees" "all things" (*OCF,* 92). He "really beholds and sees them as if actually placed before him" (*OCF,* 92). Calvin's need here to justify a scenario in which God, through vision and foreknowledge, "personally" intervenes in and determines each individual's fate—induces him to bifurcate God himself into a mind, which "conceives" and "beholds," and into some other entity upon which this perception and cognition are registered.

Arbitrary as some might find this scenario of divine predetermination of our personal fates, it occupies a decisive place in Protestant theology, serving as a foundation for the ideological planks of submission to one's lot, other-worldliness, and self-denial when it comes to the achievement of worldly aims. As arbitrary as the doctrine of predestination may seem, its impact on the theological *politics* of Protestantism is concrete and tangible.

The entire history of Western religion may be summarized as a series of hermeneutical reorientations to a handful of persistent ontotheological issues, among them ideation, mediation, and the literality or concreteness of representation in language. Calvin contributes significantly to the emerging bearing of Protestantism through his determinations regarding metaphysical issues, such as the nature and knowledge of God, the relation of the human world to the divine one, and the prospects before the human spirit. In addition, Calvin goes beyond Luther in establishing a distinctly Protestant hermeneutics: he works through the linguistic and interpretative implications of yet another major revision in the history of Western theology.

It has been suggested above that Calvin's exemplification of a rigorous, almost "scientific" interpretive practice is in keeping with Protestantism's overall tolerance for empiricism. We shall explore one example of Calvin's practice as a Biblical commentator below. In addition, Calvin's discussion of the sacrament of communion is not merely one more broadside in an overall discrediting of Catholicism; it is no quibble on a point of ritual. As Louis Marin and others have noted, the ritual of communion implicates the entire status of mediation and figurative language in Catholicism and Protestantism.[18] The Catholic belief in the incorporation of the body and blood of Christ through communion is tantamount to the literalization of a religious metaphor, while the Protestant provision of the meaning of communion amounts to an acknowledgment of the figural dimension of religious practices. The Protestant repudiation of the eucharist extends Luther's intention to eliminate (or bypass) the mediation afforded by the Church; it forces a directness in the way in which people must address Christ's martyrdom and loss; but the directness takes place on a cognitive or meditative level. The Protestant challenge to the eucharist transfers its ideological contention with Catholicism to the rhetorical and figurative spheres.

Calvin, even when he enumerates *Five Differences of the New Testament from the Old* ("On God the Redeemer," *OCF,* 61) formulates this revolution in the history of religion as much in terms of rhetorical tropes and hermeneutic practices as he does in terms of doctrinal differences:

> In the first place, the Old Testament is literal, because it was promulgated without the efficacy of the Spirit; the New is spiritual, because the Lord has engraved it in a spiritual manner on the hearts of men.

> The Old Testament is the revelation of death, because it can only involve mankind in a curse; the New is the instrument of life, because it delivers us from the curse and restores us to favor with God.

> The former is the ministry of condemnation, because it convicts all the children of Adam of unrighteousness; the latter is the ministry of righteousness, because it reveals the mercy of God, by which we are made righteous.

> The law having made an image of things that were at a distance, it was necessary that in time it should be abolished and disappear. The gospel, exhibiting the body itself, retains a firm and perpetual stability. Jeremiah calls even the moral law a weak and frail covenant. . . . Now this difference between the "letter" and the "spirit" is not to be understood as if the Lord had given his law to the Jews without any beneficial result . . . but it is used in a way of comparison, to display the plenitude of grace with which the same Legislator, assuming as it were a new character, has honored the preaching of the gospel. (*OCF,* 61)

Calvin, himself entering a comparative mode, distinguishes between the Old and New Testaments in several ways: only one of them, which determines that the Old Testament is "unrighteous" because it is condemnatory, is purely moralistic. The remainder of the points of difference all involve modes of representation and Derridean attitudes of logocentrism. In general, the New Testament falls on the side of spirituality, life, spontaneity, plenitude, and directness; the Old Testament on that of venality, death, arbitrariness, and formality.[19] But in order to posit this overall difference, Calvin has to apply some torque to his materials: he has to posit a "spiritual engraving" on the Christian heart; he has to describe, in other words, the transmission of the living Christian spirituality in a rhetoric of printing, which if pressed far enough, belongs to the "dead" and "weak" domains of the Judaic law. The printing imagery betrays some affinity for writing, intense exegesis, within the framework of Protestantism; this is, of course, at odds with the repugnance toward the formalism and death ascribed to Judaism. By the same token, Calvin declares that the gospel exhibits "the body" (of Christ) itself; yet in comparison with Judaism on the point of the "letter" of the law as opposed to the "spirit," Christianity stands on the metaphoric side of things, that is to say, the spiritual side. The Jews, in this comparison, end up as niggardly holders to the "letter," while Christians engage in the "plenitude" of the "spirit." Yet God himself is the Legislator, he who would dirty his metaphorical hands on the sullied code of legality. As jumbled as the logic of this comparison turns out to be, its most substantial elements revolve around rhetorical and representational issues: literal and figural interpretations; formalism as opposed to spiritual allegory; the figure (body) itself.

A speculative system based on contrasts can always extend itself by shifting the arena of comparisons. The issues of spirituality, literality, and figurality raised in comparison of Protestant theology with Judaism continue to operate when the point of the contrast has shifted to Catholicism. This brings us to the tight web of representational and interpretive issues implicated in the literal-figurative *Auseinandersetzung* with (or taking off from) Catholicism over the practice of communion:

> For as in baptism God regenerates us, incorporates us into the society of his Church, and makes us his children by adoption, so we have said that he acts toward us the part of a provident father of a family in constantly supplying us with food, to sustain and preserve us in that life to which he has begotten us by his word. Now the only food of our souls is Christ; and to him, therefore, our heavenly Father invites us, that, being refreshed by a participation of him, we may gain fresh vigor from day to day till we arrive at the heavenly immortality. And because this mystery of the secret union of Christ with believers is incomprehensible by nature, he exhibits a figure and image of it in visible signs peculiarly adapted to our feeble capacity; and, as it were, by giving tokens and pledges, renders it equally as certain to us as if we beheld it with

our eyes; for the dullest minds understand this very familiar similitude, that our souls are nourished by Christ just as the life of the body is supported by bread and wine. We see, then, for what end this mystical benediction is de-signed—namely, to assure us that the body of the Lord was once offered as a sacrifice to us, so that we may now feed upon it, and feeding on it, may expe-rience within us the efficacy of that one sacrifice; and that his blood was once shed for us, so that it is our perpetual drink. (*Institutes,* "On Communion with Christ," *OCF,* 117–18)

The chief irony here is that the primary means by which Calvin joins the Protestant enterprise of removing the excessive hindrance and mediation by the Church in the human relation to God is through adopting the *figural* as opposed to literal interpretation of the eucharist. Directness, in other words, in the hermeneutic sphere amounts to figurativeness rather than literality: a transfiguration of values has taken place here. The venality of Catholicism (as opposed to Judaism) is the literal meaning it has to impute to communion with Christ. God's nourishment of his human creatures is above all a *figurative* one. Since Calvin imagines God to be doing the cooking, however, He's also functioning as a mother here: "In order to fulfill the part of a most excellent father, solicitous for his offspring, he also undertakes to sustain and nourish us as long as we live" ("On Communion with Christ," *OCF,* 117). Com-munion with God takes place, according to Calvin, not by means of a hy-pothetical intersubjective directness, but through the modality of figuration. In the Lutheran discourse, by contrast, it is a question of a degraded interfer-ence with the human-divine interaction in Catholicism, as opposed to an unmediated encounter in Protestantism. If we read Calvin correctly here, in his speculations it is not so simple: in Catholicism you get literalized sacra-ments and other rituals; in Protestantism, the communion between human beings and God transpires within the figurative sphere.

Hence it is, in the passage immediately above, that "the only food of our souls is Christ" (*OCF,* 118). Christ constitutes a spiritual, figurative food. The ritual of communion, functioning as a paradigm for all explicit rituals, furnishes people, who may not all be as talented in the activity of imaginative projection as they need be, with "a figure and an image" of "the secret union with Christ." The body and blood of Christ, which people take in commu-nion in the form of bread and wine, amount to tangible "tokens and pledges" that the Savior offers people as a sign of His love (*OCF,* 118). There is a historiographical dimension to this substitution of "tokens and pledges" as well. In Calvin's account, Catholics reenact the existence and sacrifice of Christ through communion: we "may experience within us the efficacy of that one sacrifice." Catholic history becomes, in these terms, a concrete reenactment of "original" events whose primary significance is spiritual *and* metaphoric. Removing the arbitrariness of the ritual and the venality of the exchange amounts to acknowledging the figurative level on which theological doctrines and practices exist. In the Protestant world, the shortest distance to God is in the direction of replacing literal practices with figurative, metaphoric understandings. It is in this context, as well as through Protestantism's inherent sympathy for empiricism, that we can understand the importance that hermeneutic practice assumes in Protestant theology.

With this last point in mind, we proceed to a glimpse of Calvin as a scriptural commentator. It is not by accident in such a theological venture that Calvin should display some virtuosity as a textual scholar and as a rhetorical analyst. In the heavily polemical disputations among which Protestant discourse arose, textual citation and manipulation became an empirical basis for winning arguments. Not surprisingly, Calvin's gloss to Genesis 1 : 26 deliberates on (among other topoi) the distinction between *likenesses* and *images*. Genesis 1 : 26 runs as follows: "And God said, Let us make man in our image, after our likeness: and let him have dominion over the fish of the sea, and over the fowl of the air, and over the cattle, and over all the earth, and over every creeping thing that creepeth upon the earth" (*OCF,* 129). Calvin's exegesis of this verse, and the passage that it begins, runs as follows:

> 26. *In our image, etc.* Interpreters do not agree concerning the meaning of these words. The greater part, and nearly all, conceive that the word *image* is to be distinguished from *likeness*. And the common distinction is that *image* exists in the substance, *likeness* in the accidents of anything. They who would define the subject briefly say that in the *image* are contained those endowments which God has conferred on human nature at large, but they expound *likeness* to mean gratuitous gifts. But Augustine, beyond all others, speculates with excessive refinement, for the purpose of fabricating a Trinity in man. For in laying hold of the three faculties of the soul enumerated by Aristotle— the intellect, the memory, and the will—he afterwards out of the one Trinity derives many. . . . I acknowledge, indeed, that there is something in man which refers to the Father and the Son and the Spirit; and I have no difficulty in admitting the above distinction of the faculties of the soul, although the simpler division into two parts, which is used in Scripture, is better adapted to the sound doctrine of piety; but a definition of the image of God ought to rest on a firmer basis than such subtleties. As for myself, before I define the image of God, I would deny that it differs from his likeness. (*Institutes,* "On Genesis," *OCF,* 129–30)

Calvin's conclusion to this particular exegetical conundrum will be that there is no essential difference between *image* and *likeness*. This is not difficult to understand in a theology that is trying to make *figurality in general* the mode of its discourse. We should also notice a digression from this central exegetical point and pretext in the course of the immediately preceding passage. In keeping with the polemical momentum in his text, Calvin avails himself of the occasion to differ with Augustine. The latter, trying to effect a coincidence between Catholic theology and its classical heritage, links the Trinity to the Aristotelian tripartite division of the soul. Calvin dismisses this particular graft as a "subtlety," preferring a more classically Western "simpler division [of the soul] into two parts" (*OCF,* 130). The split in the soul that Calvin prefers, whether between "Father" and "Son" or between "literal" and "figurative," is in line with the overall program of binary logic underlying Protestant differentiation. Interestingly, Calvin calls Augustine out for "subtlety" during a digression, a nonessential elaboration, within his own argument. Yet the critique of excessive subtlety harbors its own particular import. While Protestant hermeneutics is to transpire on the figurative level, there are limits in the degree of elaboration (or subtlety) that this ethos will tolerate. Protestant interpretation defines itself according to a figurative modality, but Calvin's call is for an aesthetic of *plain and simple* figurality. Excessive exegetical ornamentation links the foundation of dogma in canonical texts to Catholic ornateness and interference in the encounter with the divinity. In the particular context in which Calvin's modal appeal emanates, the aesthetic of a *simple figurality* does not constitute an oxymoron. His digression concluded, Calvin sets about defining the image:

> For when Moses afterwards repeats the same thing, he passes over the *likeness* and contents himself with mentioning the *image.* Should anyone take the exception, that he was merely studying brevity, I answer that where he twice uses the word *image,* he makes no mention of the likeness. We also know that it was customary with the Hebrews to repeat the same thing in different words. Besides, the phrase itself shows that the second term was added for the sake of explanation: "Let us make," he says, "man in our image, according to our likeness"—that is, that he may be like God, or may represent the image of God. ("On Genesis," *OCF,* 130)

Moses, in this case, agrees with Calvin in tolerating no subtleties between *image* and *likeness.* Moses simply sticks with the former term. We should appreciate the care of Calvin's reading: he counts exactly how many times Moses, in his reiteration of the scenario from Genesis, uses the word *image.* According to Calvin's appropriation of Moses, the ultimate basis for the term *image* is the human being's resemblance to God. Figurality dictates more than how Protestants should approach canonical texts; it is the very modality of the human-divine interaction. People are linked to God through resemblance.

In Calvinistic Protestantism, rhetoric quickly attains the status of the lever through which the human being gesticulates to, relates to, and even manipulates God. There is nothing inherently religious about rhetoric itself. But rhetoric establishes the terrain, the field, in which it is possible for people to relate to God in a rigorous, if not scientific, way. Although rhetoric is by definition the field of all linguistic ornamentation, the rhetoric to which Calvin makes appeal is one that scrupulously, on the basis of an implicit code of honor, restrains itself to a modality and tone of "plain talk." He has made it clear in the passage above that he will not tolerate excessive subtlety. Discourse will serve God through the labor of rigorous scholarship and the controlled, instrumental deployment of rhetoric. Within the context of the particular Protestant hermeneutics and aesthetic whose principles he is enunciating, Calvin can even be explicit, can "come out," regarding his own role as a rhetorician:

> That he made this image to consist in "righteousness and true holiness" is by the figure *synecdoche,* for though this is the chief part, it is not the whole of God's image. Therefore by this word the perfection of our whole nature is designated, as it appeared when Adam was endowed with a right judgment, had affections in harmony with reason, had all his senses sound and well-regulated, and truly excelled in everything good. Thus the chief seat of the divine image was in his mind and heart, where it was eminent; yet there was no part of him in which some scintillations of it did not shine forth. For there was an attempering in the several parts of the soul which corresponded with their various offices. In the mind perfect intelligence flourished and reigned, uprightness attended as its companion, and all the senses were prepared and molded for due obedience to reason; and in the body there was a suitable correspondence with this internal order. But now, although some obscure lineaments of the image are found remaining in us, yet they are so vitiated and maimed that they may truly be said to be destroyed. For besides the deformity which everywhere appears unsightly, this evil is also added, that no part is free from the infection of sin. ("On Genesis," *OCF,* 131)

Calvin's excursus on figurality in Genesis, on the figurality of the divine image, ends with a melancholic nostalgia for a unique attunement that prevailed within prelapsarian Adam as the image of God. The melancholy of the passage stems from the condition that we shall never be able to attain or return to this unique harmony-in-the-image, in which Adam's judgment, affections, and senses were in perfect working order and in perfect alignment with each other. Adam, by the end of this passage, becomes the image for a certain perfection in imaging, in representation: in him the perfection and symmetry of God are transferred to a human being. There are images and images, just as, within the binary logic of Protestantism, there are worlds and worlds. There is the domain of the elect, and a congenitally flawed, "infected" human earth. Yet before launching into this theological equivalent of a lament, Calvin associated the unique imagery that took place in Adam with *synecdoche,* the rhetorical trope that blurs the distinction between greatness and smallness and totality and partiality, and, by implication, between priority and secondariness. Whereas Adam benefited from an attunement between his greater and lesser faculties, argues Calvin, allowing for their harmony, a "deformity" has intervened in human spirituality between Adam's day and the contemporary moment. Within this fallen and disjointed world of human endeavor, however, rhetoric and rigorous exegesis offer themselves as two primary means for "reaccessing" the kingdom of God. Like the Judeo-Christian deity Himself, rhetoric is abstract and systematic, and as a science it is neutral, detached from the particular manipulations that it describes and categorizes. Calvin adds to the bipolar religious logic an emphasis on individuation and freedom, and reiterates the call for directness in human-divine relations initiated by Luther, in part by appropriating rhetoric as a fundamentally Protestant science. It will then not be difficult by Kant's day and after to enfold linguistic and exegetical virtuosity among the most treasured qualities in the secular recasting of modern theology, among the attributes most associated with the modern artist.

~

The tension between ideology and figurality in early Protestantism serves as a backdrop to a series of transformations ultimately coalescing around the modern artist as a secular mediator to the Real or Sublime invested both with particular powers and limitations. It has already been suggested that Protestantism's self-legitimation through hermeneutical and rhetorical expertise could be displaced to the secular sphere, in which the artist of the broader modernity operates. The erudition that Stephen Dedalus demonstrates both in *The Portrait of the Artist as a Young Man* and in *Ulysses,* as well as the critical virtuosity demanded by nineteenth-century historiography, could be outgrowths of a hermeneutic ethos concretized in early Protestantism and the Counter-Reformation. I call the aesthetic contract the particular set of cultural understandings defining the creative person's role and sphere of operations. I may be wanting too much, because what I have described is a historical argument, yet the impasses and aporias that enter Luther's and Calvin's discourses, as described above, are tropological ones. The discourse of deconstruction has done much to set these systemic ambiguities in relief. From a deconstructive posture, such system-shaking rhetorical knots crop up at any time and in any culture, and belong to the ongoing repository of linguistic features in constellation with the modality of representation that Derrida terms "writing."

What is the connection between linguistically sensitive and historically specific reading? Important work in cultural studies, the New Historicism, and radical democracy has begun to ask this question. Both inside and outside the parameters of the present inquiry, the question is a crucial one.

It is possible, I believe, to approach a cultural phenomenon whose significance is attested to by its persistence and the variations upon it both ideologically and rhetorically, understanding all the time that rhetoric invariably confuses and in some cases reverses ideology, and that ideology primarily results in subjective implications. It makes sense to perform some correlation of ideological values and subjective structures and possibilities; it requires no particular leap of the imagination to see that the strongly articulate values of a culture at a particular time will impact significantly upon personal structures and actions, whether the subjective response is compliance, rebellion, or the inevitable collusion between the two. There is thus a natural affinity between subject-driven interpretations and awareness of historical specificity. At the same time, language-oriented interpretive models, directing their primary attention to the vicissitudes of rhetorical tropes and other linguistic features of an artifact, resist historical specificity, because some version of linguistic generation and distortion is taking place in any cultural arena.

If I am empowered at all to proceed both historically and rhetorically in an exploration of the emergence of the modern aesthetic contract out of an increased freedom pertaining to the Western subject at about the time of the Protestant Reformation, it is because each writing project, both "primary" artifacts and critical ones such as this, is the result of an interface between subjectivity and rhetoric. From the perspective of rhetoric, subjectivity is sometimes an illusion, but it is one whose implications can be traced in the text. From the perspective of subjectivity, rhetorical awareness can be perceived as an arcane and by no means universal level of knowledge. Yet I would argue, and the newness and strangeness of Luther and Calvin to me help in this regard, that an artifact can be submitted at the same time to historical and rhetorical, subject-based and language-oriented, interpretive models.

In terms of the texts by Luther and Calvin whose deployment in an overview of modernity we have begun to outline, the ideology that these writers formulated in their works was historically and culturally significant. Some societies repudiated their Catholicism. Wars were fought. Political figures and soldiers were motivated to fight on the basis of certain of the planks in the Lutheran and Calvinist platforms. Catholic societies, notably in Spain and Italy, initiated their own Counter-Reformation in response to various Protestant ideologies, including Luther's. Catholicism thus took on its own "Protestant" features. Chinese and Japanese societies certainly underwent fluctuations between public moods of liberality and stringency during the time frame known as the "late Middle Ages" and "Renaissance" in the West. The personal and conceptual options available to subjects in Protestant and non-Protestant societies were to some extent a function of ideological and theoretical issues worked through in theological, philosophical, and even literary texts. At all times, the impersonal and to some extent constant functions of rhetoric complicated, undermined, and even reversed the substance of these ideological claims. Culturally literate life, whether in the period under discussion or now, consisted of an interface, an interplay, between the conditions set out in prevalent ideologies and the local differences realized in each generated artifact. Walter Benjamin, for example, was able to assemble the language-based cultural anomalies resulting from early modernity under the heading "German tragic drama." This body of works is categorically complex and linguistically radical, and it nevertheless embodies significant technical and epistemological differences from bodies of works produced under other aesthetic contracts, whether they be "Imagiste poetry" or "cubist painting." (We will be pursuing Benjamin's constructions of German tragic drama and *melancolia,* its temperament, in fuller detail in Chapter 4 below.)

So I want my analysis two ways: historically specific and linguistically aware. This may be a creative endeavor or the mark of a deranged mind. Luther is my starting point because his determinations were *both* historically significant *and* benighted by their irrepressible metaphoric anomalies.

Luther established a space for an epistemological-cultural world in which the "subject," at least in certain class, gender, racial, and ethnic categories, would henceforth increase in individuation and freedom from exhaustive definition by encompassing social systems. The revised package of modern subject conditions that begins to emerge with Luther includes increased isolation, possibilities for personal liberty, and needs for internal self-regulation. The bipolar logic that we see developing in "The Freedom of a Christian" and continued in Calvin's disputations on predestination and teleology in part embodies a fusion between play and severe restraint. The received wisdom in the history of ideas is that the revised subject conditions I am ascribing to Luther begin with Descartes. In these studies, much is made of the

Cartesian toleration of faith (or the arbitrary) alongside the newly constituted sphere for empirical investigations.[20] If I take Luther and Calvin as significant departure points for my own parallel inquiry into the emergence of the modern aesthetic contract, it is for a number of not terribly closely connected reasons: there is a certain *thematic* resonance of Protestantism within a disparate body of texts all interesting in aesthetic-contractual terms. These texts are as spread out as *Hamlet,* Marlowe's and Goethe's *Fausts,* Kant's *Critique of Judgment,* Rousseau's *The Social Contract* and *Emile,* Kleist's "Michael Kohlhaas," Melville's *Moby-Dick,* Kafka's *The Castle,* Hitchcock's "Psycho," and Harris and Demme's *The Silence of the Lambs.*

There is something in Luther's *psychology,* as it has been reconstructed by readers of culture, that lends itself to the characteristic fragmentation of modern experience, and also to an object-relations conceptualization of modernity.[21] The extrapolation of cultural conditions from psychological manifestations is at best a problematical business; yet in a work such as *Young Man Luther,* Erik H. Erikson discerned in his subject fundamental conflicts related to authority, sexuality, and desire, even if these were circumscribed within the "drive-structure" model of psychoanalysis.[22] By virtue of the principle of mutually encompassing frameworks that I have sketched out elsewhere,[23] it is possible to regard psychology as a delusion of metaphysics, and, at the same time, to see intellectual-aesthetic striving as an effect of personal psychology. *All* major schools of psychoanalysis, from the outset (Freud), have had to give careful attention to the splittings of which the modern psyche is capable. As I suggested above in the Introduction, it is possible to discern among the grounding texts of Protestantism not only a characteristically modern unease regarding drives and their fulfillment, but also enabling legislation for conditions of particular interest to object-relations theorists. I think specifically of the radical splitting and the "subjective experience of emptiness" to which psychoanalysts from Melanie Klein through D. W. Winnicott and on to Heinz Kohut, Alice Miller, and Otto Kernberg have devoted such careful attention.

This was a forerunner to the notion of the artist—or the intellectual—as a hypersensitive, hyperbrilliant, singular individual who bridges the gap between normality and sublimity, an idea so well-entrenched as to be naturalized in many cultural quarters today. The ultimate precedent for this particular notion of the artist in the West is the individual who struggles directly with God over his own fate in the wake of the Protestant Reformation. This happening, in the parts of Europe that it influenced, had the effect of a megastructural *withdrawal* of a system that mediated one's relation to the Real and defined one's place in a world order. The (always hypothetical) subject who

emerges on the far side of the sometimes abstruse argumentation that under-
lay Reformation ideology is much less secure, needs to swim considerably
more on her own power, than, say, the human prototypes for the characters
in Chaucer's *Canterbury Tales*.

By 250 to 300 years after Luther's initial disputations, the artist in the West
has emerged as a superordinary individual, endowed with special powers
once reserved for the theologians and God himself. This figure of the artist,
whose lineaments can be discerned in, among other sites, Kant, Goethe, and
Schelling, emerges from a series of conceptual meditations on the relationship between the transcendental and the everyday that begins in full rigor
with Descartes, regardless of his particular theological affiliation. I'd argue
that the bipolar coexistence of religious belief and empiricism in the subject
extrapolated from Cartesian metaphysics is an aftereffect of Protestant ideology, as are the different, but always structurally parallel, empirical investigations of Locke, Berkeley, and Hume (see Chapter 3 below). The Protestant
subject, locked in a (problematically) "direct" encounter with God, is always
a bipolar construct, caught between the idealization demanded by classical
ethical behavior and the horrors of perdition. As a series of conceptual negotiations common to, among other artifacts, Elizabethan tragedy, empirical
philosophy, and the meditative poem evolves into Kantian aesthetics, the
artist emerges as the unique individual who, through his original genius, is
miraculously capable of bringing our degraded world into contact with the
Sublime, the secular Enlightenment name for God and the idealization He
embodies, or "bodies forth."

CHAPTER 3

The Knowledge of Modernity:
Tragedy and Empiricism

HAMLET: O that this too too sullied flesh would melt,
           Thaw, and resolve itself into a dew,
           Or that the Everlasting had not fixed
           His canon 'gainst self-slaughter. O God, God,
           How weary, stale, flat, and unprofitable
           Seem to me all the uses of this world!
           Fie on't, ah, fie, 'tis an unweeded garden
           That grows to seed. Things rank and gross in nature
           Possess it merely. That it should come to this,
           But two months dead, nay, not so much, not two,
           So excellent a king . . .
                 . . . so loving to my mother
           That he might not beteem the winds of heaven
           Visit her face too roughly. Heaven and earth,
           Must I remember? . . .
           O God, a beast that wants discourse of reason
           Would have mourned longer—married with my uncle,
           My father's brother, but no more like my father
           Than I to Hercules. Within a month,
           Ere yet the salt of most unrighteous tears
           Had left the flushing in her gallèd eyes,
           She married. O, most wicked speed, to post
           With such dexterity to incestuous sheets!
           It is not nor it cannot come to good.
           But break my heart, for I must hold my tongue.

                                   (I.ii. 129−59)[1]

Hamlet's tragedy of divided loyalties, subjective emptiness, and a resulting fatal inactivity is set within a decaying garden. The metaphoric tapestry-background that Shakespeare weaves for Hamlet's predicament is overgrown with images of a nature subsiding within itself, dying within itself, emptying out its own vitality and creativity. This is not a place that has lost its nature or is unnatural; rather, it is a place in which an only too natural Nature solipsistically absorbs its own energy and deprives anyone within its confines of drive or idealism. Subsequent history and theory have taught us, of course, that writing itself resides at the interstice between idealistic mystification and deflowering, between the construction of innocence and its skeptical debunking.

Fratricide and incest, major violations of human supportiveness and empathy, enclose, impart their qualities to the Garden of Death and Entropy, the garden that Hamlet describes here. The only activity that thrives in the garden is the synthesis of poetry as embodied in Hamlet's lines. Lines of poetry are evidently as inured to death as the intertwined vines of the morbid garden. The background to the action of *Hamlet* proper, ornamental as well as historical, is listless and melancholic: "weary, stale, flat, and unprofitable" (I.ii.133).

Prince Hamlet may be described as a man who can do no right. His status on the stage of Western predicaments can be seen as a constitutional incapacity to satisfy the several jurisdictions to which he belongs. Subjectivity, if Hamlet is any example, is defined at this juncture of history as the inborn *incapacity* to serve multiple rulers and the systems they represent. Subjectivity is the mark of failure and unavoidable transgression rather than a rubric for coherence and unity of character. This explains, perhaps, why Hamlet's metaphorical garden is a mortuary of entropic degeneration rather than a preserve of life. The options that the tragic hero outlines in a too-famous speech embody the listlessness of this congenitally divided subjectivity:

HAMLET: To be, or not to be—that is the question:
            Whether 'tis nobler in the mind to suffer
            The slings and arrows of outrageous fortune
            Or to take arms against a sea of troubles
            And by opposing end them. To die, to sleep—
            No more—and by a sleep to say we end
            The heartache, and the thousand natural shocks
            That flesh is heir to. 'Tis a consummation
            Devoutly to be wished. To die, to sleep—
            To sleep—perchance to dream; ay, there's the rub,
            For in that sleep of death what dreams may come
            When we have shuffled off this mortal coil,

> Must give us pause. There's the respect
> That makes calamity of so long life.
> For who would bear the whips and scorns of time,
> Th' oppressor's wrong, the proud man's contumely
> The pangs of despised love, the law's delay,
> The insolence of office, and the spurns
> That patient merit of th' unworthy takes,
> When he himself might his quietus make
> With a bare bodkin?
>
> *(III.i.56–76)*[2]

Hamlet's subjectivity is defined by his inability to be at the same time a loyal son to Hamlet Senior, a devoted son to Gertrude, a proper subject to the new king, Claudius, and an attentive suitor to Ophelia. In-difference, the placement of inherently *different* options or states of being on a par—equating wakefulness and sleep, for example—is a comprehensible counter to the exaggerated sense of different duties, and the inability to fulfill them. It is on this basis that the above passage posits an identity of life, death, and sleep, only to discover that the morbidity of sleep in dreams may rouse the morbid to unwanted life. *Hamlet* transpires under the morbid indifference of contraries that have lapsed into sameness. In this morbidity Shakespeare embodies the tragedy of options so different that they must be abandoned, of oblivion resulting from the pain of paths untaken. Life, death, and oblivion meld into the same poisoned stew or witches' potion. When the exasperated Hamlet finally does try to shake Gertrude out of her own oblivion regarding the choices she has made, he blends the perceptual senses. Blind love turns eyes into ears:

> HAMLET: Look you now what follows.
> Here is your husband, like a mildewed ear
> Blasting his wholesome brother. Have you eyes?
> Could you on this fair mountain leave to feed,
> And batten on this moor? Ha! have you eyes?
> You cannot call it love, for at your age
> The heyday in the blood is tame, it's humble,
> And waits upon the judgment, and what judgment
> Would step from this to this? Sense sure you have,
> Else could you not have motion, but sure that sense
> Is apoplexed. . . .
> Eyes without feeling, feeling without sight,
> Ears without hands or eyes, smelling sans all,
> Or but a sickly part of one true sense
> Could not so mope.
>
> *(III.iv.64–82)*[3]

The obverse of Hamlet's tragedy of choices is an indifferent blending of one perceptual domain into the next. Yet there is failure even in the hypothetical world of synergy resulting from sensual meltdown; each sense has lost what it once had to offer its "neighbor." Eyes have lost their feeling, feeling its sight, and so on. The tragedy of Hamlet is not that the prince has failed to calculate exactly the right course of action to take, but that within the subject conditions that he now inhabits, there is no difference whether he lives, dies, or sleeps. His father, by whatever cause, has abandoned him, has been reduced (or enlarged) to a creature of the imaginary; his mother, by virtue of preoccupations that would inevitably attach to something, to his father if not to Claudius, is inaccessible to him. From the outset of the drama, there has been a whiteout of the family, and more importantly, the family structure and system, that might place or guide Hamlet. Such a floating radical is Hamlet, as an exemplary subject of the recent modernity, that he has no wherewithal to sustain Ophelia's understandable familial aspirations. There has been an effacement of political lines of authority. Claudius, a pretender to the crown, is in power, and possibly in no position to repel the aggression of a foreign pretender and usurper, Fortinbras *fils*. As in the Sophoclean tragedies, the fates of family and politics are intertwined. Knowledge of political expediency is as exasperatingly unclear as Hamlet's options. Advantage and disadvantage, moral rectitude and corruption, have become as interchangeable as the domains of sense. These are the anomalies placing Hamlet, like Hieronymus Holzschuher, in the position of an early exemplary modern subject.

Walter Benjamin's term for the overall pall cast over the Renaissance character is melancholy. The thrust of his analysis, in *Trauerspiel,* as we'll be exploring in Chapter 4, is aesthetic and culture-critical. Within this framework, Benjamin's objective is not so much to extrapolate art and subject conditions in modernity, including bipolarity, radical splitting, and the borderline, as to examine how these conditions influence the vocation of writing.[4] Its overall thrust is, rather, to characterize a period-genre so anomalous as to shatter the mold of criticism constituted on those lines, requiring in its wake something different: a critical script enacting dramatically the conditions whereof it speaks. Melancholy is Benjamin's name not for a diagnostic psychopathological category that can be applied to people and certain literary characters; it is an *épistème* characterizing possibilities for thought and action in the first epoch following upon the theological redirections announced by Luther, Calvin, and others. *Hamlet* is redolent with what Benjamin would call baroque melancholy:

HAMLET: Seems, madam? Nay, it is. I know not "seems."
'Tis not alone my inky coat, good mother,
Nor customary coats of solemn black,
Nor windy suspiration of forced breath,
No, nor the fruitful river in the eye,
Nor the dejected havior of the visage,
Together with all forms, moods, shapes of grief,
That can denote me truly. These indeed seem,
For they are actions that a man might play,
But I have that within which passeth show—
These but the trappings and the suits of woe.

(I.ii.76–86)

Hamlet, in these lines, in keeping with Benjamin's spectacular specifications for German tragic drama, is as much the cipher, the emblem of unhappiness, as its subject, the person who "feels" it. Melancholy is consitituted by gesture, "havior," indulgent "acting out" far more than by sentiment: indeed, it would be most difficult for this theater or any dramaturgy to represent sentiment in any pure form. Hamlet protests to his mother that "within" he harbors pure sentiment, that "which passeth show," but for the purpose of the scenic representation, which is what fascinates Benjamin about the drama of the period, what Hamlet *is* he is by virtue of exaggeration, and melancholy is the term for the outrageously self-indulgent portfolio of traits that enable Hamlet and related protagonists in the Spanish and German theaters to claim attention when they occupy center stage. Melancholy is both the sighs and tears of human suffering and the black costume, gestures, and noises by means of which the actor dramatizes these feelings and experiences to an audience. Melancholy in turn becomes, for Benjamin, the modal basis for an entire genre, *Trauerspiel,* that measures its effect by exploding the categories of conventional historically driven scholarship, and by striding the stage of intellectual history as a pariah.

It is not entirely by coincidence, however, that Shakespeare translates Hamlet's existential and dramatic woes into a theological rhetoric of Calvinist election, just as Benjamin gravitates toward the earliest modernity for the body of dramatic works that will, as his critical discourse aspires to, shatter the mold of genre and the progression of history.

HAMLET: Why should the poor be flattered?
No, let the candied tongue lick absurd pomp,
And crook the pregnant hinges of the knee
Where thrift may follow fawning. Dost thou hear?
Since my dear soul was mistress of her choice

And could of men distinguish her election,
S'hath sealed thee for herself, for thou hast been
As one in suff'ring all that suffers nothing,
A man that Fortune's buffets and rewards
Hast ta'en with equal thanks; and blest are those
Whose blood and judgment are so well commeddled
That they are not a pipe for Fortune's finger
To sound what stop she please. Give me that man
That is not passion's slave, and I will wear him
In my heart's core, ay, in my heart of heart,
As I do thee.

(III.ii.56–71)

In this speech Hamlet reveals his fate, and accepts responsibility for it, to an intimate, his friend Horatio. He can only describe the freedom that he has usurped, and that Horatio has renounced, in Calvinist terms of election and fortune. While Horatio, as a good Calvinist, has "been / As one in suff'ring all that suffers nothing, / A man that Fortune's buffets and rewards / Hast ta'en with equal thanks," Hamlet has allowed his own soul to be "mistress of her choice." If the tragic conditions of *Hamlet* are to be extrapolated from this speech, Hamlet is now destined to suffer because, no longer able to tolerate the indifferent morass of possibilities that defines his initial position, he is determined, in clear violation of Calvinist theology, to take his Fortune into his own hands. *He* will not assume a position of flattery in which "the candied tongue lick absurd pomp" and the knee bends on its "pregnant hinges." He eschews, in other words, the radical Protestant bearing in which we can only, more or less passively, await the emergence of our predetermined Fate. Hamlet's "mistress" soul will no longer tolerate the muddle and the passivity, thus stepping into the position of Lady Macbeth, another powerful lady who betrays her man by inducing him to depart from *his* place in an implicitly Protestant world order.

Hamlet will "wear" in his "heart's core" Horatio, "that man / That is not passion's slave," but Hamlet cannot be that man himself. He is already a modern loner, a man who cannot act, but who must act, a man whose alienation from the structures of filiation and differentiation compels him to act in a manner that can only be misconstrued, to adopt a "private language" that will mystify not only Claudius and Gertrude, but Polonius and Ophelia as well. The promises and restraints of Protestant ideology define both Hamlet's predicament and his deviance. Deviance, in terms of Protestantism, is not to revert to Catholic mediation, but rather to export Protestant individuation, alienation, and privacy *outside* the framework of submission in which they attain their initial meaning. Horatio, who consistently refuses the calls of passion, is a good Protestant, one who can aspire to Election. Hamlet and his successors, by contrast, including those cowboy heroes who succeed by taking matters into their own hands, are failed Protestants to the degree that they abandon their stations of passive submission, but their actions nonetheless make sense, have meaning, only within the framework of their Protestant individuation:

HAMLET: Now I am alone.
              O, what a rogue and peasant slave am I!
              Is it not monstrous that this player here,
              But in a fiction, a dream of passion,
              Could force his soul so to his own conceit
              That from her working all the visage wanned,
              Tears in her eyes, distraction in his aspect,
              A broken voice, and his whole function suiting
              With forms to his conceit? And all for nothing,
              For Hecuba!
              What's Hecuba to him, or he to Hecuba,
              That he should weep for her? What would he do
              Had he the motive and the cue for passion
              That I have? He would drown the stage with tears
              And cleave the general ear with horrid speech,
              Make mad the guilty and appal the free,
              Confound the ignorant, and amaze indeed
              The very faculties of eyes and ears.

(II.ii.533–50)

Yet the very predicament in which Hamlet finds himself embedded offers its own means of transcendence and exultation. In the lines immediately following the above passage, Hamlet chastises himself for being "A dull and muddy-mettled rascal" (II.ii.552), who "can say nothing" (II.ii.554), "pigeon-livered, and lack gall / To make oppression bitter" (II.ii.562–63). Hamlet has, however, already given the lie to this presumed absorption in an incapacitating melancholy, in the lines cited immediately above. Hamlet, in said lines, by formulating the actor's art in terms of its simulation and dissimulation, furnishes ample evidence not only of his own aesthetic sensibility and prowess, but also of the privileged relation he maintains to linguistic facility and dramaturgical skill. Hamlet professes amazement, in these lines, at gifted actors' capacities for protesting emotions they do not feel, and he sharply distinguishes his morose inactivity from the impact the players make upon the world around them. But he himself is acting when he denies, to the players, the actors of *Hamlet,* to the literary and "live" audiences of the play, and to Shakespeare, any intention of achieving theatrical effects, such as making "mad the guilty" and appalling "the free" (II.ii.549).

Hamlet assumes the role of "A dull and muddy-mettled rascal" (II.ii.552), yet it is he who is the most fully realized poet and artist in the drama. There is a redemption to his predicament of divided jurisdictions and loyalties, and of a consequent depletion of energy, even if this compensation cannot reverse the play's tragic outcomes: political treachery, false friendship, failed and frustrated love. And this bonus, this buy-back, for acknowledging the dangers with which life in Western modernity is fraught, assumes the form of Hamlet's approximation of the figure of the artist, someone whose linguistic facility and aesthetic sense compensates the audience for the polymorphic tragedies of modern existence. Hamlet is possessed of a tongue as quick and trenchant as the blade that unwittingly murders the concealed Polonius. Language—the very same language that tempers his political effectiveness and that encloses both Marlowe's Dr. Faustus and his German counterpart in a prison-house of outmoded formulae and disciplines—language in *Hamlet* is the medium that offers any satisfaction that may be attained amid such a morass of thwarting political and erotic conditions. The character Hamlet—in keeping with the English and German Faust-figures—resides in a tragic crossfire of Derridean logocentrism: language thwarts his participation in a happy, carefree economy of spiritualized existence and communication; yet at the same time, it is language that affords him any satisfaction he is able to achieve.[5] Because Hamlet is a truly excellent poet and dramaturge (he stages *The Murder of Gonzago,* renamed *The Mousetrap,* wherein is caught "the conscience of the King" [III.i.591]), he can articulate the existential, sociopolitical, and cultural limitations of modernity at the same time that he embodies their possible transcendence or resolution. Hamlet thus prefigures the artist-figure whose ultimate systematic formulation may take place in Kant's *Critique of Judgment,* and who remains so important for Stephen Dedalus in *Ulysses,* even as Joyce attempts to realize principles of modernist aesthetics in the novelistic genre. This rather durable artist-figure, who persists at least from *Hamlet* to *Ulysses,* becomes an icon and institution of human sensibility throughout a modernity demanding enormous facility and intuition as appropriate responses to the limitations noted by Shakespeare. As a number of the artistic treatises of the age, including Lessing's *Laokoon,* make clear, the linguistic mastery of which Hamlet gives such ample evidence is the ur-facility by means of which humans may be able to generate appropriate responses to sociopolitical and epistemological configurations that deny firm knowledge or authority.

When Hamlet steps outside the bounds of his own Protestant submission, a tragedy, in the sense of his own death, has to ensue. But this is not the only possibility. The matrix of possibilities opened up by the particular revision of Western idealism that was implied by Reformation theological disputations is a particularly broad one. Shakespeare composed love sonnets as well as tragedies. The very same matrix demands harsh self-regulation by virtue of unprecedented personal discretion, within an atmosphere of sharply polarized values. But this particular configuration also allows the pleasures of circulation and experimentation taken by a liberated subject. Scientific empiricism and love poetry have an enormous amount in common: they both celebrate the capabilities of an individual subject to enter, gather, and interpret experience in a way that deploys both general (*langue*) and context-specific (*parole*) meaning. Beginning with the Elizabethan post-Protestant epoch, the domain of love becomes the most intense, personal, and intimate sphere in which the private subject, usually a male, conducts scientific research.

Hamlet establishes the morass, the inhospitable, inhuman landscape in which the alienated modern subject first negotiates the central issues of authority, privacy, and the interpretation of cultural codes. But the same moribund garden becomes, for the lover of experience, the point of departure for delightful adventures and excursions. The full spectrum of possibilities inheres in a modern subject, whose range of operation has been negotiated through the at times tenuous arguments of theological disputation.

The Canonization

For Godsake hold your tongue, and let me love,
Or chide my palsie, or my gout,
My five grey haires, or ruin'd fortune flout,
With wealth your state, your minde with Arts improve,
Take you a course, get you a place,
Observe his honour, or his grace,
Or the King's reall, or his stamped face
Contemplate, what you will, approve,
So you will let me love.

Alas, alas, who's injur'd by my love?
What merchants ships have my sighs drown'd?
Who saies my teares have overflow'd his ground?
When did my colds a forward spring remove?

When did the heats which my veines fill
Add one more to the plaguie Bill?
Soldiers find warres, and Lawyers finde out still
Litigious men, which quarrels move,
Though she and I do love.

Call us what you will, wee are made such by love;
Call her one, mee another flye,
We'are Tapers too, and at our owne cost die,
And wee in us finde the'Eagle and the Dove.
The Phoenix ridle hath more wit
By us, we two being one, are it.
So to one neutrall thing both sexes fit,
Wee dye and rise the same, and prove
Mysterious by this love.

Wee can dye by it, if not live by love,
And if unfit for tombes and hearse
Our legend bee, it will be for verse;
And if no peece of Chronicle wee prove,
We'll build in sonnets pretty roomes;
As well a well wrought urne becomes
The greatest ashes, as halfe-acre tombes,
And by these hymnes, all shall approve
Us *Canoniz'd* for Love:

And thus invoke us; You whom reverend love
Made one anothers hermitage;
You, to whom love was peace, that now is rage;
Who did the whole world's soule contract, and drove
Into the glasses of your eyes
So made such mirrors, and such spies,
That they did all to you epitomize,
Countries, Townes, Courts: Beg from above
A patterne of your love!

John Donne[6]

   As the poem specifies, the canonization in love is tantamount to the canonization in a certain religion. In one elegantly short shrift, Donne legislates
both the freedom of eroticism under subjective conditions of individuation
and the role of aesthetics as the mode for subjective play. While love has
been, within the framework of Western metaphysics, always the quintessential zone of experience, Donne supplies the erotic, with its modern (that is,
Protestant, diplomatic, commercial, and legislative) correlatives. The aesthetic, the domain answering to the specifications of the "well wrought,"

announces itself as the order optimal for the linguistic adjudication of matters of the heart, and for deliberation upon tangential themes.

As I have suggested in Chapter 2 above, modern Western ideology heightens the moral dilemma, isolation, and play accruing to the self. An increased leeway opened through a more direct engagement with the sources of authority implies greater moral responsibility and added participation in the scenario of an "ultimate" moral outcome. The domain of love, as articulated by Donne and other erotic poets writing relatively early in the modern period, constitutes the "bright side" to the moral severity. Eroticism will become a major metaphoric field for the exploration of a newly founded personal freedom. There is nothing "new" about assigning sexuality a certain centrality or essentiality in the unfolding of experience, as an ample body of poems deriving from Western antiquity attests. But there is a concentration of language in "The Canonization" and in others of Donne's lyrics that places eroticism and aesthetics in diplomatic, legal, and commercial contexts with specific nuances within an emerging modern age with an ideology of heightened personal experience.

One immediate effect of the speaker's words, at the outset of "The Canonization," will be to silence his interlocutor's speech, and allow him to get down to the "business" of love. Love in the poem functions as a nature whose being is defined by its *persistence in spite of.* The (male) lover's love will take place in spite of the interlocutor's palaver and/or reproaches and in the face of physical degeneration ("my palsie, or my gout, / My five gray haires"), death ("Wee can dye by it, if not live by love"), financial ruin ("or ruin'd fortune flout"), "the Kings reall, or his stamped face," logic ("the Phoenix ridle"), war, and legal squabbling ("Soldiers find warres, and Lawyers finde out still / Litigious men, which quarrels move, / Though she and I do love"). Love will somehow persist, win the day, whether initiated by the speaker or, as figured, as common-law property that he and his lover share; yet by the middle of the poem, the force of nature that initially authorized love has been transformed into a statute of art. By stanza four, love prevails not because of its indistinctness from nature but because its complexities can be embodied alone in utopic artifacts functioning as counterdomains to the degraded and degenerative world in which love *takes place.* Enlightened poetry will demarcate the aesthetic preserves of "sonnets pretty roomes" (32) and "well wrought" urns (33). This enclosed, though linguistically constituted, space serves as a refuge from "Countries, Townes, Courts" (44). What transpires within it is a canonization, an apotheosis, under the aegis of Love's protections and immunities. The structure of this particular canonization derives unmistakably from the unmediated encounter with the deity, the providence, freedom, and potential perdition set out in Protestant theology. The poem, the "well wrought urne," becomes the only possible collateral in a gamble that, though theologically structured, may result in a serious loss of credit, the moral and theological equivalent of bankruptcy.

Eroticism is the ultimate proving ground of the de-institutionalized self.[7] In his erotic poetry, Donne celebrates the founding of a subjectivity defined by its sexual behavior and language; at the same time, Donne is unique in pursuing the diplomatic, legalistic, and commercial implications of the erotic. Donne's love poetry thus spans the only two possible sources for ideas, according to Locke, sensation and reflection:[8] the poetry coordinates intense sensual descriptions of eroticism with metaphorical elaborations of this behavior in terms of the prevalent cultural terms into which it can be translated: law, theology, politics, and even medicine.

The importance of personal experience increases in a theology that downplays the role of mediatory institutions and practices that intervene between the worshipper and the deity. Protestant theology colonizes the realm of personal experience. This domain is potentially fecund with theological meaning. In exchange, personal experience claims a certain singularity and inalienability for itself. It is in this sense that both the religious "meditative poem" and elegies of love could be media for an emerging Protestant poetics.

Erotic poetry becomes the preeminent medium for the exploration of experience during an age in which God is either in direct communication with the subject or He has entirely withdrawn from the world. Eroticism becomes a highly charged metaphorics for the evolution of experience in general; we may not change in our citizenship or religious affiliation, but our entry into the domain of sexuality is an *initiation,* an *opening up.* Modern eroticism makes empiricists of everyone. The empiricism of Locke, Berkeley, and Hume insists that experience be, to the maximum degree possible, the source of spiritual, ideational, and ideological constructs. Experience would not be important were it not for an augmented cultural confidence in the human capability to interpret the empirical domain in a meaningful and ultimately edifying way. Experience is not distinct from its interpretation. Experience increases in its value as an occasion for human reflection in the context of a direct subjective encounter with the Transcendental. Such an encounter implies the effacement of extrinsic (for example, ecclesiastical, monarchical) institutions previously assigned responsibility in the allocation of meaning. Eroticism is merely one facet of an overall empiricist project in which knowledge increases, and the Transcendental is approached, through the survival and meaningful interpretation of a sequence of experiences. Coinciding with the entrenchment of Protestant attitudes in European societies, the European novel may be regarded, in one facet, as an empiricist experiment. Novelistic protagonists, male and female, who undergo a succession of sexual partners and marital arrangements, are readers' surrogates in a quest for knowledge and for human-derived criteria for the evaluation of knowledge. While the history of the novel of course favors male explorers in the plenitude of sexual experience as a paradigm for knowledge, it remains difficult to separate the fictionalized seriality of sexual experience from the broader empirical project. From the perspective of the emergence of empiricism from Protestant ontotheology and ideology, it is difficult to condemn the titillating dimension of the quest for knowledge through sexual experience while appreciating the underlying empirical ethos of this scenario.

From a deconstructive point of view, the empiricist enterprise may be regarded as a series of experiments incorporating at least the following features into their design: (a) an attempt to circumscribe the role of a priori metaphysical and/or spiritual constructs, such as God or the soul, to the greatest degree possible; (b) an effort to infer or extrapolate higher or more complex concepts from more simple, elementary ones, rather than the reverse, and therefore, to emphasize the synthetic or combinatorial operations of logic; (c) where possible, to derive abstract concepts and operations from physical phenomena and their effect on sensation; (d) to endow the language that is the medium of discourse with the same facticity as the (often physical) phenomena that define the structures and workings of consciousness; (e) assigning to the rigorous, controlled deployment of language the critical function of checking logic and delimiting the play of mystified and irrational (because unverifiable) constructs within the discourse; (f) starting out from the Cartesian dualism, content to function as a self-contained complex concept-game (as in Wittgenstein's "unbounded language games"),[9] *not* essentially antithetical to but coexistent with spiritually or metaphysically based systems. The greatest curiosity about this sequence of empirical experiments in which, in very different ways, Locke, Berkeley, and Hume engaged is the combination of, on the one hand, an open acknowledgment of the torque exerted by language upon thinking and writing, and on the other, a controlled deployment of linguistic possibility. Each of the concept-systems introduced by the empiricists would delimit uncertainty in a new and innovative way, only to see semiological drift disrupt the experiment from putatively insignificant and invariably surprising quarters.

Contrary to the line of demarcation between continental philosophy and its Anglo-American/empiricist Other—a line that has become so common to our schools of philosophy as to have acquired the status of Nature—it is possible to read empiricism very much within the history of idealism that

Jacques Derrida's philosophy, in an ongoing way, discloses. Empiricism is a complex model of philosophy in which the ideal is displaced from the ontological limit to the method of its progressive disclosure, which is, categorically, modest, self-correcting, and logically rigorous or severe. The idealism of empiricism assumes the form of a self-effacing *ethos* of philosophy. The ideal resides not so much in the universe, where it is to be discovered, or in the researcher, where it is to be revered, as in the method, the business of speculation and other intellectual work.[10] In empiricism, idealism receives a translation into modality, tone, prevailing ethos. Historically, we might say that empiricism is that which *came between* the Cartesian dualism, itself an effect of Protestant bipolarity, in which the scientific coexisted with the metaphysical, and the Protestant bipolarity *and* the Kantian synthesis that deployed empirical methods in reinstating, in a very limited way, the transcendental horizons of speculation. Kant's privileging synthesis as an operation epitomizing speculative and artistic originality may thus be construed as an effort on the part of systematic philosophy to uplift—*Aufheben*—and redefine the divisiveness of early modern thought. Derrida teaches us most powerfully that Western philosophy never dispenses with idealism: the trick in moving between its varied models is to read the displacements that transpire between the different ideal-based systematizations.[11] It is in this sense that we do not (as the philosophy departments have seen fit to do) need to separate either empiricism or "continental philosophy" out of the philosophical mainstream: we can instead read the models for which these categories serve as rubrics as successive (or alternate) ideal-oriented models of speculation. The discourse of Ludwig Wittgenstein can be read in one sense as an attempt to reformulate the Transcendental at the conclusion of a meta-Empirical reiteration of Empiricism.

~

Two indicative citations follow. In the first, John Locke configures the established Enlightenment constellation linking "freedom of mind," "industry," and "labor of thought." Yet in the extract that follows, David Hume engages in a theological polemic seemingly inimical to British empiricism's characteristic bearing. We are already becoming familiar with the outlines of this religious disputation.

> The *extent of our knowledge* comes not only short of the reality of things, but
> even of the extent of our own ideas. Though our knowledge be limited to
> our ideas, and cannot exceed them either in extent or perfection; and though

these be very narrow bounds, in respect of the extent of All-Being, and far short of what we may imagine to be in some even created understandings, not tied down to the dull and narrow information that is to be received from some few, and not very acute, ways of perception, such as are our senses. . . . Nevertheless, I do not question but that human knowledge, under the present circumstances of our beings and constitutions, may be carried much further than it has hitherto been, if men would sincerely, and with freedom of mind, employ all that industry and labour of thought, in improving the means of discovering truth, which they do for the colouring or support of falsehood, to maintain a system, interest, or party they are once engaged in. (John Locke, *An Essay Concerning Human Understanding, E,* 84)

The ceremonies of the Roman Catholic religion may be considered as instances of the same nature. The devotees of that superstition usually plead in excuse for the mummeries, with which they were upbraided, that they feel the good effect of those external motions, and postures, and actions in enlivening their devotion and quickening their fervor which otherwise would decay, if directed entirely to distant and immaterial objects. We shadow out the objects of our faith, say they, in sensible types and images, and render them more present to us by the immediate presence of these types. . . . Sensible objects have always a greater influence on the fancy than any other. . . . I shall only infer from these practices, and this reasoning, that the effect of resemblance in enlivening the ideas is very common. (David Hume, *An Enquiry Concerning Human Understanding, E,* 343)

The first passage is a credo of faith regarding what men, with their constitutional "freedom of mind" and in accordance with principles of "industry and labour of thought" can accomplish. A certain poignancy attends the broad scope of faith and the modest and restrained measures that will be deployed in order to fulfill it. Philosophical inquiry itself diverges, in this passage, from the Calvinist "vanity of human life" (*Institutes,* 9.1, *OCF,* 73). It will "not aspire with too much avidity after transient and uncertain riches" (*Institutes,* 9.1, *OCF,* 73).

The second citation, by David Hume, displays a surprising degree of invective against a particular conceptual and behavioral model, Catholicism, in light of the detachment and modest descriptiveness to which philosophical discourse aspires. One might even say that on this rare occasion philosophical restraint tips its cards. By the end of this paragraph, the overall aim of neutrality has regained its ground, and Catholicism is dismissed merely as one instance of practices in which conceptualization gets thrown off track through the literalization of what we today call metaphors and Hume calls resemblances. But for a moment in this passage, philosophical discourse has, unwittingly or not, metamorphosed itself into theological disputation.

In terms of the prevailing contemporary wisdom regarding the intellectual history of the age, the two passages bracket the evolution of empiricism. In a hopeful though characteristically restrained tone, Locke sets out the conditions for a conceptual protocol that proceeds from the perceptual to the ideational and from the simple to the complex, all under a credo that a precise deployment of language will unravel the perplexities that emerge along the way. By the moment of the second passage, Hume is somewhat poignantly laying bare the perplexities that not even an authentic empirical procedure can dispatch. "The *imagination* of man is naturally sublime, delighted with whatever is remote and extraordinary, and running, without control, into the most distant parts of space and time in order to avoid the objects, which custom has rendered too familiar to it. A correct *judgment* observes a contrary method, and avoiding all distant and high inquiries, confines itself to common life, and to such subjects as fall under daily practice and experience" (*Enquiry, E,* 428). With great intellectual integrity, Hume discloses the epistemological limits that not even an empirical approach will dissolve. Yet even in the forthrightness of his intellectual "investigative reportage," he holds true to the basic tenets of what has by his time established itself as an empirical tradition: in the last-cited lines, the allegiance to "common life" and "daily practice and experience" (*E,* 428). More important, even at the culmination of the decisive *Enquiry,*

> The idea of extension is entirely acquired from the senses of sight and feeling; and if all the qualities, perceived by the senses, be in the mind, not in the object, the same conclusion must reach the idea of extension, which is wholly dependent on the sensible ideas or the ideas of secondary qualities. Nothing can save us from this conclusion, but the asserting, that the ideas of those primary qualities are attained by *abstraction,* an opinion, which, if we examine it accurately, we shall find to be unintelligible, and even absurd. An extension, that is neither tangible nor visible, cannot possibly be conceived; and a tangible or visible extension, which is neither hard nor soft, black or white, is equally beyond the reach of human conception. (*Enquiry, E,* 422)

Locke, in establishing an evolutionary scenario for the emergence of concepts, posited a pivotal distinction between "simple" ideas that enter consciousness through a single sense or through perception alone (for instance, light, color, heat, cold, taste, and solidity) and those that involve some coordination between sensation and reflection (pleasure, pain, existence, unity, power, succession). Even while Berkeley has subjected the Lockean hierarchy and progressive ordering to a critique (*E,* 154), Hume holds fast to the empirical grounding of all concepts in experience. In the above passage, even extension, a fundamental intuition, ultimately derives from the senses.

Hume poignantly discloses the limits of all—even of empirically grounded knowledge. Locke hopefully builds the protocols for a progressive, human-centered science *from the ground up*. In spite of fundamental differences, in attitude and in the thrusts of their respective critiques, the empiricists maintained a very healthy skepticism toward the concepts and operations of abstraction. In light of the ontotheological issues that empiricism was addressing, even if on a subliminal level, it is not difficult to infer why this is so: abstraction is to philosophy what God is to naive (that is, pre-Protestant) religions, an autonomous, inherently arbitrary ideational point of orientation. The critique of abstraction in which Locke, Berkeley, and Hume commonly engage is tantamount to limiting the powers of a preexistent godhead who governs the universe in a particularly a priori manner. In this sense, Locke, Berkeley, and Hume may be regarded, despite the division of labor in contemporary departments of philosophy, as deconstructionists of the abstract and the a priori.

In the passage immediately above, Hume, after having questioned the received scientific wisdom of his day, including its Lockean elements, acknowledges that even so pivotal an intuition as extension emerges into abstraction only through sensory experience. In *An Enquiry Concerning Human Understanding,* Hume recurs at least five times to the image of the interchanges that take place on a billiards table in elaborating what relations of causality can and cannot tell us. The meticulous work that Hume does in delimiting the claims of causality and the inferences that can be based on those claims Berkeley invests in a multifaceted critique of abstraction itself. Ironically, of the three classical empiricists, the discourse of Berkeley is the most deconstructive in its overall debunking of ideation; yet it is Berkeley who most explicitly slips into the logocentric bias against language as the culprit in abstract misunderstandings. There is an explanation for this seeming inconsistency: a kind of speculative reaction-formation against his own intuition. So close is Berkeley to approaching the linguistic dynamics shaping all discursive formulations that, being unable to extrapolate this fully, he stops at the halfway-solution of correcting discursive error through a formally constrained, empirically tempered deployment of language. Berkeley, in his application of formally corrected language to the errors of ideation, has discovered a pre-Wittgensteinian position. Hume gives ample demonstration of how many cobwebs of abstraction and other ideational processes can be cleared away through a judicious usage of language. His analyses, in the *Enquiry,* of custom (*E,* 336), description (*E,* 341), contiguity and resemblance (*E,* 343–44), conjunction (*E,* 357, 374), and analogy (*E,* 383), in their calm descriptiveness and precision, anticipate the language-based contributions offered in the twentieth century by logical analysis, speech-act theory, and similar approaches.

Locke shapes the entire empiricist enterprise, much as subsequent psycho-analytic theory can never entirely detach itself from Freud. Locke establishes both the subject conditions under which scientific inquiry can take place and the grammar of the relations between the ideas whose ultimate source and origin is (perceptual and reflexive) experience. As suggested above, the scientist, like the Protestant, addresses the world with a sharp sense of the powers at her disposal and those withheld from her, with a dramatic sense of *liberty and necessity*.

> 8. *Liberty, what.*—All the actions that we have any idea of reducing them-selves, as has been said, to these two, viz. thinking and motion; so far as a man has power to think or not to think, to move or not to move, according to the preference or direction of his mind, so far is a man *free*. Wherever any performance or forbearance are not equally in a man's power . . . there he is not free, though perhaps the action may be voluntary. . . . So that the idea of *liberty* is, the idea of a power in any agent to do or forbear any particular ac-tion, according to the determination or thought of the mind. . . . So that liberty cannot be where there is no thought, no volition, no will; but there may be thought, there may be little will, there may be volition, where there is no liberty. (*E*, 43–44)

It is of great moment here, to the history of Western science and philosophy as well as to Locke's own work, that the exercise of liberty is tantamount to the ability to perform intellectual work. Liberty, the freedom to think or not to think, to do or forbear from doing, arises in many contexts, but never in one devoid of intellectual activity. In this sense, liberty is tantamount to thought. It is the exercise of human intellectual (the modern translation of "spiritual") capabilities. In an earlier formulation, Locke has figured this ex-ercise of agency as the ability to address (or be) "as we say, white paper, void of all characters, without any ideas" (*E*, 10). The writerly metaphor in which modern agency and intellectual development are associated with imprints upon a blank page suggests a more fundamental interaction between empiri-cal study and language than Locke is usually prepared to admit.

The blank page of consciousness and intellectual development in the modern age is pure in its whiteness. The birth of empiricism is attended by the same polarized values that were necessitated by the withdrawal of insti-tutionalized mediation in the revisions initiated by the Protestant Reforma-tion. The first sentence in the Introduction to *An Essay* runs: "Since it is the *understanding* that sets man above the rest of sensible beings, and gives him all the advantage and dominion which he has over them; it is certainly a subject, even for its nobleness, worth our labour to inquire into" (*E*, 7). Like a new Genesis, *An Essay Concerning Human Understanding* begins with the dominion of humans over other living beings, and with the polarity of mind, that uniquely human attribute, over the nonintellectual organic corporeality represented by "dumb beasts." The overall sense of bipolarity with which empiricism initiates itself continues in a section heading that is also one of *An Essay's* credos: "2. *All Ideas come from Sensation or Reflection.* . . . First, our Senses, conversant about particular sensible objects, do convey into the mind several distinct perceptions of things, according to those various ways wherein those objects do affect them. . . . Secondly, the other fountain from which experience furnisheth the understanding with ideas is,—the perception of the operations of our own minds within us. . . . The source of ideas every man has wholly in himself. . . . But as I call the other Sensation, so I call this REFLECTION" (*E*, 9–10). Empiricism will go on to try to understand reflexivity in a nonspiritualistic, intellectually responsible way, but in its Lockean *Grundprinzipe*, its fundamentals, this intellectual *modus operandi* rests on polar distinctions, arranged in chains of analogy: human/animal is to mind/body is to sources of data in reflection/sensation. To these will be added the distinction between simple and complex concepts, with the empirical emphasis on the former. Empiricism, in its own iconoclasm, its own rebuttal to the classical metaphysical configuration, may attempt to privilege the traditionally degraded complements: animal, body, sensation. But its architecture stands on a foundation of bipolar splits regardless of the particular values it advances.

So a modern science for Locke will be founded on an intense awareness of the *freedoms* of enquiry, just as Protestant faith was founded on a near-painful sense of free (because unobstructed) moral discretion. Freedom is at the heart of a nexus of subjective attributes and agencies that includes desire, will, and power. Locke underlines this centrality:

> *Liberty* is a power to act or not to act, according as the mind directs. A power to direct the operative faculties to motion or to rest in particular instances is that which we call the *will*. That which in the train of our voluntary actions determines the will to any change of operation is *some present uneasiness,* which is, or at least is always accompanied with that of *desire*. Desire is always moved by evil, to fly it: because a total freedom from pain always makes a necessary part of our happiness: but every good, nay, every greater good, does not constantly move desire, because it may not make, or may not be taken to make, any necessary part of our happiness. For all that we desire, is only to be happy. But, though this general desire of happiness operates constantly and invariably, yet the satisfaction of any particular desire *can be suspended* from determining the will to any subservient action, till we have ma-

turely examined whether the particular apparent good . . . makes a part of
our real happiness, or be consistent or inconsistent with it. The result of our
judgment upon that examination is what ultimately determines the man;
who could not be *free* if his will were determined by anything but his own
desire, guided by his own judgment. (*E,* 49–50)

While in no way suspending the liberty accruing to each modern subject,
Locke here grapples with the fact that an overall liberty can be restrained or
otherwise qualified through the division of the subject into diverse functions
or agencies. In this respect, he continues the treatment of subjectivity as a coordination of interests whose highest legislative formulation is to be found
in Kant. In this passage, desire invariably seeks happiness, yet liberty is not
synonymous with desire, because under some circumstances our better judgment can *suspend* the fulfillment of our desire. Through the inbuilt check of
suspension, or what Locke calls elsewhere in this passage indifferency, human
beings can avoid subjection to their wills and desires at the same time that
they exercise freedom.

Empirical methodology is, then, inseparable in Locke from the emergence of a new kind of subject, a modern one. At the heart of this new
subject is a new kind of grammar. The empirical subject can look at the
world in an orderly and more dispassionate way, in comparison to earlier
human emanations, in part because such a subject is preprogrammed with a
grammar that redefines experience, that explains to the subject what he or
she is seeing. There is not in Locke the tension between experience and its
grammar that will be so unavoidable in Derrida, and that will even come to
the fore in Berkeley. The grammar through which the empirical subject understands the world simply comprises part of her or his equipment, or hard-
ware. Even though we may find in Berkeley and Hume a greater tension
between the constitution of subjectivity and the grammar of reflection, the
empiricist presupposition will consistently be that the rigorous deployment
of terminology will result in greater scientific and ethical control.

It is in the context of the image of the mind as "white paper" that Locke
establishes a rhetoric of "imprinting" by which the mind receives ideas from
the outside world; as in the "variety of ideas . . . imprinted on the minds of
children" (*E,* 12), or: "Thus the first capacity of human intellect is,—that the
mind is fitted to receive the impressions made on it" (*E,* 15). The mind is not
only, rhetorically, a substance (or body) waiting to be formed or imprinted
by the intellect, it is a bounded organism (again: or body) that receives ideas
through its "inlets": "15. *Perception the Inlet of all Materials of Knowledge*"
(*E,* 33). The implicit *design* within the grammar of empiricism is toward
the treatment of the mind not as something spiritualistic or metaphysical, but

as something definite and observable, whose conditions can be controlled: in short, as a body. This displacement transpires in spite of groundwork re-affirming the classical mind/body split that Locke incorporates into the wider conceptual scaffolding supporting *An Essay.*

One encompassing design of the empiricist grammar is the despiritual-ization of conceptual processes and entities: "1. *Idea is the Object of Thinking.*" Not only does empiricism treat ideas as corporeal entities or things, it re-valorizes the value of the object in relation to the subject. This grammar does more than characterize the relationship between the "external" world and the mind, with its rhetorics of imprinting and inlets. It also speaks in terms of the combination, the "co-existence," and the agreement of ideas, as if they were physical objects that had somehow to fit within the same limited space. The twelfth chapter of *An Essay* is entitled "Of Complex Ideas."

> 1. *Made by the Mind out of Simple Ones.*—We have hitherto considered
> those ideas, in the reception whereof the mind is only passive, which are
> those simple ones received from sensation and reflection before mentioned,
> whereof the mind cannot make one to itself, nor have any idea which does
> not wholly consist of them. But as the mind is wholly passive in the recep-
> tion of all its simple ideas, so it exerts several acts of its own, whereby out
> of its simple ideas, as the materials and foundations of the rest, the others are
> framed. The acts of the mind . . . are chiefly these three: (1) Combining sev-
> eral simple ideas into one compound one; and thus all *complex ideas* are made.
> (2) The second is bringing two ideas, whether simple or complex together,
> by setting them by one another, so as to take a view of them at once, without
> uniting them into one; by which it gets all its *ideas of relations.* (3) The third is
> separating them from all other ideas that accompany them in their real exis-
> tence: this is called abstraction: and thus all its *general ideas* are made. This
> shows man's power, and its ways of operation, to be much the same in the
> material and intellectual world. (*E,* 37–38)

It is fully in keeping with the principles of empiricism that once its objects have been defined and circumscribed, the principles of their interaction should be schematized. The principles by which ideas, as atomic thought-objects, relate to each other derive from mathematics, physics, and chem-istry: addition, mixture, precipitation. Within this domain of physical acts and objects of thought, there is as yet no major suspicion regarding abstrac-tion: Locke treats it merely as one thought-act among others, separating ideas from the contingencies prevailing in their native habitats, among field conditions.

Ideas are thus objects in an empirical protocol in which the rules of their interaction derive from the hard sciences, still known as "natural history."

Yet another outgrowth of this shared attitude that Locke is initiating, this "contract," is that logic too emerges from the collisions and divergences of ideas conceptualized as atomic thought-objects: Chapter 1 of Book IV of *An Essay* is entitled "Of Knowledge in General." It begins:

> 1. *Our Knowledge conversant about our Ideas only.*—Since the mind, in all its thoughts and reasonings, hath no other immediate object but its own ideas, which it alone does or can contemplate, it is evident that our knowledge is only conversant about them.
>
> 2. *Knowledge is the Perception of the Agreement or Disagreement of two Ideas.*— *Knowledge* then seems to me to be nothing but *the perception of the connection of and agreement, or disagreement and repugnancy of any of our ideas.* In this alone it consists. Where this perception is, there is knowledge, and where it is not, there, though we may fancy, guess, or believe, yet we always come short of knowledge. For when we know that white is not black, what do we else but perceive, that these two ideas do not agree? (*E*, 75)

The ideas that constitute knowledge interrelate through a series of principles grounded simultaneously in logic and the emotions, or passions. Ideas connect, agree, disagree, and repel each other, the last term in physical and affective senses of the word. The empirical enterprise in full gear, Locke goes on to schematize the relations between ideas:

I. *Identity,* or *diversity.*
II. *Relation.*
III. *Co-existence,* or *necessary connexion.*
IV. *Real Existence.* (*E*, 76)

It is necessary, in this ideational domain perceived as a controlled environment in physics, only to *see* the relation between the ideas in order to *know* the status of knowledge. It is possible for Locke, at this stage in the unfolding of empiricism, to bracket the language-nature or linguistic dynamics of ideas whose only cultural manifestation is discursive. Relations between ideas such as identity or diversity, or coexistence alone, can characterize what transpires within the plane of knowledge. Locke can, in setting the parameters of the empirical enterprise, hold in reserve the question of the relation between the physical (or "hard scientific") picture of the interaction between ideas and the linguistic nature of conceptual formulations. Yet this question furnishes both Berkeley and Hume with enormous food for thought. Indeed, if one chooses to discern a gradual skepticism invading and co-opting the history of empiricism, it is around the question of the linguistic dimension of ideas that the doubt articulates itself. At the same time, however, both Berkeley and Hume take their participation in the empiricist "concept-contract" as an

occasion to continue the debunking of ideational presuppositions and procedures made possible by Locke's progressive, perception-based, and grammatical endeavor.

∼⌒∽

If one were to allow the reduction of Berkeley's and Hume's entire enterprises to single concept-acts, one might say that Berkeley resolutely offers a
corrective to "those absurdities and contradictions into the several sects of philosophy" (*E*, 137), while Hume furnishes a forthright *acknowledgment* of the
complexities that philosophy may never set aright. Berkeley's commitment
to the project of pointing up the absurdities in a wide range of philosophical
approaches, from idealism to materialism and including empiricism, gives his
work the greatest polemical focus among the acknowledged empiricists:

> My purpose therefore is, to try if I can discover what those principles are
> which have introduced all that doubtfulness and uncertainty, those absurdities
> and contradictions, into the several sects of philosophy; insomuch that the
> wisest men have thought our ignorance incurable, conceiving it to arise from
> the natural dullness and limitation of our faculties. And surely it is a work
> well deserving our pains to make a strict inquiry concerning the first prin-
> ciples of human knowledge, to sift and examine them on all sides, especially
> since there may be some grounds to suspect that those lets and difficulties,
> which stay and embarrass the mind in its search after truth, do not spring
> from any darkness and intricacy in the objects . . . so much as from false prin-
> ciples which have been insisted on. (*E*, 137)

> It is proper to premise somewhat, by way of introduction, concerning the
> nature and abuse of language. But the unraveling of this matter leads me in
> some measure to anticipate my design, by taking notice of what seems to
> have had a chief part in rendering speculation intricate and perplexed, and
> to have occasioned innumerable errors and difficulties in almost all parts of
> knowledge. And that is the opinion that the mind hath a power of framing
> *abstract ideas* or notions of things. He who is not a perfect stranger to the writ-
> ings and disputes of philosophers must needs acknowledge that no small part
> of them are spent about abstract ideas. These are in a more especial manner
> thought to be the object of those sciences which go by the name of *logic* and
> *metaphysics,* and all of that which passes under the notion of the most ab-
> stracted and sublime learning, in which one shall scarce find any question
> handled in such a manner as does not suppose their existence in the mind,
> and that is well acquainted with them. (*E*, 137–38)

I have cited at length these two nearly contiguous passages from the Introduction to Berkeley's *A Treatise Concerning the Principles of Human Knowledge*

because they incorporate, in microcosm, several of the major ongoing concerns in *A Treatise* and several of the characteristic stresses in the underlying architectonics. There is surely a noble tone of resolute inquiry and enlightenment about the initial passage: discovering the principles responsible for absurdities and ignorance; making "a strict inquiry into the first principles of knowledge" (*E,* 137); being willing "to sift and examine" these principles "on all sides" (*E,* 137). These are all lofty aspirations, with which only the mean-spirited would take issue.

Berkeley infuses the scene, the interior space of philosophy, with decorum, yet the villains, the threats to this domestic tranquillity, cannot be far behind. Berkeley exposes two culprits in the second passage, a major and a minor. The major villain, whose relentless debunking and criticism will afford *A Treatise* a unique focus, is abstraction itself. Berkeley will make a pet project out of discovering and announcing the delusions and abuses that emanate from abstraction under every guise and in every location. Yet at the beginning of the second passage, Berkeley cites, and then for the moment dismisses, another source of philosophical evil, "the nature and abuse of language" (*E,* 137). It will be possible for Berkeley to blame language for certain processes in abstraction, such as the generalization that invariably takes place in the process of naming or nomination. Language is, however, the medium of Berkeley's discourse, so he cannot entirely dispense with it. An unsettling mixture of tones—one would be tempted to say a bipolar mixture—pervades these early passages: extending from eloquent leavetaking and proposal to angry vilification. Thus, in the very Introduction to *A Treatise,* Berkeley announces the overall orientation of his critique—it will be against abstraction—and he identifies the linguistic whipping-boy that contributes to the specificity of his analysis and upon which, by virtue of disproportionate blame, his analysis founders.

Berkeley's analysis of abstraction, and his survey of its forms and disadvantages for philosophical discourse, are powerful, vigorous, ingenious, and in the spirit of the sustained deconstructive exposure of points of conceptual blockage and fixity. For all of Berkeley's misgivings about language, he is by far the most muscular and inventive writer among the British empiricists. He questions, with regard to color, the cognitive possibility of speaking in terms of set colors (*E,* 138). He anticipates the Wittgensteinian "family resemblance" argument in questioning the underlying abstraction in the concept "man" (or for that matter, "animal"; *E,* 139).

Berkeley's relentless pursuit of abstraction and its distortions quickly passes from the sphere of "experience" to that of prior contributions to the history of philosophy. None of philosophy's ample battery of inventions and constructs is sacrosanct: mind, spirit, soul, intuition, extension, quality, and even Being itself are made to feel the scourge of Berkeley's questioning. Below follow some characteristic Berkeleyan debunking formulations:

> For example, the mind having observed that Peter, James, and John resemble each other in certain common agreements of shape and other qualities, leaves out of the complex or compounded idea it has of Peter, James, and any other particular man, that which is peculiar to each, retaining only what is common to all, and so makes an abstract idea wherein all the particulars equally partake. (*E,* 139)

> By *matter,* therefore, we are able to understand an inert, senseless substance, in which extension, figure, and motion do actually subsist. But it is evident from what we have already shown, that extension, figure, and motion are only ideas existing in the mind, and that an idea can be like nothing but another idea, and that consequently neither they nor their archetypes can exist in an unperceiving substance. Hence, it is plain that the very notion of what is called *matter,* or *corporeal substance,* involves a contradiction in it. (*E,* 154)

> Again, *great* and *small, swift* and *slow,* are allowed to exist nowhere without the mind, being entirely relative. . . . The extension therefore which exists without the mind is neither great nor small, the motion neither swift nor slow, that is, they are nothing at all. But, say you, they are extension in general, and motion in general: thus we see how much the tenet of extended movable substances existing without the mind depends on the strange doctrine of *abstract ideas.* (*E,* 155)

> It is said extension is a mode or accident of matter, and that matter is the *substratum* that supports it. Now I desire that you would explain to me what is meant by matter's *supporting* extension. Say you, I have no idea of matter and therefore cannot explain it. I answer, though you have no positive, yet, if you have any meaning at all, you must at least have a relative idea of matter; though you know not what it is, you must be supposed to know what relation it bears to accidents. . . . It is evident "support" cannot here be taken in its usual or literal sense—as when we say that pillars support a building; in what sense therefore must it be taken? (*E,* 156–57)

> The general idea of Being appeareth to me the most abstract and incomprehensible of all other; and as for its supporting accidents, this, as we have just now observed, cannot be understood in the common sense of those words; it must therefore be taken in some other sense, but what that is they do not explain. (*E,* 157)

The above compendium of extracts demonstrates a willingness to deploy a variety of tools and approaches in opposition to a nonrigorous speculation, one whose constitutive abstractions have gone unchecked. The passages

happen to be arranged in the sequence that *A Treatise* follows. Logical disputation is what powers the objections to the abstraction of "family resemblances" out of individual family members; the displacement of ideational
categories (for instance, extension) to the matter presumably indifferent to
such specifications; and the qualities that apparently cannot decide as to
whether they inhere in the mind or in matter. In these arguments, logical
tools deriving from the tradition of scholastic philosophy are being deployed
empirically, that is, from the foundation up and with severe skepticism regarding a priori ideation. The critiques of matter and Being are immediately recognizable to contemporary students of deconstruction. Only a hair's
breadth separates Berkeley in these passages from (1) making the broad connection, like Heidegger, linking matter and Being's universality, neutrality,
and absence of qualities to other fundamentals (God, for instance) at the basis
of Western ontotheology; (2) observing, as Derrida does, that the gravitation
toward ideals in Western systematicity implies extreme distrust and loathing
toward the play and distortions programmed into the linguistic medium.
Even with his profound misgivings regarding language, Berkeley is not past
offering a linguistic explanation for the delusions of spirituality in Western
culture: "In a large sense, indeed, we may be said to have an idea or rather a
notion of *spirit*. . . . Moreover, as we conceive the ideas that are in the minds
of other spirits by means of our own, which we suppose to be resemblances
of them; so we know other spirits by means of our own soul" (*E,* 208). The
language question in Berkeley's philosophizing is particularly vexed because
a visceral logocentric suspicion toward linguistic process goes hand in hand
with an optimism, shared by other empiricists, that conceptual delusions will
be set aright by linguistic correctness.

The question of language in the process of abstraction is at play from the
inception of Berkeley's analysis, now at center stage, now fluttering about
the wings. By the end of the compendium of citations above, Berkeley is
complaining about how the conventional understandings of Being's accidents betray the ordinary meanings of the words deployed to convey those
understandings. More than any of the other British empiricists, Berkeley was
aware of how the critiques of abstraction and generalization hinged upon
linguistic usage. But so conditioned was his own intervention by the conventional identification of language as the *source* of distortion that he terminated
his analyses with the apprehension of the role that language plays in abstraction. He was unable to appreciate, or deplore, the inhibiting or dysfunctional
effect that the pretensions to generality (and for that matter, logical rigor)
exert upon communications and the realization of linguistic potential. This
defines, in a word, Berkeley's impasse regarding language—an impasse he

would not even have broached had he not been as linguistically acute as he was:

> But at the same time it must be owned that most parts of knowledge have been strangely perplexed and darkened by the abuse of words, and general ways of speech wherein they are delivered. Since therefore words are so apt to impose on the understanding, whatever ideas I consider, I shall endeavor to take them bare and naked into my view, keeping out of my thoughts so far as I am able those names which long and constant use hath so strictly united with them, from which I may expect to derive the following advantages:—
>
> 22. *First,* I shall be able to get clear of all controversies *purely verbal;* the springing up of which weeds in almost all the sciences has been a main hindrance to the growth of true and sound knowledge. *Secondly,* this seems to be a sure way to extricate myself out of that fine and subtle net of *abstract ideas* which has so miserably perplexed and entangled the minds of men. . . . *Thirdly,* so long as I confine my thoughts to my own ideas divested of words, I do not see how I can be easily mistaken. (*E,* 149)

Interestingly, this corrective, this statute of limitations imposed on words, coincides with a contract made with the discoursing self, a self-regulation to render null and void those preexisting associations between names and thoughts that so benight the powers of clear intellection. Language is clearly the invader, the external threat here. Correcting its "abuses" is tantamount to achieving the cognitive clarity itemized in Paragraph 22. The solution is not an escape, a departure from the corrupting linguistic medium (so much like the body in the founding Protestant tracts), but control, keeping things in order, applying empiricism to the linguistic medium itself.

> 23. But the attainment of these advantages doth *presuppose an entire deliverance from the deception of words,* which I dare hardly promise myself; so difficult a thing it is to dissolve a union so early begun, and confirmed by so long a habit as that betwixt words and ideas. Which difficulty seems to have been very much increased by the doctrine of *abstraction.* For so long as men thought abstract ideas were annexed to their words, it doth not seem strange that they should use words for ideas; it being found an impracticable thing to lay aside the word, and retain the abstract idea in the mind, which in itself was perfectly inconceivable. This seems to me the principle cause why those men who have so emphatically recommended to others the laying aside all use of words in their meditations, and contemplating their bare ideas, have yet failed to perform it themselves. (*E,* 149–50)

This passage entertains, and then rejects, the possibility of a divorce (a marital option again made available through the Protestant Reformation). The divorce entertained here is between abstract ideas and words. Berkeley, in light of the distortions he wants to scourge from philosophy, well understands the *wish* for the separation; in the end, however, he also acknowledges the impracticability of this marital rupture.

In the end, he accepts a settlement incorporating as its major clause the judicious—that is, empirically correct—deployment of language in the enterprise of achieving a distortion-limited discourse. This arrangement in no way silences the distrust and skepticism in his attitude toward language. His endeavor, the elimination of conceptual error through the limitation of linguistic aberration, becomes a major item on the agenda of logical analysis and related philosophical schools. It is within this context that Berkeley can propose correctives to such abuses as the abstraction implicit in nomination itself (*E*, 147); ascribing agency to ideas themselves (*E*, 163); and the free rein of "analogies, harmonies, and agreements" (*E*, 193). "We are apt," cautions Berkeley in this regard, "to lay too great a stress on analogies" (*E*, 193). Berkeley is capable, on the one hand, of reconciling his language-exasperated colleagues to continued commerce in this medium. Yet he himself would wish to steer clear of the rhetorical tropes inseparable from linguistic usage. This, in a nutshell, encapsulates Berkeley's impasse: he would like to deploy an empirically conditioned corrective to distortions entering philosophy through its ideational tendency. But the aberrations have already influenced the linguistic medium that he would employ in the scourging and the correcting.

It begins to be possible for us to place the various attempts of empiricism on the same map on which we charted an erotic poetry of conversion, diplomacy, and commercial contract in Donne. On this map can also be found the early novel of adventure, exploration, exile, and erotic discovery, whether *Robinson Crusoe, Moll Flanders,* or *Tom Jones.* This map, as we have seen in other contexts, is conditioned by unprecedented personal freedom and the resultant need for rigorous standards of self-regulation, and a thoroughly ambivalent attitude toward the language that is both an irrepressible fringe of individualism and a link to society by means of the social contract. Locke sets the agenda for an experience-based, graduated, and self-regulated philosophical speculation in keeping with modern subject conditions and understandings of language. Berkeley ups the ante, elevates the specifications, with regard to limiting the play of linguistic distortion within the already self-regulative enterprise. In attempting a reformation of philosophical discourse through purification, Berkeley also increases the pitch of the bipolar ambivalence toward the linguistic medium. Where Berkeley directs his invective at a series of aberrations implicitly figured as emanating from a *linguistic outside,* Hume adopts a confessional stance, and opts for a full and complete disclosure of the quandaries that philosophical speculation, including its empirical enterprises, will not solve. Like both his major empirical predecessors, Hume insists on a data base deriving from experience; like Berkeley, he advocates greater linguistic awareness and rigor as the primary means for circumventing further conceptual distortions. Hume's primary departure from Berkeley is temperamental and tonal rather than in the parameters of his project. Hume metamorphoses Berkeley's polemical posture and corrosive, purifying aim into a forthright confession of the limits of knowledge and an acknowledgment of the inbuilt imperfections within all philosophical instruments, including empirical ones, thus far devised.

All three major empiricists subscribe to a common epistemological ethos, one understandable in terms of the constraints that emerge under the broader modernity. If I end this survey with Hume, it is because of his notion that philosophy *adjudicates* between preexisting and in some cases longstanding positions rather than that it *elects* precisely the right one. With Hume, a linguistically aware philosophical discourse does not so much attempt to *abolish* contrary positions as, rigorously and knowingly, to *accommodate* a range of attitudes that have survived in part because they have answered to certain needs. The forthrightness and self-effacement that penetrate Hume's rhetoric as well as his attitude set the stage for a *constitutional* model of philosophy as the discourse establishing the "checks and balances" among a wide range of positions and measures. It is in this spirit that Hume calls for a precise *descriptiveness* in the elaboration of speculative postures, as when he characterizes belief (*E*, 341) and advocates a "mitigated scepticism" (*E*, 428) in the correction of earlier philosophical essays. No less than Locke or Berkeley is Hume held to a linguistic ambivalence faulting the "undeterminate meaning of words" (*E*, 429) in the failure to achieve conceptual rigor. Nor is Hume immune to his own predispositions, such as the antagonism toward Catholicism noted earlier in this chapter. But the overall tone of his aspirations is gentler than Berkeley's, and more anticipatory of the systematic philosophies of Kant and Hegel, which embrace both their own limitations and the counterpositions to their assertions. The political application of Hume's mitigated skepticism is in the direction of the liberal constitutional government that is, among other crystallizations, the outgrowth of Protestant culture. I close this placement of the attempts of empiricism on the wider map of modernity with Hume's appeal for a philosophy of ongoing but *mitigated* skepticism:

> There is indeed, a more *mitigated* scepticism or *academical* philosophy, which may be both durable and useful. . . . The greater part of mankind are naturally apt to be affirmative and dogmatical in their opinions; and while they

see objects only on one side, and have no idea of any counterpoising argument, they throw themselves precipitately into the principles, to which they are inclined; nor have they any indulgence for those who entertain opposite sentiments. To hesitate or balance perplexes their understanding, checks their passion, and suspends their action. They are, therefore, impatient till they escape from a state, which to them is so uneasy: and they think, that they could never remove themselves far enough from it, by the violence of their affirmations and obstinancy of their belief. But could such dogmatical reasoners become sensible of the strange infirmities of human understanding, even in its most perfect state, and when most accurate and cautious in its determinations; such a reflection would naturally inspire them with more modesty and reserve, and diminish their fond opinion of themselves, and their prejudice against antagonists. (*E,* 427)

CHAPTER 4

Melancholic Borders: From *Trauerspiel* to "Michael Kohlhaas"

Walter Benjamin, as he set about preserving and redefining baroque tragedy for cultural memory, and fashioning a modern/postmodern discursive medium for criticism in the process, was not unmindful of the developments I have begun to attribute to the Protestant Reformation. *The Origin of German Tragic Drama* (*Ursprung des deutschen Trauerspiels*) is a monstrous text about a monstrous aesthetic, literary, performative, and cultural phenomenon.[1] Melancholy, as elaborated in Benjamin's own extended overview of modern theatricality, writing, and subject conditions, in the guise of an advanced doctoral thesis, is not only an emotive and modal correlative to the baroque and its aftermath. It is also the overall framework in which arise such phenomena as the lateralization of the metaphor, the disqualification of extrinsic (for example, Aristotelian) constraints upon drama and other artforms, and the rise of fragmented and incoherent subject conditions and dramatic characters. Benjamin never received the *Habilitation* for which he wrote the treatise, but he established the anomalousness and complexity of early modern understandings and conditions of art. Among the many contributions made by Benjamin's exploration of an obscure corner of dramatic history is the crystallization of an allegorical critical script whose commentary on its "original" objects incorporates a sudden and violent acting out of their observed characteristic features.

Even the casual reader of this text will note that its subject, German tragic drama, is as shifting and polymorphic as the violence that this genre, in Benjamin's analysis, does to standard scientific methods of criticism and scholarship. Before Benjamin's overview is complete, German tragic drama has expanded to embrace the Spanish and English Renaissance theaters, medieval emblematics and visual iconography, and Romantic poetics. Benjamin's purported subject matter refuses to reside within the confines of its intrinsic historical and generic parameters, those of "German tragic drama." It emerges, with its allegorical performance, its polyglot heritage, and its melancholic humor, as an aesthetic category to demolish all prior ones. Benjamin's *Trauerspiel* becomes the site of an anti-aesthetic, the basis for a cultural and aesthetic monstrosity that achieves the certification of major cultural creations that violate, in their very nature, the wisdom offered by preexisting metaphysical, historical, psychological, and theme-based methods of interpretation. The very anomaly and violence that Benjamin ascribes to "German tragic drama" and allegory must be incorporated into the critical text that approaches the artifacts in question if any productive reading is to take place.

Benjamin was as aware of the divide separating language-oriented and subject-based modes of thinking and criticism as we need to be. While Benjamin demonstrates in *Trauerspiel* a healthy and productive skepticism regarding the application of subjective categories and impulses to linguistic artifacts, he did not entirely renounce the endeavor of extrapolating the subject conditions that emerged out of the historical and epistemological framework of the Renaissance. So intent was Benjamin upon reconfiguring the conditions of scholarly-conceptual criticism in accordance with the shock characterizing the productions of his own age that he held off on any ultimate repudiation of subjective categories.

Above all, the baroque German *Trauerspiel* that is Benjamin's ostensible occasion is conditioned by its anomalousness: it is anomalous to traditional understandings of beauty, ethics, the sociological functions and roles of art, human psychology, and European history. *Trauerspiel*'s intrinsic monstrosity extends to existing interpretations of it and related artifacts. By virtue of its exceptionality, vast segments of the scholarly work that has arisen to account for it undergo a decisive disqualification.

As characterized by Benjamin, "German tragic drama" and its allegorical mode of performance join a splendid tradition of monsters with revolutionary implications in the history of philosophy and aesthetics: the Romantic fragment and Kierkegaard's elaboration of the farce in *Repetition* immediately come to mind; so do *Tristram Shandy, A la recherche du temps perdu,* and *Finnegans Wake.* The *Trauerspiel* is not only a conceptually generative *exception* to existing metaphysical, historical, psychological, and thematic assumptions underlying intellectual work; it is the inaugural object, the centerpiece, in a shock-constituted counter-aesthetics and its practice.

Benjamin locates the historical home of the German tragic drama that serves him as a paradigm for a revolutionary counter-aesthetics in the Catholic Counter-Reformation. He is at the same time acutely aware of the impact of Lutheranism and Calvinism upon the epistemological conditions that were generative of this drama. I invoke Benjamin's *Ursprung des deutschen Trauerspiels* at this juncture not to give it the multifaceted appreciation that it deserves, but merely to note that for Benjamin as well, the decline of the medieval world order set the stage for a *crise de conscience et de culture* that would, after a fascinating sequence of transformations, result in the aesthetic contract prevailing in the broader modernity.

Bequeathed to the world by dramatists who have long sunk into oblivion, with names like Gryphius and Hallmann and Lohenstein, German baroque tragedy is a nightmare to the logician, the aesthetician, the historian, and the moralist alike. Even the signs of which this genre are composed are enigmatic and irregular. The allegory that is the predominant mode of *Trauerspiel's* representation deploys the "plastic symbol [*plastiche Symbol*]" (*OGTD*, 164), "the so-called symbolic or enigmatic hieroglyphs" as described by the pseudo-epigraphers (*OGTD*, 168), and even "chromatic hieroglyphs" (*OGTD*, 174). There is an enigmatic fusion between the concrete and the metaphoric in its representational mode: "With every idea the moment of expression coincides with a veritable eruption of images, which gives rise to a chaotic mass of metaphors. This is how the sublime is represented in this style" (*OGTD*, 173). The signs of which the *Trauerspiel* is composed are themselves of hybrid or bastard origin, and they are deployed in a reckless manner that would confuse their materiality with their ideational content. Even in Benjamin's aphoristic description of the violence with which *Trauerspiel's* images proliferate themselves, there is a blurring in the comprehensive historical framework: the heaping up of ideational-concrete metaphors is "sublime." Benjamin has earlier listed the "three periods in the history of the concept 'play' in German aesthetics: the baroque, classicism, and romanticism" (*OGTD*, 81–82). The enigmatic semiology that is supposedly a hallmark of the German baroque thus slides into a context of more immediate concern in Benjamin's overall body of work: Romanticism and its sublime register of expansion.

From a generic point of view, in terms of its form(s), the *Trauerspiel* is every bit as much of a minefield. Benjamin describes its affinities to virtually every subspecies of drama, poetry, painting, fiction, and discursive prose extant during its epoch. Yet the end result of each simile is dissonance and disqualification. There are affinities between *Trauerspiel* and classical tragedy, but these dissolve in consideration of a quasi-systematic violation of the Aristotelian unities (*OGTD*, 60–61). "The *Trauerspiel*, it was believed, could be directly grasped in the events of history itself; it was only a question of finding the right words" (*OGTD*, 63). But the genre history play exhausts the *Trauerspiel* no more than the martyr drama (*Märtyrtragödie; OGTD*, 70, 72, 89), the passion play (*Passionstheaters; OGTD*, 75–77), the mystery play (*Mysterium; OGTD*, 78–79), or the drama of fate (*OGTD*, 84). Benjamin sums up the relationship between *Trauerspiel* and the extant dramatic sub-genres, which shed some light but do not exhaust it, as follows: "The end of the German *Trauerspiel* is therefore both less formal and less dogmatic, it is—morally, not, of course, artistically—more responsible than that of the Spanish drama" (*OGTD*, 84). Curiously, then, there is a significant connection between *Trauerspiel*'s generic anomaly and its ability to set moral choices in relief, without in any way resolving them.

Yet when we turn to *Trauerspiel*'s success—as a moral vehicle—in delivering decisive and cogent lessons, its achievement is as muddled as its semiological or generic definition. "It was therefore quite impossible to derive an easy moral satisfaction, in the manner of the dramas of Hans Sachs, from the tyrant's end" (*OGTD*, 72). Benjamin pauses as well at the non-genre's tendency to focus on such unsympathetic characters, but these, when they fall, provide no unambiguous moral payoff. In other words, any clear moral allegory in these artworks fails: "The allegorical character of the figures is betrayed in the infrequency and the hesitancy with which the plot refers to their particular morality" (*OGTD*, 191).

The *Trauerspiel* dedicates its resources and work to following the vicissitudes of characters noble in no significant way. A disproportionate body of works in the genre surround tyrants of "the most dreadful corruption" (*OGTD*, 70), often in "the state of emergency [*Ausnahmezustand*]" (*OGTD*, 71), when "almost incapable of making a decision" (*OGDT*, 71). "The sovereign is the representative of history" (*OGTD*, 65). But the dramatis personae of repute in *Trauerspiel* also include the courtier. The organizer of the *Trauerspiel*'s plot, "the precursor of the choreographer, is the intriguer" (*OGTD*, 95). Ballet became the ultimate successor to the *Trauerspiel*, argues Benjamin, and in this progression, "The sovereign intriguer is all intellect and will-power. And as such he corresponds to an ideal which was first outlined by Machiavelli and which was energetically elaborated in the creative and theoretical literature of the seventeenth century" (*OGTD*, 95).

Benjamin situates the characterology of the *Trauerspiel* on the ground of the subjective bipolarity whose utility increases as the moral weight upon the individuated, post–Protestant Reformation subject grows. "For the 'very bad' there was the drama of the tyrant, and there was fear; for the 'very good' there was the martyr-drama and pity" (*OGTD*, 69). Among the allures of the *Trauerspiel* is the spectacle of its sharply bifurcated morality. The starkness of these moral alternatives, and the strenuous self-regulation that this splitting requires, are very much in the background of the emergence of the modern aesthetic contract; this is a historically significant point we will have occasion to return to. Within the characterology of *Trauerspiel,* the courtier emerges as a time-bomb of disillusionment. In the shock-forged enchantment of his prose, Benjamin manages to depict the courtier, whose utter cynicism makes *Othello*'s Iago a prime example, as dancing to a rhythm whose temporality ultimately derives from the king:

> "The prince develops all virtualities of the state by a kind of continuous creation. The prince is the Cartesian God transposed into the political world." [Benjamin is quoting Frédéric Atger's doctoral thesis.] In the course of political events intrigue beats out that rhythm of the second hand which controls and regulates these events. The disillusioned insight of the courtier is just as profound a source of woe to him as it is a potential danger to others, because of the use he can make of it at any time. In this light the image of this fissure assumes its most baleful aspect. (*OGTD*, 97)

As if all the above-mentioned anomalies and unpleasantnesses of the *Trauerspiel* were not enough, the entire spectacle transpires under the aura of a multifaceted melancholy bespeaking experiential unhappiness and ethical laxity. Melancholy is both the temperament of characters who abound in the *Trauerspiel* and the very *modus operandi* of astute criticism: "For the only pleasure the melancholic permits himself, and it is a powerful one, is allegory" (*OGTD*, 185). The personal attributes of the melancholic, as quoted by Benjamin from Constantinus Africanus, are not so edifying as allegorical production, yet they are part and parcel of the subject conditions prevailing in the broader modernity: "envious, mournful, greedy, avaricious, disloyal, timorous, and sallow" (*OGTD*, 145). Medical tradition in the High Middle Ages associated melancholy with a kind of hypochondria exemplifying the disillusionment in certain Melvillian characters (*OGTD*, 146).[2] Yet according to Aristotle, establishing a tradition "effective for more than two thousand years" (*OGTD*, 147), "genius is linked with madness within the concept of melancholy. . . . Apart from this, melancholy genius tends to be revealed particularly in the activity of divination. The view that prophetic ability is furthered by melancholy is an ancient one" (*OGTD*, 147).

The ambivalence evoked by melancholy places it in an excellent position as the mood under which an anti-aesthetic evolves. This is a particularly

Benjaminian position: the excess, "ostentation," and discomfort initiated by the *Trauerspiel* will also serve as a critical platform for a sensibility that is radical, revolutionary, and innovative, and that can put the shock value (*OGTD*, 163–64, 183, 185, 197) contained in the genre to good use. The melancholic ambivalence of *Trauerspiel* thus prefigures the sober delight of "On Some Motifs in Baudelaire":[3] the dynamics of demolition that the persona of the essay can bemoan become the unexpected juxtapositions that are the signatures of an exuberant, poststructural postmodernism, with its delights in, for example, technology and popular culture. From a purely clinical point of view, there is much in common between Benjamin's critical characterization of the melancholic and the substratum of ongoing, unacknowledged depression typical of the borderline and narcissistic pathologies examined by the contemporary psychoanalytic theory of object relations.[4]

What are the traits of the anti-aesthetics embodied in the *Trauerspiel*? Ongoing destabilization (*OGTD*, 65), moral indeterminacy (*OGTD*, 72), a detachment of the beautiful from the divine (*OGTD*, 160), a semiosis of jumbled proliferation rather than lucidity (*OGTD*, 173), detachment from the received balance(s) of aesthetics (*OGTD*, 176), including a questioning attitude toward the freedom of aesthetic creation (*OGTD*, 169, 205), allegory's venturing beyond beauty (*OGTD*, 178), an allegory that instigates rhetorical sensibility rather than "poetic sensuality" (*OGTD*, 198), and finally, even an agonistic bearing toward the ideal of art itself (*OGTD*, 233). As suggested above, this anti-aesthetic not only establishes the place for a neglected body of dramatic art, German baroque tragedy, within the running account of Western culture; it also establishes the modality for a twentieth-century critical practice founded on, among other elements, historical discontinuity, the juxtaposition of categorically discontinuous and heterogeneous entities, freedom from logical procedure and scientific methodology, and intense awareness regarding questions of representation.

Surely among the outstanding accomplishments of this cutting-edge critical work is the coincidence between its conceptual exploration and its writerly allegory, its performative dimension. The text *Trauerspiel* performs the anomaly and redirection that it locates in German baroque tragedy. The "mosaic" (*OGTD*, 19, 34) text that Benjamin configures, and compares to a spider's web, is jarringly heterogenous. It is impossible to remember where Benjamin's own language and the seemingly comprehensive and inexhaustible supply of apt citations begins. "Mosaic" discourse is an ideal medium for a prose that delivers its knockout punches in the form of Romantic fragments encrusted into the ongoing discursive flow.

For all the productive and suggestive demolition of deterministic historical assumptions that this treatise performs, it locates itself historically at the outset of the transformations ultimately resulting in the aesthetic contract of modernity. This coincidence is of great use to us, as are certain of Benjamin's remarks on *Hamlet* and melancholy:

> The great German dramatists of the baroque were Lutherans. Whereas in the decades of the Counter-Reformation Catholicism had penetrated secular life with all the power of its discipline, the relationship of Lutheranism to the everyday had always been antinomic. The rigorous morality of its teaching in respect of civic conduct stood in sharp contrast to its renunciation of "good works." By denying the latter any special miraculous spiritual effort, making the soul dependent on grace through faith, and making the secular–political sphere a testing ground for a life which was only indirectly religious, being intended for the demonstration of civic virtues, it did, it is true, instil into the people a strict sense of obedience to duty, but in its great men it produced melancholy. (*OGTD*, 138)

In this, perhaps *Trauerspiel*'s most extended exploration into melancholy, the condition emerges in the context of the Protestant skepticism regarding the impact of tangible actions on spiritual affairs. Protestant theology brings about an uncanny distance between people's actions and the repercussions of these acts within the ethical and spiritual domains. To Benjamin's mind, the understanding of human existence as a mere "testing ground" to a spiritual domain operating according to alien, immutable laws provokes an overbearing sense of duty in the pedestrian citizens of this world—and in its "great men," who will later emerge as the truly contemplative minds, "it produced melancholy."

Melancholy is, above all, as Benjamin characterizes it in this passage, a disease of thinking set in a world pervaded by a new and unprecedented vacuousness. Benjamin goes to great effort to describe this disorder not as one of thought or psyche, but as a malaise of reading and cultural interpretation. The tradition of psychoanalytical thought only begins to approach the void at the heart of this malady in a consistent way in the theory of object relations, which does in fact speak to the ongoing subtext of depression and the "subjective experience of emptiness" marking the loci of serious narcissistic wounds.[5] History is a subtext in Benjamin's text as well. He refers to it as often as he does to philosophy and even to *Trauerspiel* itself. The void in which melancholy arises opens for Benjamin at the outset of Protantism. Benjamin characterizes this void most powerfully as the one that opens up between our actions and our fate, leaving excessive room for speculation and

rumination; but there is a strand of thinking in *Trauerspiel* that refers this void
to the effacement of the medieval world order and its emblematic system of
knowledge:

> Even in Luther himself, the last two decades of whose life are filled with an
> increasing heaviness of soul, there are signs of a reaction against the assault on
> good works. "Faith," of course, carried him through, but it did not prevent
> life from becoming stale. "What is a man, / If his chief good and market of
> his time / Be but to sleep and feed? a beast, no more. / Sure, he that hath
> made us with such large discourse, / Looking before and after, gave us not /
> That capability and god-like reason / To fust in us unused" [*Hamlet,* IV.4]—
> these words of Hamlet contain both the philosophy of Wittenberg and a pro-
> test against it. In that excessive reaction which ultimately denied good works
> as such, and not just their meritorious and penitential character, there was
> an element of German paganism and the grim belief in the subjection of man
> to fate. Human actions were deprived of all value. Something new arose: an
> empty world. (*OGTD,* 138–39)

The character Hamlet figures in this passage as a protestant, but precisely
against the Protestant philosophy imported from Wittenberg. The bequest of
this philosophy is a distinctly modern emptiness. Benjamin repeatedly characterizes this as an alienation of people from their actions entering early
modern culture with such Protestant notions as predetermination and (Max
Weber's favorite) the notion of the calling.[6] It is most intriguing that while
constantly invoking "German tragic drama," Benjamin is fashioning a discourse whose more pressing mission is the interpretation of *hors-textes* not
included in the category. In a sense, *Trauerspiel* was written as much to read
works barely touched upon in the discourse (for instance, *Hamlet*) or not
mentioned at all (*Othello, Don Quixote*) as it was to focus upon Gryphius,
Lohenstein, and the like. In the passage immediately above, it is telling that
Benjamin designates the importance of Wittenberg in *Hamlet* as its philosophy. Benjamin's attempt, in keeping with post-Kantian skepticism with regard to psychological paradigms, is to account for melancholy in a literary-
philosophical, as opposed to a psychological, way.

> In Calvinism—for all its gloominess—the impossibility of this was compre-
> hended and in some measure corrected. The Lutheran faith viewed this con-
> cession with suspicion and opposed it. What was the point of human life if, as
> in Calvinism, not even faith had to be proved? If, on the one hand, faith was
> naked, absolute, effective, but on the other, there was no distinction between
> human actions? There was no answer to this except perhaps in the morality
> of ordinary people—"honesty in all things," "upright living"—which devel-
> oped at this time, forming a contrast to the *taedium vitae* of richer natures. For

those who looked deeper saw the scene of their existence as a rubbish heap of partial, inauthentic actions. Life itself protested against this. It feels deeply that it is not there merely to be devalued by faith. . . . The idea of death fills it with profound horror. Mourning is a state of mind which revives the empty world in the form of a mask, and derives an enigmatic satisfaction in contemplating it. Every feeling is bound to an *a priori* object, and the representation of this object is its phenomenology. (*OGTD*, 139)

Part of Benjamin's attempt to de-psychologize melancholy is to emphasize the *object,* as opposed to the subject, of contemplation. In this wider sense, there is a motif of objectivity running throughout the treatise; indeed, Benjamin's elaboration of the object in *Trauerspiel* is an anticipation of the nostalgia for handiwork and the aura around crafted things that we find in the later essays. A pictorial instance of this move away from the subject and toward the object in the melancholic sensibility that Benjamin will cite will be the prominence of the "utensils of active life" in Dürer's *Melancholy*. These utensils "are lying around unused on the floor, as objects of contemplation. This engraving anticipates the baroque in many respects. In it the knowledge of the introvert and the investigations of the scholar have merged as intimately as in the men of the baroque. The Renaissance explores the universe; the baroque explores libraries. Its meditations are devoted to books" (*OGTD,* 140). The melancholic is a sensibility thrust by the emptiness of subjective metaphysics in a post-Protestant world into the pathos of a world of things, and Benjamin's prototype for things, in the above citation, is books.

Benjamin celebrates and bemoans the world of emptiness inaugurated by Protestantism. The prevalent psychological and psychoanalytical models of his day were indeed configured by a subjective metaphysics. One would be interested to know how receptive he would be to that subsequent branch of psychoanalytical thought that approached melancholy precisely through its implicit bearings to objects, whether inert things or the introjected voices and images of significant others.

Accordingly the theory of mourning, which emerged unmistakably as a *pendant* to the theory of tragedy, can only be developed in the description of that world which is revealed under the gaze of the melancholy man. For feelings, however vague they may seem when perceived by the self, respond like a motorial reaction to a concretely structured world. If the laws which govern the *Trauerspiel* are to be found, partly explicit, partly implicit, at the heart of mourning, the representation of these laws does not concern itself with the emotional condition of the poet or his public, but with a feeling which is released from any empirical subject and is intimately bound to the fullness of an object. . . . It is determined by an astounding tenacity of intention. . . . For

whereas in the realm of emotions it is not unusual for the relation between
an intention and its object to alternate between attraction and repulsion,
mourning is capable of a special intensification, a progressive deepening of its
intention. Pensiveness is characteristic above all of the mournful. (*OGTD*,
139–40)

When Benjamin began this extended meditation on the connection between
Trauerspiel and melancholy, he noted that life itself rose in protest against the
newly founded modern void initiated by Protestantism (*OGTD*, 139). In the
extract immediately above, the contemplation that is the mark of the critic
as well as the Renaissance tragic hero (Hamlet, say) extends itself out of the
mourning attending a loss. This is the loss of clear lines of authority and any
unified sense of the meaning of life. The resolute melancholy of *Trauerspiel*
and the anti-aesthetics it implicates circumvent the metaphysics of subjectivity just as this meditation bypasses emotionality, the fluctuations between
attraction and repulsion. The contemplativeness of modernity shares the relentlessness, according to Benjamin, of tragic fate. This pensiveness continues
autonomously of its concrete implications or its emotional content or repercussions. Through his own ruminations, Benjamin dramatizes the intellectual Fall, with its unending tragic implications, its critical mark of Cain, that
took place at the outset of modernity.

Conditioned by its own grand anomalousness, "German tragic drama"
served as a historically specific stage on which to set this critical epigenesis,
this phenomenology of the critical sensibility, with its attendant modal liabilities. Yet even as broadly as Benjamin defines it, "German tragic drama"
is subject to limitations and tragic flaws. It was eventually to lose its cultural
currency and even its own life, even while the scene for sober cultural interpretation it initiated continued. The unique coincidence between "mourning and ostentation" (*OGTD*, 140), that is, its inbuilt aesthetics of excess,
carries the genre forward and to some extent defines its contribution. *Trauerspiel* is extended as well by a repetition compulsion indicative of its gamelike
qualities. From the perspective of the "great constellations of the worldly
chronicle" (*OGTD*, 140), melancholic self-absorption, its pretentious fluctuations between "mourning and ostentation," "seem but a game" (*OGTD*,
140). So to some degree, *Trauerspiel* extends its life through repetition. But
even in comprehensive outrageousness and its compulsive self-perpetuation,
Trauerspiel is fated to its own tragic death. It is on this note that Benjamin
culminates his analysis of *Hamlet:*

> In the German *Trauerspiel* the characteristic attitude is that of the reaction of
> the Counter-Reformation, and so the determining factor in the creation of
> dramatic types is the medieval scholastic image of melancholy. But in its for-

mal totality this drama diverges fundamentally from such a typology; its style and language are inconceivable without that audacious twist thanks to which the speculations of the Renaissance were able to recognize in the features of the sorrowful Contemplator the reflection of a distant light, shining back from the depths of self-absorption. This age succeeded (at least once) in conjuring up the human figure who corresponded to this dichotomy between the neo-antique and the medieval light in which the baroque saw the melancholic. But Germany was not the country which was able to do this. The figure is Hamlet. The secret of his person is contained within the playful, but for that very reason fully circumscribed, passage through all the stages in this complex of intentions, just as the secret of his fate is contained in an action which, according to this, his way of looking at things, is perfectly homogeneous. For the *Trauerspiel* Hamlet alone is a spectator by the grace of God; but he cannot find satisfaction in what he sees enacted, only in his own fate. His life, the exemplary object of his mourning, points, before its extinction, to the Christian providence in whose bosom his mournful images are transformed into a blessed existence. Only in a princely life such as this is melancholy redeemed, by being confronted with itself. The rest is silence. (*OGTD*, 157–58)

Hamlet the character is fated to a unique apotheosis. At the last moment, he succeeds in Christianizing, as no German character does, the otherwise hopeless fate of *Trauerspiel*. A remote, beclouded source of illumination is a quintessential Benjaminian image for the integration of diverse cultural manifestations and the vocation of criticism in the fallen—that is to say, de-idealized—world of the broader modernity. Hamlet ponders and acts under the stigma of this impeded illumination, but in the very last instant, he allows Christian ideology and mythology to co-opt the otherwise unredeemable malaise of melancholy. Which means that mainstream Western culture *thinks* that it accommodates the particular negativity defined by the radical discontinuity between hopes and possibilities. Hamlet falls down leaving alive the faintest hope of deriving redemption from the vacuities and despairs defining the position of the critic. Not even this glimmer remains when it comes to the fate of the *Trauerspiel* itself:

> It is only in this prince that melancholy self-absorption attains to Christianity. The German *Trauerspiel* was never able to inspire itself to new life; it was never able to awaken within itself the clear light of self-awareness. It remained astonishingly obscure to itself, and was able to portray the melancholic only in the crude and washed-out colours of the medieval complexion-books. What then is the purpose of this excursus? The images and figures presented in the German *Trauerspiel* are dedicated to Dürer's genius of winged melancholy. The intense life of its crude theatre begins in the presence of this genius. (*OGTD*, 158)

In the tradition of the philosophy of writing that takes as its mission to reach *writerly* formulations of conceptual and aesthetic conditions, Benjamin's implicit history of modernity eschews psychological and sociological frameworks of explanation. Benjamin composes both a history and a phenomenology of modernity by assembling a constellation of the traits of what was at best a hybrid and shapeless, all-but-forgotten adventure in the evolution of literature. Benjamin's story sets off, as mine does, with Protestantism's registering the death-knell of a medieval European world order that to some extent delivered what it promised: a comprehensive metaphysical, sociological, and structural map. For all Benjamin's attempt to depsychologize his utterly literary account of the rise of modernity, melancholy is a highly personal experience, even when intellectual to the core.

There is, I believe, a significant contribution that the allegory of *Trauerspiel* has to make to subject-oriented models of criticism that address modernity, that is, to New Historical, cultural studies, and radical democratic approaches. Like the rest of Benjamin's erudite, generative, and generous contribution to the calling of criticism, *Trauerspiel* sheds an illuminating light upon the distinguishing aporias and pitfalls of criticism today, even in a world heavily conditioned by the discourse of postmodernism and the economics of late capitalism.

Whether our framework is historical or structural, "consciousness," once the European Renaissance has established its distinctive aesthetic contracts, is henceforth and forevermore defined by gaps and fissures rather than wholenesses; by the failure to satisfy multiple allegiances rather than by identities based on perfect affiliations. The historical rendition of this story runs this way: once the comprehensive placement furnished by the "medieval world order,"[7] in which there is a parallelism between military, ecclesiastical, and socioeconomic orders, breaks down, an entire range of individuals, among them businesspeople and freed serfs, begins to exist and thrive (and suffer) outside this order. It is interesting that the very lineaments of this order resemble a graduated speculative system in which the ideal or transcendental value resides at the top. The shape I imagine for the medieval world order that determines ecclesiastical, political, and socioeconomic hierarchies is that of an inverted tree-diagram, with the position of God, Pope, King, and Lord on top. Among the factors cited in historical accounts of this change are the rise of towns, which sustain activities and possibilities not encompassed by either ecclesiastical or feudal orders; the emergence of market economies, which are impervious to ideology; and the development of the trades, which are professionally rather than metaphysically driven. I would add to the factors contributing to the dissolution of this unique and oppressive parallelism of hierarchical orders the Protestant Reformation, whose founding texts may on one level be read as theologically grounded attacks on medievalism. The structural or epistemological way of telling the same story, as Foucault has done it in *The Order of Things,* involves characterizing the obsolescence into which certain medieval ways of knowledge, including similitudes, analogies, and allegories, eventually fall.[8]

One could argue that tragedy, even in its paradigmatic classical artifacts, is an entire genre dedicated to embellishing the fissures in identity. Yet I would rejoin, even with the demonstrated importance of Greek tragedies to the English and Spanish Renaissances, that the earlier artifacts are characterized by a structural economy and purity limiting the number of conflicting allegiances—and fragments—into which subjectivity falls. Such ancient tragic characters as Oedipus and Antigone are divided in their obligations and prospects, but the dramatic artifacts in which they figure incorporate balance and symmetry into the central dramatic conflicts.[9] By the time of *Hamlet,* a work with curious resonances throughout Heinrich von Kleist's "Michael Kohlhaas," the tragic work incorporates glimpses of the the angry Poles knocking at the gates of Denmark. By *Hamlet*'s moment and forever after, the fragmentation accruing from the conflicting calls of family, nation, public life, private life, and sexuality is truly catastrophic. Postmodern life has even exacerbated the panoply of demands upon the individual: the airwaves and the cybernetic, print, and phonic media remind us at every turn that "on top" of our "classical" allegiances—to family, nation, and possibly to affiliation groups—we should, for the general good, be ideal consumers, dressers, and sexual performers.

"Michael Kohlhaas," like E. T. A. Hoffmann's later "Mademoiselle de Scudéry," is an early-nineteenth-century work of fiction that accomplishes enormous measures through its selection of historical materials: the setting, characters, and details of history that it elects to incorporate within its framework. While Hoffmann will adapt the overall excess remembered as prevailing throughout the reign of the French Sun King as a backdrop for the atmosphere following the Reign of Terror, Kleist, in composing a fable of bureaucratic outrages and impossible shifts in jurisdictions and allegiance, veers toward the Protestant Reformation as his favorite historical alternate world, and even goes so far, in this text, as to include Martin Luther among the dramatis personae. In the very center of this novella, Kohlhaas, who is depicted as a basically fair-minded and reasonable private entrepreneur, but who can, like a typical rational individual, be driven into a fury when faced with impossible demands, actually confronts Luther, who has written him off as "a rebel and no warrior of the just God" (*MO*, 150).[10] Kohlhaas's aim in relation to Luther is "To prove that you are wrong in thinking me an unjust man [*ungerechter Mann*]!" (*MO*, 152). In Kleist's rendition, Kohlhaas is a man whose sense of justice "was as fine as a gold-balance [*Goldwaage*]" (*MO*, 120); a character who would immediately choose justice over self-aggrandizement, or who at very worst sees the two interests as inextricably linked. " 'I call that man an outcast [*Verstorene*],' " Kohlhaas answers Luther, "clenching his fist, 'who is denied the protection of the law! For I need that protection if my peaceful trade is to prosper; indeed it is for the sake of that protection that I take refuge. . . . Whoever witholds it from me drives me out into the wilderness among savages. It is he—how can you deny it?— who puts into my hands the club I am wielding to defend myself' " (*MO*, 152). Kohlhaas's particular appeal here to Luther is successful. He has taken up arms because, owing to the differences between and intrinsic bureaucratic complexities of the competing German principalities, he has been abused: his horses have been wrongfully possessed and starved, his servant has been expelled and seriously wounded, and, indirectly, his wife killed. The result of Kohlhaas's appeal to Luther, an example of a tangible historical graft incorporated into a work of fiction, is temporary leniency on the part of a few of the myriad political authorities with whom Kohlhaas has dealings in the novella. Yet Luther contributes to the overall problem even in seeming to (partially) solve it. He constitutes yet another form of the religious and political authority that proliferates, twists, bifurcates, and contradicts itself as it wraps itself around and ultimately stymies Kohlhaas, a private entrepreneur in animal husbandry and horse-breeding, the most natural sort of cultivation. The problem upon which the novella focuses in its historical framework is the mad proliferation of authority and bureaucracy that takes place with the Holy Wars occasioned by the Protestant Reformation. As Kleist makes even clearer in "St. Cecilia or the Power of Music," also set at this time, it is not as though Protestant authority represents a solution to Catholic abuses, or vice versa. Power, not its particular ideology, is the corrupting force. This major historical event serves Kleist as a mega-metaphor for a dual crisis, in cultural codes as well as in subjectivity, that arises when people are caught *between* conflicting and unresolvable systems of idealism and authority. Both in "Michael Kohlhaas" and well beyond it, the crisis of residing between conflicting jurisdictions becomes the very modern definition both of subjectivity and of the deployment of language and cultural codes.

To recapitulate the bewildering sequence of Electors, princes, chancellors, counts, Junkers, abbesses, chamberlains, imperial attorneys, magistrates, barons, knackers, wardens, and stewards to whom Kohlhaas must have recourse in order to redress the injustices that have been perpetrated upon him, his family, and his business, would be tantamount to retelling the story. Indeed, the contrast between the apparatus of officials and subalterns that Kohlhaas must deal with and the simplicity of the business at hand, which merely involves the return to their owner of two black workhorses in their original condition, is one of the sustaining ironies upon which the entire architecture of the novella rests. To simplify the tortuous path that Kohlhaas must take between and around officials, let me just say that certain of the high officials are exemplary in their dealings and personal integrity, while others, who have sided with Kohlhaas's aggrieved opponents, are unsympathetic to his cause. I can also say, speaking generally, that the serious conflicts of authority in the novella are initiated by middle-ranking officials, who on their own volition usurp newly claimed authority for the first time. This is precisely what happens at the beginning of the story, when Junker Wenzel von Tronka, a local landholder, claims the right to issue permits and levy tolls for the passage of people and goods through his territory. Speaking generally again, the relatively higher officials depicted in the novella fulfill their responsibilities with efficiency and dispassion. Overt acts of abuse, instances of "acting out," are confined to lower-level officials who are in effect testing uncharted waters, and even more so to *their* subalterns (such as Wenzel von Tronka's chamberlain and steward). The novella details how the sociopolitical institutions and jurisdictions of the highest order can be mobilized and polarized by relatively inconsequential acts. The novella is politically and historically specific in its depiction of a Central European society in which local authority and jurisdiction far outweighs any centralized authority or cultural vision. The novella's allegory is timed for a moment when, as the result of the Protestant Reformation, questions of authority were even more "up for grabs" than usual in a political region highly resistant to the centralized political control that eventually regulated France, England, and Spain.

Within the context of the present study, the demonic and mechanical quality with which the powers that be in the novella fragment, undermine, supplant, and oppose each other is of greater import than the particular sequence of reasonable and unreasonable rulers and their subordinates that Michael Kohlhaas confronts. In "Michael Kohlhaas" and other works, Heinrich von Kleist anticipates other major writers of the nineteenth century, including E. T. A. Hoffmann and Edgar Allen Poe, who will elaborate that particular species of irony inhering in the depiction of deliberate and rational orders when they are overcome by a loss of subjectivity, when they submit to a rational, mechanical process.[11] The world of Kleist's fiction is saturated with accidents, coincidences, and physical freak occurrences bespeaking the limit of rationality, both in human and physical spheres, and in their understanding. One of the most curious instances of the violence pervading Kleist's fictive world is the (unmediated) suddenness with which certain events succeed each other.[12] "But hardly had he passed beneath the barrier when a fresh voice cried out from behind the tower behind him: 'Stop there, horse-dealer!'" (MO, 115). "Kohlhaas regained his composure. A sudden terrible deluge of rain, beating down on the cobbles of the courtyard, extinguished the torches and relieved the anguish in his tormented heart" (MO, 142). Kafka, who paid close attention to the anomalies pervading Kleist's fictive world in one major novel, The Castle, and in two characteristic brief tales, "The Knock at the Manor Gate," and "A Country Doctor," appropriated this violent suddenness, particularly in the two shorter works.[13]

Like much of the most memorable literature of modernity, then, including Sterne's, Conrad's, and Kafka's novels, we have in "Michael Kohlhaas" a text that is unusually satisfying both in its subjective, characterological dimension and in its machine-work of arbitrary human designs gone awry, the ultimate model for a deranged system being textuality itself. An allegory of Reason, of what happens to a man when he is shuttled in and out of reasonable conditions, is interfused with an allegory of Order, concerning lines of authority and jurisdiction that efface, supplant, and challenge one another at every turn. The historical framework that Kleist selects for this relentlessly disconcerting novella is that of the outset of European modernity, a moment of stark increase in the burden upon selfhood owing precisely to political and theological developments taking place in the novella's "wings."

In order for the novella's crises in jurisdiction and authority to work to their fullest effect, the "personality" of Michael Kohlhaas must be represented as inherently reasonable and good-willed. This is precisely Kleist's strategy with regard to his title character. Set against the basic idealism of a character who would gladly lose the monetary value of his two black horses in exchange for some public acknowledgment of the righteousness of his claim (MO, 120) are the abuses of power and blatant displays of indifference to rectitude that begin with a local Junker and his underlings and then shift to authorities of both higher and lower status. (Here I refer to the ultimate embroilment with at least two Electors and the brigand Johann Nagelschmidt.) There is already a sharp divide, I am arguing, in Kohlhaas's experience (on the "empirical" level) between those who abuse him and those who would redress the injustices he has suffered. The parallel movement in the novella's allegory of displaced authority is across literal borders, between hostile and protective jurisdictions. There are far more ways for authority and administrative responsibility to be displaced and deranged than there are for attitudes of "good faith" or its contrary to be determined. Michael Kohlhaas's allegories of spiritual trial and jurisdictional dispute run parallel for a long time but then part ways at the point where the confusions of authority and allegiance *far* outnumber the binary possibilities for either Kohlhaas's betrayal or his advocacy. In this regard, the novella suggests that the administrative, political, and ultimately hermeneutic complexity opened up by modernity and its theological subtexts is far more daunting than the spiritual tribulations within the newly founded modern Protestant soul.

The remaining task for the present section will be to chronicle the parallelism between subjective and jurisdictional allegories in "Michael Kohlhaas," as well as the "parting of the ways" that leaves any remaining simulacrum of a modern subject in a demonic and mechanistic nightmare of indeterminate allegiances. Since in Kleist's text these two allegories seamlessly interpenetrate each other, my own account of these developments will follow a loop. I will begin by pointing out just how fundamental borders and officials of many stripes are to the novella; then proceed to the fluctuations, encoded subjectively, between a basic good faith on Kohlhaas's part, in which we must believe, and an escalating rage. Only briefly, precisely in the center of the novella, is the possibility for justice and basic benevolence withdrawn from Kohlhaas's character: when he assumes a grandiose persona as "a freeman of the Empire and the world, subject to God alone" (*MO*, 143) and as "an emissary of the Archangel Michael" (*MO*, 148). Irrational though this posture may be, and despite the fictionalized Luther's basic repugnance toward Kohlhaas, Kohlhaas's resolve here, to take matters into his own hands, akin to a vigilante of the U.S. West, is understandable in a context of Protestant hermeneutics. The final gesture in my own appropriation of "Michael Kohlhaas" in an account of the emergence from modernity of the broader Western attitudes toward the artist will be to return to the novella's jurisdictional disputes, in the hope of demonstrating how maddening they "really" are.

All of these shifts and developments are compressed into the novella's initial scene. The first sentence in the text, for example, begins with specifications regarding Kohlhaas's time, geographic location, and social class; it goes on to detail a distinctive and characteristic polarization in his soul. "About the middle of the sixteenth century there lived beside the banks of the River Havel a horse-dealer called Michael Kohlhaas, the son of a schoolmaster, who was one of the most honourable as well as one of the most terrible men of his age" (*MO,* 114). Kohlhaas's location places him in Brandenburg, also not far from modern Berlin. Indeed, much of the novella's administrative and jurisdictional craziness can be ascribed to the uncertainties, at this particular moment of history, arising from his doing much business and holding property, including a second residence, in the adjacent Land of Saxony. Kleist also includes some specifications regarding Kohlhaas's background in this initial, somewhat paradigmatic "snapshot": when he later resorts to armed resistance, we cannot mistake him for a peasant rebel, because his father is a schoolmaster, a member of the middle and cultivated classes. The first sentence also inscribes a certain equation indicating a profound underlying split of character. Kohlhaas "was one of the most honourable as well as one of the most terrible men of his age." The Enlightenment symmetry between honor and terror in the first sentence is a setup for what we learn by the end of the paragraph: that "his sense of justice made him a robber and a murderer" (*MO,* 114).

The primary scene of injustice and abuse of power that sets the novella's mad escalation of jurisdictions and ambiguities into play takes the issues of borders and levels of authority fully into account. J. Hillis Miller, in his suggestive study *Topographies,* which explores the spatial dimensions of a wide range of literary settings, elaborates the implications of these borders in "Michael Kohlhaas." [14]

> One day he was riding out of Brandenburg with a string of young horses, all of them well nourished with glossy coats. He was just considering how he would invest the profit he hoped to make from them at the markets—partly, as a wise businessman does, to yield fresh profit, but also partly for present enjoyment—when he reached the Elbe and, close to a magnificent castle on Saxon soil, encountered a toll-gate that he had never seen on this road before. . . . The horse-dealer told him to open the barrier. "What's happened here?" he asked when the toll-gate keeper finally emerged from the house. "State privilege, conferred on Junker Wenzel von Tronka," said the latter. (*MO,* 114)

> "Well, what's going on here?" Kohlhaas asked himself as he brought the horses to a halt. The warden, still fastening a waistcoat across his capacious body, came up and, bracing himself against the wind and rain, demanded the horse-dealer's permit. "My permit?" asked Kohlhaas. . . . The warden, looking askance at him, replied that without a state permit a dealer bringing horses could not be allowed across the border [*Grenze*]. (*MO,* 115)

The text makes us, along with Kohlhaas, exquisitely aware of borders, the identity of administrators (Junker Wenzel von Tronka has claimed the right to issue permits upon his father's death), and regulations. The text specifies as well that based on jurisdictional determinations, the conditions for life as for doing business can change radically from one moment to the next. "The horse-dealer assured him that he had crossed the border seventeen times in his life without such a document. . . . But the warden retorted that he would not slip through for the eighteenth time, that the regulation had only recently been made for precisely that reason" (*MO,* 115–16).

Kohlhaas's fundamental difference with the Junker, his underlings, and the new regulations defined, the novella's initial and paradigmatic scene becomes a bit chaotic; that is to say that Kleist, in his own fictive experimentation, introduces more lines of action and distraction than we are normally accustomed to in fictive scenes whose construction follows the classical Aristotelian unities. Exasperated "by these illegal and extortionate demands" (*MO,* 116), Kohlhaas decides to take the matter up with the Junker directly. The Junker is initially loth to interrupt his carousing with his cronies (one example of the venality if not the corruption of the midlevel administrators who assert most of the authority in the novella); the rain that has been falling since the outset miraculously stops. Attention is drawn to Kohlhaas's magnificent horses themselves. Some very tentative testing regarding the horses' price and value begins. Amid all this action—and a lot of it has opened up within the scope that we expect from conventional fiction—"Kohlhaas noticed the warden and the steward whispering together and throwing knowing glances at the blacks, and prompted by an obscure foreboding he did his utmost to get rid of the horses to them" (*MO,* 116–17).

A shadow has crept across the positive expectations that Kohlhaas, as a good businessman and Protestant, reserved for himself as he set out on his journey. And the shadow has assumed the form of a plot hatching in the collusion between two underlings whose own possible predilections for corruption are not exactly checked by their employer's example. Kohlhaas catches wind of this semi-private conference between the warden and the steward and its providential meaning for himself because in his business, he needs good horse sense. This aside, this play-within-the-action that can come to no good is the paradigmatic instance of the acting out that, along with overt indifference and insolence, constitutes the primary forms of abuse that bring Kohlhaas, and all readers of good faith, to the point of rage. We can never know if, in the logic of "The House that Jack Built," the unjust appropriation and misuse of the two black horses that might have originated in this conversation are the ultimate cause of the novella's drama and untoward events. But the possibility occurs to Kohlhaas himself, as a providential shadow cast over the scene.

Let us pause for a moment at the indifference that constitutes as vile a

manifestation of the abuse of power as injustice itself, as it is predicated for
the entire novella in the first elaborated scene:

> Kohlhaas asked how much he would have to deposit in money or in goods on
> account of the blacks. The steward muttered into his beard that he might just
> as well leave the blacks themselves. "Of course," said the warden, "that is the
> most practical solution; once he has bought the permit he can come and col-
> lect them whenever he likes." Taken aback by such an unconscionable de-
> mand, Kohlhaas pointed out to the Junker, who was wrapping the tails of his
> jerkin round his freezing body, that he wanted to sell the blacks. But at that
> very moment a gust of wind drove a great sheet of rain and hail through the
> gateway, and to put an end to the matter the Junker shouted: "If he refuses to
> leave the horses, throw him back over the toll-gate." (MO, 117–18)

This passage marks the conjunction between human injustice and meteoro-
logical chance. Two kinds of arbitrariness mix: the human variety, which is
avoidable, forces Kohlhaas to leave the two black workhorses as a deposit on
the others, which will then be conducted to his Saxon property and sold; the
natural happenstance, which is forgivable precisely because of its inevitability,
allows the Junker to terminate his considered deliberation on the matter, and
to dismiss Kohlhaas in a particularly crass and unsympathetic way, one that
emphasizes the arbitrary deployment of force. This dismissal sets a precedent
for a series of outrages including the "scornful" laughter with which the
warden repudiates Kohlhaas's claim, in front of the Junker, of willful damage
to the horses (MO, 120), the lies with which the warden and steward have
Kohlhaas's servant Herse expelled from the Junker's pigsty (where he has
been housed; MO, 122–26); and the overeagerness with which the Elector
of Saxony's bodyguard staves Kohlhaas's wife, Lisbeth, on the occasion of her
petition (MO, 135–37).

The vectors of force and conflict that, in keeping with the laws of quan-
tum physics, will unleash a vast quantity of energy and violence, have been
seeded in the novella's initial scene. These forces, as J. Hillis Miller notes,
tend to be triggered at border-crossings and other points of exchange.[15] The
field on which this energy is generated, stored, and expressed is Kohlhaas's
own character, which has been represented from the outset as "fair and
square" in the best modern sense. Kleist takes pains to establish that Kohlhaas
is *both* of the utmost good faith *and* sensitized to abuses of power such as the
ones to which he has already been subjected.

The narrator therefore repeatedly represents Kohlhaas as a man who
wishes to regain no more than has been taken from him; as a man who will
relinquish any aggressiveness in his stance as soon as he has received reassur-

ance that impartial deliberation prevails; and generally, as an individual of an unusually positive and optimistic outlook:

> A few weeks later, with the string of horses he had brought with him sold to his satisfaction, he returned to Tronka Castle with no more bitterness in his heart than one might feel at the sorry state of the world. (*MO*, 118)

> Kohlhaas would have gladly sacrificed the whole value of the horses to have had the groom at hand and to be able to compare his statement with the statement of this loud-mouthed castle warden. (*MO*, 120)

> For despite the insults he had suffered, experience had already given him a realistic sense of the imperfection inherent in the order in the world, and this feeling inclined him to accept the loss of the horses as a just consequence. (*MO*, 121)

> He then recounted to Lisbeth, his wife, the whole course of the story in full explanatory detail, and declared that he was determined to seek redress in a public court of law. . . . With the aid of a lawyer with whom he was acquainted, he drew up a statement. . . . He demanded punishment of the Junker in accordance with the law, the restoration of the horses to their former condition, and compensation for what both he and his groom had suffered. (*MO*, 126–27)

These extracts do not describe a man with a hidden agenda of repressed and possibly unconscious aggression toward the world when he sets out on his business trip at the beginning of the novella; they characterize, rather, a man who prides himself on the sense of fair play he has gained from his experience, and with a sound, philosophical attitude toward life's inevitable reversals. The narrative rarely ventures into psychological commentary; when it does so, it is in order to assess the emotional cost that Kohlhaas's run-ins with the authorities, which are not of his creation, exact from him. The text specifies that, as a result of the somber tone his business dealings have taken, and in cognizance of the feelings these events have aroused, Kohlhaas contemplates putting down his business and selling his property. It is only the existential considerations raised by Lisbeth that make him persist, both commercially and in his desire for justice:

> Kohlhaas, who could now take no further pleasure in breeding horses, or in his home and farm, or scarcely even in his wife and children, waited through the next month with a feeling of despondency and foreboding. (*MO*, 130)

> A feeling of repugnance such as he had never experienced [*wiederwärtigsten*] before filled his heart as he looked toward the gate whenever he heard a sound in the courtyard, expecting to see the Junker's men appear. . . . Well

schooled in the world's ways though he was, this [having the starved nags returned to him] would have been the one eventuality to which his feelings could have found no fitting response. (*MO,* 130–31)

He invited a neighbor to call on him, a local magistrate. . . . and when this man had seated himself Kohlhaas asked him what price he would offer for his properties in Brandenburg and in Saxony, house and land. . . . At these words his wife Lisbeth paled. (*MO,* 131)

"Let me forgive the Electors, my two sovereigns, the warden and the steward, the lords Hinz and Kunz and whoever else has done me wrong in this affair; but, if it is possible, let the Junker be compelled to fatten my blacks for me again." (*MO,* 155)

No sooner had Kohlhaas received from Dr. Luther a copy of this proclamation, which was displayed everywhere in the principality, than notwithstanding the conditional character of its undertakings he disbanded his men, sending them away with gifts, expressions of gratitude and suitable admonitions. He surrendered all the money, arms, and equipment he had taken as booty to the courts at Lützen as Electoral property. (*MO,* 160–61)

These passages indicate that Kohlhaas continues to desire, at most, what is due him; that facing a set of arbitrary and inflexible conditions, he is willing to adjust his entire way of life; and that even after he has succumbed to his enraged impulses, and mounted a campaign of vengeance, he decommissions and disarms his men at the first assurance that his affairs will be adjudicated with impartial legality.

We should bear in mind that narrative is at all times a treacherous medium in the Romantic conventions of fiction that Kleist helps initiate. In "Michael Kohlhaas," the narrator's attestations to the title character's basic good faith are particularly conspicuous. The counterforce to Kohlhaas's presumed innocence is a sequence of abuses, displacements, and fragmentations in authority and jurisdiction that ultimately result in a tragic standoff between him and the law: "The relationship now existing between him and the state seemed quite intolerable" (*MO,* 171). These territorial disputes achieve an intricacy that Benjamin would call truly baroque. I am arguing that in terms of the negotiations that Western culture conducts with the artist over the broader modernity and in the wake of the Reformation depicted in the novella, it is the fractured jurisdictions and subjections to multiple authorities in the novella that constitute its enduring contribution. We have seen the attention to territories and their borders in the very *foundation* (inception) of the novella. It is worthwhile now to pause over the complexities that these disputes achieve, both early in the novella when Kohlhaas is a legitimate plaintiff, and later, when, having given in to his aggressive impulses, *his* actions require judicial deliberation.

The response to Kohlhaas's initial appeal to the (Saxon) court in Dresden, regarding the appropriation of his horses and the injury to Herse, his employee, establishes a pattern for responses from authority in the novella. Authority is itself starkly split, between extensions of the Junker's corruption and exemplary officials who are, as it were, extensions of Kohlhaas's projected good faith. After a year of deliberation, Kohlhaas's attorney informs him that his suit is hopeless because

> Junker Wenzel von Tronka was related to two noblemen, Hinz and Kunz von Tronka, one of whom was Cupbearer to the sovereign and the other actually his Chamberlain. He advised him to attempt no further court proceedings, but take steps to recover possession of the horses, which were still at Tronka Castle . . . in conclusion he requested that Kohlhaas, if he were not content to let it rest there, should at least excuse him from acting further in the matter. (*MO,* 128)

Justice is immutable in this situation not because of its transcendence but because of the impenetrability of the shield of affiliations protecting the Junker. The lawyer not only declares the hopelessness of Kohlhaas's case, but excuses himself from any further legal representation of him. Yet just as Kohlhaas receives this thoroughly disheartening and cynicism-reinforcing letter a different type of official happens to be present, a coincidence of the kind resounding through the novella:

> The governor happened to be present, standing beside the bath in which Kohlhaas had laid Herse and giving some instructions, when a messenger brought the horse-dealer his Dresden lawyer's disheartening letter. . . . While he was talking to the doctor, the governor noticed that Kohlhaas let fall a tear on the letter he had received and opened; whereupon he approached him in a cordial and friendly manner and asked what misfortune had befallen him. When the horse-dealer handed him the letter without a word, this worthy man . . . clapped him on the shoulder and told him not to lose courage; he would help him, he said, to obtain justice. . . . He told him that he need only compose a petition to the Elector of Brandenburg accompanied by a brief account of the incident and his advocate's letter, and requesting his sovereign's protection against the injustices done to him on Saxon territory. (*MO,* 128–29)

The novella thus establishes a dichotomy between "good cops" and "bad cops" existing in uncanny complementarity to the dichotomy between Kohlhaas's good faith and his potential rage against perceived abuse. (I myself, knowing never to trust the narrator, knowing that Kafka himself often adopted the technique of the narratorial "thumb" that tips the scales, cringe at the term "worthy" applied to the governor. Subsequent events in the novella, however, substantiate the abyss between worthy and untrustworthy authority.) As a dutiful and consistent official, the Grand Chancellor of the High Court, Count Wrede, will be the governor's successor (*MO*, 163).

We should be aware that the governor's well-intentioned counsel to Kohlhaas escalates the legal battle. The governor's advice now leverages the Elector of Brandenburg into the conflict: his counter as the supreme authority in the principality is the Elector of Saxony. One round into the match (score that the Junker 1; Kohlhaas 0), and the battle is now German principality against German principality. We must factor in that at least one additional administrative tier, including courts, princes, and their subordinates, has now been triggered to contribute to the matter. Plus, as suggested above, there is the across-the-board authority, furnished at no extra cost, from the religious sphere, from Luther—marginal, but somehow also at the heart of things.

Two scenes in particular illustrate the demonic textual web of conflicting authorities in which Kohlhaas has gotten caught and in which his quest for justice has embroiled a vast host of others. Were these scenes painted canvases, characters and objects would be pouring beyond them onto the frame and into the viewer's space. This is a characteristically Kleistian "painterly" style: to fill the canvas to overflowing with characters, details, and fields of force, not unlike the effect achieved in the apocalyptic works of Brueghel and Bosch. I would argue that the overflowing of events, terms of opposition, ironies, and displacements in Kleist's fiction constitutes the performative dimension of the prospects that he envisages for order, reason, and subjective tranquillity in the modern world.

The verbal canvases in the two scenes I have in mind do incorporate, in the manner of diptychs or triptychs, plays between opposed fields of force, themselves complicated and involuted: these are the Saxon and Prussian fields of influence that Kohlhaas's just but sorry affair has set into motion against each other. The first of these scenes represents a meeting between an array of officials on both sides who, for a time, deliberate on Kohlhaas's fate. The second brings us to the marketplace in Dresden, where all kinds of tensions flare during a second parallel deliberation, over the two black horses, the material substrate of the whole issue and of the set of actions that it engenders. The horses, serving the novella as a Lacanian "petit objet a,"[16] have miraculously emerged from the Junker's burning castle, and through a set of coincidences and transactions have arrived in a place occupied by Kohlhaas and a number of friends and enemies of different ranks, in a very real sense to haunt them.

Kleist pays a lot of attention in the novella not only to the composition and receipt of letters and other dispositions, but to who happens to be present in the setting when they happen to arrive. The first scene that I cite in illustration of the uncanny, uncontainable, and non-Newtonian play of forces activated by the Kohlhaas affair is one that takes place when Luther's final statement on the matter, in the form of a letter, reaches the Elector of Saxony:

> When the Elector received this letter there were present at the palace Prince Christiern of Meissen, the Imperial Marshal and an uncle of Prince Friedrich of Meissen who had been defeated at Mühlberg and was still laid up with wounds; the Grand Chancellor of the High Court, Count Wrede; Count Kallheim, President of the State Chancellery; and the lords Hinz and Kunz von Tronka, respectively Cupbearer and Chamberlain, both of them childhood friends and intimates of the sovereign. The Chamberlain, Lord Kunz, who in his capacity as privy councillor looked after the Elector's privy correspondence and had authority to use the name and seal, was the first to speak. (*MO*, 156–57)

Simply in the list of those present at the letter-reading are ample indications of the complexity of the bureaucratic structure and the lines of allegiance and affiliation that are becoming polarized around the Kohlhaas affair. The scales have always been tipped against Kohlhaas because of the familial affiliation (cousinship) between Wenzel von Tronka and his cousins Hinz and Kunz, high officials of the Saxon Elector. The assonance between "Hinz" and "Kunz" is an example of the crazy mechanics that can take off when sense gets separated from sound, like the play of names in Poe's "The Spectacles." The passage indicates not only a pair of von Tronka cousins (like the pair of horses that occasion the affair); there is also a pair of princes of Meissen, Friedrich and Christiern. Normal human procreation can generate duplication and confusion in the human system of kinship and in the administrative system that is based upon it.[17]

What is so interesting about this scene as it continues is that, on a substantive level, it describes a considerable qualification and even softening of the positions in the conflict as it has evolved. The conflict has achieved a life of its own. It is homeostatic. The substantive points—who is right, to whom the horses belong, what retributions or compensations must be made—are far less significant than the fact that conflict, proliferation, and displacement have evolved into a counter-system of their own, a system that is counter to the logic, determination, and felicity with which human affairs in this society (or these societies) are ordinarily governed. In short, the situation can aggra-

vate itself even when its original positions undergo considerable amelioration. When Chamberlain Kunz von Tronka, a cousin, as we know, of the
Junker's, initiates the discussion, he in fact wraps a major concession in the
packaging of a continuation of the hard line:

> He [Chamberlain Kunz von Tronka] explained at length that he would never
> have decided on his own responsibility to dismiss the case brought to the
> High Court by the horse-dealer against his own cousin the Junker, had he
> not been deceived by false information into regarding it as a wholly ground-
> less and idle piece of trouble-making. Coming to the present situation, he
> observed that no law either of God or of man authorized the horse-dealer to
> exact, as he was presuming to do, such monstrous personal vengeance for this
> judicial error. It would, he insisted, lend prestige to this accursed reprobate if
> they were to treat him as with a lawful belligerent. The disgrace that would
> thereby be reflected upon the sacred person of the Elector was, he added in a
> burst of eloquence, so intolerable to him that he would rather bear the worst
> and see his cousin the Junker taken to Kohlhaasenbrück to fatten the blacks,
> in accordance with the mad rebel's decree, than have Dr. Luther's proposal
> accepted. (MO, 157)

From the perspective of the von Tronka clan, a new subtext has entered the
brew: a desire to circumvent Martin Luther's authority has made a reversal of
the refusal to fatten the blacks preferable to the acceptance of the proposal
that has just arrived from Luther. The von Tronka clan continues to press for
its perceived self-interest, even when the means of doing this reverse themselves. Yet the positions in the conflict not only soften and reverse in themselves: new counter-positions are generated, with the effect of adding further
confusion:

> The Grand Chancellor of the High Court, Count Wrede, half turning to
> him, expressed his regret that the Chamberlain had not shown the same deli-
> cate solicitude for his sovereign's reputation when this unquestionably em-
> barrassing matter first arose as he was now showing when it had become
> necessary to clear it up. He indicated to the Elector the reservations he felt
> about invoking the power of the state to enforce an obvious injustice. He
> alluded significantly to the horse-dealer's ever-increasing following in Sax-
> ony, pointed out that this thread of violence threatened to spin itself out in-
> definitely, and declared that there was no way to sever it and extricate the
> government from this ugly situation except plain fair dealing: they must im-
> mediately and without further scruple make good the wrong that had been
> done. (MO, 157–58)

The fault line dividing opinions regarding the disposition of Kohlhaas's claim
takes off from a basic value judgment as to whether civil tranquillity or

justice is more important. Those who favor Kohlhaas's restraint and punishment, for the considerable violence and even death that he has inflicted, at least implicitly advance the value of civil peace. The Grand Chancellor of the Court, whose discourse is reproduced above, takes the juridical high road, and advocates that legal deliberation focus on redressing misusages of justice. Score so far, then: Kohlhaas 1; Tronka clan 1. The tie is immediately broken by one of the "twin" Princes of Meissen, Christiern, who claims Kohlhaas's wrongs have so compromised "the interests of Wittenberg and Leipzig and indeed the whole of the country ravaged by the horse-dealer" that "principles of jurisprudence" are beside the point (*MO,* 158). Kohlhaas should be either captured or destroyed. Please note that in simply describing an impromptu meeting that convenes itself around mail-call, Kleist has now involved at least four discrete and different levels of authority, capable of competing with each other: imperial, involving the Electors; feudal, whose officers are princes, barons, and the like; juridical; and religious, for we know that the von Tronka clan would not be unhappy to evade the growing authority of Luther. In the case at hand, any and all of these relations are compromised by the blood relations that link the Junker to the Elector, and that "tilt the table" against Kohlhaas. In any architecture involving so many stresses and strains, and I think we can speak in terms of a decadent Gothic architecture here, one in a state of collapse, conflict is bound to erupt. It indeed does so, both in this scene and in the one immediately following, in the Dresden marketplace:

> The Chamberlain, bringing over two chairs from the wall and politely placing them in the room for the Prince and the Elector, said that he was glad to find that a man of the Prince's integrity and perspicacity agreed with him on the question of how best to settle this perplexing affair. Holding the chair without sitting down, the Prince looked straight at him and said he had no reason at all to be glad, since the proposed course of action inevitably entailed that he, Kunz von Tronka, should be arrested and put on trial for misuse of the sovereign's name. For although it might be necessary to draw a veil, before the seat of justice, over a whole series of crimes which had proliferated until they were simply too numerous to be called to account, this did not apply to the first of them, which had led to all the rest; and not until the Chamberlain was arraigned on this capital charge would the state be entitled to suppress the horse-dealer, whose grievances, as they well knew, were perfectly just. . . . At these words the Junker looked in dismay at the Elector, who turned away, blushing deeply, and moved over to the window. After an embarrassed silence on all sides, Count Kallheim remarked that by such means they would never break out of the charmed circle in which they were caught. (*MO,* 158–59)

In this instant, even in a setting of exemplary *politesse* and restraint, the stresses and strains in the novella's baroque architecture of jurisdictions and hierarchies break out. The *signs* of the violence of the disagreement are ironically slight: a prince refuses seating in a chair proffered by a chamberlain; an Elector blushes and moves toward a window, away from the disputant who happens to be a relative of his. In the towns of Saxony, blood has run and houses have burned in the name of this conflict: yet its restrained manifestations, in the seat of Saxon government and civility, are barely perceptible.

The second scene illustrative of this utterly baroque play of forces is the one containing the determination of the horses' fate. The black horses in question, bizarrely, serve as one of the chief forces for narrative coherence in the novella. They are like cats in their seeming ability to arise from deadly situations and pursue Kohlhaas. A second consummate episode demonstrating the jurisdictional perplexity that the novella generates concerns the final disposition of the two horses. These were led away from the Tronka Castle, which Kohlhaas was in the act of burning; a character called "the knacker from Döbbeln" purchases them from the shepherd who led them away in a town called Wilsdruf; the "facts" in these eventualities are embroidered with rumors and alternate accounts, which Kleist has been only too willing to incorporate into the narrative (*MO*, 164–65). The horses end up in the marketplace at Dresden, where they will be subjected to "ocular inspection" (*MO*, 168) by Kohlhaas, to determine if these specimens are in fact the horses in dispute. They have been moved from Wilsdruf to Dresden through the intervention of (Saxon) Chamberlain Kunz, who, as we remember, is Junker Wenzel von Tronka's cousin; only now that Kohlhaas has succeeded to some extent in discrediting the Junker, Kunz has distanced himself from von Tronka. The scene in which the opposing parties meet and the horses are appropriated is a masterpiece of chaotic fictive overdetermination. It is striking in large measure because it is so exasperating to read. But what it demonstrates, I am certain, is the complexity of the jurisdictional affiliations that the property dispute between Kohlhaas and the Junker has generated.

The reason overt hostility breaks out in this second scene, in a nutshell, is that so many individuals have been dragged into the conflict, direct interaction between the von Tronka and the Kohlhaas parties becomes inevitable. This is precisely what happens when Chancellor von Wrede directs Kohlhaas to inspect the horses, on whom the knacker from Döbbeln now has some claim. I quote the passage at some length because it dramatizes the environment of proliferating violence and complexity, and because I could not recount the events any better than Kleist.

It happened that Kohlhaas, summoned by a court messenger to give certain explanations that were needed concerning the property deposited at Lützen, was in the Chancellor's room when the Baron entered with his message. The Chancellor rose from his seat with an air of annoyance and left the horse-dealer, whom the Baron did not know, standing on one side with the papers in his hand; the Baron then told him of the embarrassing situation in which Kunz and Wenzel von Tronka found themselves. The knacker from Döbbeln, acting on inadequate instructions from the Wilsdruf courts, had turned up with a pair of horses in such a miserable condition that Junker Wenzel understandably hesitated to identify them as those belonging to Kohlhaas; for this reason, if they were going to be taken to the knacker for the purpose of attempting to re-fatten them in the family's stables, ocular inspection by Kohlhaas would first be necessary to remove all doubt on the point. "Would you therefore be kind enough," he [Baron von Wenk] concluded, "to have the horse-dealer fetched from his house and taken to the market-place where the horses are." . . . He [the Chancellor] then introduced him [Baron von Wenk] to the horse-dealer who was standing behind him, and requested him, as he sat down and put on his spectacles again, to consult the horse-dealer himself on the matter. Kohlhaas, whose expression revealed nothing of what was passing through his mind, said that he was prepared to follow the Baron to the market-place to inspect the horses. . . . As the Baron turned round in amazement towards him, he returned to the Grand Chancellor's desk and having given him, from the documents in his wallet, several pieces of information concerning the property in Lützen, he took his leave. The Baron, who had blushed scarlet and crossed to the window, did likewise; whereupon, escorted by the three lansquenets acting on the Prince of Meissen's orders, and accompanied by a crowd of people, they walked to the palace square. (MO, 167–69)

Eventually, in a civil setting, Kohlhaas has to come face to face with a member of the opposing party, in this case with a Baron Siegfried von Wenk, who has earlier been introduced as "a friend" of Chamberlain Kunz von Tronka (MO, 167). The baron *misrecognizes* Kohlhaas:[18] he thinks that the latter is at home when he is standing behind him unnoticed. As in the previous scene, the slightest of gestures, out of the aesthetic of gesture that Benjamin, in *Trauerspiel*, extrapolates from German tragic drama, conveys the most violent kind of opposition: turning around suddenly, blushing. There are other parallels between these two central scenes: the latter scene also begins with the receipt of a message—from the chamberlain, telling Kohlhaas to inspect the horses in the marketplace. An unexpected person—in this case Kohlhaas—is also there when the message arrives. The baron, upon learning that this hated adversary to his clique is present, and that the two may have to inspect horses together, crosses to the window (*MO,* 168). These parallels between scenes suggest that the veneer of civil cordiality in the novella is beginning to buckle; violence has been seeded in so many locales of signification that it is about to break out even in the unlikeliest places. Yet the subliminal violence in the grand chancellor's house is nothing compared to what breaks out in the marketplace:

> He [Kohlhaas] stopped at a distance of twelve paces from the animals, which were standing unsteadily with their heads bowed to the ground and not touching the hay put down for them by the knacker, glanced at them briefly, then turned back to the Chamberlain and said: "My lord, the knacker is quite right; the horses tied to his cart belong to me." With that he looked round at all the gentlemen, raised his hat again and, escorted by his bodyguard, left the square. As soon as the Chamberlain heard this he strode across to the knacker so quickly that the plume of his helmet shook, threw him a bag of money, and while the fellow, combing his hair back from his forehead with a lead comb, held the bag in his hand and stared at the money, he ordered a groom to untether the horses and lead them home. . . . But hardly had he taken hold of their halters to untether them when his cousin, Master Himboldt, seized his arm and shouting: "Don't you touch those knacker's nags!" hurled him away from the cart. Then rather uncertainly stepping back across the pile of dung towards the Chamberlain, who had stood speechless at this incident, he told him he had better get himself a knacker's man if he wanted an order like that carried out. Foaming with rage, the Chamberlain glared for a moment at Himboldt, then turned round and shouted over the heads of the noblemen surrounding him, calling for the guards; and as soon as an officer with some Electoral guardsmen appeared from the palace at Baron von Wenk's behest, he gave him a brief account of the outrageous riot which the citizens of the mob were presuming to instigate, and called on him to arrest the leader of the mob, Master Himboldt, whom he seized by the shirt. . . . Skilfully twisting himself free and pushing the Chamberlain back, Himboldt said: "My lord! Telling a lad of twenty what he should and should not do is not inciting him to riot!" (*MO,* 169–70)

Not only violence but irony proliferates as Kohlhaas and Chamberlain Kunz von Tronka, bitter adversaries, find themselves for once on the same side. And their present adversary, Master Himboldt, is merely questioning the chamberlain's high-handed repurchase of the horses so that justice accorded Kohlhaas, in the form of compensation, can lead to just retribution against him. Ironically, in questioning the forced purchase of the horses, Himboldt is displaying the same individualism that has characterized Kohlhaas's quest for justice. The scene thus violently shifts the valences that have prevailed throughout the novella. The chamberlain, who wants to punish Kohlhaas, turns out to be an enemy of the common man. Himbolt's populism is an extension of the Lutheran creed, even though Luther basically opposes Kohlhaas. The novella here suggests that history has arrived at a time when the democracy implicit in Protestantism is already the property of every individual man. Kohlhaas and the chamberlain, who a moment before were confirmed adversaries, now both desire the repossession of the horses so that the mechanisms of justice can get under way and work to their end. Once again the novella dramatizes the *telos* of violence implicit in the scenario of a fictive surrogate, Kohlhaas, who must deal with the predicament of owing allegiance to too many jurisdictions, themselves logically incompatible:

> When the young man, retreating into the crowd, diffidently answered that the horses would have to be made decent again before that could be expected of him, the Chamberlain pursued him, snatched off his hat which bore the family's coat of arms, stamped on it, drew his sword, and raining furious blows on him with the flat of his blade, instantly drove the groom out of the square and out of his service. Master Himboldt cried out: "Down with the murderous tyrant!" and as the people, incensed by this scene, pressed together and forced the guard back, he threw the Chamberlain to the ground from behind, tore off his cloak and collar and helmet, wrenched his sword out of his hand and with a savage sweep of the arm hurled it away across the square. . . . This incident, little as the horse-dealer was in fact to blame for it, nevertheless aroused throughout the land, even among the more moderate and well-disposed, a feeling that was highly prejudicial to the successful outcome of his case. (*MO*, 170–71)

Over and opposed to the fragmenting authorities vying over the Kohlhaas affair stand the people, a kind of political Real. Despite the purported overthrow of the "medieval world order," the authorities of the empire, the principalities, the vestigial feudal landowners, the courts, and religion are arranged hierarchically in relation to the people, of whom Master Himboldt is an outspoken representative. Even Michael Kohlhaas, and his meaning, belong to a still-hierarchical autocracy.

Many unexpected factors, not merely this incident, contribute to Kohlhaas's ultimate and inevitable demise. There is the Johann Nagelschmidt subplot. Nagelschmidt, in his guise as a self-motivated loner who takes what he wants, is an imitator of Kohlhaas; but he has neither Kohlhaas's fine sense of justice nor his desire for legitimation. Kohlhaas's fading credibility is in effect done in by a collaboration with Nagelschmidt that seems far greater than it is. But what really makes Kohlhaas's existence impossible is what has made everyone's existence, in the West, impossible since the morning star rose on the broader modernity: being caught between simultaneous, multiplying, self-displacing, fragmenting, self-doubling, and self-undermining sources of authority.

I close my reading of this tale with two notes, minor addenda, really. Names in the novella, proper and geographical, form a self-contained hermeneutic system functioning alongside the story much like the numerical register in Wittgenstein's *Tractatus Logico-Philosophicus* supplements its argument. The name of the venal von Tronka clan contains the word for throne. Grand Chancellor of the High Court Count Wrede's name, in addition to being the most ridiculously extended appellation in the text, harbors the word for speech or discourse. The knacker who is one-time owner of the immortal and ubiquitous horses comes from Döbbeln, a place name that highlights the doubling in the novella's ironies, meanings, and affiliations. The play, arbitrariness, and violence in the work's system of names parallels the same qualities predicating the relations of affiliation and authority. Indeed, if the historical period that the novella chronicles brings about the withdrawal of plausible institutional forms of authority, such as feudalism and the Catholic Church, then the register of language, which structures the displacements in naming and meaning, rushes to the fore in their replacement as the paradigm for Western thought and culture.

It is perhaps beginning to emerge that *Trauerspiel,* with its emphasis on the *gestus* that reigns in German baroque tragedy, could be a gloss on "Michael Kohlhaas" as on several other implied texts. In the spirit of Kleist's graft of the Reformation period within the novella's historical framework, let us pursue, for an instant, a gloss within the framework of "Michael Kohlhaas" upon another implied text, in this case Shakespeare's *Hamlet,* which also figures prominently in *Trauerspiel.*

Saxony, the locus of so much of Michael Kohlhaas's rage and agony, also includes Wittenberg. An entire treatise could be devoted to the status of this town in cultural history and literary semiology: in addition to its role in "Michael Kohlhaas," Wittenberg serves as home to Marlowe's Dr. Faustus and as college town to Hamlet. "Now it happened at this time that the Kingdom of Poland, for reasons not known to us, was involved in a dispute with the house of Saxony, and was repeatedly and urgently pressing the Elector of Brandenburg to make common cause with the Poles against the Saxons" (*MO,* 186). An even more devastating blow to Kohlhaas's prospects than the purported Nagelschmidt conspiracy consists in changes that take place when, in consideration of the international situation, the jurisdiction of his case is shifted from Saxony to Brandenburg. Once again, the issue of jurisdiction is central, both to Kohlhaas's status as a fictive "subject" and to the narrative resolution of the novella. It may well be that the narrator is ignorant of the terms of the conflict between Saxony and Poland because the graft of *Hamlet* as a period and issue model, a text also touching on the predicament of subjectivity at the outset of modernity, is more important than the "factual" details. "Poland was already amassing an army of five thousand men on the Saxon frontier" (*MO*, 187): the Poles are also very much on the scene at the tragic culmination of *Hamlet*. In a performatively compelling as well as narratively complex and historically "true" way, then, "Michael Kohlhaas" "reproduces" the aesthetic and subjective conditions of the broader modernity, by invoking, in a multifaceted way, their sources.

CHAPTER 5

Kant and the Anointment
of the Modern Artist

In a certain bizarre sense, if Judaism's failure, at the outset of Christianity, consisted in its formalism and literality in carrying out rules, Kant's third Critique, *The Critique of Judgment,* plays the Christian role of a corrective to the first Critique, *The Critique of Pure Reason,* humanizing and personalizing its own rather cold alignment of the transcendental and empirical spheres. The much more human and therefore Christian interface between the spheres (and we may think of these latter as late-Enlightenment distant descendents of Western idealism and the mind/body split) is no longer Christ, but the artist himself. Curiously, the "humanized" and "applied" dimensions of *The Critique of Judgment* place *The Critique of Pure Reason* in a relatively "Judaic" position within Kant's corpus. This is despite strikingly ambivalent pyrotechnics with regard to Judaism and smug dismissal of all cultures (for instance, African, Polynesian) at some anthropological remove from the mainstream of European-Christian culture that we find throughout *The Critique of Judgment.* I want to state very clearly at the outset of this chapter that philosophers and writers of the Enlightenment and Romantic periods were unable to entirely dispense with metaphysical notions of spirituality and transcendence, in spite of massive amounts of discourse, argumentation, and artwork generated to demonstrate the limits of theology, arbitrary political power, and a priori biases in looking at the world. The artist, as he emerges from the discourse of Immanuel Kant, is an exceptional person invested with extraordinary powers to see into the intellectual operating system built into the universe and to mediate, as in a theological sphere Christ once did, between the transcendental and human registers. An enormous amount of

work, in Lessing, Rousseau, Kant, Schelling, and Hegel, goes into establishing the secular pedigree of the artist and her close relative, the thinker or the
intellectual. This secularization is in keeping with the intellectual rigor of
some brilliant philosophers and writers; it also reaches toward the effort to
set out the lineaments of a post-Revolutionary (referring to the American as
well as the French Revolution) religion in states that moved quickly, some
found alarmingly, toward antiestablishmentarianism. I am arguing that despite the secular nature of the theological void the artist was constructed to
fill, according to the aesthetic contract of modernity, the artist and the intellectual are encrusted with metaphysical values so persistent that we are labor-
ing at their productive illumination even today.

The artist, the subject or agent of the aesthetic contract, emerges in a fully
articulate form at the turn of the nineteenth century in the wake of a varied
and wonderful set of experiments that rush to fill in the void created for
Benjamin during the age of *Trauerspiel* (although for some, this age is not
initiated until the famous dualism of Descartes). The artist is the human-born
deity of creative and intellectual endeavor. An elaborate set of agreements
reached by accord in the cultures and societies that pursued these developments determined who the artists were, what constituted valued aesthetic
products, the considerable privileges and risks that accrued to the artist. A
figure of giftedness and inherent transcendence, the artist became as much
an embodiment of sanction, scorn, monstrosity, and deviance as of reverence.
But the aura surrounding the artist is definitely theological, even in a secular
religion of art. With respect to Hegel, Derrida points out the special accom-
modations made for and offered to the artist by revealed religion:

> Art includes its own proper religion, which is only a stage in the spirit's lib-
> eration, and has its destination in "true religion," truth of the past art, of
> what art will have been. In the fine arts, the content of the idea was limited
> by the sensuous immediacy and did not manifest itself in the universality of
> an infinite form. With *true* religion (the true, the Christian religion, that of
> the infinite God), the sensible, finite, and immediate intuition passes into the
> infinite of a knowing that, as infinite, no longer has any exteriority, thus
> knows itself, becomes present to itself. Presence (*Dasein*) that knows itself
> since it is infinite and has no outside, truth that announces itself to itself,
> resounds and reflects itself in its own element: the manifest, the revealed,
> *das Offenbaren*.[1]

It is not only the artist's unique *presence,* formulated in this passage so well
by Derrida, that qualifies her as a secular prophet, if not a divinity. In the
late-Enlightenment systematic philosophy anticipating artificial intelligence's
quest for an evolutionary, self-generating, self-revealing human intelligence,

the artist is distinguished by intuition, sensibility, perspicacity, and social exemplarity as well as by the presence and immediacy that Derrida notes. In the Kantian *précis* to the Hegelian revelation of art, as we shall see, public taste restrains artistic flight at the same time that it provides for aesthetic celebration.

A broader view of the aesthetic contract, its formulators and examplars, and the best artworks that allegorize its conditions, will follow in Chapters 6 through 9 below. Kant's placement of art and the artist within the context of a truly systematic overview of human and nonhuman intellectual structures, infrastructures, and cognitive faculties was done so well, and exerted such a pull over subsequent nineteenth- and twentieth-century aesthetics, including that of Hegel, that the purpose of this section will be a sketch of the emergence of the aesthetic contract in *The Critique of Judgment*.

If I can have passably made four points, placed them in some reasonable alignment, and marshaled the appropriate textual material in their justification, I will have succeeded in my endeavor: (1) Kant devotes a surprising and apparently disproportionate amount of labor in his treatise on aesthetics to elaborating the issues of freedom and its artistically gauged statute of limitation, purposiveness. I would argue that the very space for this free play and willfullness is the teleological uncertainty, individuation, and resultant sense of polarized moral drama introjected into Western culture at the time of the Protestant Reformation and Counter-Reformation. (2) Kant selects the domain of art and the constant evaluation of beauty that attends it both in formal discourse and in "everyday experience" as a context for and contrast to the emergence of the sublime. I would argue that both the logical and cultural necessity for the sublime entails a shift of the metaphysical values attending art to a secular sphere. The sublime is a topos or setting that allows a continuation of the Western cultural discussion regarding the magnificent and the transcendental, but in a discourse cleansed of sectarian claims. (3) Human manifestations of sublimity, that is, sublime attributes incorporated within the sphere of the modern subject, extend from creativity and the imagination to "original genius" and inspired madness. Artists, intellectuals, and creative thinkers constitute the human interface between the transcendental and the empirical, that horizon possibly an extension of the Western mind/body split, toward whose elaboration Kant's systematic works devoted themselves. In a secular domain, the artist occupies the position reserved in earlier Western ontotheological configurations for priests, seers, and prophets. (4) There is a legislative thrust to Kant's systematic thought extending to his work on aesthetics as well. Kant, whether working out the interplay between cognitive faculties or intellectual fields, endeavors to elaborate the working relationships between the entities or agents in question. In the case of the aesthetics of *The Critique of Judgment,* Kant works through the implicit and explicit social and cultural understandings surrounding the figure of the artist as the new exemplary transcendental-empirical mediator. So powerful are Kant's speculations in this regard that they provided an extended Western, Enlightenment-Romantic format for what I am terming the aesthetic contract.

Art and Freedom

So much attention and work does Kant devote to the formulation of conditions of freedom and purposiveness at the outset of *The Critique of Judgment* that one could characterize these issues as the cornerstone of his aesthetics. At the very beginning of the Introduction, Kant specifies: "Now there are only two kinds of concepts, and these admit as many distinct principles of the possibility of their objects, viz. *natural concepts* and the *concept of freedom*" (*CJ,* 7).[2] The universe of concepts itself, with concepts as the very units of philosophical thinking, or "idemes," if you wish, is divided between the arbitrariness of nature and the freedom to which thinking gives us access. Freedom could not be more basic to Kant, and the freedom that Kant elaborates, as his system grows, is increasingly one predicated by conditions of subjectivity first crystallized by Luther, Calvin, and other thinkers of the Protestant Reformation.

Yet an enunciation of the possibilities of freedom, of any sort, even a purely intellectualized freedom, cannot remain too far from a counteractive citation of the Law. Without the Law, the freedom made possible by such phenomena as the Protestant Reformation and Cartesian dualism would be agoraphobic, unsettling, even maddening. "We must, however, remark, that *separation from all society* is regarded as sublime if it rests upon ideas that overlook all sensible interest. . . . Evidence of this is afforded by the propensity to solitude, the fantastic wish [*phantastische Wunsch*] for a secluded country seat, or (in the case of young persons) by the dream of the happiness of passing one's life with a little family upon some island unknown to the rest of the world, a dream of which storytellers or writers of Robinsonades know how to make good use" (*CJ,* 116–17).

The freedom declared by Enlightenment thinking immediately launches an appeal for moderating legislation on the part of the reasonable, moderate hypothetical philosophizing subject. In psychological terminology, the invocation of repressive devices in the face of instinctual gratification is called "reaction-formation," the defense mechanism whereby we abjure, and on occasion take up behaviors to counteract, the very satisfactions that drive us on. One of the most distinctive qualities permeating the vast systematic undertakings of the Enlightenment-Romantic period, as well as the fictive works modeled on them, is a breathless exuberance regarding the inbuilt powers and potentials of systems themselves. I would argue that these systematic aspirations are tempered, from the outset, by a "massive cultural reaction-formation," a painful suspicion toward the freedoms liberated by newfound systems. This cultural reaction-formation is a subtext sobering the tone of the expansive works by Rousseau, Melville, and others that celebrate expansion and liberty:

> Legislation through natural concepts is carried on by means of the understanding and is theoretical. Legislation through the concept of freedom is carried on by the reason and is merely practical. It is only in the practical [sphere] that the reason can be legislative; in respect of theoretical cognition (of nature) it can merely (as acquainted with law by the understanding) deduce from given laws consequences which always remain within [the limits of] nature. But, on the other hand, reason is not always therefore *legislative* where there are practical rules, for they may only be technically practical. (*CJ*, 10–11)

Where freedom is a possibility, legislation cannot be far behind. Note that whereas the understanding that performs empirical experimentation is a splendid faculty for the administration of "natural concepts," "Legislation through the concept of freedom . . . is merely practical." Freedom, while it predicates an entire domain within the conceptual world, is not a very profound context for legislation. Freedom-inspired legislation is reasonable and eminently practical. Freedom will sparkle not so much in the world of legislation as in the domains of taste and aesthetic judgment. "The concept of freedom is meant to actualize in the world of sense the purpose proposed by its laws, and consequently nature must be so thought that the conformity to law of its form at least harmonizes with the possibility of the purposes to be effected in it according to laws of freedom. There must, therefore, be a ground of the *unity* of the supersensible, which lies at the basis of nature, with that which the concept of freedom practically contains; and the concept of this ground . . . nevertheless makes possible the transition from the mode of thought according to the principles of the one to that according to the principles of the other" (*CJ*, 12). At the level of the very widest infrastructure on which Kant builds this element of his system, he needs to invoke both a principle of freedom and (an ultimately repressive) unity within the supersensible: the former will sustain the play of art as the new faculty of the encounter of the human with the Transcendental; a supersensible principle will still, as in *The Critique of Pure Reason,* serve as the basis for the interface that unifies the vertically hierarchical Transcendental and empirical realms. At the outset of the treatise, then, Kant will have things both ways: he will establish a domain for the play of freedom and in the same gesture will regulate that play by invoking "the *unity* of the supersensible [*der Einheit des Über-sinnlichen*]" (*CJ*, 12). The play of freedom will be a determining factor in the nature of art and in the complex of cultural attitudes and behaviors surrounding it. Yet all the time this play will have a role in something greater, in the wider nexus of metaphysical assumptions and attitudes that will have shifted from the sphere of ontotheology to that of aesthetics.

In getting *The Critique of Judgment* "on its feet," so to speak, Kant devotes considerable energy to the curious term "purposiveness" (*Zweckmässigkeit*). To speak of the purpose of a phenomenon is to place it within some context of meaning without ascribing to it an exhaustive, predetermined, utterly final—teleological—place in the universe. Purposiveness, in other words, performs for the free will / determination dyad exactly what art does as the architectural foundation for the sublime: it admits some degree of free play into an overall context of determination. This mix is absolutely crucial to Kant's conception of and scenario for art: there are some objective criteria for beauty, but the overall experience of art must highlight the spontaneity of the experience, its seeming to result from a *free* interplay with the world. Purposiveness enables some degree of legislation and public consensus to enter what might otherwise be purely playful and decadent cultural experiences; it counteracts the wasteful "spilling of seed" within the intellectual sphere. Kant's "Analytic of Beauty" will derive much of its distinctive flavor from a striptease between the play and the teleological aim that come together in the notion of purposiveness: beauty seduces, but not for no Reason whatsoever. For this reason, Kant specifies: "The principle of the purposiveness of nature (in the manifoldness of its empirical laws) is a transcendental principle [*transcendentales Prinzip*]" (*CJ*, 18).

> The transcendental concept of a purposiveness of nature is neither a natural concept nor a concept of freedom, because it ascribes nothing to the object (of nature), but only represents the peculiar way in which we must proceed in reflection upon the objects of nature in reference to a thoroughly connected experience, and is consequently a subjective principle (maxim) of the judgment. (*CJ*, 20)

Purposiveness of nature is a concept that does not occur in nature; but neither is it a "concept of freedom." Yet it is so crucial for Kant to make the provision in his speculative system for something that is not quite free but is also not teleologically predetermined that he elevates this notion to the level of a "transcendental concept" (*CJ*, 20). Kant, in trying to determine where this overall purposiveness lies, disqualifies the possibility of its being inherent to an external thing. Subjectivity, so far as he is concerned, is the sphere in which the purposiveness of things is to be hashed out: "Now the purposiveness of a thing, so far as it is represented in perception, is no characteristic of the object itself (for such cannot be perceived) although it may be inferred from a cognition of things. . . . Hence the object is only called purposive when its representation is immediately combined with the feeling of pleasure, and this very representation is an aesthetical representation of purposiveness" (*CJ,* 26).

Purposiveness, an abstract attribute if there ever could be one, becomes associated with the aesthetic experience in Kant on the basis of two steps: a disqualification of the *object* as the possible locus of purpose, and a pre-Freudian sense that some pleasure underlies the human apprehension of a purpose in something (just as in classical psychoanalysis some *desire* must underlie even the most horrific dream images). The incorporation of the notion of purposiveness (or one much like it) into Kant's aesthetic schema is crucial because it establishes a volitional ambivalence that becomes the basis for an aesthetic experience and judgment defined by self-contradiction, enigmatic teasing, hovering, and, to incorporate a gender identification, by fickleness. Let us bear in mind that the sublimity to which the artist and the original genius have unique access derives its transcendental overview from the qualities rehearsed as inherent to the process of aesthetic judgment. Hence I dwell on the notion of purposiveness, and incorporate Kant's initial and most abstract exposition of the term:

> If, now, in this comparison the imagination (as the faculty of *a priori* intuitions) is placed by means of a given representation undesignedly in agreement with the understanding, as the faculty of concepts, and thus a feeling of pleasure is aroused, the object must then be regarded as purposive for the reflective judgment [*reflektierende Urteilskraft*]. Such a judgment is an aesthetical judgment upon the purposiveness of the object, which does not base itself upon any present concept of the object, nor does it furnish any such. In the case of an object whose form (not the matter of its representation or sensation), in the mere reflection upon it (without reference to any concept to be obtained of it), is judged as the ground of a pleasure in the representation of such an object, this pleasure is judged as bound up with the representation necessarily, and, consequently, not only for the subject which apprehends this form, but for every judging being in general. The object is then called beautiful, and the faculty of judging by means of such a pleasure (and, consequently, with universal validity) is called taste. (*CJ,* 26–27)

Kant is particularly concerned, as he lays the conceptual groundwork for a scenario of a free choice that may involve all sorts of allurements, with two issues: the relationship between an object's representation and the pleasure it arouses; and a salutary harmony between the cognitive faculties that is a primary basis for any possible pleasure. "In the case of an object" cited immediately above, its form has been sufficient to produce a reflexive pleasure (short of some conceptual evaluation), and this pleasure is related part and parcel to the object's mode of representation. In this case, two conditions for beauty have been achieved: beauty has achieved a reflexive state without extending over into conceptualization; and there has been a harmony, a conformity, between the law of judgment applied in the case and the object's mode of representation, or (we may interject) its form. The situation of beauty described here in the most abstract possible way involves a striking, we might almost say teasing, *almostness*: the object is a form, not a sensation or representation; it tickles reflexivity, but does not bring down upon itself conceptualization (or judgment). *And* it brings about a most pleasing harmony, "of the object with the faculties of the subject" (*CJ,* 27).

Purposiveness is that quality that allows this almostness and harmony to happen, but which stops short of applying deterministic preconditions to the aesthetic. Purposiveness is itself an ambivalent notion deriving from an onto-theological predicament in which the same freedom that can lead to damnation can be taken up, apperceived, as an object of pleasure in itself. The entire aesthetic domain in Kant becomes colored by the play, the collusion, the duplicity, and the mutual seduction rehearsed here on the conceptual level under the rubric of purposiveness.

Indeed, we learn that "*Beauty* is the form of the *purposiveness* of an object, so far as this is perceived in it *without any representation of a purpose*" (*CJ,* 73). The most asexual of writers, Kant nonetheless endows his antinomies with the greatest intensification of the fickleness, seductiveness, and ironic self-contradiction that the Western tradition ascribes to women. Kant's rapture with the thing of beauty, and beauty itself, constitutes the Kantian emanation of a recurrent event in the philosophy of writing, namely, the Joyous Seduction of the (Male) (Rigorous) Philosopher at the Hands of a Figurative Language (or Figurality in General) Quintessentially Female (and Alogical) in Nature.

So Beauty crystallizes itself only in (female) antinomies, just as, in *The Critique of Pure Reason,* the Transcendental, in the medium of a bizarrely uncanny illumination or light, glimmers back into the understanding from beyond only in the form of equally duplicitous antinomies.

> We are not concerned here with empirical (*e.g.* optical) illusion, which occurs in the empirical employment of rules of understanding that are otherwise correct, and through which the faculty of judgment is misled by the

influence of imagination; we are concerned only with *transcendental illusion* [*transzendentalen Scheine*], which exerts its influence on principles that are in no wise intended for use in experience, in which case we should at least have had a criterion of their correctness. In defiance of all the warnings of criticism, it carries us altogether beyond the empirical deployment of categories and puts us off with a merely deceptive extension of *pure understanding*. (*CPR*, 298)

Logical illusion, which consists in the mere imitation of the form of reason . . . arises entirely from lack of attention to the logical rule. . . . Transcendental illusion, on the other hand, does not cease even after it has been detected and its invalidity clearly revealed by transcendental criticism (*e.g.* the illusion in the proposition: the world must have a beginning in time). . . . We therefore take the subjective necessity of a connection of our concepts, which is to the advantage of the understanding, for an objective necessity in the determination of things in themselves. This is an *illusion* which can no more be prevented than we can prevent the sea appearing higher at the horizon than at the shore, since we see it through higher light rays; or to cite a still better example, than the astronomer can prevent the moon from appearing larger at its rising, although he is not deceived by this illusion.

    The transcendental dialectic will therefore content itself with exposing the illusion of transcendent judgments, and at the same time taking precautions that we be not deceived by it. . . . There exists, then, a natural and unavoidable dialectic of pure reason. (*CPR*, 299–300)

Waxing metaphoric in these pivotal passages from *The Critique of Pure Reason,* Kant characterizes a (natural and inevitable) illusion that arises from an objectification of fictions that have intuitively arisen in subjective (or psychological) accounts of experience. The transcendental illusion amounts to a taking literally, for the sake of convenience, the bendings of reality that arise in the untested deployment of the inbuilt constructs of the understanding. Through his own deployment of metaphors, Kant endows the transcendental illusion with a decidedly visual bias: both of his examples are illusions at the horizon, the bourne and orientation of vision. One illusion involves the seeming "rise" of the visual field toward the horizon; the other, the "magnification" of astronomical bodies at horizon level. Kant, through the examples selected for a pivotal passage, reinforces an implicit hallucinogenic and, in Lacanian terms, imaginary basis for Western speculative thought. Systematic thinkers from Plato to Kant and Hegel may invoke sensation in general as the foundation, the breeding ground for abstraction, but within the manifold of sensation, vision, images, and imagination occupy a privileged position as the paradigm for thought.

    As formulated by Kant, transcendental philosophy will furnish a corrective to the illusions that have inevitably risen in the literalization of constructs of the understanding. The questions that the transcendental philosophy will undertake are so general, so deeply enmeshed in the operating systems of thought and the universe, that they can be posed only as antinomic possibilities, as a thesis and an antithesis. Dialectic, for Kant, becomes neither a logical nor an empirical *instrument,* but a deep-structural format for questions posed at the limits of understanding and systematic possibility. It is in this sense that Kant can write:

> Since the cosmological idea has no bearing save upon an object of experience which has to be in conformity with a possible concept of the understanding, it must be entirely empty and without meaning; for its object, view it as we may, cannot be made to agree with it. This is in fact the case with all cosmical concepts; and this is why reason, so long as it holds to them, is involved in an unavoidable antinomy. (*CPR,* 436−37)

Holding to the anthropocentric bias of his age, Kant pursues human thinking from its bases in sensation and intuition out toward the conceptual limits of the universe, pictured in a visual way. He applies the gaze of human reason to successively more sublime objects of scrutiny until the process itself has arrived at the Transcendental, at which point the horizon of abstraction begins to glare back at the human investigators in a distinctly uncanny way. The "spaced-out" canvases of painters as varied as Caspar David Friedrich and J. M. W. Turner may be understood as illustrations of the uncanny gaze cast by the Transcendental itself back upon the empirical world from which its exploration and investigation emanated. The plot of the "monster story," whether in literature or film, pursues the trajectory of the Kantian inquiry. The scientists' pursuit of "The (uncanny) Thing" describes only one half of the story; the *dénouement* inevitably dramatizes the aroused monster's counterpursuit of its seekers. The monster's shattered visage is, in a Kantian-Lacanian sense, the very eye of the Transcendental, gazing back into an empirical domain of human endeavor and folly that it can now freely terrorize. Only as antinomies, as irresolvable dialectical conflicts, do the ultimate speculative questions —those situated at the horizon of abstract capability— articulate themselves, as Kant specifies in the citation immediately above. These deliberations predicate Kant's meditations on beauty and its relation to the sublime.

Beauty, in its third inherently paradoxical position within the Kantian analytic, is the appearance of an object's purpose or design, but without any commitment to this purpose. Beauty thus acquires a certain basic fickleness: in terms of longstanding Western gender stereotypes, it becomes female to the core. The other antinomies of beauty tinkle as well to this tone of playful, seductive almostness. "*Taste* is the faculty of judging of an object or a method of representing it by an *entirely disinterested* satisfaction or dissatisfaction. The object of such satisfaction is called *beautiful*" (*CJ,* 45). The playful treacheries here, of course, are that something that could arouse us would be represented in an "entirely disinterested" way, and that taste can dispatch dissatisfaction and satisfaction with equal disinterest. In its Second Moment, beauty is that which can please "universally" without requiring the universality (and formalization) of a concept (*CJ,* 54). The nature of beauty is to hover, to retract its conceptual promises, but in exquisite witticisms, to be the conceptual correlatives to Lord Henry Wooten's self-contradictory aphorisms in *The Picture of Dorian Gray*.[3] In the analytic's Fourth Moment, "The *beautiful* is that which without any concept is cognized as the object of a *necessary* satisfaction" (*CJ,* 77). Here, beauty manages to assert necessity, but stops short of the high-powered, logical deployment of concepts. Thus on several planes sublimity, the medium for artistic and original genius, derives its dynamic if not its tone and implied gender from the beautiful.

Kant is the philosopher who thought through the transcendental-empirical horizon—a primary feature of Western idealism—most rigorously. In order to survey this borderline of decisive importance, culturally and ontotheologically as well as philosophically; in order to complete his survey with utmost rigor, Kant fashions a conceptual architecture in which pivotal weight rests on hinge-concepts, the Derridean *brisure* or hinge.[4] There is something of this spanning quality to crucial concepts in *The Critique of Pure Reason* such as representations, apperception, the copula, and even concepts themselves. In *The Critique of Judgment,* these hinge-concepts, such as beauty, become humanized, personalized, and even gendered. The cumulative effect is, *within reason,* to emphasize the degree of freedom prevailing within the domain of the beautiful as an everyday (and secular) instance of the philosophical (in our lives). The freedom itself, the ongoing play against a background of predetermination, as well as the increasing responsibility accruing to the human subject in the mediation, in the encounter with the Real are concerns that attain their modern form only with the decline of the medieval world order and the rise of Protestant ideology.

The Sublime and the Beautiful

If we pause at the interface between the beautiful and the sublime in Kant's construction of a secular, aesthetics-based religion, it is because the sublime is that modality of thought and invention that modern artists and people of imagination and creativity enter. We would have to characterize the relationship that the sublime maintains to the beautiful as one of infrastructural sublation: the sublime structures itself after the beautiful while emptying out its tone and contents; the sublime vastly enlarges the scope of the beautiful by speaking at the level of its deep-seated cognitive conditions. While achieving breathtaking *scope* of thought, the sublime installs itself as the underlying phenomenological, cognitive, and even psychological operating system implicit in human creativity, imaginativeness, and originality.

For the purpose of tracing this development, we do well to recall a fundamental passage, early on in *The Critique of Judgment*, in which Kant sets down three basic modes of discrimination in which the human apprehension of the world and judgment take place:

> The pleasant, the beautiful, and the good designate then three different relations of representations to the feeling of pleasure and pain, in reference to which we distinguish from one another objects or methods of representing them. And the expressions corresponding to each, by which we mark our complacency in them, are not the same. That which *gratifies* a man is called *pleasant;* that which merely *pleases* him is *beautiful;* that which is *esteemed* [or *approved*] by him, i.e. that to which he accords an objective worth, is *good.* Pleasantness concerns irrational animals also, but beauty concerns only men . . . and the good concerns every rational being in general. . . . We may say that, of all these three kinds of satisfaction, that of taste in the beautiful is alone a disinterested and *free* satisfaction; for no interest, either of sense or reason, here forces our assent. Hence we may say of satisfaction that it is related in the three aforesaid cases to *inclination, to favor,* or to *respect.* Now *favor* is the only free satisfaction. An object of inclination and one that is proposed to our desire by a law of reason leave us no freedom in forming for ourselves anywhere an object of pleasure. All interest presupposes or generates a want, and, as the determining ground of assent, it leaves the judgment about the object no longer free. (*CJ*, 44)

This passage begins with a wonderful largesse concerning the wider domains within which humans evaluate their experience; but it ends with legalistic (I would venture: contractual) specifications concerning which satisfactions are formally free, a central issue, as we have seen, with respect to beauty. Beauty's role, in contrast to the good and the pleasant, is to be "disinterested and *free.*" Beauty, itself a mark of distinction, confers upon its possessors certain privileges of choice, discretion, and favor.

The passage cited immediately above serves as a format for the third Critique because its stages function as a nuclear accelerator for the emergence or manifestation of the sublime. By the end of this passage, Kant has arranged three attitudes or bearings that correspond to the three earlier dimensions of judgment: inclination, favor, and respect. We incline toward the pleasant; this initial dimension falls out of the picture fairly soon because it pertains to animals as well, and Kant wants to limit his discussion to anthropocentric processes. Beauty calls forth our favor, as we have seen; and the good inspires respect.

The sublime emerges out of the beautiful both *sequentially* and *exponentially*. The sublime is intended to evolve from the beautiful, but then to raise it by several powers as well. When Kant arrives at the analytic of the sublime, this modality will in effect be the fourth in a sequence preceded by the "pleasant, the beautiful, and the good." The respect evoked through apprehensions and judgments of goodness serves as the architectural platform, within the domain of the beautiful, for the subjective experience of awe characterizing the sublime. But awe is not merely a next attitude in a sequence; it is a (theologically derived) intensification and magnification of the respect that attends apprehensions of the good. There are not merely a few literary instances in which something magical or wonderful emerges from the "world of realism" both in a sequence and in a revelation. My favorite, a thoroughly theoretically aware example, is the apprehension that opens up "among the boundless odor of the eucalypti," in Borges's "Death and the Compass," in which Red Scharlach ensnares the rationalistic Lönnrot in an expanding network of patterns and associations.[5]

"The beautiful and the sublime agree in this that both please in themselves. Further, neither presupposes a judgment of sense nor a judgment logically determined, but a judgment of reflection" (*CJ*, 82). Kant begins the analytic of the sublime with the sublime and the beautiful largely in agreement: the domains are self-contained and reflexive. "But there are also," he writes, "remarkable differences between the two" (*CJ*, 82):

> The beautiful in nature is connected with the form of the object, which consists in having [definite] boundaries. The sublime, on the other hand, is to be found in a formless object, so far as in it or by occasion of it *boundlessness* is represented, and yet its totality is also present to thought. Thus the beautiful seems to be regarded as the presentation of an indefinite concept of understanding, the sublime as that of a like concept of reason. Therefore the satisfaction in the one case is bound up with the representation of *quality,* in the other with that of *quantity.* . . . For this [the beautiful] directly brings with it a feeling of the furtherance of life, and this is compatible with charms and with the play of the imagination. But the other [the feeling of the sublime] is a pleasure that arises only indirectly; viz. it is produced by the feeling of a momentary checking of the vital powers and a consequently stronger outflow of them, so that it seems to be regarded as emotion—not play, but earnest in the exercise of the imagination. Hence it is incompatible with [physical]

charm. . . . But the inner and most important distinction between the sublime and beautiful is, certainly, as follows. . . . The sublime of art is always
limited by conditions of agreement with nature. Natural beauty (which is
independent) brings with it a purposiveness in its form by which the object
seems to be, as it were, preadapted to our judgment, and thus constitutes in
itself an object of satisfaction. . . . The feeling of the sublime may appear, as
regards its form, to violate purpose in respect of the judgment, to be unsuited
to our presentative faculty, and as it were to do violence to the imagination.
(*CJ*, 82–83)

Form, boundary, quality, quantity, satisfaction, pain (the latter as in "no pain,
no gain"): these are the defining terms that offer themselves as Kant launches
his elaboration of the sublime, a modality of experience, thought, and even
creative work that will live up to the specifications of apprehending the Transcendental in an age of secular anti-authoritarianism. *How* is the sublime in
relation to the beautiful in this crucial transitional and defining passage: in
brief, it confronts reason with a distinctive boundlessness, quantitative mass,
violation of conventional charm, and disruptions to our normal comfort and
self-interest, our sense of physical proportion, and our reassurance as to the
inherent purposiveness and rationality of events. Kant's attribution of "a
checking of vital powers" to the sublime anticipates the loss of the will to live
that music-lovers will experience when enthralled by their favored medium,
according to Schopenhauer. The sublime violates the beautiful. Within the
implicit sexual allegory that Kant, whether knowingly or unknowingly, in-
terjects into the schema of his aesthetics, this is an aggressive response to
beauty's gentle teasing.

The sublime is thus beauty's antithetical, monstrous, aggressive, male-
gendered, violent, out-of-control, and in large measure unconscious double,
though the two domains, that of thinking and of experimental endeavor, are
dynamically interrelated. Sublimity qualifies not the object of cognition, the
thing-in-itself, but the subject of thought and judgment. "We hence see also
that true sublimity must be sought only in the mind of the [subject] judging,
not in the natural object the judgment upon which occasions this state" (*CJ*,
95). The sublime does indeed confront us with something: and that something is awesome, inhuman, magnificent, and, as I have argued elsewhere,
possibly grandiose.[6] "We call that *sublime* which is *absolutely great*. . . . But to
cognize *how great*" the sublime "always requires some . . . magnitude" other
than number "as a measure" (*CJ*, 86). Sublimity initiates a vertiginous dwarf-
ing of any units of measurement that can be invoked in the effort of quanti-
fying its extent (*CJ*, 95). "The feeling of our incapacity to attain to an idea
which is a law for us is *respect*" (*CJ*, 96). Respect, originating in judgments of

the good, just begins to describe the awe prompted by the sublime. It is but a logical step from this bounded respect to "an extension" that the Sublime "acquires. . . . *Astonishment* that borders on terror, the dread and the holy awe which seizes the observer at the sight of mountain peaks" (*CJ*, 109). We will return to the undercurrent of religiosity in this sublime imagery below. The magnificence that Kant attributes to the sublime hammers at the threshold of pain:

> The feeling of the sublime is therefore a feeling of pain arising from the want of accordance between the aesthetical estimation of magnitude formed by the imagination and the estimation of the same formed by reason. There is at the same time a pleasure thus excited, arising from the correspondence with rational ideas of this very judgment of the inadequacy of our greatest faculty of sense. . . . The mind feels itself *moved* in the representation of the sublime in nature, while in aesthetical judgments about the beautiful it is in *restful* contemplation. This movement may (especially in its beginnings) be compared to a vibration, i.e., to a quickly alternating attraction toward, and repulsion from, the same object. The transcendent (toward which the imagination is impelled . . .) is for the imagination like an abyss in which it fears to lose itself. (*CJ*, 96–97)

Inhuman though the sublime is, its cognitive and even affective impacts are all too human. "The feeling of the sublime" may be painful, but there is a pleasure in the rational acknowledgment of its definitive transgression. The depiction of this vacillation is a "vibration," with inbuilt sexual innuendoes, between pleasure and pain. This is the basis for the Lacanian apprehension of a crucial liaison between "Kant avec Sade." [7]

The home of the sublime is philosophy. Kant's thinking out of the sublime participates in an overall Enlightenment-Romanticism experiment in deriving all abstract and higher (in the sense of value) constructs out of an intellectual place of endeavor human in its very essence. Sublimity is a human-initiated (as opposed to divine) approach to the Transcendental and the Real. The home of sublimity is intellection, philosophy, but when Kant characterizes this interface, it is endowed with too-human movements, fluctuations, even emotions. Sublimity evokes pain as well as pleasure. It situates itself in the interstice between attraction and revulsion. Its consummate pleasure, experienced on an intellectual level, of course, is the post-orgasmic relaxation of an imagination drawn back into itself after the extremest stretching possible. The visitor to St. Peter's in Rome, for one, experiences this relaxation: "For there is here a feeling of the inadequacy of the imagination for presenting the ideas of a whole, wherein the imagination reaches its maximum, and, in striving to surpass it, sinks back into itself, by which, however, a kind of emotional satisfaction is produced" (*CJ*, 91; also 114, 118).

Kant goes to church, to the cathedral of cathedrals, in order to locate an image for a noncelibate pleasure of the sublime. (His situation of a sublime-orgasmic experience under the cupola of St. Peter's confirms the intensity of the massive cultural reaction-formation that I am attributing to the Enlightenment-Romantic period.) Kant's sublime plays itself out on two facets: as the secular version of Christian theology, and as a domain of intellectual violence and even implicit sexuality. His basic definition of the sublime posited, Kant goes on to catalogue the many contexts to which this modality has applications. He displays an uncharacteristic looseness in extending sublimity to contemporary disciplines, artifacts, and even aesthetic styles. The "sublime" reading of religion reveals quite dramatically the onto-theological subtext lurking just beneath the surface of the *Critique's* secular pretensions:

> We are accustomed to represent God as presenting Himself in His wrath and yet in His sublimity, in the tempest, the storm, the earthquake, etc.; and that it would be fooling and criminal to imagine a superiority of our minds over these works of His and, as it seems, even over the designs of such might. . . . In religion in general, prostration, adoration with bent head, with contrite, anxious demeanor and voice, seems to be the only fitting behavior in the presence of the Godhead, and hence most peoples have adopted and still observe it. But this state of mind is far from being necessarily bound up with the idea of the *sublimity* of a religion. . . . The man who is actually afraid . . . is not in the frame of mind for admiring the divine greatness. For this a mood of calm contemplation and quite free judgment are needed. . . . Even humility, in the shape of a stern judgment upon his own faults . . . is a sublime state of mind, consisting in a voluntary subjection of himself to the pain of remorse. . . . In this way religion is essentially distinguished from superstition. The latter establishes in the mind, not reverence for the sublime, but fear and apprehension of the all-powerful Being to whose will the terrified man sees himself subject, without according Him any high esteem. (*CJ*, 102–3)

Here is philosophy, sometimes bordering on anthropology, redefining religion. This is a new direction, but it is not clear from this passage that the (long established) reverse is not also true; that religion is still informing philosophy. In this passage true religion, described from a philosophical point of view, is to be distinguished from any visceral fear of a deity or superstition in a fashion similar to the distinction between viewing a natural catastrophe or wonder *on the scene* or contemplating it at some distance or from safety ("We must regard ourselves as safe in order to feel this inspiriting satisfaction"— *CJ*, 101). Yet the passage admits, even with this specification, that the attributes of the divinity of Judeo-Christianity as they have been transmitted since the Pentateuch have a special affinity to the sublime. Some of Kant's ambivalence toward Judaism, as toward all exemplary material not Euro-Christian in origin, emerges as he tries to think through the sublimity of God. "Perhaps there is no sublimer passage in the Jewish law than the command, 'Thou shalt not make to thyself any graven image, nor the likeness of anything which is in heaven or in the earth . . .' This command alone can explain the enthusiasm that the Jewish people in their moral period felt for their religion, when they compared themselves with other peoples, or explain the pride which Mahommedanism inspires" (*CJ,* 115). While professing admiration for the Judaic (and parallel Muslim) prohibition against the representation of God, Kant has a page earlier excoriated "that false humility which sets the only way of pleasing the Supreme Being in self-deprecation, in whining hypocritical repentance, and in a mere passive state of mind" (*CJ,* 114). Kant knows perfectly well that the Judaic stance toward the deity is a penitential one. His "admiration" toward this religion is qualified as being limited to "its moral period," whenever that epoch prevailed.

Were I held to one word in order to characterize the sublime, that one word would be "disruption." The sublime is a dimensional, modal, architectural, cognitive, and emotional disruption to, among other things, commonsense logic, existential comfort, and authoritarian ideology and governance; it is a radical disruption announced, characterized, and celebrated in order to bring about what Foucault would call an epistemological break. On the far side of that break—and the sublime itself—stands a culture defined by principles of philosophical speculation and aesthetics. The sublime stands in a problematical relation to the beautiful, because the latter is something that it violates at the same time that it is structured by the investigation into beauty. The sublime interpolates a dimension of disfiguration and even ugliness into the beautiful (*CJ,* 154–55). This is in the enterprise of the kind of paradigmatic expansion that I have touched upon above. Upon a background of beauty, sublimity declares itself the official religion in a secular, philosophy-oriented world. Artists, creative individuals, and thinkers will be the priests in this new religion.

Sublime People: Artists and "Original Geniuses"

> *Genius* is the talent (or natural gift) which gives the rule to art. Since talent, as the innate productive faculty of the artist, belongs itself to nature, we may express the matter thus: Genius is the innate mental disposition (*ingenium*) *through which* nature gives the rule to art. . . . Beautiful arts must necessarily be considered as arts of *genius.*
>
> For every art presupposes rules by means of which in the first instance, a product, if it is to be called artistic, is represented as possible. But the concept

of beautiful art does not permit any judgment upon the beauty of a product to be derived from any rule which has a *concept* as its determining ground. . . . Therefore beautiful art cannot devise the rule according to which it can bring about its product. . . . nature in the subject must (by the harmony of its faculties) give the rule to art; i.e., beautiful art is only possible as a product of genius. (*CJ*, 150)

Ingeniously, Kant situates the concept of genius on a ground of nature under the administration of rules. In the above passage, Kant demonstrates that artistic invention and intuition cannot derive from any preexisting rule system. Beautiful art, possibly by virtue of its inherent female gender identification, is incapable of generating its own intrinsic laws. These come *gratis* nature; and one of the compelling aspects of geniuses, then, is that they incorporate—they sublate, in a Hegelian sense, they preserve and uplift—some fringe of nature that has become inaccessible to the rest of us. The genius is *between* nature and the rule. Nature "gives the rule to art" through *him*. The genius is a secular, intellectual Jesus, who implictly invokes the issues of mediation and formalism coming to the fore in Christianity's initial revision of Judaism.

Having raised these issues, Kant renders them formalistic and statutory in a recapitulating passage characteristic of his writing: he in effect "gives the rule" to his own exposition:

We thus see (1) that genius is a *talent* for producing that for which no definite rule can be given; it is not a mere aptitude for what can be learned by a rule. Hence *originality* must be its first property. (2) But since it also can produce original nonsense, its products must be models, i.e., *exemplary*, and they consequently ought not to spring from imitation, but must serve as a standard or rule of judgment for others. (3) It cannot describe or indicate scientifically how it brings about its products, but it gives the rule just as nature does. Hence the author of a product for which he is indebted to his genius does not know himself how he has come by his ideas; and he has not the power to devise the like at pleasure or in accordance with a plan, and to communicate it to others in precepts that will enable them to produce similar products. (Hence it is probable that the word "genius" is derived from *genius*, that particular guiding and guardian spirit given to a man at his birth, from whose suggestion these original ideas proceed.) (4) Nature, by the medium of genius, does not prescribe rules to science but to art, and to it only in so far as it is to be beautiful art. (*CJ*, 150–51)

This passage fits well into a Kantian schema whose major issues, the synthetic versus the analytical, a transcendental operating system some of whose principles can be intuited and some learned, are familiar to most readers of his works. But there is a personal cast about this passage as well.

The first logical anomaly that Kant must confront in the passage is a social tension, between originality and eccentricity, between invention and gibberish. An *originality* not constrained by specifications of *exemplarity* might indeed constitute a purely whimsical linguistic or cultural playfulness. Genius has to occupy a didactic or exemplary role as well if its productions are to rise above this potential eccentricity. Once again, in a Kantian negotiation, a legislative principle enters: here the paradigmatic imperative that saves genius from supporting wilfullness and idiosyncracy.

In this consideration, Kant uncannily anticipates the "private language argument" that played such a pivotal role in the disputations of logical analysis.[8] We ask our artists and other creative people to improvise something new, but at the same time, there are intrinsic limitations upon improvisation set by the limits of legibility and recognizability of words and other cultural units of signification. In the age initiated by the Protestant Reformation and the Counter-Reformation, based on the scenario of an individuated subject with increased liberty, the artist receives an upgraded mandate for creative exploration. The artist is sundered between the counterimperatives of achieving originality and singularity, on the one hand, and performing services of social utility, on the other. In a post-Protestant world of enhanced individuality and sensitized moral awareness in the personal sphere, this dual imperative joins an overall context of radical intrapsychic splitting to which creative people are susceptible. I will explore in fuller detail, in Chapter 7, "Maxima Moralia," certain implications of Kant's placement of the genius between improvisation and the statute of exemplarity.

As Kant elaborates in the passage cited immediately above, the genius is an innocent in certain crucial respects. He "does not know himself how he has come by his ideas" (*CJ,* 151). This means that the genius is also a dupe. He is not responsible for having the traits that set him apart from his fellow people, who then, if they chose to be envious, would be in the position of "not knowing what they do." The genius has to innovate, but under the framework of some recognizable format, in keeping with a certain contract. In matters relating to art, this is the place of the aesthetic contract, the occasion of this essay. The genius is masterful but extraordinarily vulnerable, because he did not place the power that links him to the Transcendental in a most special way into his own hands. The genius is a messiah in search of a cross.

Kant anticipates and joins the nature/nurture debate of culture in the passage under consideration: he speculates if the *genetics* etymologically linked to *genius* does not mean that the genius is *born* with her special trait(s). If the improvisation of the genius is inborn, then it cannot be taught. Can geniuses teach or be taught?, Kant asks in this crucial defining passage. The answer that Kant chooses on this occasion is that genius is nontransferrable, even though this implies a limit on the genius: he cannot teach his gift. Another limitation that Kant posits in this passage concerns the division of labor among the disciplines. Nature, through genius, only prescribes its rules to art, not to science, and only to beautiful art (*CJ*, 151). This is a Kantian regulation in whose violation creative people have reveled since its pronouncement. At least since Victor Frankenstein on, and in an entire strand of Hollywood creations, the mad scientist is a Kantian artistic genius.[9]

The above pivotal passage on genius contains self-referential nuance as well. Especially in *The Critique of Pure Reason*, Kant performs for philosophy and culture the functions he ascribes to the genius. He elaborates and formulates those intellectual principles that have been installed into the operating system of all nature. He attends carefully to mathematics in the first Critique, because numbers are the notation in which these overarching and profound principles have been inscribed. Only a very few minds have had access to this secret and subliminal code, and they have reached it by means of a very special intuition, for which nature also has provided. Kant has not only had access to these codes; he has mapped their place in a system accounting for the role, function, and place of human intelligence in a universe split, according to the old mind/body dualism, between Transcendental and empirical spheres. Kant does not claim to have achieved a comprehensive systematization of all underlying physical and intellectual principles in the universe; but what he claims to know, he knows. Kant's system, then, is a work of genius on the order of other creations of genius that Kant describes; but Kant is also a teacher who would presume to disseminate not only his special knowledge but his operating principles.

Whether Kant acknowledges himself as genius or not, he endows his meditations on the interface with the Transcendental achieved in art with a philosophical character by exploring the interaction between the various faculties involved in aesthetic creation. Imagination and the understanding are the "mental powers . . . whose union . . . constitutes genius" (*CJ*, 160). It is indicative of the Kantian aesthetic's legislative mandate and its "classical" proportions (in Foucault's sense) that genius should as much reflect the "happy relation" (*CJ*, 160) between the faculties it involves as any particular discovery or innovation. Genius arises at the intersection between inspiration (imagination) and intellect (understanding). Kant's definition of the imagination links together the images of excess production and dynamic, restless movement: A "representation of the imagination . . . occasions in itself more thought than can ever be comprehended in a definite concept and . . . con-

sequently aesthetically enlarges the concept itself in an unbounded fashion"
(*CJ*, 158). Imagination, as pictured in this passage, generates more thoughts
(later cognitive scientists will say associations)[10] than can be retained by a
bounded ("definite") concept, here imaged as a physical container. The proliferation of ideational material necessitates an "aesthetical enlargement": an
expansion very much in line with the opening up of a chasm or void producing first terror or awe and then relaxation in the modality of the sublime.
"Creative" imagination brings about this accelerated generation of material
and a subsequent enlargement of "the concept itself in an unbounded fashion" (*CJ*, 158). It is no mean feat, then, for genius to yoke this "wild and
wooly" imagination to the intellectuality of understanding, and to pay as
much attention to the "happy relation" between faculties as to Yeats's "mon-
uments of the unaging intellect"[11] or to Pound's "high deeds in Hungary."[12]

> Thus genius properly consists in the happy relation [between these faculties],
> which no science can teach and no industry can learn, by which ideas are
> found for a given concept; and, on the other hand, we thus find for these
> ideas the expression by means of which the subjective state of mind brought
> about by them, as an accompaniment of the concept, can be communicated
> to others. This latter talent is, properly speaking, what is called spirit; for to
> express the ineffable element in the state of mind implied by a certain repre-
> sentation and to make it universally communicable—whether the expression
> be in speech or painting or statuary—this requires a faculty of seizing the
> quickly passing play of imagination and of unifying it in a concept (which is
> even on that account original and discloses a new rule . . .) that can be com-
> municated without any constraint [of rules]. (*CJ*, 160–61)

Genius here thus consists not merely in creative achievement, but also in the
salutary alignment of faculties that it brings about, and in the *communication*
of unprecedented material. Kant speaks here to the necessity of coordinating
the countertemporalities of imagination and conceptualization. Imaginative
work is a "quickly passing play," while the unification achieved by concepts
implies a stabilization of some duration. Genius thus not only coordinates
different faculties; it exists in different time frameworks or warps. Interestingly, not only must imagination be unconstrained in order to fulfill its im-
provisatory purpose; the product or expression of genius must be released
from the standard constraints upon communication. The amalgam of ephem-
erality and duration in genius results in a "concept . . . that can be communicated without any constraint [of rules]" (*CJ*, 161).

Kant is building here toward a libertarian notion of the play of faculties
and concepts in the production of eccentric/exemplary works of genius.
"Genius is the exemplary originality of the natural gifts of a subject in the *free*

employment of his cognitive faculties" (*CJ*, 161). The insistence upon this freedom and what it might reasonably imply is understandable both in the broader context of a post-Reformation exacerbation of awareness of individuation, personal liberty, and personally imposed constraint, and in the more immediate background of political emancipations (for example, the American and French Revolutions) from a priori theological and monarchical authority. Artistic geniuses, then, do more than produce new and original productions; they actualize unprecedented freedom and liberty as well. This founding document in the evolution of the aesthetic contract of the broader modernity thus makes provision for an unprecedented artistic license, at least for persons of genius. As we shall see below, while in keeping with genuine talent, this special artistic license is a liability to those who would protest it. In different ways, Emma Bovary and Captain Ahab will become fictional victims of the new freedom that Kant announces and rationalizes here.

Kant's final summative statement on the genius unites those elements that will speak for the *"free* employment" of the "cognitive faculties." *Genius* "is a talent for art, not for science, in which clearly known rules must go beforehand and determine the procedure. Secondly . . . it presupposes a definite concept of the product as the purpose . . . but it also presupposes a representation of the intuition" (*CJ*, 161). In his last comprehensive run-through of the powers and privileges of genius, Kant emphasizes the grounding of its exercise in known rules and the coordination of being (product) and becoming (process) in its activation and fulfillment. Genius occupies the position of a seer, prophet, or avatar who negotiates, in a mode of free play or discovery, the (sublime) transition (or chasm) between the known and the imagined, the existent and the yet-to-become:

> Thirdly, it shows itself, not so much in the accomplishment of the proposed purpose in a presentment of a definite concept, as in the enunciation or expression of aesthetical ideas which contain abundant material for that very design; and consequently it represents the imagination as free from all guidance of rules and yet as purposive in reference to the presentment of the given concept. Finally, in the fourth place, the unsought undesigned subjective purposiveness in the free accordance of the imagination with the legality of the understanding presupposes such a proportion and disposition of these faculties as no following of these rules . . . can bring about, but which only the nature of the subject can produce. (*CJ*, 161)

As it closes, the passage emphasizes the unboundedness and potentiality in the aesthetic exercise of genius. Creativity is a state of potentiality more than actuality. Imagination is free and purposive. It adheres to proportions, yet "no following of . . . rules" can bring about its fulfillment. It is rooted in knowledge, but its ultimate location is in the subject.

The liberty and inventiveness of the genius are awesome but fraught with liabilities. We've already touched upon a passage in which Kant links such literary phenomena as *Robinson Crusoe* to a sublime isolation that "naturally" accompanies the invention of genius. Kant prophesies as well the sublimity of the monomaniacs who abound in modern literature, from Melville's Ahab to the political fanatics in Conrad's *The Secret Agent.*

> For the *inscrutableness of the idea of freedom* quite cuts it off from any positive presentation, but the moral law is in itself sufficiently and originally determinant in us, so that it does not permit us to cast a glance at any ground of determination external to itself. If enthusiasm is comparable to *madness,* fanaticism is comparable to *monomania,* of which the latter is least of all compatible with the sublime because, in its detail, it is ridiculous. In enthusiasm, regarded as an affection, the imagination is without bridle; in fanaticism, regarded as an inveterate, brooding passion, it is without rule. (*CJ,* 116)

Kant here prefigures a potential dramatis personae of "original geniuses" as they might be depicted in works of fiction. This is so even if he excludes from the honor roll of sublimity the monomaniac, of which Hoffmann's René Cardillac and Melville's Captain Ahab comprise splendid examples. Masterful fiction writers could indeed create characters of genius and fascinating obsession that avoided the stigma of laughability.

Artistic creativity plays such a pivotal role in the conceptual evolution of the sublime because art is a universal phenomenon in human societies that has been with us since the "origin" of such communities. Art demonstrates the existence, activity, and importance of transcendental concepts in our world. It thus also serves Kant as a "proof" of the elaborate schema characterizing the interaction between transcendental and empirical worlds in *The Critique of Pure Reason.* Art is an "everyday" example of something that would not be possible were it not for the existence of intuitions, concepts, representations, and the various human faculties as Kant represents them. Especially gifted individuals, who perform aesthetic creation, are necessary to access "the supersensible substrate of all . . . faculties" and "to harmonize all our cognitive faculties" (*CJ,* 189). The person who serves as the interface to the Transcendental in art, this universal cultural phenomenon that nevertheless exemplifies the operation of the Transcendental in the sectors of the everyday and the nonsectarian, is the original genius, or the artist. A certain sublimity attaches to this figure herself. Intimacy with "the supernatural substrate of all . . . faculties" may come at a certain cost: monomania (Captain Ahab), impractical romantic exploration (Emma Bovary), physical disfiguration (Poe's Hop-Frog and Hoffmann's René Cardillac). But after Kant, who was quite convincing in these matters, the artist became the priest or messiah in a secular religion whose values, sought-after objects and experiences, and notions of Being and existential purpose were articulated in terms deriving from the enterprise of artistic creativity.

Taste, Common Sense, and the Aesthetic Contract

The Critique of Judgment hangs suspended between the greatest possible play of the imagination in aesthetic creativity and a recurrent definition of the rules and conditions under which art arises, captures something of the Transcendental, and is evaluated. Its legislative imperative controls, and to some extent clips the wings of, the radical aesthetic improvisation of which it furnishes an account. I would argue that the aesthetic play and the legislative purview, rather than being mutually contradictory, in fact necessitate each other. In terms of my historical argument, Kant's fascination with legislation is a defensive reaction against the potential anomie that may ensue from the unprecedented Western freedom and discretion of action associated with the artist—but it is also part and parcel of overall post-Reformation subject conditions. Individuation, greater personal freedom, and the need for personal self-regulation go hand in hand with a constant concern for legislation. Kant's obsession with the rules, I am arguing, comprises part of the overall evolution of the Freudian superego made much more urgent by the subjective crisis announced by theologians such as Luther and Calvin. Kant's disclosure of the rules according to which human faculties, institutions, and behavior operate reflects, within my overall scheme, the "massive cultural reaction-formation" that becomes a very prominent part of European culture, particularly in the eighteenth and early nineteenth centuries.

The Freudian superego may be taken as a necessary implication of modern individuation and freedom. The cataclysmic punishment meted out by the superego to borderline subjects, as described by the contemporary psychoanalyst Otto Kernberg, is merely an extension of a pressing need for self-regulation that began with a distinctively Protestant trial of the soul. Luther and Calvin speak to the needs and conditions of the subject in an age witnessing the withdrawal of the mediation to the Transcendental (or the Real) that was furnished in Western societies by the Catholic Church; Kernberg articulates the conditions of a self that has witnessed the withdrawal of the mediation that had been furnished by an ego with an arsenal of classic defensive neuroses at its disposal. Borderline conditions emerge when it is a liabil-

ity to have a self; they are the outgrowth of an upbringing in which the
mediation of the ego has been disqualified by the need for sharply polarized
values, all-good and all-evil. Among the descendents of Kant's constant concern for the activities and criteria of legislation, then, are first the Freudian
superego,[13] which exercises control over the subject during an age when
neuroses characterize failures in instinctual gratification; and then the contemporary borderline personality, which indicates a self whose coherence has
been shattered by a particularly vicious internal oversight and judgment.[14]

When Kant ponders the rules and agencies involved in the judgments we
make about taste—and remember that taste, whether individual or collective, is a fundamental factor in the reception of art—he finds that taste is as
anomalous and difficult to pin down as the several self-contradictory aspects
of the beautiful that he explored. Kant demonstrates some overriding duty
to analyze taste. If, indeed, the apprehension of beauty and the related disruption of dimensions and values embodied in the sublime are going to serve
as paradigms for judgment and a secular theology in an intellect-driven society, then Kant has assumed some obligation to specify what is going on as
individuals and the public determine aesthetic and cultural values.

Any difficulties attending the process and judgments of taste, therefore,
are parallel to the enigmas installed in Beauty and the Sublime. Kant labels
"judgments of taste" as "peculiar." He devotes two segments of *The Critique
of Judgment,* Sections 32 and 33, to their "peculiarity." Before he elaborates
these peculiarities, he characterizes the conditions confronting "judgments
of taste" on the most abstract level:

> We have before us in the latter case no cognitive judgment—neither a theo-
> retical one based on the concept of a *nature* in general formed by the under-
> standing, nor a (pure) practical one based on the idea of *freedom,* as given *a
> priori* by reason. Therefore we have to justify *a priori* the validity, neither of a
> judgment which represents what a thing is, nor of one which prescribes that
> I ought to do something in order to produce it. We have merely to prove for
> the judgment generally the *universal validity* of a singular judgment that ex-
> presses the subjective purposiveness of an empirical representation in the
> form of an object, in order to explain how it is possible that a thing can please
> in the mere act of judging it . . . and how the satisfaction of one man can be
> proclaimed as a rule for every other. (*CJ,* 122)

Kant is in search here of the *a priori* operating principles underlying judgments that give pleasure in their own right and that do not claim an objective
basis in "sensation or concept" (*CJ,* 122). It is not surprising that in formulating the rules underlying such "calls," Kant should be confronted with
issues of universality versus particularity (or singularity) and of objectivity as

opposed to subjectivity. Understanding the matrix out of which such judgments arise is tantamount to proving "the *universal validity* of a singular judgment that expresses the subjective purposiveness of an empirical representation in the form of an object" (*CJ*, 122). This is the operational phrase in the characterization of the conditions pertaining to judgments of taste; it describes a highly difficult feat: How can there be a lucid explanation of judgments collectively understood (if not binding) that arise amid the singularity of the individual subject? Of judgments, by the same token, that in evaluating objects, things, and treating them empirically, incorporate *subjective* conditions? Such judgments determine the *purposiveness* of these (aesthetic) objects from a subjective (private) point of view.

The mediatory factor in such judgments, which creates an interface between the universality and singularity, the objectivity and subjectivity, involved in this judgmental process, is taste. Taste is, like many interstitial categories in Kant, those that interrelate presumably binary contraries, inherently enigmatic and self-contradictory. The "First Peculiarity of the Judgment of Taste" involves the imputation of general assent to evaluations that are subjective and personal at best: "The judgment of taste determines its object in respect of satisfaction (in its beauty) with an accompanying claim for the assent of *everyone,* just as if it were objective" (*CJ*, 123). Kant's example for the upping of the ante in judgments of taste from personal experiences to class predications is an assertion of the beauty of a particular flower. Curiously, Kant emphasizes not so much the weakness of this particular claim as that it may be jeopardized by other forms of output from the flower's synesthesia: "By the pleasantness of its [the flower's] smell it has no such claim. A smell which one man enjoys gives another a headache" (*CJ*, 123). In setting out parameters for judgments of taste, Kant is arguing for a certain trait-specificity, such that controversy can be directed toward a specific criterion (of an object) and not be displaced along a chaotic multiplicity of traits. So a judgment of taste involves an imputation of beauty to an object "just because of that characteristic in respect of which it accommodates itself to our mode of apprehension" (*CJ*, 123).

Yet each of us, each thinking subject, is empowered to make such judgments. "It is required of every judgment . . . that the subject shall judge by himself, without needing to grope about empirically among the judgments of others" (*CJ*, 123). To the extent that we are not bound either to empirical protocols or to the cumulative wisdom of others in making such determinations, each of us is inherently fitted out, endowed, "hardwired," with the faculties and apparatus necessary in the making of such determinations. To paraphrase a comment in *Ulysses* about Bloom: there's a touch of the artist in each of us.[15] Since the judgments that Kant describes here involve aesthetic principles, human beings are inherently endowed with some capacity to intuit or infer transcendental principles through aesthetic experiences. This judgmental capacity is a constitutional right, in two senses of the word. It belongs to the properties inherent in human subjectivity by virtue of a philosophical Declaration of the Rights of Man (with cognitive and phenomenological elements). Yet human beings, fitted out as they are with this suffrage, need examples and gathered wisdom in order to help them in their choices of taste. (Once again, Kant immediately subjects a human liberty to legislative controls: here, the need for examples constrains the universal right to make judgments of taste.) Kant immediately cites religion as a body of knowledge that numbers among its inherent workings an impressive collection and deployment of examples (for instance, Christ's parables). This is another instance of the Kantian ambivalence toward theology. Religion is a source of the authoritarian *doxa* that will be circumvented in a secular, intellect-driven culture; it is very often, as well, the hidden model, a "secret sharer," in this brave new Enlightenment culture. "Even in religion . . . there is never as much accomplished by means of universal precepts . . . as by means of an example of virtue or holiness . . . exhibited in history. . . . But of all faculties and talents, taste, because its judgment is not determinable by concepts and precepts, is just that one which most needs examples" (*CJ,* 125). Once again, a Kantian construct in the overall complex of libertarian disruptions to established orders and newly released energies submits immediately, akin to the child in Margaret Mahler's "separation–individuation subphase," to a severe schooling, in this case at the University of Examples.

Kant's examples of judgments of taste tend to involve senses lower than vision in the traditional hierarchy of the senses, as if to signal that taste is a more bestial matter than an implicitly sight-oriented cognition. When Kant arrives at the "Second Peculiarity" of these judgments, he deploys tongue and ear as well as eye. His concern here is that these determinations do not rest on proofs or other "objective" criteria:

> I try the dish with *my* tongue and my palate, and thereafter (and not according to universal principles) do I pass my judgment.
>   In fact, the judgment of taste always takes the form of a singular judgment about an object. The understanding can form a universal judgment by comparing the object in point of the satisfaction it affords with the judgment of others upon it. . . . But then this is not a judgment of taste but a logical judgment. . . . That judgment, however, in which I find an individual tulip beautiful. . . . is alone a judgment of taste. Its peculiarity consists in the fact that, although it has merely subjective validity, it claims the assent of *all* subjects,

exactly as it would do if it were an objective judgment resting on grounds of knowledge that could be established by a proof. (*CJ*, 126–27)

It is pivotal to my argument here that Kant's almost exaggerated rhetoric of legislation and judgment is in the enterprise of making the transcendental philosophy speak to conditions of subjectivity and empowerment in a secular culture. Issues of the apprehension of beauty, sublimity, and aesthetic creation refer to the rights and privileges with which the citizen in such a world is inherently endowed; issues of taste, consensus, and the *sensus communis* characterize social participation and control in such a world. This is an implicit community whose values are arrived at through cultural debates, themselves fitted out with, as we have seen, transcendental-empirical negotiations mediated within the domain of the aesthetic. Participation in the elections of taste gives every citizen "a touch" of the original genius. The forum of taste, on the other hand, subjects the dynamic and possibly radical energy released in creativity to a salutary control. The influence of art upon society, and the participation of the artist within it, generate the Kantian equivalent of a social contract, which is negotiated by judgments of taste. Viewed from the perspective of the artist, this social contract has certain implications for the creative process itself. In this sense, the Enlightenment social contract generates an aesthetic contract characterized by Kantian (implicitly Protestant) modern ambivalence toward the artwork and its producer. The most significant passage in *The Critique of Judgment* in this regard is the following:

> Taste, like the judgment in general, is the discipline (or training) of genius;
> it clips its wings, it makes it cultured and polished; but, at the same time, it
> gives guidance as to where and how far it may extend itself if it is to remain
> purposive. And while it brings clearness and order into the multitude of the
> thoughts [of genius], it makes the ideas susceptible of being permanently,
> and, at the same time, universally assented to, and capable of being followed
> by others, and of an ever progressive culture. If, then, in the conflict of these
> two properties in a product something must be sacrificed, it should be rather
> on the side of genius; and the judgment, which in the things of beautiful art
> gives its decision from its own proper principles, will rather sacrifice the free-
> dom and wealth of the imagination than permit anything prejudicial to the
> understanding.
>   For beautiful art, therefore, *imagination, understanding, spirit,* and *taste* are
> requisite. (*CJ*, 163–64)

If I am right in my assertion that Kant is a decisive thinker in the evolution of a modern aesthetic contract itself heavily conditioned by the subject conditions initiated by the Protestant Reformation, then the passage immediately above is pivotal to the finalization of this contract. Certain paradigmatic rights, licenses, and domains of operation inhere in the artist, who himself becomes an exemplary although privileged subject. The other side of the unprecedented freedom enjoyed by the artist, the freedom in which ordinary people vicariously participate through him (although in their own judgments of taste they experience "a touch" of the artist) is as follows: discipline, the "clipping" of wings (a resonant image given the pictorial representations of Psyche), sacrifice of genius in any hypothetical conflict between its interests and momentum and social welfare. This is the "down side" of the aesthetic contract of modernity, assuming that freedom, exuberance, and *jouissance* in artistic creativity are positive values. Henceforth, the artist will hover (or hang) between these two modes of operation: the exuberant, which Kierkegaard will dramatize in the figure of his hypothetical and operatic aesthete; and a bleak world of moralistic constraint, which Kierkegaard, in the same work, *Either/Or*, will distill into the pronouncements of Judge William.[16] The artist will hang in a schizoid way between the jouissance of play and freedom and the disparaging glance of social welfare: "Don Giovanni: Il Dissoluto Punito." We will all still need to admire the artist: this figure is sublime, magnificent, with the touch of genius. But he or she is also a deranged genius (Victor Frankenstein), a maniac (Captain Ahab), a whore (Emma Bovary), a monstrosity (Gregor Samsa). From the side of these artists, a preserve, a sanctuary is necessary to protect and shield their unique talents: the Magic Mountain, the Trapeze Artist's private trains.[17] A standoff is arrived at between these rare innovators, without which Western idealism loses its momentum, loses the possibility of undergoing Kuhnian paradigm shifts, and the continuity of social momentum and welfare becomes the Iron Law of Oligarchy.[18] The artist pays the price, first of living on the edge, then of sinking into the mediocrity Flaubert so relished depicting, and possibly of being annihilated.[19] Such are the terms of the aesthetic contract prevailing during the broader modernity. It arises during the tendentiousness and moral severity of the Protestant Reformation; during Foucault's "classical age" of the seventeenth and eighteenth centuries, it builds toward what I have termed "massive cultural reaction-formation"; in the twentieth century, art begins to digest and, kaleidoscopically, to rearrange its own forms: exuberantly, in modernism; in-differently, in postmodernism. Even these postures, extreme though they may seem, fall within the purview of the aesthetic contract of the broader modernity. Throughout its duration, the artist is there, on the edge, capable of influencing the transcendental operating system itself, but also subject to dismissal and degradation, as well as to self-generated delusions of grandeur and magnificence.

PART TWO

Untimely Propositions
on the Contracting of Art
in Modernity

CHAPTER 6

Corollaries to the Aesthetic Contract

So what *is* the aesthetic contract? Philosophically, it is the understanding regarding the the role and functions of art and artists in (Western) societies prevalent during the broader modernity. This general understanding encompasses such issues as art's relation to religion and other value systems, and the privileges and/or penalties assessed against the artist. Chapters 2 through 5 of this exploration dedicated themselves to these wider (Western) cultural attitudes and assumptions regarding the enterprise of art. This sense of the contract comes out slightly differently depending on whether its effective date begins with Luther or Descartes, or perhaps the Enlightenment.

In any particular modern context, the aesthetic contract is a framework for understanding cultural history in a way that doesn't overlook the linguistic nature and dynamic of all cultural productions and that does not rely on Romantic scenarios, such as Kant's, of the artist as a unique genius whom we honor by remembering. An aesthetic contract defines the problems and solutions that discourse and artistic invention are willing to address for a certain time. The conventions or terms of the contract are precisely those problems an artistic or intellectual community is willing to undertake for the duration of the contract. Examples of particular aesthetic contracts include "German tragic drama," "the Elizabethan sonnet," *décadence,* modernism, and postmodernism.

To be sure, there are aesthetic and conceptual innovators who arrive at certain solutions that an entire community or school is then willing to undertake. But this anticipation of the rules of a complex art game, paralleling Wittgenstein's notion of complex language games, is not a function of Kantian "original genius" or other Romantic notions of art such as transcendence but merely a coincidence, an arrival at the particular terms of a plausible artistic working-through before others.

The aesthetic contract is in effect so long as its always provisional and tentative solutions are to problems whose relevance is agreed upon by some consensus. There are indeed what we call historical determinants to the problems that the aesthetic contract addresses or attempts to work through. A new order of government or a new system of production or technology may so alter living and thinking conditions as to invalidate a particular aesthetic contract in effect. This is what we mean when we say that the dissemination of literacy among certain classes of individuals spurred on and shaped the development of the novel; or, along with Neil Schmitz, that the rise of photography spelled the end of the Romantic or transcendental novel in the United States.[1]

Particular aesthetic contracts come into effect because, at the level of mimesis, they pose and answer questions about knowledge and experience better than alternate models. Artworks hold interest because they sustain a certain uneasy balance between public discourse and idiosyncratic personal usage. A prevailing aesthetic contract *incorporates* particular images, sounds, literary styles, and so on in part because they are as yet publicly *undigested,* not yet reformulated as truism. Artworks that become the basis for aesthetic contracts hover between an exciting hypothesis regarding possibility and a plausible analysis of existing conditions. The definition of cultural journalism is the discourse that, appearing almost coincidentally with artworks that shift terms in the prevailing aesthetic contract, affords the public terms for coping with the artworks' unfamiliarity and invention.

⟿

Artists and intellectuals do not adapt, that is, abide by the terms of a particular aesthetic contract only because of the brilliance or innovation in the experiments themselves, but because the experiments have obtained a certain public sanction, and the sanctioned modes of production function as settings for intellectual and artistic endeavor. In abiding by the contract, artists and intellectuals relinquish a certain amount of their creative freedom and personal idiosyncrasy. They do so in exchange for a certain degree of recognition, affirmation, and in some cases, material benefits. "Creative freedom" is itself a clause deriving from one particular aesthetic contract, a late-Enlightenment-Romantic one discussed in the preceding chapter, whose terms are elaborated, among others, by Kant, Schlegel, and Kierkegaard.

The more successfully the aesthetic contract addresses cultural unknowns and suggests possible answers, the more numerous and significant are the subclauses, or spinoffs, that it generates. Understanding the wider aesthetic contract in which an artwork participates, if this participation is a plausible inference, is a useful context for its illumination. A problematic subexperiment, say Mondrian's austere paintings of squares, "lights up" hermeneutically, and attains validation for the duration of the wider contract, in this case, that of cubism.[2] The kaleidoscopic experimentation in cubism, in turn, becomes a basic clause within an even broader aesthetic contract, that of modernism.[3] Such issues as form and style may be understood as the particular working through of the provisions in a prevailing aesthetic contract.

Artists relinquish a certain degree of individuality in order to produce Elizabethan sonnets, or cubist paintings, or postmodern novels, but in return they are accorded a certain degree of recognition and an audience for their creative activity.[4] There may be purported originators of aesthetic experiments: Braque may have produced the "first" cubist paintings, or Édouard Dujardin may have been Joyce's model for the interior monologue—but in terms of a contractual understanding of artistic and conceptual production, the *origination* of the terms of the contract is much less important than the contract's *duration,* the period of time over which it answers better than other endeavors basic questions that groups of people have about knowledge and experience.

Like other time-specific documents, contracts go in and out of effect. Collectivities of writers and thinkers abandon certain projects, or the public evinces indifference toward them, not because of inherent flaws in these large experiments, but as a result of circumstantial changes, including changes in technological and socioeconomic paradigms, and wars. As the result of such developments, an existing aesthetic contract may no longer satisfy a community's interest in knowledge and experience to the same degree as an alternate enterprise; or there may be durations when no paradigm for aesthetic invention satisfies these needs. The aesthetic contract declines as well as rises; it can coexist with other prevailing contracts as well. It guarantees public attention to certain stylistic and generic innovations. It protects artists from oblivion; it protects artists from each other, furnishing more or less explicit conditions of mutual recognition and sanction.

The aesthetic contract relies significantly for its format on stipulations made by Rousseau in *The Social Contract.* The discursive correlative of the aesthetic contract is the critical contract, the conditions by which a (Western) society makes itself receptive to discursive commentary.

What does it gain us to describe the histories of literature and art as a succession of sometimes dialectically counterpoised and sometimes mutually indifferent aesthetic contracts? I would argue that the notion of the aesthetic contract keeps us out of a number of uncomfortably confining situations: (1) It is a useful construct in demystifying and denaturing art as an implicit ontotheological setting, as a model for all creative or productive work, and as a fundament in a moral philosophy. The demystification of the aesthetic enterprise, through an appreciation of the sociological motivations for certain styles, schools, and genres, can lead toward a more realistic appreciation of the claims and social dynamics falling under the aegis of the critical contract. (2) The notion of the aesthetic contract takes as the unit of study not a particular author or artifact but a varied body of works/texts that can be illuminated in being read as variants upon each other. The works do not so much arise out of their authors' essences or intentions as out of the exigencies of doing creative work in the historico-sociopolitical world of production, combined with the epistemological and experiential issues that the aesthetic improvisation answers. This enables a statute of limitations to be placed around such Romantic constructs as "original genius" and the unique access to the "sublime" that such "world-historical individuals" exercise.[5] What opens up in place of this idealistic, spiritualistic, and teleological model, which can still operate institutionally even where it has been supplanted conceptually, is the scenario of a productive, though sometimes conflictual cultural interplay among and between the producers and users of art. (3) The construct of an aesthetic contract avoids the pronounced disregard for historical specificity that became associated with language-based critical models, which would illuminate artifacts in terms of their ultratemporal and ultrageographical dynamics of language, communication, and related activities.

Yet the purview of the aesthetic contract is not entirely historically specific, for it inquires into the workings of an entire body of artworks themselves responding to complicated historical, epistemological, experiential, and sociological conditions. So the inquiry into the aesthetic contract operative for a set of works responding to some meaningful grouping principle is both specific and general, that is to say, heterogenous in a theoretically productive way.

It is inherently arbitrary to identify what constitutes the *particular terms* of the aesthetic contract under whose rubric some meaningful grouping of artifacts appears to emerge. The assertion of the terms of any aesthetic contract invariably involves generalities. These generalities may include formalistic assumptions about rhetorical tropes, literary genres, or subgenres; historical conclusions as to which conditions and events were telling at a certain time, and their influence on the social and intellectual climate; subjective assessments as to which artists and artifacts "speak" most compellingly regarding an "era," whose coherence itself is a fiction. Each of these abuses is involved in the attempt to achieve some "snapshot" of the grouping qualified by an aesthetic contract, its mode of operation, and its meaning, both in and somewhat out of context. The alternatives to these abuses involve assumptions regarding the universal qualities of either language or people. Every artifact then becomes an allegory of certain rhetorical principles that never change, or an allegory of a set of psychoanalytical agencies and features that never changes. As soon as a rhetorical or psychoanalytical reading of an artifact adjusts itself in order to account for particularities that are functions of time, place, authorship, technology, or prevailing *épistèmes,* it becomes possible, in the background, to discern the operation of an aesthetic contract.

∽

We could say, then, of time-specific modernism (c. 1890–1945) that its characteristic works managed to incorporate an apprehension of the priority of language; an analysis of constituent parts down to the level of the structure; a *jouissance* in the recycling, updating, and disfiguration of historical source materials, the remoter the better; a mood of nostalgia in the face of dramatic and inevitable social and technological change; a psychology of sexual release and oedipal fascination; a playfulness in the kaleidoscopic reorganization of structures; a relentless exploration of the possibilities and variations in perspective and perspectivism; the intuition of synesthesias and synergies making the arts and traditional genres translatable into each other in unanticipated ways. If the above constitute major, but by no means exhaustive, clauses in the aesthetic contract of modernism, this contract can already account for cultural manifestations as diverse as cubist painting, improvisational jazz, Freud's early schemata for the organization of the "psychic material," Kafka's parables, Joyce's *Ulysses,* Proust's *Recherche,* Stein's *Ada,* Woolf's *The Waves,* Faulkner's *The Sound and the Fury,* Eliot's *Wasteland,* Pound's *Cantos,* Barnes's *Nightwood,* Benjamin's "mosaic technique," Lévi-Strauss's "structural analysis" of myths, Barthes's understanding of *mythologie* as recycled language whose tensions and play have, for ideological reasons, been placed on hold, Mahler's and Ives's musical pastiches, Sullivan's and Wright's "referential" architecture, and so on. I arrive at the terms of the contract deductively, through a "fieldwork" that consists of sifting and sorting through the material. There may appear to be an empirical dimension to this enterprise; yet the contract is as much informed and empowered by its exceptions and anomalies as by the artifacts it may seem to order. It is possible that some of the contractual terms I have assembled above functioned as explicit aesthetic and productive specifications at the time when thinkers and writers of all sorts adjusted their efforts in the name of modernism. But it is merely a matter of coincidence if the terms of a particular aesthetic contract happen to reflect an artist's (or a group of artists') intentionality. While it is possible to extrapolate the wider art or concept-games comprising the major clauses in an aesthetic contract, this process has meaning only when these formulas are the result of meticulous readings and comparisons of the artifacts involved. The validity of the terms in an aesthetic contract is in direct proportion to the meticulousness with which the works falling under it have been read and interpreted.

We could say, then, that sublimity is the name of a dominant clause in the aesthetic contract characterizing European and American art and literature over a period extending roughly from 1790 to 1860. Sublimity establishes, as we have observed in the passage devoted to the Kantian aesthetics above (Chapter 5), the ambience for a field of conceptual and representational work enormous in its own right. One thread holding a significant body of sublime "manifestations" together is the opening up of a vast chasm of magnificent and impersonal temperament, whether in the phenomenal, imaginary, semantic, or emotional fields. The eruption of this vastness transpires autonomously of human wishes, tendencies, and faculties, even where the sublimity is situated in a human context or experienced subjectively. The *indifference* of the sublime to human needs and capacities explains its affinity to the Freudian uncanny, in which intimacy and monstrous impersonality are always catching each other short, substituting themselves for each other. There is an emphasis in the sublime on the grandiose and awful rather than on beauty and pleasure. Its apprehension demands a strenuous adjustment on the part of its perceiver, who can then relax or enter a state of unconsciousness in the wake of this opening; its sites, as described by Shelley, may be "remote, serene, and inaccessible." The aesthetic contract of sublimity establishes a setting in which art and the experiential components that inspire it achieve a distinctive purity, grandeur, and masculinity; these qualities are transferred to the artist *him*self. Sublimity achieves a vibrant interface between the inner, which we ordinarily associate with the psychological, and the outer, the characteristically vast and male-coded landscape of Romanticism. Sublimity therefore allows for psychological formulations to be displaced to the landscape, and conversely, for the landscape to be psychologized, all within a comfortably masculine and heterosexist environment. Sublimity allows the emotional convolutions of artwork to be undertaken by real men. Because of the relatively fluid interior/exterior interplay that it establishes, sublimity becomes a human feature as well: the bushy brows of the Sandman in Hoffmann's tale of the same title; Hop-Frog's exaggerated shoulders; Ahab's monomania; Moby-Dick's hump; the demented expression in Caspar David Friedrich's self-portrait.

Jean-François Lyotard would invoke the sublime in explanation of the postmodern; and indeed, there are sublime aspects of representation, of language's impersonality, that emerge at every moment of cultural history. There are certain advantages to be gained from treating sublimity as a transepochal phenomenon, as Lyotard does, and some to be derived, on the other hand, from assessing sublimity's role(s) in the specific aesthetic contracts in which it plays. Lyotard's updating of this still-suggestive notion emphasizes the sublime features of the contemporary world: cybernetics, the deployment of science in political legitimation, the subjugation of political ideology to multinational economics, and so on:

> Modern aesthetics is an aesthetic of the sublime, though a nostalgic one. It allows the unpresentable to be put forward only as the missing contents; but the form, because of its recognizable consistency, continues to offer to the reader or viewer matter for solace and pleasure. Yet these sentiments do not constitute the real sublime sentiment, which is an intrinsic combination of pleasure and pain: the pleasure that reason should exceed all presentation, the pain that imagination or sensibility should not be equal to the concept.
>
> The postmodern would be that which, in the modern, puts forward the unpresentable in presentation itself; that which denies itself the solace of good forms, the consensus of a taste which would make it possible to share collectively the nostalgia for the unattainable; that which searches for new presentations, not in order to enjoy them but in order to impart a stronger sense of the unpresentable.[6]

But the problem with this approach is the appropriation of a term, "sublimity," with indifference to the contractual context in which it makes the most sense, namely, the arrangements of late-Enlightenment-Romantic aesthetics. The sublime, as Lyotard invokes it, does help account for the technologically driven, overpopulated, multinational aspects of contemporary life; but the thrust of the above passage imperceptibly shifts from the issue of sublimity to that of representability, a cornerstone to the aesthetic contract of modernism that does not receive its full philosophical elaboration until Derrida and poststructuralism. Lyotard appeals to sublimity, an equally fundamental element in the aesthetic contract of Romanticism, only to redefine it in terms of the poststructuralist problematic of representation. He takes sublimity out of context; he inserts a clause from one very important aesthetic contract into another.

~

Could we begin to assemble the terms in an aesthetic contract for postmodernism? And could we think of some of these clauses not merely as antitheses of modernist conditions, but as the enabling legislation for an aesthetic paradigm with its own distinctive temperament? It may be that the modern/postmodern boundary best articulates itself as a sea-change, a modal counterpoint, a borderline at the boundary of concurrent supplemental moods. We know we have crossed the frontier in the same sense in which we come to know whether a day will be spent under the sunlight of exuberance or the dark sun of depression.

Crucial from the perspective of the readings I have done is the postmodern self-sustaining discourse of indifference and relentless self-correction: the renunciation of teleological aspirations, nostalgic affect, oedipal pretensions. Postmodernism spells the end of irony, for irony, as I understand it, arises in the disjunction between different levels of knowledge, and in postmodernism this differentiation has been neutralized. In postmodernism there may be humor but no irony. The endless, teleologically unmarked, self-sustaining discourse of postmodernity gravitates toward the aphoristic and bombastic extremes of expression. There is room for Wittgensteinian propositions, Kafkaesque aphorisms, Heideggerian expansions, Beckettian monologues—but no room for discourse that metes itself out in well-proportioned sentence units. The undifferentiated fenestration of the International Style was postmodernism's initial, architectural avatar. (In architecture postmodernism anticipated modernism; this is always a possibility.) In psychology, the line of demarcation between modernism and postmodernism falls between the neurotic and the borderline personality. Literary characterization, in a postmodern context, gravitates toward what I have called "creatures of the text" that are anything but human surrogates. Kafka's subterranean rodent of "The Burrow" and the environment of Beckett's *The Lost Ones* (*Le Dépeupleur*) furnish splendid examples. In music a working modern/postmodern line of demarcation falls between the bricolage of Mahler and Ives and the atonal works of Berg and Schönberg; in painting, between the exuberant cubism and collage of Braque, Picasso, and Léger and the silent canvases of Mondrian, the geometry of Albers, the painterly outpourings of Pollock; in discourse between Barthes's pointed semiological slices of life in *Mythologies* and

Blanchot's ruminations on writing as the extension of death. Postmodernism is fated to hover in the wake of infrastructural modifications that have been made at the very architectural foundations of systematicity. It is both supplemental to modernism and autonomous from it. As a system it is conditioned by soft structure; not quite chaotic, not quite coherent. It produces characters that are not quite simulacra of subjectivity; plots that refuse to link an initiation to an endpoint; poems that never quite get over the materiality of their language; culture that cannot quite separate itself from the everyday objects of existence; essays that cannot manage to reach some conclusion. This near-systematic incompletion is not due to default or foreclosure,[7] but is a major element in an aesthetic contract, a cultural understanding that allows artists and intellectuals to go about their work, and that establishes a space in which people can consult and consume art in the search for knowledge and illumination regarding the conditions and possibilities of their experience.

The infrastructural play or modification of postmodernism is not a simple erasure, or "finding" absence where there was "presence" or "plenitude." In the case of the discourse of *Finnegans Wake,* for example, one can speak of the "half-reference" to which Joyce rises,[8] something both less and more than was prevalent in the aesthetic contracts for modernism. Atonal music is still articulate; it still "fills the air" (and time) with sound even if certain of the formal and melodic expectations have been modified. It is striking in postmodernism, even with the gravitation in this megacontract toward minimalism and hyperbole, that the contractual constraints *can* be known; that there is even some contract answering to *its* experiments.

For every time-specific aesthetic contract I can formulate, I can find exemplars that fall out of the epoch I am presumably characterizing. The existence of these anomalies does not disqualify the efficacy of the contract's specifications. There are postmodern qualities to works that have been characterized as "Menippean satires"; "Romantic" dimensions to works—for instance, *Don Quixote*—that long preceded historical Romanticism; a "cubist" analysis of space in certain paintings that anticipated the twentieth century considerably. In the spirit of Borges's "Pierre Ménard Author of the *Quixote,"* imaginativeness demands both that we read such anomalies within the context of the age that produced them and that we celebrate and reenact the historical leaps involved in their creation and productive illumination. Within the overall purview of the aesthetic contract, certain transtemporal or transhistorical subcontracts emerge, whether the Menippean satire or the Bakhtinian carnival.[9] These transhistorical contracts work in productive supplemental relation to more age-specific ones; there is no need to see the two kinds of contracts as stealing each other's thunder. Sterne's writing *Tristram Shandy* does not predetermine the futility of informed attempts to work out the aesthetic contract(s) prevailing in postmodernism; characterizations of postmodernism do not in themselves disqualify historically specific accounts of the generation of *Tristram Shandy*.

Indeed, the aesthetic contract, to the degree that it contains provisions for its own displacement and succession, falls within that tradition of Western idealism that regards the present, and all the efforts that have gone into perfecting it to the highest degree possible, as a sacrifice to even more striking productions in the future, whether these be scientific, ethical, juridical, or aesthetic in nature. The pathos of Western teleology consists in the self-effacing drive to produce a perfection that is in no way perfect, and that is at best provisory. The highest innovation of which we are capable becomes tragic but noble fodder for the next generation.

The future of the aesthetic contract becomes assured only by its strident violation. This deviance arises, on the one hand, as a transgression; but there is patently room for such contractual violation within the scenario of evolving aesthetic and cultural forms. Each time the aesthetic contract is broken and a significant body of convention-linked works becomes bankrupt, there is initially a loss of orientation and the pain that we associate with divorce. Yet at the infrastructural level, this dissolution has always already been written into the contract. It is in this sense that Benjamin can write, "All great works of literature found a genre or dissolve one." [10] Art producers who survive the disqualification of the enterprises to which they have struggled to contribute experience major contractual modifications as a form of annihilation. Members of the avant-garde occupy the vacated territory with militaristic *jouissance*. Despite the powerful emotions that attend paradigm shifts within the ongoing aesthetic contract, such dramatic changes are programmed implicitly within the scenario of a contractual setting and mode of change. Cognizant artists suffer piteously when the contractual understandings under which they have labored change; from the perspective of "creative" improvisation, the aesthetic contract winks at this tragic melodrama.

Subsequent versions of the aesthetic contract establish themselves on the ruins of prior understandings through a revisionary tactic of predatory "reading in." The manna of a new aesthetic contract is the problems an old one didn't answer; the experiential dimensions that it didn't encompass. There are so many dimensions in which an existing aesthetic contract can be deficient that the protest lodged by a new project and the innovations it marshals are unpredictable. As opposed to scientific procedure, the terms of a new aesthetic contract are not responsible for maintaining the solutions that were achieved in the old model. The new aesthetic contract can thus go off at a skew from the old one. It answers certain deficiencies in the old one, but not in a comprehensive or progressive way. It is frequently not clear which purported deficiencies in an aesthetic project the new contract is answering.

By their inherent nature, aesthetic contracts generate strategies; the different stages in the "life" of an aesthetic contract have some bearing upon how, at least "intentionally," the artist will situate his or her work. The game of "fort/da" that Freud describes in *Beyond the Pleasure Principle*,[11] which developmentally corresponds to what Margaret Mahler calls the "separation-individuation subphase," is indicative of some of the characteristic attitudes that artists manifest toward the aesthetic contract. Early during the period of its validity, when it introduces currency into the marketplace of interest, the aesthetic contract induces artists to espouse it. This espousal takes place in the interests of gaining recognition and protection. Yet the same contract that once evoked revolutionary manifestoes on the part of its adherents can be transformed, over time, into an oppressive, patriarchal law that begs to be violated and cast aside. That attitude of the artist toward the aesthetic contract in its full effect and effectiveness may well be one of avant-gardist defiance and improvisation.

It is the very *purpose* of the aesthetic contract, then, to be broken, but not by everyone. Art's bad boys and girls stream into the margin of violence and transgression only at exactly the opportune moment.

So it is misleading to speak in terms of any "preprogrammed," sequential "life" (or duration) of the aesthetic contract. Which contractual attitude prevails at a given moment, running a full gamut from treasuring and repudiating what was, promoting and disavowing what will be, is a function of the *interaction* between the degree of entrenchment of the aesthetic contract in effect and the conservatism/progressiveness prevailing in the world at large. It is edifying to think of artists in a constant state of violating "things as they are" and advancing their state. I am not arguing that this doesn't happen; merely that this doesn't happen all the time, in spite of the modern belief in art-as-transcendence. In *other* phases of the aesthetic contract, artists greedily anticipate the rewards that will accrue from alignment with one megaartgame or another. The "separation-individuation subphase" describes a moment of development at which adventuresomeness and fears of catastrophe are exaggerated.

~~

It is edifying for modern artists to think of their activity as making the world anew, as clearing away the rubble of outmoded experiments. Yet as I am beginning to think in these paragraphs, this predatory innovation is only one part of the attitudinal scope of the aesthetic contract. The aesthetic contract is also a rubric for restraint, conservatism, and the assumption of collective responsibility in creative endeavors.

To understand the terms in which the artwork "thinks" and articulates itself is to infer the clauses in the aesthetic contract(s) to which it adheres, to which it may relate through affirmation, disfiguration, denial, or other attitudes. The artwork may espouse the contract or distance itself from it. A different aesthetic contract may apply to the artwork than the artwork "thinks." The relationship between an artwork and the contract(s) that may qualify it is invariably problematical. The variables involved in the assessment of intentionality and design and in the artwork's "meaning" are confusing in their multiplicity. Yet all of these variables in assessment do not definitively preclude certain benefits that accrue from a contractual understanding of artistic and creative activity. The notion of an aesthetic contract emphasizes the collective work that may underlie the impression of "single-author" production. Collaborative work may play as large a role as "originality" in the synthesis of new forms of art and discourse. The contractual conception also lengthens the units of cultural history from artists' lives (or the portions of those lives devoted to "careers") to the "lifespan" of projects conceptualized broadly, in terms of their underlying specifications.

Indeed, the "bore" of aesthetic contracts can be adjusted such that one contract may address parameters prevailing over a long period of time, say over "modernity" since the Protestant Reformation, while a finer-tuned variant may be much more time-specific and address, say, cubist painting. In their differing degrees of finitude, both kinds of contract can be artwork- (or text-) based, so that the large scope of a particular contract is not necessarily "wrong." Elsewhere in this study I suggest that conceptions of individuality and freedom, bipolar logic, and the need to conceptualize both individuated and collective mechanisms of self-regulation are crucial elements in a mega–aesthetic contract prevailing from the outset of the latest modernity (however that is determined) until at least well into what we call modernism. Thinking in terms of this contract will not gain us, in specificity, what we will gain from contractual studies of "the eighteenth-century novel" or "the Romantic elegy." But it may offer us something—if nothing else, a sense of the relatedness of phenomena that may merely seem to be floating together in space.

Breaking the contract, conceptually as well as legalistically, is as crucial as "making" (formulating) it. Breaking the contract does not destroy the specific benefits that a contract-conception brings. Over spans of history long enough to be noteworthy, the production of art and discourse transpires between moments of contract formulation and dismantling. The notion of the aesthetic contract is itself a construct of very limited and specific validity, application, and usefulness. To the degree that it too rises and falls in its power and value, the aesthetic contract is very much a creature of the modern theory and art that it might hope to amplify. The very characteristics of this modernity permit the conception of the aesthetic contract to rise, work itself through, and dissolve, having offered the field of knowledge a certain specific purview, and having otherwise caused little harm.

CHAPTER 7

Maxima Moralia:
Millennial Fragments on the
Public and Private Dimensions
of Language

Suicide.[1] The event of a suicide arises in a superfluity of shameful signifiers that cannot be processed through the existing resources of the self. The occurrence of a suicide is a testimonial to a failure in the "Penelope-work of forgetting." A certain healing of old wounds, a cancellation of accumulated debts (or, in German, *Schulden*) has not transpired. A suicide may be understood as an accretion of misrecognitions. A suicide destroys a self at the same time that it stays the hand of writing. I write here knowing full well that the notion of a stable self with a sense both of personal history and future expectations is as much a construct as an empirical veracity. Yet it is the self that is destroyed in the act of suicide, the self nearly indistinguishable from the signatory of the signature. Jacques Derrida opens this possibility in "Signature Event Context" and other essays. We may be tempted to gloss over, for academic purposes, the self that is lost in the act of suicide; yet what other than a self takes credit, in the act of signature, for "original" or "creative" authorship?

We can never fully understand someone's suicide (any more than we could comprehend our own). This is because the suicide marks the place of the nonassimilation of circumstances and conditions that were tolerable to the rest of us who chose to remain alive. We cannot fully plumb the depths of the private language in which the suicide agent/victim thinks. There is "in" each of us a register of private language, occupying a position analogous to Saussure's *parole,* so idiosyncratic, so singular, that it "means," makes sense, only to us. Of course, we are conversant at the most exclusive margin of this personalized language even when we do not commit suicide. Suicide, bodies, sexuality, food, men, women; people of various national, ethnic, racial, age categories; physical objects—all mean, on one band of the register, something special to us. To think about suicide is not to commit it. To think about suicide may be one way of conceptualizing our nonexistence in a way that may have something in common with other people's fantasies, but that inevitably also carries meanings and nuances special to ourselves. Thinking about suicide may comprise one effort in the enterprise of conceptualizing our singularity. Thinking about suicide is not terribly dramatic.

Every "self" is a system to the degree that more or less stable patterns of behavior and thought have formed. Even where, through circumstance or unfavorable conditions of upbringing, a more or less stable self has not been allowed to develop, the erosion of the self is understood in comparison to the relative perdurance of a formed system. Psychologically, and in terms of the kind of moral philosophy described by Charles Taylor, this places so-called unstable or inconsistent selves at a disadvantage.[2] They are always being judged against a norm. These inconsistent selves may be great intellectuals, or artists, or social reformers, but their achievement takes place under the stigma of moral suspicion and failed responsibility.

The self resides at the intersection of the public language or codes prevailing in the culture(s) in which the person has been socialized and that person's singular private language.[3] The self's private language consists in the nuance and torque that its particular and not always easily communicated experience imparts to the signifiers composing the communal *langue*.

Our associations regarding gender, race, ethnicity, and class have a significant bearing on how we function as sociopolitical creatures. The best hope we have of functioning as ethical individuals in a diverse, multicultural society resides in our access to an educational process that will allow for the questioning and culling of our initial heritage of attitudes, even if part of this baggage, in retrospect, turns out to have been reasonable. To emerge as viable citizens in an age whose demographic stress sorely tests the ideals of Enlightenment emancipation, we need access to a second education that can, in certain instances, undo and disqualify our first one, assuming this initial one to include a significant share of received, local, and untested attitudes. One term that we might apply to this supplemental acculturation, in an implicit Rousseauan scenario, is "cultural psychoanalysis," a term that will be elaborated below.

Developmental psychologists and educators know that we do not have to be very old before our associations are nuanced in important ways by the received "wisdom" of our initial cultural milieu. Lacan's "mirror stage" surely represents a crossroads. After this moment of psychological structuration, high levels of linguistic usage and conceptualization are possible; prior to it transpire the emotional and experiential assaults that threaten, according to contemporary object-relations theorists, the integrity of the self, that result in such phenomena as lifelong introjections and sudden and violent swings into mystical states and physico-spatial disorientation.[4] Some of our associations we can trace to our earliest experiences of socialization, and some to inferences we drew on the basis of that training. Some of our associations seem "acultural" or "pre-social" because they arose amid a relative dearth of interpersonal contact or cultural mediation.

Given the multiplicity of sources and nuances of our attitudes toward gender, race, ethnicity, and class, it may be unrealistic to demand, from a perspective of "political correctness," that individuals display, from the outset of their social lives, the beginning of their schooling, an a priori Enlightened neutrality with regard to these matters. It may be more practical to think of elementary education and beyond as the setting in which the individual is afforded an ample opportunity to plumb the depths of, and unravel, his or her attitudes. Under this conception, education becomes, among other things, a prolonged cultural psychoanalysis, in which individuals are given occasion and encouragement to retrace, redefine, and rethink the meanings of their gender-related, racial, ethnic, and socioeconomic stereotypes.

Cultural psychoanalysis is retrospective and integrative. It retraces the formation of attitudes, but does not operate, exactly, on the individual, or the individual "spirit." The subject of cultural psychoanalysis is a self residing at the interstice of language operative for some community and language that has been personally nuanced or appropriated.

The self encompasses public and private language. There are considerable social sanctions that reward keeping public and private language to their proper spheres, and that punish misplacements and confusions in this regard. Yet practically, from a linguistic point of view, the public-private barrier is a hopeless compartmentalization. It might seem that we punish exhibitionists because the meaning of their private parts *to us* might get "out of control." But perhaps what exhibitionists display is not as shocking as our inability to fathom what their presentation means to *them*. We reward poets, even the author of *Finnegans Wake,* for their inventiveness only when a social consensus arises to *define* their achievement, to assign their improvisation a certain, though possibly false, meaning. The greatest achievement of behaviorism has been to characterize the processes of conditioning by which the elements of experience establish "private" meaning. This is what "learning theory" does.[5] Empiricism errs not in establishing a process of conditioning but in presuming to determine particular sequences of causation. So many factors are involved in an individual's learning of meaning that a significant proportion of her semiological repository is individual and private. The greater the social stigma accruing to a particular meaning-lexicon—for instance, if it encompasses sexuality or matters of social prestige—the more room it provides for nuanced idiosyncratic meaning.

No twentieth-century author reads the collision between conditioned learning and private meaning more hilariously than Thomas Pynchon. A good measure of *Gravity's Rainbow*'s humor and wonder consists in the fictive hypostatization of a universe in which Slothrop's conditioned sexual responses can predicate German rocket attacks. The sexuality that *Gravity's Rainbow* highlights is "marginal": heavy on S/M and anality. Through a fictive condensation linking the science that makes the military-industrial complex possible to the wildness of "deviant" sexuality, Pynchon underscores the dynamic tension between public and private spheres in the landscape of postmodernity.[6]

~⌐

There is nothing you can do with your personal parts that is "deviant" in itself. In keeping with the overall cultural progression in the West over the broader modernity, lurid and "deviant" sexuality is more conducive to the expression of personal liberty than conventional or "assumed" sexuality. This is why Lacan places "Kant with Sade," why Derrida, in *Glas,* frames modernity within a supplemental, tympanic vibration that communicates between Hegel and Genet. If Victorian writers, whether George Eliot or Henry James, declined to invest in the explicit representation of sexual practice, this is because they assumed a sexual knowledge so literal and public that its literary representation was beside the point.

In a world with a global Internet and the possibility of omnipresent surveillance, personal sexual activity becomes a matter of political choice and expression. The fetishization and commodification of sexual activity, whether deemed conventional or not, has as much to do with Personal Pan Politics as it does with the essentials of partnership or lifestyle. The politicization of sexuality coincides with its cultural identification with the dismantling of restraints upon personal liberty. The issues surrounding the ingestion of restricted substances, and the experiences that presumably ensue, comprise, as Avital Ronell has dramatized in her splendid *Crack Wars,* a particularly suggestive area of inquiry.[7] The current cultural fascination with male homosexuality and lesbianism involves the public colonization of a hitherto private, subversive, scandalous, and restricted sphere as much as it does the discovery of some "new" kind of empirical sexual behavior.

The distinction between "public" and "private" operates not as a static opposition but on a continuum. Private language distinguishes itself not qualitatively but in degree of relativity. Private language is *relatively* more impenetrable, discrete, and nuanced than public language. Yet a distinctive atmosphere or mood prevails when we veer off into the heavily privatized extreme of a person's, or an artist's, discourse. It is as if a heated argument erupts while we are visiting a new family; or we are accosted by an "ancient mariner" who displays highly individualistic cognitive or linguistic habits as he addresses his discourse to us. Public and private language are in communication with each other on a continuum, but we encounter different climates of communality and loneliness as we journey along this continuum. "Linguistic loneliness" is measured by the degree to which we or someone we observe has recourse only to a discourse at the private extreme of the continuum.

So I go out into the world doing my best to adhere to salutary social codes, assuming some sort of gravitation to the good described by moral philosophers, yet equipped with a self-system certain of whose elements are highly discrete. These private elements consist of a language formed by a conditioning (the place for an informed empirical discourse in a discussion of language and culture has been suggested above) and a span of events and memories that only *I* can know and remember, even though I cannot do so fully. The degree to which I am capable of knowing and remembering the key events constitutive of the private facet of my self-system is a function both of the vividness of these events (Freud would say their "traumatic" nature) and the hardiness of my intellectual and psychological constitution.

~

Certain institutions and situations favor conformity to the community's public codes; others favor the elaboration of private language. The poet wins no laurels for sounding like the Brooklyn telephone directory or for demonstrating adherence to the discursive statutes defining medical, legal, or administrative parlance. Professionals in the latter fields will lose their certification to function for adopting highly eccentric behaviors and language, just as the poet will lose her audience if she begins to compose verse as predictable as a tax-return form or an equipment requisition.

"Creatives"—those who mark themselves as qualifying for the aesthetic contract, or its close critical correlative—are torn between the implicit values of public and private language. Finding a location on the map demarcated by some public discourse is a necessary condition for the recognition of their work; yet their uniqueness, or nonetheless-decipherable eccentricity, is the very margin or index of our individuality, or interest. Indeed, the not entirely excessive margin between conformity to existing cultural codes and innovative nondecipherability may be taken as the most significant measure of the artist's value to Western society over the broader modernity.

The aesthetic contract to which artists and intellectuals subscribe is the overall set of statutes providing for creative work in the above-named cultural arena and time. It is colored heavily by conditions of individuation, freedom, and "personal" conflict that were accentuated by the revisions in Western ontotheology that prompted the Protestant Reformation and its epistemological correlatives in Cartesian philosophy and science. The contract achieves a definitive formulation in Kant's enduring scenario of an artist who both embodies and transcends distinctly modern conditions of subjectivity and writing.

In modern times, at least since the Protestant Reformation, there has been some confusion between the artist's *status* and *performance* as a subject who embodies and intensifies the human predicament. Through inborn capabilities that may be the immanent equivalents to the divine rights of kings, the artist both intensifies the modern conditions of human *subjectivity* (allegiance to conflicting jurisdictions, radical splitting, and so on) and possesses innate facility in media and relations (language, music, mathematics) circumventing human limits. The artist is a human prodigy and a virtuoso in the cultural forms that bypass the specifications of human subjectivity.

The artist opens and exercises a freedom to which not every person may rise. She or he marks and registers a parallel need for "internal" subjective constraints and regulation discernible in characterological representation over the span between Luther, Calvin, and Shakespeare and Flaubert, Melville, and Nietzsche. From the outset of the Western modernity of which I write, a facility with language defines the artist's freedom and distinction— and the moral perdition and psychological disintegration to which such a person is uniquely susceptible. An intimacy with language is both the artist's privileged escape-hatch from the inevitable divisions of subjectivity and the mark of Cain that will assure her punishment and degradation. It is no accident, then, that at least two Fausts—Marlowe's and Goethe's—spend too much time in their studies. The enclosed library is the unnatural garden hatching damnable achievements and discoveries of a distinctly linguistic nature. We have here, of course, another version of Derridean logocentrism, but what is so modern in this particular rendition is the association of linguistic evil with private cloistering. Through distinctively modern infrastructural processes of chiasmus, the artist's facility in a "public" medium, language, defines the imprisonment in "private" meaning that constitutes her secularized Hell. Precisely at the interstice between subjectivity and language, the modern dimensions of publicity and privacy become confused, reversed.

What, then, transpires when two individuals interact? We would most want to think of their interaction more as the location of shared discursive registers than as some behavioral event. When people relate to each other they have established some register of common interest, and this interest is culturally— that is, linguistically—defined.

The more intense the encounter, the more numerous, dense, and redundant are the common discursive registers. There seem to be no end of common interests and discursive topoi with individuals with whom one is in a basically constructive familial or collegial rapport. When I bring my bank deposit to a teller with whom I am not acquainted in any other social context, the basis of our interaction becomes the legibility of my deposit slip and the accuracy with which I have calculated checks and currency. Of course, my interest in my bank teller will accrue dramatically if she chooses to disclose to me that she's from Mars.

When I am engaged in conversation with a stranger sitting next to me in a public conveyance, the intensity and length of the discussion will be determined, in no simple empirical way, by the degree and commonality of the discursive registers we share. As "free" modern selves, my neighbor and I have every opportunity to construct together a vibrant world of mutual associations and interests. How often does this happen? What are the constraints against this happening? Is this as likely to happen now as it was thirty years ago?

Each discursive register upon which I act (or negotiate, or elaborate, or broker) with another human being consists of terms themselves arrayed on a continuum between public and private meaning. My neighbor and I in a public conveyance, or my spouse and I, may have worked efficiently in constructing registers of common interest and knowledge. But what I can never know—or can learn only through elaborated intimacy—is the degree to which the "subject areas" covered by my interlocutor are nuanced by very particular associations and memories, possibly accessible only to that person. The singular and private nuance of a discursive topic is in antithetical relation to the degree of its public "hashing out" or "working through." Men, and increasingly women, in contemporary U.S. society spend a lot of time talking about sports, and not only because the subject matter bears certain implicit reassurances regarding (hetero-) sexual orientation. This subject recurs also because of the high degree of dependable shared meaning that can be expected from discussions extending from it. In a relatively unstructured or impromptu situation, we would expect a much more unsettling and possibly conflictual discussion to extend from the discursive topoi "condoms" or "women" than from "National League pennant race." This is because the terms of the pennant race, whether its teams, its major stars, or the latters' contract negotiations, have had ample opportunity to be negotiated in public forums, including the broadcast media and journalism. These media are increasingly becoming arenas for the discussion of heavily personalized and controversial issues such as race, religion, and gender. I would nonetheless expect greater reluctance on the part of most people to broach their particular sexual habits to strangers than to pronounce on the National League pennant race. The delicacy of issues related to sexuality, race, class, and religion accrues from the conflicts in which they place the modern subject, who is defined from the outset of this epoch by her *inability* to satisfy the terms of the various social contracts in which she figures. This fundamental conflictuality explains both the pains and symptoms of modern subjectivity and the reason why linguistic facility is the distinguishing mark of the modern artist. Linguistic facility is an escape clause enabling the specially endowed artist, the secular version of the Judaic and Muslim prophet and the Christian priest, to finesse this conflictuality by dancing with impunity on its multiple and proliferating sides. We *expect* discursive topoi encompassing race, religion, gender, and socioeconomic status, by virtue of their inherently conflictual nature, to be highly nuanced by meanings toward the private end of the significatory spectrum.

Every time we discuss something with someone, we carry certain expectations about the social objectivity with which the topic is perceived. Yet each self is a discrete, more or less consistently operating system that, by memory, learning, conditioning, and association, has attached personal, singular meaning to each of the component elements, or "signemes," comprising the given subject area. Hence, in each interaction, even one based on the most commonly discussed topic, even with a lover, lifelong friend, or mental-health professional, we are shooting in the dark, we are in a blind created by the difficulty of determining the degree of publicly understood or privately inaccessible meaning.

Given this unavoidable predicament, which spans linguistic, sociological, psychological, and epistemological conditions, it is amazing in fact how efficient families, friendships, and even societies often are. Even with my domestic mate, it is not always easy to arrive at common understandings, even on such relatively trivial topoi as "telephone" or "lateness." Yet significant interactions encompass and condense thousands of understandings, on terms as trivial as these, and on ones of far greater moment. Given the degree of private, that is, potentially inaccessible, nuancing that may condition each term within each discursive register, it is wondrous that relationships take place at all, that certain nuclear families persist, that organizations run.

What transpires when two individuals interact? Two self-systems, each reserving for itself potential private signification on every possible term of common interest, address each other.

The artist is hopelessly stranded on the thin, ever-disappearing shoal situated between the turbulences of public and private language. To one side, the artist faces platitude; to the other, madness and unmediated idiosyncracy. When the shoal dissolves, the artist has been transfigured into Melville's Pip, waiting for his ship to arrive.

We demand that the artist earn our interest by venturing into the extraordinary, yet should an artist offer us artifacts of purely personal word-salad, we might recommend that he or she seek mental counseling. The artist must deploy language less than fully publicly but more than purely privately. Idiosyncracy is adorable; incomprehensibility sublime and monstrous, constitutive of a public menace. These are the terms of the aesthetic contract of the broader modernity, with regard to the coordinate of incomprehensibility. Incomprehensibility, since Kantian "original genius" set the horizon for artistic and creative achievement, is the sun in whose face the artist, as Daedalus, constantly flies. Society dresses the artist in a flying-suit, so that he or she may (exhibitionistically) challenge the sun, but then imprisons her or him in the double message that has at one extreme social utility and at the other, privately nuanced signification. *Also sprach* the aesthetic contract of modernity.

~

In his provision for "The Mutability of the Sign," Saussure characterizes the evolution of language as the stately negotiation between two spheres of meaning, one relatively public, the *langue,* and one less established, the *parole.* While Saussure, an early and pivotal modernist, prefers the spatialized, "horizontal" perspective of synchronic linguistics to the banal historical determinations of its diachronic counterpart, he nonetheless furnishes a scenario for change in language. In this model, language is constantly sifting and sorting, adapting and disqualifying variants and misusages that do not enjoy the social legitimacy characteristic of the *langue.*[8] Language evolves as the *langue* incorporates and legitimates misusages and improvisations that originate at the forefront of anomie in the *parole.* We could think of artistic invention as a dual idealization/deviance that takes the already restricted domain of the *parole* as the horizon of its possibility. Art is the meta-*parole* of the *parole.* The artist still needs to be legitimized—that is, contained under some category of public knowledge and meaning—but within the aesthetic sphere, as a modern, post-Renaissance, post-Reformation, and Enlightenment temple of displaced religion, the artist is applauded for her (possibly imperialistic) quest toward the "outer" limits of meaning, the hypothetical "non-meaning" that meaning, in its alienation and alterity, can precipitate out of itself.

Twentieth-century philosophy, when it faced the monstrosity of a private, alogical language, chose only to address the *possibility* of such a language: it could not relinquish logic in interrogating a phenomenon it knew already to be logic-indifferent. Wittgenstein's approach to private language is an "unbounded concept-game" in its own right. Among the game's extrinsic specifications are depsychologization—that is, the despiritualization of intellectual processes and the ordination of the steps ("moves") undertaken in the investigation, in sequence and magnitude, such that the exoskeleton of the process mimics, in the sense of *mimesis,* the structure of logic itself. About describing intellectual processes in a way that does not presuppose a "psyche" or the interiority that such an agency implies, Wittgenstein is resolute. The "private language" investigation is fraught with absolute boundaries and distinctions. Not so the issue of figurative or poetic language: here Wittgenstein demonstrates that he is capable of aligning contraries on continua. We can say that in the *Tractatus Logico-Philosophicus* logic and figurative language are, for the most part, remote from each other. By the *Blue and Brown Books* and the *Philosophical Investigations,* however, Wittgenstein has begun to dramatize a scenario I call "the poignant seduction of the (male) philosopher by poetic language, figurative speech, and their inevitability."

If Wittgenstein can demonstrate the home in philosophy for such figures as the color red, pain, and the pain of strangeness to a language;[9] if he can deploy what he calls "family resemblance" not only as a logical construct but as a metaphor for thinking and seeing in a certain way; then he should be able to conceptualize "private language" not as a strictly insular entity, but on a spectrum, a continuum. He should be able to place "private language" on a continuum with its Other, discourse. In this case, language would be either more or less public, more or less private. This of course would rob of its drama the game of seeing whether or not a purely idiosyncratic language could exist.

Again, we revere the singularity of private language if it can be shown to be in alignment with an aesthetic design, or if an explanatory discourse (journalistic or critical) arises to furnish the deviant usage with a setting or context. But we excoriate the same language if it seems to be the product of psychological or neurological damage. The words of *Finnegans Wake* are reverentially recited in reading groups celebrating its creativity and innovation; but how do we, amid the social disaffectation and indifference of the late 1990's, react to the homeless individual reciting its passages on a sidewalk in a big city, especially when we cannot identify the literary source? Wittgenstein's depsychologizing account of intellectual processes makes it impossible, in his schema, to evaluate private language as a psychological manifestation; the analytical thrust of his investigations marginalizes the sort of sociological observations and explanations that would emerge from fieldwork. So instead of an analysis of where public language evokes boredom (the telephone book, a menu, possibly a newspaper); where private language evokes physical revulsion (evesdropping on "word salad" in a confined space); and the aesthetic interface where idiosyncracy is not only tolerated but even demanded—instead of this spectrum of potential language-games, Wittgenstein and followers content themselves with the *possibility* of an aberration that cannot be separated from the comprehensive repository of *langue* in any event. Logocentrically—as in Derrida's critique of Saussure[10]—Wittgenstein's particular debt to empiricism keeps him situating the locus of language in the body.[11] The pain that we either do or do not succeed in communicating becomes the example *célèbre* of a "private" language situation, in part because the instance claims a corporeal source and grounding. But a pain is no less describable than a phantom; no more substantial than any other perceptual stimulus of similar intensity. Wittgenstein does not elude the illusion of interiority in basing the possibility for a private language on the metaphor of pain; he merely substitutes a corporeal interiority for a metaphysical one. The relentlessly logical operation and the situating of private phenomena in the body merely comprise a tribute to two particular offshoots of empirical methodology that have insinuated themselves into the Prolegomena for a Logical-Analytical Philosophy.

In fact, Wittgenstein, in certain formulations in the *Philosophical Investigations,* does treat private language as on a continuum with its Other:

243. A human being can encourage himself, give himself orders, obey, blame and punish himself; he can ask himself a question and answer it. We could even imagine human beings who spoke only in monologue; who accompanied their activities by talking to themselves.—An explorer who watched them and listened to their talk might succeed in translating their language into ours. (This would enable him to predict these people's actions correctly, for he also hears them making resolutions and decisions.)

But we could also imagine a language in which a person could write down or give vocal expression to his inner experiences—his feelings, moods, and the rest—for his private use?——Well, can't we do so in our ordinary language?—But that is not what I mean. The individual words of this language are to refer to what can only be known to the person speaking; to his immediate private sensations. So another person cannot understand the language.[12]

I cite the section in its entirety, for it functions as a microcosm of several of Wittgenstein's options. The beginning of the second paragraph is the place where, from my point of view, Wittgenstein concedes that there could be, relatively, *more* and *less* privacy in language usage. This in contrast to many of the participants in the "Private Language Argument,"[13] who treat private language as an exclusively idiosyncratic matter, and who concern themselves largely with the conditions of its possibility. In his phrasing here Wittgenstein equates "private sensations" with "what can only be known to the person speaking." Wittgenstein does acknowledge a facet of experience and language best, if not exclusively, grasped by the individual.

But in this section, Wittgenstein explicitly dissociates himself from any integrative interplay between the (relatively) more and less private dimensions of language. "But that is not what I mean." He himself is interested only in the case where the "individual words . . . refer to what can only be known to the person speaking." This is a rather demanding epistemological criterion: a language of reference known to only one speaker. Even clinical cases of word salad are (usually, most likely) rooted in a language accessible to a community of speakers, even if no larger than a family. Because Wittgenstein's last specification in this section, that the hypothetical private language be such that "another person cannot understand" it, is so stringent, it is not difficult to understand why he and his followers can so easily dismiss the very possibility of a private language.

But there is more to Paragraph 243 than this. Wittgenstein's meditations on language insist on its service as a *communicative medium*, its operation in relation to some Other. Wittgenstein does show some interest in what the psychoanalysts of object relations would call "introjections," emotionally charged language learned early on from the environment that acquires the status of an automatic caption regarding the self;[14] but in the context of the operational modality of language games, Wittgenstein and Wittgensteinians find themselves compelled to dismiss any link between communication and ordering, blaming, or asking oneself; to repudiate communication with the self as Other. It is with the prescription that language be other-oriented that Paragraph 243 begins. In the middle of the section, an "explorer" succeeds in "cracking" the monologic language of human beings "who accompanied their activities by only talking to themselves" by watching and listening to them talk, that is, through intense behavioristic scrutiny. This translation belongs to the tribute that Wittgenstein pays behaviorism at several points in the *Philosophical Investigations,* suggesting that one of the few ways in which we can infer what people are thinking or experiencing is through the observation of their behavior.[15]

Two other characteristic Wittgensteinian attitudes are to be discerned within the dense compass of Paragraph 243. When Wittgenstein imagines the "language in which a person could write down or give vocal expression to his inner experiences," there is a certain stress upon the tenuousness of *inner* experience. One overarching purpose of extrapolating the human predicament through very careful attention to the usages and misuses of language is a critique and delimitation of a whole range of metaphysical constructs, including the notion of psychic interiority. Wittgenstein's skepticism toward the spirituality that can be situated "in" this interior is one line of questioning that logical analysis shares with deconstruction. Wittgenstein's conclusion to Paragraph 243, "So another person cannot understand the language," referring to a hypothetical private language as Wittgenstein has framed it, is a rather stark conclusion. It is a conclusion that a philosopher who has been as meticulous as Wittgenstein could "feel" that he has earned; the decisiveness of the conclusion may even be one that on some ethical level Wittgenstein "feels" compelled to articulate. But the entire issue of whether the private language can be understood by another person is indicative of a bipolar logic which is another feature of the Wittgensteinian signature.

Paragraph 243 is a place in the *Philosophical Investigations* where Wittgenstein is somewhat open to the idea of a spectrum or continuum in the play between *relatively* public and private languages, which I see as a major factor in such issues as human socialization, psychopathology, and aesthetic production as understood both within and beyond the framework of the aesthetic contract of the broader modernity. In this paragraph, he is briefly open to a spectral interplay between languages that are "more" and "less" private. While he veers away from this option, he nonetheless uses the occasion to register certain of his other assumptions and attitudes: that the communicative function of language makes communicating with one's self and related operations insignificant if not impossible; that behavior is one of the few legitimate ways we have of inferring what people think or what is "behind" their language; that the rhetoric of personal interiority is a metaphysical error correctible through rigorous language use and behavior observation; and that, logically, if a state of affairs cannot be confirmed, then it need not be considered, because it has been abolished. Each of these attitudes is involved in a disinterest that Wittgensteinian discourse manifests toward the interplays between public and private language, and between normativity and deviance, that are absolutely crucial in approaching understandings about art that emerge over the broader modernity.

~

Whether we choose to think of ourselves as language users or subjects, then, we *regularly* compose some formulations toward the extreme of thoroughly digested discourse and others toward the extreme of incomprehensible word salad. General obedience to the Law gains us a wide berth in thinking odd thoughts and making odd formulations. The tradition of aesthetics has furnished the "transvaluation of values" that sanctions behaviors and productions that would otherwise be received as uncanny deviance. In brief, the relatively private extreme of nuances with which we approach language and people makes it possible for us at any moment to access, to approach, the limit, the edge. But because even the idiosyncratic extreme of our language and associations is culturally mediated, this is an edge we can never fully go over. Even at moments of personal or intellectual extremity, we are fated to hover near the edge of the cataract without falling over.

So what happens when two people interact? Two quasi systems, whether thought of as personal or linguistic in nature, address each other. The metaphor of a system speaks to the relative consistency accounting for a person's "character," "identity," or the like. To a certain degree, the signs through which the individuals interact are mediated culturally, that is, they have some identifiable predetermined meaning. But there is another register of the interaction in which each of the partners in the interaction is placing an individualized nuance or torque on the signs constituiting the interaction. This means that there is a limit on what each partner knows regarding the significance of each other's communications, and regarding her own communications. Wittgenstein very admirably phrased this epistemological limit:

> 272. The essential thing about private experience is really not that each
> person possesses his own exemplar, but that nobody knows whether other

people also have *this* or something else. The assumption would thus be possible—though unverifiable—that one section of mankind had one sensation
of red and another section another. (*PI*, 95e)

Even while eschewing the notion of a continuum between the more and less
private extremes of language, Wittgenstein phrases the limits of an interlocutor's knowledge regarding her Other's meaning with finesse. Indeed, as I
have attempted to elaborate elsewhere,[16] Wittgenstein's pinpointing of certain phantasms informing Western metaphysics shares much with that of deconstruction; both approaches could not be more solicitous to the precisions
of language as the *way out* of certain persistent metaphysical biases. Ironically,
at times Wittgenstein's adherence to empiricist principles ostensibly antithetical to metaphysics results in a reinstatement of logocentric attitudes that
Derrida avoids by playfully deferring the possibility of any definitive conceptual closure. Wittgenstein's most powerful examples of both the exasperation
and precision that language can furnish involve the communication of perceptions (the color red, for instance), sensations (such as toothache), and illusions (or metaphors: a centaur, the King's College fire). Wittgenstein and
Derrida both insist on a certain irreducible corporeal dimension to language,
but to markedly different effects. The tympanic vibrations reverberating
through the hymen of language give the lie, in Derrida's articulations, to the
corporeal denial and sublimation characterizing logocentric conceits. For
Wittgenstein the body is something else: a foundation to philosophical formulations as well as a source of stimulation and sensation. Perceptions and
sensations, as well as vocal communication (even in its broader sense), are
firmly rooted in the body, which is also the taking-off point of the empiricist
project. Wittgenstein would disencumber classical philosophy of some of its
ingrained metaphysical attitudes through a manfully rigorous deployment of
language, but the examples he enlists in his cause often betray logocentric
bias. I think of the exasperation of the linguistic outsider whose plight Wittgenstein—however analytically—chronicles; the pain of the toothache suf-
ferer withheld even from the symbolic relief that would be afforded by unambiguous expression; the pathos of uncertainty surrounding the implied
subject of the last reflections. Wittgenstein thus lets metaphysics in through
the back door after banishing it from his front portals.

⁓

What happens in psychoanalysis (or now, increasingly, psychotherapy), in
terms of the interplay along the spectrum joining public and private language? It must first be said that a significant portion of the healing that oc-

curs, regardless of the prevailing theoretical paradigm, is a direct function of the statute of privacy in keeping with which the interaction must prevail. Like all privacies, this is a relative privacy. The therapist promises confidentiality surrounding the secrets, memories, observations, judgments disclosed; yet with the client's permission the therapist may consult analytical supervisors regarding the case. What is being promised, and I think delivered with a remarkably high degree of reliability (although I cannot know this), is *privacy within the psychotherapeutic sphere*. That is, the client delivers himself of meaningful quantities of personal information about himself so that it may be interpreted by the therapist, so that it may be "worked through" mutually by him and the therapist, and possibly, so that there will be a measure of catharsis taking place simply in the exposure of the shameful or otherwise discomfiting material. And I am saying that a significant achievement of psychotherapy, one built upon the tradition of religious confessional practices (for instance, the Catholic sacrament of confession), consists simply in the *communication* of heavily nuanced private discourse to a neutral, judgment-reserving public situation, a "conversation" with an Other. And though the mores of confidentiality attending clients' communications are strict, the client is speaking both to one individual, the therapist (my discussion, for the moment, excludes the model of group therapy), and to the psychotherapeutic sphere, the more extensive apparatus that provides support to the therapist. Both the therapist and the psychotherapeutic sphere promise the confidential reception of personal, confidential, and possibly damaging material. On one level, then, we may define psychotherapy as the transportation and displacement of "psychic material" and discourse from the domain of the individuated self, where it has become shameful, painful, and disconcerting, to a public sphere defined by certain ethical statutes and clinical protocols.

The client does not always necessarily experience the "material" making up her therapeutic discourse as painful or dysfunctional at all. Some therapies assert the salutary effect of "restoring" a pain, which has become effaced, to certain memories, actions, and personal tendencies.

The client brings his pains, personal disclosures, and personal language to the therapeutic situation where the therapist interprets it, to some degree with the collaboration of a psychoanalytic system that the therapist has espoused. The therapist's interpretive paradigm may be Freudian, Jungian, Lacanian, object-relational, existential, interactive, and so on. The therapeutic situation opposes a self-system to an interpretive system. The client presumably effects some modifications of the self-system through the expression of "personal material" to which the therapist reacts, both as a sympathetic individual and as the operator of a particular psychoanalytical interpretive system. The therapist interprets the material both "instinctively" and through the deployment of a certain psychoanalytical model—and chooses which elements of the interpretations, and how much of them, to in turn disclose to the client. The therapist tests the validity of the psychoanalytical model she has mastered against her ability to foster productive change by means of the model.

The psychoanalytical encounter thus brings a client with a self-system some of whose inconsistencies or particularities may be painful or shameful face to face with a therapist whose being and range of operation are also split between a systematic and a singular dimension. The psychotherapist is, both as an individual person and as the exponent of some psychoanalytical interpretive model or combination of models, vulnerable to the client. The patient is to some degree vulnerable to the therapist's interpretations and worldview. From a viewpoint of truly distant, possibly annoying abstraction, then, the psychoanaytical encounter involves reciprocal displacements and interchanges both on a systematic level and on a personal one. The encounter holds, in different ways, the self-systems of the therapist and the client, as well as the therapist's operating system, in reserve. The major asymmetry in psychoanalysis is that the therapist's reactions—the interchanges and adjustments between her system and her "self"—do not have to be expressed. They do not have to enter the very limited and controlled quasi publicity of the psychoanalytical situation. The psychoanalytical interchange receives its impulse and direction from the expression of significant and possibly discomfiting accounts, thoughts, memories, and judgments by the client. Were we to introject the terms of Hegel's master-bondsman dialectic here, we would say that the psychoanalytic encounter is bondsman-driven, but that the therapist's clinical posture incorporates a "passively attentive intervention."

Where the client "goes public," the therapist guards her silence. The client publicizes his marginal experiences to the therapist; she is most reticent to the patient regarding the reactions ("the countertransference") his discourse evokes in her. At her discretion, she can disclose some of her countertransference, but this is calibrated carefully, and only done to achieve some educational effect.

Some of the effect achieved by psychotherapy consists simply in the heuristic effect of the client's "hearing himself speak." This dimension of the healing takes place independently of the therapist's interpretive interventions. With regard to this aspect of self-correcting expressiveness, the therapist's standing and qualifications, "who" she is, count more than specific observations she makes or the analytical framework within which the observations achieve some strategic utility.

Psychotherapeutic healing transpires to some extent with the help of theoretical frameworks and to some extent independently of them. It is not clear (though it is possible) that the most intellectually edifying psychoanalytical discourses (the Lacanian, for instance) are the most useful in effecting healing.

What is (psychoanalytic) healing? From the perspective of our mode of exchanges along the continuum between (relative) publicness and (relative) privacy, healing consists of the "outing," the making public, of expressions which in the domain of individuation are distressing, disconcerting, saddening, and so on. We should remember that the particular publicity given to upsetting private language is a controlled one, in the sense of "controlled" experimental conditions. The sadness and tragedy of life achieve reality, verifiability, testability, and correctability in their expression. In this aspect of healing, consisting in reification and editing through expression, the therapist's skepticism, her resistance to sudden new schemata for organizing states of affairs, is a crucial and indispensable resource for the therapeutic process.

The client expresses hitherto private (or hitherto unorganized) material. The therapist both systematizes the material to some degree—according to its intrinsic particularities—and reads this individuated system against the interpretive models she has appropriated. The client begins to discern the conceptual system underlying the therapist's interpretations. From the perspectives of both mental health seeker and provider, psychotherapy then becomes a process that is inherently speculative and theoretical. As the client becomes stronger and healthier, she can express and withstand more of the notions that have underlain her behavior and fantasy life. The product of years of psychotherapeutic working through may be nothing more impressive or gaudy than a bounded set of propositions, stunning in their relevance and authenticity.

Many of these propositions do not involve the importation of theoretical frameworks of psychotherapy to experiences, memories, fantasies. Many of these propositions, whose discernment and expression constitute the significant work of psychotherapy, consist in simple observations: for instance, "my father rejected me," "my family was polarized in such and such a way," "an incestuous undercurrent prevailed at certain times in the household." These propositions may even change in the course of therapy. What keeps the therapy on course is the patient's ability, even if slow and gradual, to arrive at and express propositions regarding the meaningful dimensions of life. (Sometimes the seemingly trivial *is* the most meaningful dimension of life.)

What is psychoanalytical healing? It is the public accommodation, acknowledgment, and forgiveness of the private—so long as the process in-

volves the productive formulation and reformulation of narratives and propositions. The therapist's theoretical affiliation is less important than it might
seem, because from the point of view of expression, formulation, and reformulation, the theoretical framework serves only the purpose of logic at
the end of the *Tractatus Logico-Philosophicus:* a heuristic device, a fiction, that
Wittgenstein figures as a ladder, whose realization is as much contained in its
being set aside as in its formalization. The initiation and maintenance of a
creative process of expression, editing, and productive reformulation of basic
life-propositions holding "true" for the client is the aim of (psychodynamic)
psychotherapies.

～◦

The psychotherapist is, whether she wants to be or not, implicitly a literary
critic; the client is a philosopher. Teachers of literature and culture are in
effect cultural psychoanalysts: they expose their students to the gender, race,
ethnicity, class, and age-based determinants of their lives. But the specificity
of the analysis proceeds no further than the level of the group. The clinical
psychoanalyst orchestrates a self-scrutiny or self-interpretation that takes the
above factors into account, but whose finitude goes all the way to the client's
personal experiences, associations, and memories. A culturally astute educational system, then, should transform every student into a cultural critic and
a philosopher of her collectivity's experience.

The borderline patient imposes upon the world a language that has not
been culturally mediated. This is what Kernberg means when he stresses the
hostile projective fantasies to which borderline patients are prone.[17] The borderline patient acts upon fantasies that he has not validated in conjunction
with disinterested people, with people who can distinguish their own interests from situational reality. The borderline personality, whether Norman
Bates in *Psycho* or Jame Gumb in *The Silence of the Lambs,* imposes a highly
idiosyncratic language upon people for whom the language does not make
sense, and for whom it is in fact dangerous and life-threatening. It takes a
long time, and significant interaction with someone, including a borderline
personality, before it is possible to determine whether his language is nuanced
in a particularly idiosyncratic way. The borderline personality uses the same
language that you do. Speaking the same language as the borderline personality, you make yourself vulnerable to his imposing his highly nuanced personal language on you. If what I am writing is true, your ability to arrive at a
common and therefore quasi-public understanding with a person as to the
value and meaning of terms, events, conditions, and symbols pertinent to

your shared interactions is one of the most fundamental and crucial ways you have of assuring yourself of that person's goodwill. Your gaining this reassurance is therefore tantamount to your avoidance of submersion in situations programmed by Another's highly privatized, nuanced semiology. The non-negotiability of interpersonal terms is the best indication that you have erred into a borderline situation.

Groups—for instance, societies engaged in genocide—can collectively adapt highly nuanced language; they can make this language the basis of their current social contract. This is what the Germans did during World War II, and what the Serbs of the former Yugoslavia are doing even as I write. It is a chicken-and-egg game as to whether individuals or societies can take credit for such thoughts as "the world will be better off if all Muslims (or Jews, or people of color) are eliminated," or "it is a capital offense to burn a national flag." It is clear that genocidal thinking is less dangerous to the lives of certain populations and to any transcendental value of human life if it is confined to the "relatively private": to individuals or very small groupings. Borderline conditions are achieved on a societal scale when extreme and nonnegotiable thinking is incorporated into the prevalent social contract. In the case of genocide, the very existence of a societal subgroup is being singled out both as the nature of its offense to the society and as the condition that punitive action will deny. Under these circumstances, involving the utter nonnegotiability of the terms by which a pariah subgroup has been culturally defined, societywide borderline conditions have been achieved. I need hardly add that this predicament is highly dangerous for the subgroup marked in this fashion. When this condition of linguistic nonnegotiability has been reasonably well established, ethical constraints to comply and even interact with the agent dictating these highly idiosyncratic, nuanced conditions, whether this agent is an individual or a social agency, have been dissolved.

One way of describing ethics is as the set of linguistic conditions under which it is imperative, fair, salutary, and productive to interact with people, whether as individuals or groups, in order to negotiate issues of common knowledge and concern. By privately and unilaterally determining the meanings operative within a situation unethically, the borderline personality usurps control over the situation; the only ethical response to this coerciveness is either exiting or bracketing the situation.

From a private-language purview, psychoanalysis constitutes an individual's effort and willingness to negotiate the terms of her privately nuanced language with an exemplary representative of a certain society. The implicit society of psychoanalysis is the historical descendent of the libertarian society born at the time of the Western Enlightenment. This Enlightenment ide-

ology stresses, among other tenets, universal enfranchisement of human beings, personal liberty, and freedom from certain extrinsic systems of authority
and control. The psychotherapist is empowered as the representative of this
Enlightenment society who will negotiate symbolism that has become painful to the client, or that has been a factor in the client's inflicting pain on
others, as the result of a certain formation or education. Psychoanalytic education stresses the voluntary nature of the treatment; the possible damage
brought about by the therapy itself; the delicacy of psychotherapeutic interactions; the centering of the process on the patient, and its orientation toward the patient; as suggested above, the confidentiality and *relative* privacy
of the interaction; the client's gradual assumption of responsibility for his
actions, at the same time that the process may involve the attribution of
blame for extenuating circumstances that have influenced his life; a certain
value inhering in knowledge or attentiveness itself, whether this attentiveness
is conceptualized as a making conscious of what is unconscious or as an integration of "self-fragments" that have become detached. Let us pause, for
an instant, at the fact that psychotherapies presuppose some societal commitment on the part of both client and therapist. A psychotherapeutic protocol
based on the above assumptions will be attenuated to the extreme by pronouncedly antisocial attitudes, whether on the part of the therapist or the
client. One possible way of defining borderlinearity is as antisociality translated to the symbolic sphere. The borderline personality imposes heavily nuanced private language on situations that presuppose a large degree of mediation and disinterestedness in linguistic usage. The clinical literature suggests
that it is the neurotics, who are often literally taken aback by their symptoms,
whether of an anxious, obsessive-compulsive, depressive, or other nature,
who will seek therapeutic intervention in the effort to ameliorate these manifestations. From the perspective of the same literature, the borderline personality's highly idiosyncratic collation of meanings and values has served as
an effective mechanism of adaptation. Why should the individual place this
system under therapeutic scrutiny, where it may be jeopardized, *except* under
legal or medical constraint? Generally speaking, it takes a long time before
the borderline personality finds it in his interest to initiate psychotherapy.

State-administered psychiatry, as arose under Soviet government in Rus-
sia, represents the attempt of political institutions to usurp control over private language; psychotherapy inhabits the space where, on the basis of personal volition, the client negotiates her private language with an individual
determined to be, through disciplinary oversight, disinterested; borderline
conditions, which increasingly set the tenor for institutional life in "ad-

vanced" societies and are represented in mass artifacts, are tantamount to the nonnegotiability of *some* of some people's private language.[18]

～

One way of thinking about ethics in a world of increasingly sublime complexity is to ask the degree to which we are obligated to enter or conform to another individual's private language. The entire tradition of Western ethics takes for granted our being bound to, connected with, certain other human beings. But what if another person's private language defines us, our value, and our utility in collective activities in a way that is utterly beyond our assent and collaboration? If the ethical is defined by a notion of personal responsibility, then relationships nuanced by the highly private language of another deprive me (or anyone) of the possibility of conducting myself ethically. One way of rethinking ethics is as a range of possible collaborations with one's fellow human beings. Within this conception, the degree to which the language articulating the interactions is situated toward the "public" or "private" end of the continuum is a decisive factor.

Human beings are citizens of the middle ground between the relatively more singular and relatively more mediated extremes of their language. What is the nature of this middle ground? It is not merely the register upon which I as self-system can, under controlled conditions, interact with an Other self-system; it is also the register upon which I can productively communicate with myself. For I speak a language to myself that is every bit as communicative and signifying as any that I share with an Other. Psychoanalysts of object relations characterize the language with which I address myself as introjective in nature. From a clinical point of view, this particular language, arising from an early developmental stage and carrying vestiges of "archaic" memories and values, is highly charged. Salutary maturation involves, according to these theoretical frameworks, a "toning down" of the extremity and bipolarity with which the language of introjections is inherently endowed. In different ways, Klein, Winnicott, and Kohut furnish scenarios for what may be described as a "taming" and integration of value-laden primitive language addressed to the self.[19] Psychotherapy picks up in this process of the amelioration of private (introjective) language where parents and other significant others leave off.

Psychological efficiency (if not health) may be defined as the ability to assimilate the disjunctive language that the self and the world address to the self. In the case of psychological health, the individual benefits from a personal "catcher in the rye" capable of gathering in and processing disjunctive language more or less as it arises. People under various degrees of disturbance are subject, on the occasions of failure, error, criticism, social ostracism, and so on, to be thrown into relatively greater extremes of disequilibrium than people with functioning "catchers in the rye." What we call psychological health is, relatively speaking, the ability of a hypothetical internalized public language to accommodate a hypothetical internalized private (introjective) one. Constructs such as "introjections" and their "integration" therefore presuppose the internalization of the dynamics operating along the continuum between relatively mediated and relatively singular language.[20]

∿

What we call healthy interpersonal relations are those in which the differences between two somewhat individuated self-systems are negotiable, eventually arriving at some agreement even in a process involving some degree of conflict and hostility. The conditions that sustain us from psychological and social points of view are all situated in what I'm calling the middle ground. As we have seen, however, these conditions may not be the ones most directly involved in our composing a symphony or a splendid sonnet. In fact, the conditions most supportive of our doing liminal creative work may well be situated at the extremes of the creative borderline.

The difference between the borderline of creativity and the borderline of psychological splitting, projective fantasies, exploitative behavior, apparent but superficial affability, and so on, is in many cases and under many conditions difficult to discern. But we can say this: the integration of the incommensurate tends to generate writing, as Derrida articulates it; whereas the existential traces of the borderline, in radical splitting, cold manipulativeness, and the like, void writing and its possibilities. As a marginal, interstitial medium, writing thrives at the frontiers between incommensurate thoughts, phenomena, and conditions. The splitting that has been a feature of subjectivity since the inception of the broader modernity and that is accentuated in the borderline personality achieves a high level of fragmentation, whether described as between "self-fragments" or as situated in the field of cognition. Radical splitting in effect quells the communication between fragments whose most comprehensive medium is writing. "Integration," whether transpiring in psychoanalysis or creative work, is *not* a devolution to the point of banal homogeneity; it is, rather, the always fragile and tenuous communication between differends.[21]

The middle ground between the (relatively) singular and mediated spheres is in fact a free-trade zone, a locus of negotiation, barter, exchange. In an age of depleted space and resources, it becomes increasingly crucial to define and elaborate this middle ground. At certain moments in history, the nineteenth century, for example, the middle ground is equated with a difference-leveling mediocrity, and comes to be seen as a cultural and ethical travesty.[22] At other moments, and I think here of postmodernism, the middle ground in fact devours any other possible extremes, and there appears to be nothing outside. There is, in other words, the conservative attitude toward the middle ground, and the liberal one.

It can be argued that a continuum consists *only* of a middle ground. The present essay can be read in one sense as an argument in defense of continua (as opposed to binary terms or their blanket rejection). Continua may not offer definitive results, but they provide for *ranges* of possibility and activity. The notions of "privacy" and "publicity" in language may be utter fictions, but the continuum between them may have a lot of light to shed on how people invoke language and behave. Continua do provide for extremes of thought and behavior; they just place those extremes in relation to the more "moderate" forms. Continua are the conceptual models that do the work of integration as it takes place in the psychoanalytical sphere.

Much of the cultural work being done today—Judith Butler's work on gender, say—inserts a spectrum model where previously there had been a binary opposition—say, female-male. And work on postcolonial theory (and in the teaching of "world civilizations") places national and ethnic groupings in one vast arena in questioning earlier ideological constructs of differentiation.

Continua do not by their very nature solve all problems located within their spheres. But their deployment is an implicit vote for integration, as opposed to pat ideology-based hierarchy, in the attempt to address and solve problems.

In a world of sublime overcrowding and tenuous supply, how human beings do as a species is integrally linked to how well they inhabit the middle ground. The interval between what has been known as "private" territory and the public sphere is, conceptually speaking, one of the continua whose exploration can be most fruitful. The self-sustaining, endlessly self-correcting discourse of postmodern literature (Beckett, the late Kafka and Joyce, Blanchot, Bernhard) and psychoanalysis (in different ways, Lacan, Kernberg) may in part be understood as an adaptation to the need to inhabit the middle ground. Within this middle ground, we will need to learn to tolerate and understand each other, to integrate our own skewed tendencies and interests,

even as the world has to accommodate more of us, with a corresponding
diminution of individuated "private" space "around" us.

~

The philosophy of writing is the discursive space inhabited by the middle
ground. The philosophy of writing is the interface linking the philosophical
discourse that has acknowledged (and to some extent dramatized) the figurality of its language and the literary discourse that has elaborated the concepts
that it has implicated. Twentieth-century critical theory has given the philosophy of writing a relief and explicitness that it has rarely achieved; but
this is not to say that the philosophy of writing is unique to the twentieth
century.

"The philosophy of writing": what is the meaning of this phrase? "The
philosophy of writing" suggests that the artifact's status as a written document, whether philosophical or aesthetic, constitutes a significant portion of
its working through, a significant measure of what it is about. Even the formal and stylistic aspects of an artifact concern, to some degree, its written
status. We do not have to claim any exclusivity for writing as the only worthy
subject in works of literature and philosophy. These works may address other
issues as well, for instance, the quests for truth and meaning, and possibly for
an albino whale. My purpose is more than adequately served by devoting
some attention to the artifact's sensitivity to (and technical elaboration of) its
own status as a poetic, fictive, or discursive written document.

Philosophy and writing would seem intuitively to share some special relation, an intimacy, perhaps even a conspiracy. After all, writing is the notation in which philosophical concepts make themselves known; and philosophy is the epochal operating system capable of cutting through the plethora
of figurative uses of language at any particular moment—able to disclose the
most fundamental and general questions underlying poetic variety. We can
think of Philosophy and Writing as a single comedy team, in which the former plays the straight man to the latter's jokester.

No one in our time has been more astute regarding the possibilities liberated in this partnership than Jacques Derrida; indeed, despite an early insistence (above all, in *Of Grammatology*) that deconstruction goes off on a radical
tangent from the *technique* of writing, one of deconstruction's enduring and
most important contributions consists in its elaboration of writing as a philosophical category—its delving into the spatiality, rhetoric, logic, semantics,
and even politics of writing in a philosophically rigorous way. Indeed, Der-

rida's work begins with a devastating critique of a scenario that I invoked a moment ago in order to launch my own discussion of these terms: with Philosophy a country theologian and Writing a drunken sailor. The rapport, as Derrida has demonstrated again and again, is not nearly as simple as this. The relation between Writing and Philosophy is very similar to that between Kierkegaard's unnamed aesthete and Judge William in *Either/Or*. The effervescent music-lover gets to make most of the noise, but sometimes the *rhetoric* deployed by the marriage-oriented moralist is more treacherous, more interesting, in a literary sort of way.[23]

The interplay between philosophy and writing—between the more logical and the more playful facets of discourse—is well under way, as Derrida illustrates in "Plato's Pharmacy," by the time of the Platonic dialogues. Such Greek texts as these, joined by the classical texts of Judaism (many codified in the Old Testament), launch Western culture on its headlong and distinctive fidelity to rationalistic idealism. Yet this privileged intimacy or conspiracy between philosophy and writing—whose interplay Derrida would characterize as supplemental—cannot be generalized or totalized. As in an extended liaison between lovers, there is no typical moment of the relationship that is more authentic than others. In describing an extended, complex, intense, and ambivalent liaison, one articulated temporally, we cannot distill essences. The most we can come up with is a compendium, a menu, of different attitudes and postures that the relationship between philosophy and writing at times assumes. These intersections, dances, thrusts-and-parries, transpire on what I have been calling the middle ground, the ethically bounded space also extending between the private and public extremities of language, recognizing that the endpoints of this continuum are at best hypothetical constructions.

As the scribe of this interplay, I'll conclude this paragraph with a partial list of attitudes between philosophy and writing so prominent and recurrent as to have joined the classical repertoire and baggage of Western civilization:

- Philosophy as straight man; writing as comic. Philosophy as logic; writing as myth, art, madness, or some other form of delirium.

- Writing, in the form of parables or stories, as a quasi-magic *revelation* that can break out in a work of reasoning; and that can accelerate progress to the truth which is the occasion for the discourse.

- Logic, by virtue of its scientific purpose, as something designed to *resist* playfulness, invention, distortion, and sensuality. Philosophy is to resist language that, by virtue of its figurality, draws attention to its play and indeterminacy, in the way a virtuous man, who has taken a vow of celibacy, is to stave off the seductiveness of a beautiful and sexually aroused woman.

Philosophy as the discourse that, after a magnificent effort at resistance, falls prey to the figurative playfulness it has struggled to resist. Philosophy as that which *surrenders itself* to the enigmaticness and intractability of figurative language, but which, through its intrinsic logical and scientific mission, can now uplift the marginality, madness, femininity, Jewishness, homosexuality, and so on, of writing to some level of acceptability.

Writing, by virtue of such features as synonymy, homonymy, polysemy, and aphoristic compression, as that which can debunk and lay low philosophy's system-building pretensions.

Philosophy as that which, although apparently stodgy and repressive, can in fact be the most subversive, seductive, and playful discourse of all (see Kierkegaard, *The Concept of Irony, Either/Or*).[24] Logical arguments can be posited and made compelling, for example, through nothing more substantial than metaphors.

Issues of logic, reasoning, and conceptual rigor in general, which we normally associate with philosophical discourse, may in fact come to the fore more powerfully, strikingly, and rigorously in an artwork showcasing writing than in a work of philosophy. We all have our favorite instances of this "anomaly." Mine include Swift's *Gulliver's Travels,* Goethe's *Faust,* Kafka's "A Common Confusion" and "A Crossbreed [A Sport]," Proust's *A la recherche du temps perdu,* Borges's "Tlön, Uqbar, Orbis Tertius,"[25] and Calvino's "t zero," "The Chase," and "The Count of Monte Cristo."[26]

Each one of these positions is an inevitable way station in the inquiry known as "The philosophy of writing," the study of the positions emerging between the relatively codified and relatively singular dimensions of language.

The most significant, and perhaps the only liberty exercisable over the broader modernity is the liberty of writing, in Derrida's sense of the term. The very same liberty that, in concert with the idea of determination, from Plato through Luther, Calvin, and Descartes conditions the bipolar logic which is the ultimate nemesis to integration and creativity, finds its ultimate home and refuge in the play and dynamics of writing itself. It is fundamentally anomalous that the idea of freedom, worked through in writing—despite its long history as the enabling construct to bipolarity—could comprise

the ultimate margin of liberty available to us: this in a world of overpopula-
tion, shortage, and environmental stress of sublime proportions. Liberty is
still available to us. According to the ethos of the Enlightenment, it is incum-
bent upon us to exercise this potential. Writing remains the ultimate margin,
dynamic, and preserve for the exercise of human liberty.

PART THREE

The World at Large:
Systematic Expansionism on the Threshold of Modernity's Realization

CHAPTER 8

From Social to Aesthetic Contract

I want to evoke with you a time and an ("advanced," Western) world when the possibility of (human-evolved) systems went hand in hand with a vast expansion of technological capability and imperialistic control. My posture here is nothing more than evocative. I want to try to re-create with you the sense that there must have been of unlimited capability and expansion in North America and certain European countries, above all in England, France, and the German Lands, at the dawn of the nineteenth century. At the very largest scale, the American and French Revolutions had institutionalized the ethos of individual freedom, the human source of the higher orders of abstraction and thought, and the need for collective and personal self-regulation, which had been a potential since the outset of the broader modernity. My main point here is that the systems of the period, whether of abstraction or government, combine a certain exuberance at the expectation of human-originated solutions to problems of sublime proportions with the possibility of a self-regulation whose extrinsic (ecclesiastical and feudal) instruments have been discredited for some time. A writer such as Rousseau encompasses both sides of the collective desire expressed by this systematic status: in *The Social Contract* he can speculate as to the optimal proportionality between the executive and legislative branches of a hypothetical government; while in *Emile* he (or his Savoyard vicar) can appeal to nature and conscience as capable, intrinsic forms of personal self-regulation. The narrator of *The Confessions* can both dramatize and epitomize the inevitable bad faith resulting when the subject militating for its desires has to regulate and, under certain conditions, chastise itself.

I am concentrating here on a specific Euro-American exuberance at systematic expansionism, and at the contradictions that inevitably go with it. A variegated community of my colleagues has undertaken the analysis of the world that this Euro-American force expanded into, and of the sociopolitical, cultural, and exegetical effects resulting from this expansion. The more I think of this postcolonial review of phenomena naturalized within Western idealism, the more I am convinced of its radical potential, methodologically and theoretically as well as to supply material and points of view neglected within a Western framework. For at stake in the explicit articulation of the West's Other(s) is the neutral inner sanctum from whence all Western truth issues and to which it is oriented. This inner sanctum, whether the laboratory or the logical constraints through which philosophical discourse would establish a purified, neutral space for itself, may constitute a zone of mystification. But it has succeeded in establishing a *surround* of relatively "objective" trials and tests to which Western science, jurisprudence, philosophy, and even art have subjected themselves. Western science, for example, has progressed more quickly than any other because of the altruistic submission of its results to the legislative purview of the *future*. Yet the statutes of precedent and accountability that have spurred Western science and jurisprudence on to such achievements come at some cost, specifically the cost of the maintenance of the hypothetically neutral zone in which advanced thought, systematization, experimentation, and even art are allowed to transpire (presumably "on their own," like a Rousseauan "noble savage"). Even contemporary critical theory appeared, at its outset, as a method of methods, as a privileged citizen of the rarefied neutral zone. Barthes's notion of metadiscourse serves as an example of a radical theoretical idea that nonetheless situated itself within the traditional *preserve* for advanced work. To the degree that my colleagues in the field of postcolonialism have begun to explore the implications of Western idealism within the field to which this procedure was exported, they have embarked upon an inquiry that may requalify the neutrality upon which my entire battery of theoretical models has been based. With excitement and trepidation I await further developments from this field. My current attempt to evoke the expectations and failures of Western systematicity in the nineteenth century only begins, alas, implicitly, to incorporate a postcolonial perspective, which is being more than capably elaborated and amplified by my colleagues.[1]

The totalizing systems of Kant and Hegel are imaginary, conceptual simulacra of institutions of authority that once prevailed in the European ecclesiastical and political domains. These post-Enlightenment systems are immanently rather than externally motivated; they are attributed to a human rather than a divine origin. Yet on a cultural level they perform the same defensive functions as religious ceremonies and political hierarchies. They suggest people's status in the universe; they furnish moral standards. They exemplify a certain rationality that can be taken as a counter to madness. These systems, both by their own account (see the Preface to Hegel's *Phenomenology of Spirit*) and that of others (say, Foucault), incorporate a certain organicity: they are synecdochically intertwined; they are endowed with the capability to grow of their own accord attributed to artificial intelligence.[2]

The systems of Kant and Hegel have already co-opted a certain element of anti-authoritarian motivation and sentiment—yet they are systems. They also exercise totalization and the potential for generalization and repression. It is inevitable that these systems should occasion ambivalence. Ambivalence is what they are made of. The expansionism intimated by Rousseau's panorama of gentle self-regulation for Emile, or painted more boldly by Melville in *Moby-Dick,* gives rise to a parallel, closely related ambivalence: Melville's Pip resides at the center of it. Where is the guarantee for sanity and measure in this rapidly expanding world (the Derridean *garde-fou* of *Of Grammatology*)?[3] The outbreak of delirium and its social correlatives is but a finger's breadth away from human-based immanently proceeding systems of knowledge and authority. Pip is an African-American, from Alabama (*MD,* 27; 121).[4] Is an African-American more susceptible to the potential derangement lurking in nineteenth-century systems than a white man?

The following remarks are devoted to the uneasy coexistence between exuberance and terror in Romantic systematicity. Within this alignment, the original genius lives in mortal terror of himself. The aesthetic contract of the broader modernity has evolved to a situation in which a constraint once deemed intolerable has emerged as the ideal at the horizon of an incestuous, self-engendered system. Men seek protection in systems they once abhorred, because these systems have been endowed with the aura of intuitiveness, of being homemade. The discourse and technology of fragmentation arise to combat systematic pretensions, in literature as well as philosophy. But it is difficult for the disavowed remains (or refugees) of systems ever to characterize fragmentation purely in fragmentary terms; something of the systematic homeland adheres to the fragment.

The late-Enlightenment-Romantic impulse to imitate systems, in literature as well as philosophy, may be taken as an instance of massive cultural reaction-formation: an appeal is made to the system to structure the liberty that is so disorienting, so potentially chaotic, and so desired. The same voyage of discovery that leaves the constraints of home and measure behind can encompass a system as defensively reassuring as it is vast. This is the joy I want to share with you: of (from a Western point of view) a geographic and administrative expansion that coincided with an increase in the scope and power of conceptual systems. Yet there is a somber tone underlying this *jouissance:* in each of its emanations, the aesthetic contract of the broader modernity transpires under a logic and mood of bipolarity.

Two of the authors we will surely want to consider carefully from this point of view are Rousseau and Melville. In different ways, both of these writers inscribed the *jouissance* of a world whose expansiveness was achieving a certain tangibility; yet this breathless *opening up* initiated a set of anxieties of its own. These anxieties were themselves formative to the massive cultural reaction-formation that becomes a distinctive talisman and central defense mechanism of the late-Enlightenment-Romantic age.

Rousseau himself manages at least three discourses that can be partially understood in the context of the stresses and strains brought about by the expansion that is the occasion of this essay. In his *Discourse on the Origin and Fundaments of Inequality* and *The Social Contract,* Rousseau carries forward the concern for proportion and balance that are, according to Michel Foucault, distinctive marks of knowledge during the "classical" *épistème* of the broader modernity. In the latter work, Rousseau very precisely describes optimal demographic and political conditions for a government more or less corresponding to a small-scale participitory democracy, that is, one originated in a community and oriented to it to the greatest degree possible: the political correlative to subject-originated systems of philosophy and knowledge.

Yet in addition to these concerns with measure and proportion in government and thought, Rousseau is a master in at least two other supplementally related discourses. One is a discourse of Nature, in which knowledge, intelligence, and authority shift to a human basis. (The issue of what kind of authority should be the basis of educational, romantic, and cultural decisions is at the heart of *Emile* and *La nouvelle Héloïse.*) And Rousseau follows up his fictive-discursive attempts to formulate a human-based, intuition-guided epistemology and ethics with the only kind of discourse that can result from such an enterprise, namely, the discourse of bad faith articulated so memorably in *The Confessions.* If knowledge of good and evil ultimately arises from faculties and intuitions that emanate from "within," and if we all continue to make mistakes, which we do, then it is bad faith, whose terms Rousseau so tellingly sets forth in *The Confessions,* that plays such a central role in human consciousness. We may define this bad faith as human knowledge's failure to satisfy its own stipulations; as the unavoidable *décalage* between what we know and what we do.

Rousseau is best remembered for his discursive explorations and for his admonitions regarding the diversion of human institutions from their sources in human nature. Yet the scenario of bad faith is inseparable from the seemingly constructive languages of proportionality and Nature. Pure consciousness and the "beautiful soul" are as short-lived in Rousseau as they are in Hegel: bad faith and the lurid experience and experimentation that inspire it are endemic to the expansive world that has severed its ties to a priori moral certitude.

This package of three related but very different discourses gives Rousseau's work a highly distinctive feeling: paeans to Nature and efforts to further its interests in education, diet, clothing, and so on; dramatizations, in fiction and discursive prose, of the tragedies inherent to human romantic life, except when the ideal collusion between desire, education, and an approving society arises; speculations, as we have seen, regarding the ideal demographics and proportions of government; and the unmasking of the inevitable self-delusions that arise when human beings presume to specify their own criteria of judgment. (The Rousseauan sensitivity to rhetoric and its displacements comes to the fore in his examinations of bad faith, which is, quintessentially, a rhetorical situation, in which language "knows" more than the mind can allow itself to apprehend. This is not to say that Rousseau's other discursive projects are free of rhetoric. Surely Rousseau deploys rhetoric to the same degree when he posits relations of sameness, difference, and proportion; and when he appeals to the inherent adequacy of human nature. But the Lacanian *misrecognition*[5] that is systematic throughout bad faith gives the Rousseauan discourse of confession a particular rhetorical nuance and intensity.)[6]

These discourses in Rousseau are all quite different, but they arise out of the same heady atmosphere in which human beings take responsibility for epistemological, social, and even environmental affairs to a hitherto unprecedented degree. *Jouissance* defines the situation in which people can generate their own criteria for sexual coming of age and marriage; when inbred intuitions can solve moral quandaries better than can extrinsic theological or perhaps political creeds. Yet it may be, in different ways, that concern for proportions in government and the cognitive faculties, and the compulsion to admit the fruits of bad faith, comprise defensive measures necessary to restrain *jouissance* lest it overwhelm all propriety and limit.

The same questions come into play when we ask how Melville could have followed *Moby-Dick,* his greatest tribute to and exploration of the sublime, with the domestic travesty of *Pierre* (not that the latter work lacks sublime dimensions). Melville's own "dialogic" response to a novel celebrating the vastness of our planet's oceans, the magnificence of its whales, and the enterprise of hunting them is *Pierre,* in one of its dimensions an exploration of the structurally inbred treacheries within (and outside) domestically sanctioned marriage. We know that Melville wrote this novel in a conventional romantic vein in part to "penetrate" the sizeable female reading market. I am speaking on a very general level here, but I would argue that the domestic melodrama of *Pierre* is also a counterweight that Melville finds necessary in his milieu—precisely to the joyous expansion that might otherwise madden the culture of his day.

I will graft one additional major artifact of the era to this framework, an artwork so monumental as to become a cultural icon of the predicaments of subjectivity and the possibilities of aesthetic production for its age: Goethe's *Faust.* Expansion, in this cultural artifact of multifaceted significance, proceeds in a direction opposite to the sequence that leads from *Moby-Dick* to *Pierre,* specifically, from the existential drama of desire, seduction, freedom from ethical constraint, and the emergence of "empirical" negative consequences in *Faust I* to a phantasmatic repetition of the major aesthetic and ethical issues rehearsed in the base-drama but set in a temporally uncertain domain of sublime expansion. The stages for the action of *Faust II* are nothing less than a "Spacious Hall," the "Upper Peneios," "The Inlets of the Aegean Sea," the "High Mountains," and "In the Foothills," among others.[7] So much a staple of European culture is *Faust I* already, so obvious are its existential outcomes, that we could argue *its* relative dearth of dramatic plot, in the sense of outcome-uncertainty. In this light, *Faust II* can be typecast as a sublime masque or spectacle, or choral poem, as opposed to a dramatic artwork. Crucial to its effectiveness as a fresco of the individual and collective predicaments of the moment in European culture is the enormous setting that its issues and questions have occupied.

The responses of both Rousseau and Melville—in the context of unprecedented human systematic capability, one encompassing speculative, technological, scientific, and administrative dimensions—are reminiscent of Kant's metaphoric act of "clipping the wings" of the artist-as-genius whom *The Critique of Judgment* has, only "an instant before," fully empowered (*CJ,* 163). Kant adds understanding, judgment, and taste to the baggage that the artist has to carry. These additional interests weigh down the intuition that is the artist's mark of distinction, lest the artist, like the mad geniuses and psychopathic authority figures of Hollywood, "take flight" in his own direction, not for the good of the *sensus communis;* lest the artist become a version of "bad writing," or decadent ornament for its own sake.[8]

The prominent thinkers and writers of the late-Enlightenment-Romantic age thus play a game of "fort-da" with the unprecedented human power and centrality that they appropriate. With an imperialistic, missionary fervor, they claim every right and power they can for the human (and the subjective); yet within range of this usurpation, they divest enough of this liberty to achieve a certain reassurance. The need to *deny* a certain degree of liberty that has already been won constitutes a complex move on rhetorical, psychosocial, and cultural levels.

One way of defining the project of the Romantic fragment is as the enterprise which, by focusing only on language's (and humanity's) concentration, play, and resistance to overarching schemata, successfully avoided the systematic aporias outlined immediately above. By leaving so much unstated in the margins *around* the fragment, the Romantic masters of this discourse bypassed the conceptual "bad faith" involved in the vacillation between the power of the aphoristic kernel and the rationalization furnished by the systematic surround. Yet the Romantic fragment's "purity" only elides the systematic bad faith taking place everywhere around it, in the rhythm between the usurpation of unprecedented human power and centrality and a cautionary divestment of this power, no doubt prompted by a certain collective vertigo, indigestion, or nausea.

～

"The passing from the state of nature to the civil society produces a remarkable change in man," writes Rousseau near the outset of *The Social Contract* (*SC*, 64).[9] Indeed, contraction—shrinkage, reining in—may be an exemplary way of characterizing this remarkable change.[10] The notion of the contract that Rousseau elaborates is not limited to the carrying out (or carrying with) of mutual pledges and obligations; it includes a transition to small scale, an acceptance of restraint, presumably in the *gain,* the interest of something. "Since men cannot create [*engendrer*] new forces, but merely combine and control [*unir et diriger*] those which already exist, the only way in which they can preserve themselves is by uniting their separate powers [*de former par agrégation*] in a combination [*somme*] strong enough to overcome any resistance, uniting them so that their powers are directed by a single motive and act in concert" (*SC,* 59–60). This sentence is itself a remarkable machine, beginning in the physics of the conservation of energy and ending in the mathematics of a stochastic augmentation of force through unity. The calculus of social contraction produces liberty through voluntary subjection; the enlargement of power through finitude; "Freedom is slavery" (Orwell).[11]

The rhetorical correlative to the contraction at the basis of the social contract is the maxim, the bare-bones fragmentary statement that is so self-contained that it is autonomous of its context. By Rousseau's day, the maxim occupies a significant place in the history of French letters; Rousseau's discourse abounds with examples. Within the pedagogical scenario of *Emile*, these take on the quality of moral teachings, furnishing an interesting contrast to the Rousseau of spontaneity and repulsion toward arbitrary restraint. The maxims of *The Social Contract* are often paradoxical, and assume the logical form of aporias. Where Rousseau's discourse summons itself to utterly compressed, definitive truths, it capitulates to the same bipolar apperception with which the empirical discerns the Transcendental in Kant: "Man was born free, and he is everywhere in chains [*dans les fers*]" (*SC*, 49). "Since each man gives himself to all, he gives himself to no one [*à personne*]" (*SC*, 61). "Whoever refuses to obey the general will shall be constrained to do so by the whole body, which means nothing other than that he shall be forced to be free" (*SC*, 64). "There is no man so bad that he cannot be made good for something" (*SC*, 79). "The constant will of all the members of the state is the general will; it is through it that they are citizens and free" (*SC*, 153). Most curiously, the fragmentary compression epitomizing—for a range of writers including the Schlegels, Kierkegaard, and Wordsworth—the *freedom* of aesthetic invention, in Rousseau's parlance becomes a rationalization for submission to the general will. One could indeed argue that the political maxim in Rousseau, the speech-act of social contraction, constitutes a rhetorical illustration of Kant's Fourth Antinomy: "*Thesis:* There belongs to the world, either as its part or as its cause, a being that is absolutely necessary. *Antithesis:* An absolutely necessary being nowhere exists in the world, nor does it exist outside the world as its cause" (*CPR*, 415).

The political interpretation of Rousseau has been polarized between "liberal" and "reactionary" camps, this depending on whether the emphasis in the social contract's fundamental trade-off—power for individuality—falls upon the former or the latter quantity. In different ways, Nietzsche and Freud sound an alarm at the repression implicit in this contraction. For Nietzsche, the tribe of Rousseau's noble savages is a prototype for the moralistic masses who have become insensible to creativity and intolerant to transcendental ethics. The Rousseauan social contract is a pre-Freudian repressive situation the bedrock of "civilization and its discontents."

The subjection of singularity to unity augments freedom and power, but only within the framework of the bipolar logic institutionalized by modern theology and crowned by the Kantian antinomies, the only tangible medium through which we discern the Transcendental Illusion. Rousseau frames the contraction of human powers and pretensions in modernity within the format of a balance sheet, but this amiable proportionality does not mask the fact that his logic has yoked expansion to contraction; the gigantic to the miniature; the macrocosm to the microcosm; Brobdignag to Lilliput. "The road of excess leads to the palace of Wisdom," wrote William Blake. "Just as nature has set bounds [*a donné des termes*] to the stature of a well-formed man, outside which he is either a giant or a dwarf, so, in what concerns the constitution of a state, there are limits [*bornes*] to the size it can have if it is to be neither too large to be well-governed nor too small to maintain itself" (Rousseau, *SC,* II, chap. 9, 90). The stipulations of the social contract are in the interest of securing anthropocentric control within the social and speculative sciences through the renunciation (sublimation? repression?) of human violence. The ease with which Rousseau attaches gigantism to minute control contributes to an uneasy sense that cultivation and civility are at all times in close proximity to gigantism and violence.

The balance sheet of the civilization that the clauses of the social contract condition and demarcate reads as follows:

> Suppose we draw up a balance sheet, so that the losses and gains may be readily compared. What man loses by the social contract is his natural liberty and the absolute [*illimité*] right to anything that tempts him and that he can take; what he gains by the social contract is civil liberty and the legal right of property in what he possesses. If we are to avoid mistakes [*ne pas se tromper*] in weighing the one side against the other, we must clearly distinguish between *natural* liberty, which has no limit but the physical power of the individual concerned, and *civil* liberty, which is limited by the general will; and we must distinguish also between *possession,* which is based only on force or "the right of the first occupant," and *property,* which must rest on a legal title [*titre positif*]. (*SC,* 65)

Rousseau's social contract is a tabulated matrix of compromise, illustrative in all dimensions of the uncanny collusion between expansion and contraction, whose mechanisms include psychoanalytical sublimation, rhetorical substitution, and deconstructive supplementarity. In the above passage, Rousseau assumes the guise of the (psychoanalytical) "good-enough" father: although not yet Emile's stringent but empathic tutor, he affects a "weaning" of the hypothetical human subject from the "hallucinations" of unlimited freedom and possession through a bargain in which civil liberty substitutes for natural freedom and property for possession. The underlying mathematical "formula" (*SC,* 62) that enables this logic to operate is that once the reduced scale of civilized life is a *fait accompli,* the protections attending civil liberties and property rights do constitute an expansion of what might otherwise be the case. The imposition of limit can constitute an enlargement of possibility, once civilization is defined as repression and the thrust of this teleological scenario is seen as inevitable.

The above passage, as an instance of the ratios and formulae that abound throughout *The Social Contract,* explains how this work could serve as a major precursor to Michel Foucault's characterization of Europe-based knowledge in the seventeenth and eighteenth centuries in terms of proportionality, tabulation, and visibility:

> Resemblance, which had for long been the fundamental category of knowledge—both the form and content of what we know—became dissociated in an analysis based on terms of identity and difference; moreover, whether indirectly . . . or directly . . . comparison became a function of order; and, lastly, comparison ceased to fulfil the function of revealing how the world is ordered, since it was now accomplished by the order laid down by thought, progressing naturally from the simple to the complex. As a result, an entire *épistème* of Western culture found its fundamental arrangements modified. (*OT,* 54) [12]

> The activity of the mind . . . will therefore no longer consist in *drawing things together,* in setting out on a quest for everything that might reveal some sort of kinship, attraction, or secretly shared nature within them, but, on the contrary, in *discriminating,* that is, in establishing their identities, then the inevitability of the connections with all the successive degrees of a series. In this case, discrimination imposes upon comparison the primary and fundamental investigation of difference: providing oneself by intuition with a distinct representation of things, and apprehending clearly the inevitable connection between one element in a series and that which inevitably follows it. (*OT,* 55)

Looking ahead toward the classical *épistème* to which Rousseau's work remains a distinctive contribution, Foucault chronicles an archaeological moment in which resemblances and similitudes, and the comparisons that constitute them, have become an inadequate basis for knowledge. (Or rather: when the knowledge generated by comparisons no longer satisfies the questions that science and experience generate.) Discrimination, not comparison, becomes the intellectual activity that powers the "classical age," the Europe-based seventeenth and eighteenth centuries, on to its signature achievements.

With an unwavering commitment to *mathesis* and *taxinomia,* to measurement and definition, and the orders that emerge from these operations, Foucault's classical age goes on to perform wonders in the gathering, organization, classification, categorization, storage, comparison, and condensation of knowledge. The age will eventually even take its chance with monstrosities and lapses in nature with which there is no comparison; but its efforts all transpire under the aegis of a commitment to measurement, order, and proportion: "All Classical knowledge, in its most general form, maintains with the *mathesis,* understood as a universal science of measurement and order" (*OT,* 56).

> The fundamental element of the Classical *épistème* is neither the success or failure of mechanism, nor the right to mathematicize or the impossibility of mathematicizing nature, but rather a link with the mathesis which, until the end of the eighteenth century, remains constant and unaltered. . . . This relation to *Order* is as essential to the Classical age as the relation to *Interpretation* was to the Renaissance. (*OT,* 57)

Foucault's classical age stands at the center of his tripartite epistemological account of what I have been calling the broader modernity. In Foucault's world, knowledge is constituted less by historical happenstance, technology, social and material conditions, and the like, than by prevalent modes of interpretation. In the passages on comparison and discrimination above, a "baseline" age, roughly corresponding to the Renaissance, in which knowledge stands on a series of parallelisms between the mutable and transcendental worlds, is about to be supplanted by an age whose epistemological practices revolve around structures and bespeak structuralism. Foucault characterizes the modernity that will supplant this classicism by its fascination with the forces—labor, life, the unconscious—that elude the organizationally and structurally meticulous instruments of knowledge generated during the seventeenth and eighteenth centuries. Three interpretive practices thus parallel and confront each other—naive allegory, structuralism, and linguistically sensitive exegesis—as Foucault archaeologically chronicles the transition between the ages that they exemplify—the Renaissance, the classical age, and his modernity (the nineteenth and twentieth centuries).[13]

The age responsible for producing both the primary organizational principles of knowledge and the framework on which Foucault's own study is arranged is, as stated above, the classical. It can be argued that the structuralist procedure at the heart of this age is itself a crucial but occasional and by no means exclusive protocol within the menu of exegetical practices that we still deploy on an ongoing basis. "The centre of knowledge, in the seventeenth and eighteenth centuries, is the *table*" (*OT,* 75). Again:

> The Classical age gives history quite a different meaning. . . . The documents of this new history are not other words, texts or records, but unencumbered spaces in which things are juxtaposed: herbariums, collections, gardens; the locus of this history is a non-temporal rectangle in which, stripped of all commentary, of all enveloping language, creatures present themselves one

beside another, their surfaces visible, grouped according to their common features, and thus already virtually analyzed, and bearers of nothing but their own individual names. (*OT,* 131)

Foucault's understanding of the table, with its implicit emphasis on the visual, as the paradigmatic knowledge-generator of the classical age constitutes one of the archaeological and theoretical triumphs of *The Order of Things.*

As extrapolated from crucial seventeenth- and eighteenth-century artifacts and as characterized by Foucault, the classical table is a structuralist machine. Structures are at once the table's raw materials, constitutive parts, and end products.

> To observe, then, is to be content with seeing—with seeing a few things systematically. . . . Visual representations will now at last be able to provide natural history with what constitutes its proper object. . . . This object is the extension of which all natural beings are constituted—an extension that may be affected by four variables. And by four variables only: the form of the elements, the quantity of those elements, the manner in which they are distributed in space in relation to each other, and the relative magnitude of each element. . . . These four variables, which can be applied in the same way to the five parts of the plant—roots, stem, leaves, flowers, fruits—specify the extension available to representation well enough for us to articulate it into a description acceptable to everyone: confronted with the same individual entity, everyone will be able to give the same description; and, inversely, given such a description everyone will be able to recognize the individual entities that correspond to it. In this fundamental articulation of the visible, the first confrontation of language and things can now be established in a manner that excludes all uncertainty.
>
> Each visibly distinct part of a plant or an animal is thus describable in so far as four sets of values are applicable to it. These four values affecting, and determining, any given element or organ are what botanists term its *structure.* (*OT,* 134)

Uncertainty can be eliminated from the "confrontation of language and things" (*OT,* 134) through the application of common values to the object of scrutiny and the comparison of different objects on the basis of these values. Nowhere is Foucault's understanding of classical epistemology more lucid than in his analysis of natural history during this period. But the procedures that he discerns underlying the naming, classification, and ordering of plants and animals during this age also apply to political economy and linguistics, the other two areas of "fieldwork" that he pursues from the Renaissance through the more recent modernity as the basis for his epistemological generalizations. The object of scrutiny is analyzed into its structures on the basis of their form, their quantity, the manner of their distribution, and their relative magnitude. Each object (in natural history, each plant or animal) as a compendium of structures can be compared with any other entity incorporating the same structures. The result of the analysis will be a vast map, broken into the broadest groupings possible, in which space will be made for every variation upon the structure, and in which values of magnitude will be placed in a graduated order:

> By virtue of structure, the great proliferation of beings occupying the surface of the globe is able to enter both into the sequence of a descriptive language and into the field of a mathesis that would also be a general science of order. And this constituent relation, complex as it is, is established within the apparent simplicity of a *description of the visible*. . . . The plant and animal are seen not so much in their organic unity as by the visual patterning of their organs. They are paws and hoofs, flowers and fruits, before being respiratory systems or internal liquids. Natural history traverses an area of visible, simultaneous, concomitant variables, without any internal relation of subordination or organization. (*OT,* 136–37)

Rousseau's concern in *The Social Contract* with the optimal organization of government, and with the proper magnitude, power, and interface between its constitutive elements, is very much in the spirit of his classical heritage, as Foucault has defined it. His interest in the local particularities of a given situation (what Derrida, in reference to Rousseau's *Essay on the Origin of Languages,* terms its local difference) [14] and in the organic interrelation of the composite of governmental offices and agencies foreshadows the interests of Foucauldian modernity. In supplementary fashion, Rousseau intertwines organic, developmental scenarios for government and statehood with specifications regarding scale and proportion of a far more classical hue. In this sense, Rousseau already resists the state he is in the act of (conceptually) founding; the "inalienable," human-originated liberty he extols has, before the fact, been measured out in mathematical—that is, a priori—quantities and proportions.

On the one hand, the state is an architectural construction, inorganic, subject to foregone conditions of scale and materials. "Just as an architect who puts up a large building first surveys and tests the ground to see if it can bear the weight, so the wise lawgiver begins not by laying down laws good in themselves, but by finding out whether the people for whom the laws are intended is able to support them" (*SC,* 88). Here, the "wise lawgiver" (a cousin, as we shall see, to the Kantian "original genius") is reluctant to impose a priori laws ("in themselves"—*an sich*) before testing the people, the organic party in the state partnership. Yet Rousseau cannot entirely dispel the impersonal architecture from his scenario of human-originated governmental self-regulation. In the chapter following his architectural metaphor, he specifies: "A state if it is to have strength must give itself some solid foundation, so that it can resist the shocks it is bound to experience and sustain the exertions that it must make to preserve itself" (SC, 92). Rousseau's hovering between an inert *mathesis* of law and government and an organicist rhetoric of immanence, development, and expansion is fully evident in this sentence: Rousseau appeals to a "solid foundation" to support a homeostatic system of governmental self-regulation.

Although Rousseau eschews "the exact mathematical proportion" (SC, 93) between territory and people, he nonetheless bases his metaphoric projection of optimal government on mathematical representations:

> There are two ways of measuring a body politic, by the extent of its territory and by the number of its people; and there must be a certain balance between these two dimensions if the state is to achieve its best size [*véritable grandeur*]. Men make the state and the soil nourishes men; thus the right balance demands that there be land enough to feed the inhabitants. . . . It is in this proportion that the maximum strength of a given number of persons is brought forth; for if there is too much territory, care of it is burdensome, cultivation inadequate and produce excessive . . . while if, on the other hand, there is too little land, the state must live on what it can import at the discretion of its neighbors, and this soon becomes the cause of offensive wars. (SC, 93)

Even while "the soil nourishes men" a preordained mathematical proportionality exists between territory and population. In the very next paragraph, Rousseau insists on the impact of local differences—"the different characteristics of different places, different degrees of fertility, in the nature of produce, in the effects of climate" (SC, 93) upon this formula. But the Rousseauan governmental *mathesis* persists throughout the treatise with a life of its own, as a simulacrum or the "artificial person" with which Chapter 4 of Book II begins (SC, 74)—as a counterweight from the sphere of quantity to the indeterminacies of human self-regulation and organic development. It is in utter reliance upon this mathematics that Rousseau can specify: "No one of these three terms [sovereign, government, state] can be changed without destroying the ratio. . . . Lastly, as there is only one geometrical mean between two extremes, there is only one good government possible for any state" (SC, 103). In this dictum, proper proportionality translates into exclusivity in the rectitude of governmental form. The *dénouement* of *The Social Contract* abounds in maxims on propriety, in its mathematical sense, in government, meaning in collective human self-regulation: "For a monarchy to be well governed, its size and extent ought to be proportionate to the talents of those who govern. . . . However small the state may be, princes are almost always inadequate" (*SC,* 119). "When the ratio of prince to sovereign is greater than that of people to prince—this lack of proportion has to be remedied by dividing the government" (*SC,* 123).

There is something mutually reinforcing here between the form of the maxim and its underlying rationale in mathematical formulations. A certain moral imperative ultimately rooted, as Kant would say, in quantitative intuitions saves the "inalienable rights" of individual and collective men from devolving into utter whimsy or madness. We have yet to explore the terms in which Rousseau articulates this unprecedented, because ignored, freedom. For now it must suffice to suggest the ongoing need for an underpinning in mathematical givens and moral imperatives to *coincide with* the expansive evolution of human solutions to human predicaments *from within.* This is not a question, as a somewhat naive reading of *The Order of Things* might suggest, of Rousseau's being able to dispense with an antiquated concern with *mathesis* and proportionality in favor of a new, organically constituted epistemological paradigm as he moves from eighteenth-century to Romantic concerns. Instead, I am arguing, throughout the Enlightenment-Romantic period, stringent mechanisms of self-regulation, some but not all mathematical, insinuate themselves in every instance of expansionism, collective transcendence, revolution.

The epistemology, then, of this late-Enlightenment-Romantic moment, poised between the classical table and the sublime potentials of organicism, finds itself confined to exasperating constraints. Knowledge and power must be human-originated, but still backed by some transcendental authority. In Foucauldian terms, man is about to assume (or resume) a position of centrality within the allocation of knowledge and authority; but relations of power and precedence maintain their ages-old vertical configuration: this because a man-centered regime still wants to claim an ineffable, absolute authority. The a priori, despite Kant's insistence on its human apperception and its emergence as the result of a deduction, persists as the orientation point of speculative systems. For Rousseau, the superiority of the Transcendental remains as a structure even where this projection has lost its cultural validity. His discourse is far from the brokerage between nuances of expression that are more singular or less so, a brokerage that will become characteristic of language-based conceptual systems. The discourse of *The Social Contract* still mediates between a superior domain of the Law, pictured as a vertically stratified layer, and the people. Rousseau implicitly posits a parallelism between the vertical configurations of political power and conceptual abstraction. Rousseau's lawgiver is a force *hors système,* a deus ex machina, who nonetheless aligns the sociopolitical system according to its internal, immanent authenticity. The lawgiver's authenticity is a function of his disinterest, his removal from the "loop" of self-aggrandizement. It requires an intervention from outside the system to express the system's most inherent, authentic nature. In this respect, Rousseau's lawgiver is a political correlative to Kant's "original genius," who, precisely by virtue of *his* communication with sublimity, the judgment system's *outside,* is able to restore the human faculties to their inherent "harmony":

> The lawgiver is, in every respect, an extraordinary man in the state. Extraordinary not only because of his genius, but equally because of his office [*emploi*], which is neither that of the government [*magistrature*] nor that of the sovereign. The office which gives the republic its constitution has no place in that constitution. It is a special and superior function which has nothing to do with empire over men; for just as he who has command over men must not have command over laws, neither must he who has command over laws have command over men; otherwise, the laws, being offspring [*ministres*] of the legislator's passions, would often merely perpetuate his injustices, and partial judgements would inevitably vitiate the sanctity of his works. (*SC,* 85)

"Giving" laws constitutes something of an exception, like the original genius's acuities, while it also defines an ongoing function in the state. Indeed, by foregone ratio, in which command and legislative purview are mutually exclusive, the lawgiver's position is defined by an extreme idealism abjuring interest in worldly negotiations.[15] The lawgiver exercises an exceptional influence *inside* the state because of his *marginal* status; he impacts upon the *artifice* of the state by virtue of something in his *nature.* This is the sense in which Rousseau can imagine citizens under the jurisdiction of the social contract in the condition of being *stripped naked.* "In a word each man must be stripped of his own powers [*qu'ils ôte à l'homme ses forces propres*], and given powers which are external to him" (*SC,* 85). The citizen, under the sublime inspiration of the lawgiver, loses one nature in order to gain another. The nature that he gains is akin to the one often celebrated in sculpture from Praxitiles on: the idealized nakedness that is a sublimation of the condition of being without one's clothes.

Rousseau's lawgiver joins the roster of bona fide Romantic Heroes—one that includes Kant's original genius, Goethe's Faust, P. B. Shelley's Prometheus, M. W. Shelley's Victor Frankenstein, E. T. A. Hoffmann's Nathanael, and Melville's Ahab—who do business with an ontologically superior realm at the same time that they comprise and initiate disruptions to the system of the Law itself. Dead-on in his intuition, marginal in his interest, naked in the substratum of the natural to which he retains a higher fidelity than the rest, the Rousseauan lawgiver is a sociopolitical counterpart to the artist of the broader modernity: he occupies an analogous position, but the contract to which he adheres is drafted in legal and administrative terms. From a position of natural but unprecedented freedom, he reaches toward an externality to the System that will purify, sanctify it from within; but he retains an onto-theological baggage and sublimity that hearkens from the very history, and system, that he would supplant. The margin from which the lawgiver emanates is the native land of the intellectual estate. Throughout the age that the Rousseauan lawgiver both exemplifies and initiates, the intellectual will renounce wealth and power in exchange for a certain credibility in enunciating ethical statutes in accordance with a higher (if not specifically religious) authority. The scenario of the lawgiver, with this figure's intuition, lack of political clout, and marginality, harbors within it the seeds of an exquisite and devastating martyrdom. Socrates, for one, pursued this martyrdom to its conclusion. It may be said as well that Rousseau, demonstrating an affinity with Blake, reinscribes the position of the biblical prophet within the parameters of the aesthetic contract of the broader modernity.

And what is the teacher, if not the actual lawgiver within the existential sphere? And what's in an education, in terms of that sector of the aesthetic contract that Rousseau is most willing to fill in? In Foucauldian terms, education will eventuate in a certain *discipline,* but in keeping with epistemological considerations, with the specifications of the prevailing aesthetic contract, Emile or Any-student's discipline will be born more of instinct and immanent predilections than restraint; it will be self-generated and self-directed as well as furnished from outside. Yet the constraints of moralism, the closure both substantively asserted and rhetorically dramatized by maxims, persists within the liberal education whose modern emanation *Emile* rehearses. *Emile* is a text whose ideology is distinctly at odds with its rhetorical performance. In this respect, it is the textual simulacrum of a highly conflicted and guilt-ridden modern self. *Emile*'s authoritative narrators preach liberality; its maxims and lessons perform restraint; through the text's increasingly complex allegory, one facet of its rhetorical performance belies another; moral adages bespeaking mythological closure in the Barthesian sense find themselves upstaged by progressive intricacy in the text's narrative framework. Through Rousseau, late-Enlightenment-Romantic liberality asserts its demands and censures; yet an infrastructure of restraint is already in place to measure the degree of liberation. *Emile* is in this sense a privileged environment for observing its age's "massive cultural reaction-formation."

Yet *Emile,* for all its a priori restraint, is quintessentially a *synthetic* text, effecting a merger between the analytic and the synthetic in Kant, and forming a bridge linking the classical and the modern in Foucault. *Emile* is configured by what I have elsewhere termed the superimposition of discourses and modes of subjectivity and rhetoric.[16] The parameters of its discourse, as in the varied cases of Goethe's *Wilhelm Meister* and Hegel's *The Phenomenology of Spirit,* are multiple and polymorphic.

What is the dimensionality of *Emile*? In exploring the parameters of its discourse we would do well to open seven interrelated files. *Emile* is a work of *sociopolitical* and *moral* theory; it is a conspicuously *literary* exercise, with up-to-date attention to its *rhetorico-linguistic* design, taking part in an overall *aesthetic* enterprise reaching its full conceptual force only in the Enlightenment. To the degree that *Emile* extrapolates the subject conditions of a historically specific or timebound hypothetical personage, it is inherently *psychological,* or in the literary world we would say *psychoanalytical,* in its purview. To the degree that *Emile* considers conceptual, moral, and psychological topoi on their own terms, it may claim, in the moment of its appearance, to join the body of *philosophy.* In order to write a work predicating education and indicative of his empowerment as a writer, Rousseau, in other words, had to craft a text opening up and coordinating sociopolitical, ethical, aesthetic, rhetorico-linguistic, psychological, philosophical, and literary dimensions. There is an expansive joy in the multiplicity of discourses whose requirements *Emile* satisfies. The works for which Rousseau is best remembered—*La nouvelle Héloïse, The Social Contract,* and *Emile*—appeared in quick succession (in 1761 and 1762). Through his unique writerly polymorphousness, Rousseau made a claim on the territories of human enterprise constituted by writing.

Indeed, *Emile* is powered by a versatility, a successive penetration of different discursive arenas on a scale with the prodigious freedom that Rousseau celebrates, delimits, and protects. The writer's license to expand on related topoi is tantamount to a liberty belonging to (and appropriated by) the intellectual estate, whose exemplar is the lawgiver. From the perspective of Rousseau's project, this liberty needs to be earned; it is not a given. Rousseau earns the discursive freedom that becomes a model for Emile's human-evolved prerogative and constraint by installing within his discourse the *features* of a multifaceted and evolving text. The features that implement the liberty that the expansive discourse of *Emile* would claim include the following: *Citations from the classics and modern "blockbusters":* These endow a literary environment with a pronouncedly historical mission. *A social-individual linkup or coordination:* This is no more than an analogy, really, but in Rousseau's discourse it acquires special force. In the West, this superimposition goes back to the emblematic explorations of character in Greek drama, in which agency and function are not sharply delineated. The character Emile is both a child and an exemplar of his times. His individual achievements and concerns at all times register the stages of his social involvement and participation. *A developmental scenario:* As the treatise extends itself, its title character ages; as he ages, he becomes wiser. What is education itself if not the fusion of a certain cognitive development with a certain ethical development? This temporization of human experience and capacity has roots deep in the empiricist project; it furnishes a precedent as well for the narrative framework of Hegel's *The Phenomenology of Spirit.* The Hegelian text, however, as a primarily speculative work, does not allow for characters, except the very occasional emblematic one such as Antigone, and it relegates nature to a single phase of consciousness and sociopolitical organization. One implication of *Emile's* developmental scenario is that subsequent stages increase in length as the title character encounters considerations of increasing abstraction and moral complexity. There is thus *a linkage between developmental growth and moral complexity. Emile,* then, in keeping with both the unprecedented writerly liberty that it embodies and its own systematic aspirations, demands *a hybrid discourse of mixed media* consisting, at least, of classical and modern literary sources; conceptual-philosophical deliberation; rhetorical demonstration; novelistic characterization and development; psychological inference and commentary; sociopolitical theory; and moral preoccupation. The writerly correlative to Rousseau's Enlightenment freedom consists in his ability to operate and pass freely between these generic prototypes. The illustrations incorporated into the text's earliest editions open a pictorial dimension to the text. The freedom that Rousseau both exercises and constrains (the latter in the interest of *good education*) thus directly implicates a full exploitation of the resources implicit in the book medium.

It is impossible to imagine education without development. As *Emile* elaborates itself, its literary and rhetorical performance increases in complexity, so that by Book IV, we find moral maxims implanted into narrative; staged dramatic dialogues; and such a long, complicated, and pivotal digression as the "Profession of Faith of the Savoyard Vicar." An evolution of rhetorical and generic forms parallels Emile's hypothetical growth from infancy to childhood, yet a rhetorical "education" cannot become complex in any simply incremental way. The writerly growth paralleling the transition from childhood to youth to adulthood consists in exercising the *liberty* to jump laterally across an inclusive palette of literary genres and discursive modes.

Which brings us to nature, the metaphoric zero-point of the endeavor, akin to the simplicity with which empiricists begin their disputations. Nature may well occupy in *Emile* the place assigned to God in Descartes's *Discourse on Method* and *Meditations,* that is, the role of a (by no means simple) "black box" or fudge factor. Rousseau often ascribes a simplicity to nature, but this fundamentality is akin to the one that supposedly prevails between individuals and their mothers, a relation by no means free of its complexities. The centrality of Rousseauan nature does not consist in its simplicity, which often is not the case, but in its service as a hypothetical zero-point for all developmental models and in the multiplicity of situations in which natural "benefice" is involved. Yet through its ongoing invocation, nature does acquire some general semantic content on a thematic level. And here Rousseau can take some responsibility for inventing what corresponds to a Romantic abhorrence of cities and institutions: an idealization of the simple life, packaged as a commodity, that has prevailed ever since. The desirability of natural foods and flights into "nature" (outfitted by L.L. Bean and Eastern Mountain Sports) is the construct of a conscience-stricken meditation on liberty in which any possible release from constraints must be presanctified by transcendental values.

The education that is *Emile*'s broadest subject "comes to us from nature or from men or from things" (E, 38).[17] Education is the supplemental second nature that serves a function for people analogous to that which horticulture does for plants: "Plants are shaped by cultivation, and men by education" (E, 38). Yet much as *Emile* is conditioned by a merger-fantasy either with the Mother to whom it is lovingly dedicated (E, 37–38) or the Nature which is the ultimate rubric or prototype for nurturing, from the outset of the treatise neither nature nor education can claim the simplicity with which it is conventionally associated. The pupil of the modern age "is thus formed by three kinds of masters" (E, 38)—nature, people, and objects—and thus receives "three different educations" (E, 38). So too is Emile, the subject of education, Rousseau's generic name for the epistemological child of his times, sundered—in the tradition of Hamlet, baroque Benjaminian melancholics in general, and Michael Kohlhaas—among multiple and conflicting sources of authority. Even while Emile, as education's child, moving toward symbiosis with the second nature, if not the first, would seem the least susceptible to conflict and splitting of all the examples mentioned.

We see from the outset that, conceptually speaking, Rousseauan nature is inherently divided and fragmented: there is the first nature of phenomena and the second nature of education. Yet in terms of the explicit ideology that Rousseau feels empowered to advance as a lawgiver, nature is an inalienable substratum, an origin of human essence that orients productive human enterprises and delimits the possibility and value of artifice, cultivation, and representation. While counterposed to artifice, nature nonetheless serves as a base and point of orientation against which to measure human institutions and enterprises. These are accorded legitimacy within the Rousseauan ideology to the degree that they manage to preserve within themselves, in the manner of the Hegelian *Aufhebung,* an adequate degree and authenticity of nature. It is no accident that recent critics hover in their political assessment of Rousseau as a liberal or a conservative: the Rousseauan ideology is inherently conservative in its recourse to a substratum of human essence; it is liberal in its identification of this substratum as the uncultivated, unfettered, and inalienable. From the outset of *Emile,* Rousseau intertwines the vicissitudes of (human) nature and education:

> Therefore, when education becomes an art, it is almost impossible for it to succeed, since the conjunction of the elements necessary for its success is in no one's control. All that one can do by dint of care is to come more or less close to the goal, but to reach it requires luck.
> What is that goal? It is the very same as that of nature. . . . But perhaps this word *nature* has too vague a sense. An attempt must be made here to settle on its meaning.
> Nature, we are told, is only habit. What does that mean? Are there not habits contracted only by force which never do stifle nature [*qui n'étouffent jamais la nature*]? Such, for example, is the habit of the plants whose vertical inclination is interfered with. The plant, set free, keeps the inclination it was forced to take. . . . The case is the same for men's inclinations. So long as one remains in the same condition, the inclinations which result from habit and are the least natural to us can be kept; but as soon as the situation changes, habit ceases and the natural returns. Education is certainly only habit. Now are there not people who forget and lose their education? Others who keep it? . . . If the name *nature* were limited [*borner*] to habits conformable to nature, we would spare ourselves this garble. (*E,* 38–39)

The dialectic of nature and habit is a complicated one indeed. Rousseauan education is tantamount to a reconciliation with one's *natural* inclinations. Education is as much an archaeological excavation *beneath* secondary, acquired habits as it is the annexation of something new, additional, not present at birth. Rousseauan education, according to analogic connections in the above passage, will restore natural tendencies as a plant, liberated from artificial bracings, will return to its proper inclinations, the postures of its inbred heliotropism.

Such formulations play havoc with identifications of primacy, secondarity, and supplementarity. In these terms, education is a supplement restoring the true primacy of the primary. The true service of education, as the secondary, the human supplement to nature, is to the primary, nature. The given condition of humanity (in effect, the human "presenting complaint"), which might appear to be primary, amounts to an aberration, a distortion effect in urgent need of correction. So nature, within the educational field defined by Rousseau, quickly moves from obscured, abjected origin to restorational supplement, medicinal cure. But Rousseau's orientation to a nature, a zero-point, a ground, within a human nature, or a nature defined as a manifold of ongoing human traits, never wavers.

The essentialism inherent in Rousseau's educational theory demands, at least in certain situations, that (human) nature be situated at the level of sensation, what Hegel terms "sensible certitude" (*sinnliche Gewissheit*), and that higher levels of cognitive function such as reflection and judgment involve the corruption and possible degeneration of the natural givens. Judgment and reason, the very faculties whose care is given over to the educational process, become the sources of cognitive derangement and moral corruption. This is precisely what happens as Rousseau's meditation on nature's relation to education continues:

> We are born with the use of our senses [*sensibles*], and from our birth we are affected in various ways by the objects surrounding us. As soon as we have, so to speak, consciousness of our sensations, we are disposed to seek or avoid the objects which produce them, at first according to whether they are pleasant or unpleasant to us, then according to the conformity or lack of it that we find between ourselves and these objects, and finally according to the judgments we make about them [*nous en portons*] on the basis of the happiness or of perfection given us by reason. These disputations [*dispositions*] are extended and strengthened as we become more capable of using our senses and more enlightened; but constrained by our habits, they are more or less corrupted by our opinions. Before this corruption they are what I call in us *nature*.
>
> It is, then, to these original [*primitives*] dispositions that everything must be related; and that could be done if our three educations were only different from one another. (*E*, 39)

Habit, the product of our educations, corrupts; the continuation of our individual dispositions, above all in the form of sensation, might spare us the delusion and the corruption. In quasi-Hegelian fashion, sensation evolves into "consciousness of our sensations," and at an even higher level of function, into reason. To the degree that we can preserve, in the fashion of *Aufhebung*, a *sensibility* in the judgments that involve the higher functions of reason, these judgments will be valid. In Manichaean fashion, the basic disputations through which we work out our ethical stances and social attitudes are suspended between sensation and habits, between primary and secondary, between the Derridean origin and supplement. Rousseau's pronounced fidelity to a substratum of human nature as the orientation of all inclinations and enterprises is in keeping with the treatise's original and melodramatic dedication to "Maman" (*E*, 37–38).

From the outset of *Emile* Rousseau has specified the tripartite source of education, "from nature or from men or from things" (*E*, 38). The subject of educational cultivation, like her *semblables* over the span of the broader modernity, is suspended between multiple and incongruous sources of authority at odds with each other. Education leaves in its wake a unifying, homogenizing effect, setting its subject off from the multiplicity of sensations and individuals acting strictly on their own behalf; it eventuates at the cohesion of ethics and altruism, the ideology of voluntary renunciation at the heart of the social contract. The trajectory of education that Rousseau formulates early in *Emile* leads from an inherently divisive Nature (nature for an instant turned bad) to the paradox of voluntary self-renunciation and restraint that occupies so much of the discursive terrain in *The Social Contract*:

> Every particular [*partielle*] society, when it is narrow and unified, is estranged from the all-encompassing society. Every patriot is harsh to foreigners. They are only men. They are nothing in his eyes. This is a drawback, inevitable but not compelling. The essential thing is to be good to the people with whom one lives. . . .
>
> Natural man is entirely for himself. He is numerical unity, the absolute whole which is relative only to itself or its kind. Civil man is only a fractional unity dependent on the denominator; his value is determined by his relation to the whole, which is the social body. Good social institutions are those that best know how to denature man, to take his absolute existence from him in order to give him a relative one and transport the *I* into the common unity, with the result that each individual believes himself no longer one but part of the unity and no longer feels except within the whole. (*E*, 39–40)

Natural man is a *Ding an sich* in search of a denominator, a manifestation of irreducible singularity. Participation in the social contract is akin to the mathematical search for elective affinities or for factorial commonalities. Rousseau's characterization of this process is replete with ambivalence. The (hypothetically free-standing individual's) entrance into the community is a denaturing, a deprivation of the "absolute" Nature whose preservation in society is, in other contexts, so crucial. The ritual reenactment, in the West and other cultures, of this domestication or "downsizing" by the community may well be circumcision. Man is cut down to where he belongs to others, to where his nature is severed from its possibly dysfunctional singularity, to where the loss of his mathematical unity and uniqueness allows his membership in demographic sets. The symbolic renunciation of singularity is the pretext to society; yet the alienating Nature sacrificed in this process becomes in other contexts the definition of humanity. Thus in Rousseau does the Kantian artist, in the guise of "noble savage," undergo the "clipping" of his wings.

This drama of the betrayal and preservation of nature, of the loss and gain of social identity, is on a course toward tragedy. Mathematical thinker that he is, Rousseau sets out the eventualities in this calculus:

> He who in the civil order wants to preserve the primacy of the sentiments of nature does not know what he wants. Always in contradiction with himself, always floating between his inclinations and his duties, he will never be either man or citizen. . . . He will be one of these men of our days: a Frenchman, an Englishman, a bourgeois. He will be nothing.
>
> To be something, to be oneself and always one, a man must act as he speaks; he must always be decisive in making his choice, make it in a lofty style, and always stick to it. I am waiting to be shown this marvel so as to know whether he is a man or a citizen, or how he goes about being both at the same time.
>
> From these necessarily opposed objects come two contrary forms of instruction [d'institutions]—the one, public and common; the other, individual and domestic. (E, 40)

The two vertically configured strata of the fraction, the particular over the general, become the very structure of Rousseauan education. It is only the fraction, the particularity of the modern person, that can encompass both the tug of unprocessed nature and the mores of the social community. To the degree that Enlightenment culture underscores the individual's confrontation with her particularity-as-nature, every class member, bourgeois or otherwise, and every national will be, precisely, "nothing." Under these conditions, the task of public education becomes the filling in of this void or emptiness; "private" education, the promotion of individuality, goes on independently. Rousseauan education thus takes on the form of the implicit subject whose societal interactions it mediates, and the division into public and private registers that this implies.

Rousseau's recourse, however paradoxical it may be, to a Nature that is both a substratum and point of orientation for human endeavors carries with it a suspicion toward the artificial, the contrived, the tangential, and the extrinsic. Anyone who has read *Of Grammatology* understands the placement of the ideological ambivalence that could both appeal to education as a second and human nature and rail against pedagogical contrivance within Western culture's longstanding conflictedness with regard to the linguistic intractabilities that Derrida associates with writing. It is worthwhile to pause for a moment at the suspicions toward the extrinsic, the artificial, the urban, and the constrained in *Emile* both because these attitudes comprise fundaments within an encompassing liberal Enlightenment ideology and because they are so intimately intertwined with Rousseau's appeal to a Nature, however human its gauge may be.

The maxim is the rhetorical unit within the morality of Nature that pervades *Emile*. (It is also a discursive unit in the history of French letters, specifically that history coincident with a relatively free-ranging subject in need of memorable, compressed moral truisms.) It is no accident, then, that the text of *Emile*, particularly toward the beginning, is studded with maxims addressing the issues of freedom, cities, social institutions, and artificiality as they pertain to education:

The body must be vigorous in order to obey the soul. (*E*, 54)

A frail body weakens the soul. (*E*, 54)

It is especially in the first years of life that air acts on the constitution of children. . . . I prefer his going to breathe the good air of the country to her breathing the bad air of the city. (*E*, 59)

Cities are the abyss [*gouffre*] of the human species. At the end of a few generations the races perish or degenerate. They must be renewed. (*E*, 59)

Children's first sensations are purely affective. (*E*, 62)

The only habit that a child should be allowed is to contract none [*de n'en contracter aucune*]. (*E*, 63)

Unfailingly, a child whose body and arms are free will cry less than a child bound in swaddling [*dans un maillot*]. (*E*, 68)

In general, children are overdressed, especially during their early age. They should be hardened to cold rather than to heat. Very cold weather never indisposes them [*ne les incommode jamais*] if one lets them be exposed to it early. (*E*, 128)

Everything is only folly and contradiction in human institutions. (*E*, 82)

It follows from this that children's lies are all the work [*sont tous l'ouvrage*] of masters. (*E*, 102)

> Appearing to preach virtue to children, one makes them love all the vices.
> The vices are given to them by forbidding them to have them. Does one
> want to make them pious? (*E*, 103)

Dispersed as they are throughout the first half of *Emile,* these pronouncements are sutured together by several common strands. As suggested above,
their pointed rhetorical form goes hand in hand with their ethical decisiveness. These statements deploy formal and rhetorical compression, a simplicity
bespeaking the innocence of childhood, in the interest of resisting a variety of externally applied constraints, whether excessively tight clothing,
moralism itself, the close confines of cities, or the duplicity necessitated by
human institutions. All of these constraints violate an original unfetteredness
at the core of human nature. One could argue, of course, that maxims,
through their compression and decisiveness, reinstate, at the level of grammar and logic, precisely the constraint against which Rousseau ideologically
poses them.

The above compendium of extracted maxims begins with the aggravated
body-mind split that is, from the ages of Luther, Calvin, and Descartes on,
an existential zero-point; the optimal conditions that the narrator of *Emile*
wishes for his charge involve an amelioration, if not the abolition, of this
split. Childhood appears here as a temporary, fragile state of grace that needs
nurturing and protection itself; the fragility of the child becomes displaced to
his or her puerile state. Even where he argues for robust living and tolerance
for a wide range of climatic conditions, Rousseau ushers in the culture of
childhood as a state with special repercussions for the whole person and the
entire duration of existence. Childhood becomes a prototype for one's rapport with Nature, the degree to which Nature, as the optimal, preordained
substratum, persists within the individual. Corruption is tantamount to los-
ing one's Nature, to a failure within one's second nature, one's education, in
fostering the inclinations implicit within that primary heritage.

Constraint within a field of motion: artificiality plays this role in a scenario
of resources and materials. Indeed, Rousseau directs his first aphoristic salvo,
at the very outset of the body of his tract, against the artificial as the inherently profane: "Everything is good as it leaves the hands of the Author of
things; everything degenerates in the hands of man. . . . He turns everything
upside down; he disfigures everything; he loves deformity, monsters" (*E*, 37).
In keeping with a fidelity to the salutation inherent to the natural substratum,
the narrator of *Emile* lauds the virtues of natural products relatively free of
adulteration; he becomes an early proponent of "green" causes:

> My principle aim [*objet*] in teaching him to feel and to love the beautiful of all
> sorts [*dans tous les genres*] is to fix his affections and tastes on it, to prevent his

natural appetites from becoming corrupted, and to see to it that he does not one day seek in his riches the means for being happy—means that he ought to find nearer to him. (*E, 344*)

From this immense profusion of goods which cover the earth I would seek what is most agreeable to me and what I could best make use of. To that end, the first use of my riches would be to purchase leisure and freedom, to which I would add health, if it were for sale. . . .

I would always stay as close as possible to nature, in order to indulge the senses I received from nature—quite certain that the more nature contributed to my enjoyments, the more reality I would find in them. In choosing objects for imitation, I would always take nature as my model; in my appetites I would always give it preference; in my tastes I would always consult it; in foods I would always want those which are best prepared by nature and pass through the fewest hands before reaching our tables. I would prevent myself from becoming the victim of fraudulent adulterations by going out after pleasure myself. My foolish and coarse gluttony would not enrich an innkeeper. . . . My table would not be covered with a display of magnificent garbage and exotic carrion. . . .

For the same reason I would not imitate those who are never contented with where they are and thus always put the seasons in contradiction with one another and the climate in contradiction with the season. These are the people who seek summer in winter and winter in summer, who go to Italy when it is cold and go to the north when it is warm. . . . I would remain where I was, or I would take exactly the opposite course. I would want to extract from each season all that is agreeable in it. (*E, 345–46*)

Maxims of the natural life persist as Rousseau enters the utterly intangible domain of taste. In matters of preference, the attitudes of Nature are to hold sway. Nature is thus to dominate culture regardless of its signification in context; it is a point of reference as much as any particular meaning. Its function as a marker is substantially different from its (ideological or moral) *value.*

Nature stands available as the truest and best consultant in the occasions for judgment that pervade modern life. It is a universal and intrinsic "home reference work" at hand to serve us in our decisions regarding food, clothing, and other issues of consumption. Whether Nature serves Rousseau best as an *empirical* set of raw materials or as a culturally determined and varying *value,* the citizen is free to fluctuate between these two deployments of the term, so long as his orientation remains "natural." Of course, it is in matters of consumption where the ideological pretenses underlying the economy are stripped bare. Nature and home decor may at first seem strange bedfellows, yet Rousseau is a pioneer in establishing Nature as an arbiter of judgment in tangible matters, an attitude whose modernity has not yet been exhausted. Nature is humankind's original and hardwired Encyclopaedia Britannica, its original Sears catalogue:

In the setting of my table and the decorating of my dwelling, I would want to imitate the variety of the seasons with very simple ornaments and to extract all its delights from each season without anticipating the ones that will follow it. It takes effort—and not taste—to disturb the order of nature, to wring from it involuntary produce which it gives reluctantly and with its curse. Such produce has neither quality nor savor; it can neither nourish the stomach nor delight the palate. Nothing is more insipid than early fruits and vegetables. It is only at great expense that the rich man of Paris succeeds, with his stoves and hothouses, in having bad vegetables and bad fruits on his table the whole year round. If I could have cherries when it is freezing and amber-colored melons in the heart of winter, what pleasure would I take in them when my palate needs neither moistening nor cooling? . . .

In order to be well served, I would have few domestics. (*E,* 346)

Nature is above all a system that is both a *source* (of energy, inclinations) and an *education.* The tendency of this system (like ideological, epistemological, and political aspirations in Europe during this period) is expansive. There is ample space here for great and small, for matters of home decoration and for ultimate spiritual questions—even for God. The systematic thinkers of this particular age are the first structuralists. They experience and express a discernible joy at the iterability and near-universal applicability of the key tropes their systematic explorations unearth. Rousseau joins Hegel in this respect. Lest the Jean-Jacques Rousseau of *Emile* seem too pretentious for attributing such a grandiose scale of application to his own discourse, he introduces the figure of the Savoyard vicar as the text's "man" in a certain theological "Havana":

> Always remember that I am not teaching my sentiment; I am revealing it [*je l'expose*]. Whether matter is eternal or created, whether there is or is not a passive principle, it is in any event certain that the whole is one and proclaims a single [*unique*] intelligence. . . . This Being which wills and is powerful, this Being active in itself, this Being, whatever it may be, which moves the universe and orders all things, I call *God.* I join to this name the ideas of intelligence, power, and will which I have brought together, and that of goodness which is their necessary consequence. But I do not as a result know better the Being to which I have given them; it is hidden equally from my senses and my understanding. . . . I know that my existence is subordinated to its existence. . . . I perceive God everywhere in His works. I sense Him in me; I see Him all around me. But as soon as I want to contemplate Him in Himself, as soon as I want to find out where He is, what He is, what His substance is, He escapes me, and my clouded mind no longer perceives anything. (*E,* 277)

The vicar's supreme Being joins Kant's Transcendental and Hegel's Absolute Knowing as a version of a secular God. The manifestation here described by Rousseau still fits within the compass of the loving embrace endowed by

Nature. The vicar is on a sufficiently human scale to issue his "sentiment." This inner inclination he "reveals." In the quandary surrounding God in an antiecclesiastical Enlightenment setting, and within the framework of his educational treatise, Rousseau prefers to err on the side of caution: there may still be a certain utility in retaining God within the Universe. An enlightened clergyman, the Vicar disclaims intimate or detailed knowledge of God. He nonetheless retains God's strong possibility. In spite of the full narratological complexity of the interplay between Jean-Jacques and his textual surrogate, the Savoyard vicar, it appears that Rousseau has made provision at least for a Supreme Being. Yet no sooner are the parameters of divinity articulated than they are appropriated to people. The ultimate residence of divine attributes in *Emile* is within the subjects of a liberal Englightenment age:

> If man is active and free, he acts on his own. . . . The supreme enjoyment [*jouissance*] is in satisfaction with oneself; it is in order to deserve [*mériter*] this satisfaction that we are placed on earth and endowed with freedom, that we are tempted by the passions and restrained [*retenus*] by conscience. What more could divine power do for us? (*E,* 281)

Nowhere does Rousseau come to a more concise and modest formulation of the conditions of subjectivity during the broader modernity that begins with Luther, Calvin, and *Hamlet* and ends "one fine morning" with Joseph K.'s arrest.[18] There is the unprecedented freedom (and loneliness) arising with cities, a market economy, and the debunking of monarchal and ecclesiastical ideologies. Conscience in *Emile* becomes the Derridean guardrail preventing this freedom from coming to no good. Rousseau is pre-Freudian in understanding the repressive impact, within the psychological sphere, of conscience.[19] It is impossible to overestimate the importance of conscience in maintaining the good of social welfare during the age that, in different ways, Rousseau and Melville initiate. We should bear in mind the support that a construct of conscience has behind it at a moment of high systematic aspiration, one held in common by the likes of Rousseau, Kant, Hegel, and later, even by Freud. In this milieu, conscience is not only an ethical-social guardrail: it is a function within a more or less integral psychic or social economy. We can only begin to fathom the importance that conscience assumes in Western cultures as these systematic confidences founder. The dependable conscience elaborated by Rousseau metamorphoses itself into the vicious superego lording it over Kernberg's "subjective experience of emptiness":

> In continuing to follow [*suivant toujours*] my method, I do not draw these rules from the principles of a high philosophy, but find them written by nature with ineffaceable characters in the depth of my heart. I have only to

consult myself about what I want to do. Everything I sense to be good is
good; everything I sense to be bad is bad. The best of all casuists is the conscience; and it is only when one haggles with it that one has recourse to the
subleties of reasoning. The first of all cares is the care for oneself. Nevertheless how many times does the inner voice tell us that, in doing good at another's expense, we do wrong! We believe that we are following the impulse
of nature, but we are resisting it. In listening to what it says to our senses, we
despise what it says to our hearts; the active being obeys, the passive being
commands. Conscience is the voice of the soul; the passions are the voice of
the body. Is it surprising that these two languages often are contradictory?
And then which should be listened to? (*E, 286*)

Rousseau's scenario of conscience is fitted out with an apparatus that begins
to be familiar for the age initiated by Luther, Calvin, and *Hamlet*. The rules
of his method itself, within which conscience is one agency, are not extrinsic
and formal, deriving from "high philosophy" (*E, 286*). These rules constitute a hybrid communication transcending the conventional attitudinal differences directed at speech and writing. Conscience effects a synthesis between an immanent script "written by nature with ineffaceable characters in
the depth of my heart" (*E, 286*) and "the voice of the soul" (*E, 286*). In its
immanence and interiority, conscience can neutralize the alienation of writing and assume the intimacy of the most primitive introjections. Conscience
is the "voice of the soul" (*E, 286*) that can silence the immoderate demands
posed by our "passions . . . the voice of the body" (*E, 286*). Conscience
resolves this shouting-match spiritually. Martyrlike, it plays to an unappreci-
ative audience, which despises "what it says to our hearts" (*E, 286*). Conscience plays between the active and passive bearings of our activity. Its coordinates are the same ones that condition subjectivity in Plato's *Phaedrus* and
Luther's "The Freedom of a Christian." The conscience that Rousseau invokes is loving and gentle. It pricks our remorse, but in a maternal way. In
the passage below, Rousseau contrasts the conscience that is in accordance
with Nature to the implicitly masculine superego capable of inflicting severe
punishment in the Freudian, let alone Kernbergian, world:

We speak of the cry of remorse which in secret punishes hidden crimes and
so often brings them to light. Alas, who among us has ever heard this impor-
tunate voice? We speak from experience, and we would like to stifle this ty-
rannical sentiment that gives us so much torment. Let us obey nature. We
shall know with what gentleness it reigns. (*E, 288*)

There is in the depths of souls, then, an innate principle of justice and virtue
according to which, in spite of our own maxims, we judge our actions and
those of others as good or bad. It is to this principle that I give the name
conscience.

But at this word I hear the clamor of those who are allegedly wise rising on all sides: errors of childhood prejudices of education, they all cry in a chorus. Nothing exists in the human mind other than what is introduced by experience, and we judge a thing on no ground other than that of acquired ideas. They go farther. They dare to reject this evident and universal accord of all nations. And in the face of this striking uniformity in men's judgment, they go and look in the shadows for some obscure example known to them alone—as if all the inclinations of nature were annihilated by the depravity of a single people, and the species were no longer anything as soon as there are monsters. (*E*, 289)

Rousseau's invocation of a more or less universal conscience whose inherent gentleness would allow people, left to their own devices, collectively as well as individually, to be good—the pervasiveness of this conscience is in the spirit of those mathematical and aesthetic human capacities and apprehensions in Kant serving to confirm the ubiquitousness of the Transcendental. Conscience here is "innate," but "Nothing exists in the human mind other than what is introduced by experience" (*E*, 289). Quite noticeably, Rousseau is not in a position here to resolve the contradiction between a moral sense whose innateness is a function of its universality but that is also a social construct and hence, if in no other sense, *communally* arbitrary. He allows the contradiction in the overall endeavor of ascribing bad judgment to the secondary, the socially mediated, and, implicitly, the educational. Any goodness that humankind manages to produce arises in spite of the very educational contrivance that is the true subject of *Emile*.

Despite the gentleness and easy accessibility of conscience, real people persist in being outcasts from the United Nations that conscience, precisely *implicitly*, convenes. They do so in the context of a Rousseauan quest for origins and immediacy whose principles have been so meticulously elaborated by Jacques Derrida.

~~~~~

Do not attempt to imagine the charms and graces of that enchanting girl. You would not come near to the truth. Young virgins in the cloisters are not more fresh, seraglio beauties are not so sportive [*vives*], the houris of paradise are less enticing [*piquantes*]. Never was such sweet pleasure offered to mortal heart and senses. (*C*, 300).[20]

I entered a courtesan's room as if it were a sanctuary of love and beauty; in her person I felt I saw the divinity. I could never have believed it possible to feel anything like the emotion she inspired in me, without my also feeling a respect and esteem for her. . . . Suddenly, instead of the fire that devoured me, I felt a deathly cold flow [*courir*] through my veins; my legs trembled [*me flageolent*]; I sat down on the point of fainting [*prêt à me trouver mal*], and wept like a child. (*C,* 300)

"There is something incomprehensible about this. Either my heart deceives me, deludes [*fascine*] my senses, and makes me the dupe of a worthless slut, or some secret flaw that I do not see destroys the value of her charms and makes her repulsive to those who should be quarreling for possession of her." I began to seek for that flaw [*Je me mis à chercher ce défaut*] with a singular persistence [*avec une contention d'esprit singulière*], and it did not so much as occur to me that the pox [*la vérole*] might have something to do with it. The freshness of her flesh, the brightness of her colouring, the whiteness of her teeth, the sweetness of her breath, the air of cleanliness that pervaded her person, so completely banished that idea from my mind . . . (*C,* 301)

But just as I was about to sink upon a breast which seemed about to suffer a man's lips and hand for the first time, I perceived that she had a malformed nipple [*téton borgne*]. I beat my brow, looked harder, and made certain that this nipple did not match the other. Then I started wondering about the reason for this malformation. I was struck by the thought that it resulted from some remarkable imperfection of Nature [*cela tenais à quelque notable vice naturel*] and, after turning this idea over in my head, I saw as clear as daylight that instead of the most charming creature I could imagine I held in my arms some kind of monster, rejected by [*le rebut de*] Nature, men, and love. I carried my stupidity so far as to speak to her about her malformed nipple. First she took the matter as a joke and said and did things in her skittish [*folâtre*] humour that were enough to make me die of love. But as I still felt some remnant of uneasiness, which I could not conceal from her, I finally saw her blush, adjust her clothes, and take her place at the window, without a word. I tried to sit down beside her. She moved and sat down on a couch, then got up the next moment and walked about the room, fanning herself. Finally she said to me in a cold and scornful voice: "Gianetto, lascia le donne, e studia la matematica." (*C,* 301–2)

How is it that the sordid tale of a "malformed" nipple and the social codes of decency with which it collides could crown Rousseau's *Confessions,* the body of confessions to which a great intellectual and *littérateur* of his times feels constrained to give vent? On the most superficial level, the story comprises a joke upon its author. The humiliated courtesan, whose human imperfection belies her otherwise celestial beauty, nonetheless manages a comeback: "Johnny, study mathematics, not women!" The joke might seem to be on Rousseau.

But I would suggest, within the purview of the broader modernity, that the joke of free consciousness catching itself short, the joke making men who ought to know better tell on themselves, is a joke on all who buy into the

Enlightenment's myth of transcendence through intellectual genius. Does the speech-act of confession preserve Jean-Jacques's genuine intellectual contributions—in Giulietta's words, his "mathematics"—from his excesses, his infidelities, his parental neglect? In which case the metaphor of the pox at the basis of the story of degraded beauty and the inability to cope with it is perfect: the Great Man of his age tells on himself so as to inoculate his possibly genuine achievements against the pox of adverse public opinion.

The confessional story reveals an imperfection on the part of the Great Man, who, as an intellectual public figure of the broader modernity, is obliged to surpass on all planes: "No, Nature has not made me for sensual delight" (*C,* 300). But could we argue, along with Freud, that the act of compulsive confession surely encompasses its own secondary gain?[21] And wouldn't the confession enabling Rousseau to salvage the substantial part of his work from moral outrage offer, as its "underlying" pleasure, the martyrdom implicit to self-disclosure and self-censure themselves, prompting Slavoj Žižek to explore the "Stalinist" dimension of psychoanalysis?[22] The martyrdom of confession rejoins the exercise in *franchise* to the grandiosity of free intellectual creation during the epoch of Romanticized creativity.

The episode of Giulietta's nipple brings the substratum of confession that has been building since the outset of this text and that has accounted in significant measure for its thematic coherence to a certain orgasm—this despite Jean-Jacques's need for sexual prowess. There are the matters of the ribbon, interpreted so powerfully by Paul de Man (*C,* 86–89);[23] participation in a group copulation with Klupffel's mistress (*C,* 331); parental rejection (*C,* 332–35); and overall indiscretion (*C,* 574). But in no other section does Rousseau so crassly depict such a rude breakdown in the empathy implicitly demanded by his own social contract. Again, the gains made possible by the confessional mode add up at least to equal the losses: confession unifies material for yet another immortal work by the Great Author; it deflects censure from nonconfessional works; it defines its own genre of modern martyrdom and transcendence. (Paul de Man, as a great reader of Rousseau, may have known this. With regard to the controversy that arose regarding de Man's presumed wartime ethical lapses, in a specifically Rousseauan context, his eschewing confession may well have occupied a higher ethical plane than its alternative.) The passage I have quoted at length above from *The Confessions* is quite specific in the manner in which it links the besmirching of idealism with the confessional mode. It deserves to be pursued further.

Within the purview of the broader modernity, there is no "pure" consciousness. Faith is tantamount to bad faith. As we have observed above with regard to Kleist, there are more sources of authority and points of obligation than can be possibly satisfied. To exist is to fail in certain registers. To think is to fall from the protocols of idealism into the shame of perversity. This is how Rousseau's mathematical thought, as exemplified by the proportionality of *The Social Contract* and the *Discourse on the Origins and Fundaments of Inequality,* could coexist with his idealization of nature and the discourse of confession. Rousseau is sincere in his effort to evolve an epochal ethos of social responsibility from the governmental speculations of *The Social Contract.* Rousseau distills a social contract in whose terms he knows his own behavior has failed. The rhetoric of *The Confessions* bridges the gap between the modern aesthetic contract, in which existential constraint and failure can be transfigured under the purview of secular intellectual achievement, and the critical contract, in which the performatives of disclosure, interpretation, and debunking furnish all human achievements, even aesthetic ones, with a delimiting framework. In *The Confessions,* Rousseau becomes the critic of his prior life, its achievements, and ultimately of himself. Rousseau's impulse to add confession as yet another dimension of his discourse suggests that the criticism arising in the late Enlightenment and the Romantic age falls under the aspirations that the aesthetic contract defined by Kant and others nourished for the artist. The critical contract exists in a supplemental relation to the aesthetic one, much as the aesthetics of the broader modernity supplements certitudes once furnished by theology and highly structured modes of sociopolitical organization.

But I neglect the details in a key episode in the life of modern confession here, a telling one in the rapport between idealization, prowess, and critical commentary. The overall scenario, of course, is one of broad sexual possibility. The libertine in a very real sense is an adventurer in license and liberty. The libertine is an individuated, free modern subject set loose within the wonderland of sexuality. His or her adventures there combine the whimsy of play with the deliberation of scientific experiment. Discoveries unearthed within the field of sexual exploration are rarely fatal. The knowledge gained in this fieldwork becomes the basis for future adventures. Sexual knowledge thus belongs to the temporality of repetition and the dramaturgy of comedy. The episode of Giulietta transforms the aggression that the narrator manifests toward his sexual quarry and the shame that is both the beginning and the end of the episode into self-awareness celebrated under the ethos of altruism and a new beginning for the narrator whose ultimate aesthetic paradigm is comedy. It remains for critical scrutiny to determine whether the quite deliberate and obstinate perpetrator of Giulietta's shame deserves to be let out of the episode with a comedic slap on the wrist and new material for his next adventure.

For indeed, there is something self-fulfilling about this episode, which begins in search of a flaw, a reason for sexual disgust, and ends with its discovery: "I began to seek for that flaw with a singular persistence" (*C,* 301). Giulietta's breast is the monstrous counterpart to the good breast that, in accounts ranging from Freud's to Klein's and Winnicott's, the infant hallucinates.[24] It functions for the adult Jean-Jacques as a defense mechanism projected "externally." "If the 'divine' beauty can be discovered to possess some overwhelming flaw," so runs the logic of the defense, "then there will be a way of resisting her overpowering feminine allure, and feminine attraction generally." But the defense, of course, is already installed within the individual who, at a moment of sexual triumph, in the intimate presence of a magnificent woman, seeks it, desires it. The defense has always already been installed within the sexual libertine, the individual whose historical moment, social status, and culture empower him or her to undertake sexual voyages of discovery.

This defense underlies the imaginary quality of the evil breast that materializes, in the fashion of the infantile "good" one, just when the subject hallucinates it, at the moment of hunger. The appearance of the flawed breast falls under the temporality of a fulfilled prophecy. But another pivotal temporality holds sway in this episode: the belligerent repetition of insult. "I carried my stupidity so far as to speak to her about her malformed nipple. First she took the matter as a joke" (*E,* 301). It takes real deliberation, sometimes, to hammer home an insult, because people are not always disposed to expect social aggression. The scene depicts the narrator's efforts in making sure that Giulietta is aware of his discomfiture regarding her breast's *natural* formation. During a moment of sexual lightheartedness, Giulietta does not expect such a hit. The moment of registered and confirmed insult ("I still felt some remnant of uneasiness, which I could not conceal from her," *E,* 301) transforms a sexual (could we say "victimless"?) trespass into a human and social act of considerable aggression. The aggravation of sins in the episode goes nicely with the mode of confessional revelation that frames the text: as the crimes, first of body and then of mind, become more lurid, confession becomes more dramatic, difficult, forgivable.

According to the results of this lurid experiment, the shame discovered is merely the shame at the start; it takes some real persistence to commit the ultimate act of demoralizing, one which shames others. Confession would presume to set right these excesses of a world in which the subject has been free and is conflicted enough to commit them; but by the logic of reciprocity, confession joins the universe of bad faith that it is contrived to mark and set aright.

CHAPTER 9

Between Sublimities:
Melville, Whaling, and the
Melodrama of Incest

Rousseau's characteristic circumlocutions—whether the celebration of liberty, the minute measurement of its possibilities, constraints, and proportions, or the bad faith that is the modal and cognitive correlative to its exercise—form a splendid, even inevitable backdrop for aporias that assume sublime dimensions in Melville's fictive world. For Melville too, who writes both as an utterly tangential as well as exemplary citizen of his age, the Transcendental, the Sublime, the Big Pleasure, penetrates through to our sensibility, but only in the form of an aporia, a double bind. At the flanks of the Melvillian aporia reside, in utter rawness, expansion and contraction themselves; the coexistence of these modalities is defined by writing, whose sinuous trajectory and production comprise the borderline between them. *Moby-Dick,* though in no sense unidirectional, performs a spectacle of expansion before a culture in an expansive mood. It thus becomes the constatement and performance of expansion, the testing and penetration of limit in an allegorical mode. Texts such as *Pierre* and *The Confidence-Man* frame this allegory, in architectural and Kantian-Derridian senses of the term.[1] In these texts, the constraints of civility in its symbolic and semiotic modes measure the chasm in language that *Moby-Dick* might otherwise seem to celebrate.

Moby-Dick constitutes the United States' imaginary colony in the empire of the sublime. Whale-hunting, the sea, Ahab, and the White Whale itself are in turn invested with the grandiosity and gaping vacuousness of sublimity. The Other of *Moby-Dick*—whether understood to be Queequeg, the whale, the sea, or Ahab—is invested with the deep-structural, overdetermined significance inherent to the Lacanian *objet a.* The systems of *Moby-Dick,* the human instruments devised to mediate the Real or the Transcendental, themselves become endlessly expansive or sublime. The objects, faculties, and human enterprises of *Moby-Dick* become endlessly, and uncannily, expansive. Pip's definitive psychosis and the solitude of "Ishmael's" survival describe the existential impact of this multifaceted expansionism, whose material underpinnings incorporate developments in technology, nationalism, political administration, and military control throughout the nineteenth century. The expansiveness that the text of *Moby-Dick* seems to celebrate is personally, psychologically devastating.

Melville grafts his most expansive sea story onto the modern history that has been the occasion for the present study. Captains Peleg and Bildad, the shipowners who inscribe Ishmael and Queequeg into the *Pequod*'s crew, are Quakers, Protestants who first in the colonies and later in the the States became stereotyped for their industriousness, skill at trade and commerce, and parsimony. "For some of these same Quakers are the most sanguinary of all sailors and whale-hunters. They are fighting Quakers; Quakers with a vengeance" (*MD*, 16: 73). Peleg—whose biblical name may also connect him to the Pelasgian creation myth—is an uncanny prefiguration of Ahab's uncanninesses: "He was brown and brawny, like most old seamen, and heavily rolled-up in blue pilot-cloth, cut in the Quaker style; only there was a fine and almost microscopic net-work of the minutest wrinkles interlacing round his eyes" (*MD*, 16: 70). While Peleg "cared not a rush for what are called serious things . . . Captain Bildad had not only been originally educated according to the strictest sect of Nantucket Quakerism, but all his subsequent ocean life, and the sight of many unclad, lovely island creatures, round the Horn—all that had not moved this native born Quaker one single jot, had not so much as altered one angle of his vest" (*MD*, 16: 74). Through figures such as Peleg, Bildad, and Ahab himself, Melville inscribes this novel within an overall American cultural history of opposed and bipolar impulses and defenses. The same sensibility that revels in unprecedented American liberties and commercial possibilities invokes "internal" and "external" retaliatory mechanisms of some severity. In chapter 16, "The Ship," Peleg and Bildad banter about each other's consciences, the "internal" liberty regulator. "But as thou art an impenitent man," quips Bildad to Peleg, "I greatly fear lest thy conscience be a leaky one" (*MD*, 16: 77). Within the architecture of *Moby-Dick*, Melville constructs his exemplary subjects' encounters with the sublime, the uncontainable, and the Real upon a foundation of a vivid American Protestant sensibility to the dangers within late-Enlightenment liberty and enterprise.

Some of Melville's most vivid descriptions in *Moby-Dick* move forward

with the unflappable certainty of advertisement language, the code of public
cliches:

> But here is an artist. He desires to paint you the dreamiest, shadiest, quietest,
> most enchanting bit of romantic landscape in all the valley of the Saco. What
> is the chief element he employs? There stand his trees, each with a hollow
> trunk, as if a hermit and a crucifix were within; and here sleeps his meadow,
> and there sleep his cattle. . . .
>   And as for going as a cook . . . yet, somehow, I never fancied broiling
> fowls;—though once broiled, judiciously buttered, and judgmatically salted
> and peppered, there is no one who will speak more respectfully, not to say
> reverentially, of a broiled fowl than I will. (*MD*, 1: 4–5)

Perhaps the most hidden and ironic expansionism in the novel is a language
of utter predictability attaining breakneck speed through its formulae. The
Romantic landscape and cottage of "Looming" (chap. 1) are postcard stuff;
the broiled chicken anticipates menu copy of a far later moment. While the
statue of Ahab is surely cast in the genius model, a certain portion of the
novel's unique power derives from the banal: the commercial language at
the core of the Melvillian notion of "confidence," a system of recognitions
whose entrenchment and speed, if not complexity, are prodigious.

Melville's anticipation of the linguistic mechanisms of mass capitalism
joins—it does not counteract—the collocation of sublimities that the novel
stages. Even the semantic dimension of the novel, in passages, borrows the
inevitability of the sublime and the sea. The upshot of this multifaceted encounter—with Nature; with one of its monstrosities, the White Whale; with
a human monster in the mold of the Kantian original genius and the Rousseauan lawgiver, Ahab—is utter devastation and solitude, the solitude which
for Blanchot and other philosophers of writing is the native land of inscription. The sublimity of writing will go out to answer, is the only counter to,
the sublimities of the Transcendental and the Real.

Pierre, as we shall see, issues forth with its own sublimities, but these are,
precisely, of the homebred variety. The impenetrability of sexual knowledge
is the domestic correlative to the sublime in a world depicted externally.
The only counter to the sublime in nature is an immense uncertainty on a
household scale. *Pierre* (and the shipboard setting of *The Confidence-Man*) is
a counterweight, a Derridean guardrail, to the seemingly objective (because
"external") sublime of Melville's sea tales. *Pierre* exists to *Moby-Dick* as Pira-
nesi's interior architecture exists to Friedrich's landscapes and Turner's sea-
scapes. The self to be extrapolated from the world of Melville's fiction is
poised between two sublimities: the disruptive chasm that surrounds us in

"external" nature and the one that underlies domestic "sensible certitude." Subjectivity, during Melville's epoch, whether we call it the nineteenth century, Romanticism, or late Romanticism, is a suspension between two counterpoised versions of the uncanny, one leading in the direction of dispersion and disintegration (anticipated by Poe's *Eureka* and related texts), the other pointing toward domestic treachery and constriction (that bind women every bit as much as men). We will pursue the sublimity of *Moby-Dick* through its natural, systematic, and psychological dimensions.

> It was a sight full of quick wonder and awe! The vast swells of the omnipotent sea; the surging, hollow roar they made, as they rolled along the eight gunwales, like gigantic bowls in a boundless bowling-green; the brief suspended agony of the boat, as it would tip for an instant on the knife-like edge of the sharper waves, that almost seemed threatening to cut it in two; the sudden profound dip into the watery glens and hollows; the keen spurrings and goadings to gain the top of the opposite hill; the headlong, sled-like glide down its other side;—all these, with the cries of the headsmen and the harpooners, and the shuddering gasps of the oarsmen, with the wondrous sight of the ivory Pequod bearing down upon her boats with outstretched sails, like a wild hen after her screaming brood;—all this was thrilling. (*MD*, 48: 223)

There is no more vivid picture of the expansion that Melville celebrates, to which he gives expression, than this one. Fluidity of dimension and motion merge here: the ocean's waves, sounds, and movements are immense; the boat is at most a stylus leaving faint and instantaneously disappearing traces upon an empirical manifold that it can never master, contain, or record. The ship's relative tininess and fragility indicate the weak hold that writing exercises over the phenomena that it modifies and elaborates, yet that it radically displaces. And in return the sea, with the "knife-like" edges of its waves, will register an indelible legend upon the ship and its characters.

The expanses of water are "watery glens." The tumult of the waves is reminiscent of a deafening crash of pins issuing from a bowling-green. Anticipating Proust and the impressionist painters who were the model for his Elstir, Melville measures the sea with terrestrial imagery, and vice versa.[2] The extent of a sea voyage can only be comprehended on land. This means that domesticity, the seeming antithesis of voyages of conquest and discovery, harbors its own immensity, and that this vastness too moves in waves.

But at the moment of "The First Lowering," constraints such as these form only the faintest subtext to the magnificence and sublimity that the narrative celebrates. We see, in the passage immediately above, the sea that *Moby-Dick* is remembered for embroidering: wild, uncontainable in its motion and energy, relentless. There is something in Melville's occasion that empowers him to access this uncontainable sea: a whale industry that has become a match for the ocean itself in its extent, its knowledge, its technology. Melville's paean to the sea is *only* in the context of a human economy and system-making that rival the ocean in their expansiveness.

It is only because the system of whales—the science, mythology, and pictorial and discursive representation—has achieved a dimension of sublime, possibly grandiose expansion, that more narrative attention is devoted to these mediations and qualifications than to the facts and mechanics of the whale-hunt itself. From its initial reception onward, readers of *Moby-Dick* have been bemused by its seemingly endless archival and encyclopaedic excursus.[3] Melville intertwines his sea adventure with a systematic whale encyclopaedia whose pretension to comprehensiveness is as grandiose as the sea and the sea monstrosity known as Moby-Dick.[4] The monomania that the narrative attaches to Ahab is not limited to the domain of characterization. Beyond one specifically unforgettable character, who plays an indispensable role in the drama of literary surrogates, the monomania of *Moby-Dick* extends to the claims of its internalized system of whaling, which, like human consciousness in the Hegelian systematizations, not only ultimately embraces everything, but *expands* as it evolves itself out of itself.

The ultimate sublimity that *Moby-Dick* celebrates is the expansive potential of human knowledge and dominion in the era of its composition. For this reason, Melville signals the sublimity of the *object* and occasion of the whale system, the sperm whale itself:

> In some particulars, perhaps, the most imposing physiognomical view to be had of the Sperm Whale, is that of the full front of his head. This aspect is sublime.
>
> In thought, a fine human brow is like the East when troubled with the morning. In the repose of the pasture, the curled brow of the bull has a touch of the grand in it. Pushing heavy cannon up mountain defiles, the elephant's brow is majestic. Human or animal, the mystical brow is as that great golden seal affixed by the German emperors to their decrees. It signifies—"God: done this day by my hand." But in most creatures, nay in man himself, very often the brow is but a mere strip of alpine land lying along the snow line. Few are the foreheads which like Shakespeare's or Melancthon's rise so high, and descend so low, that the eyes themselves seem clear, eternal, tideless mountain lakes; and all above them in the forehead's wrinkles, you seem to track the antlered thoughts descending there to drink, as the Highland hunters track the snowprints of the deer. But in the great Sperm Whale, this high and mighty god-like dignity inherent in the brow is so immensely amplified, that gazing on it, in that full front view, you feel the Deity and the dread powers more forcibly than in beholding any other object in living nature. For

you see no one point precisely; not one distinct feature is revealed; no nose, eyes, ears, or mouth; no face; he has none, proper; nothing but that one broad firmament of a forehead, pleated with riddles; dumbly lowering with the doom of boats, and ships, and men. Nor, in profile, does this wondrous brow diminish; though that way viewed, its grandeur does not domineer upon you so. In profile, you plainly perceive that horizontal, semi-crescentic depression in the forehead's middle, which, in man, is Lavater's mark of genius.

But how? Genius in the Sperm Whale? (*MD,* 79: 346)

A pivotal point of the sperm whale's sublimity is its gaze. Detaching this head (as it has been physically severed from the sperm whale's body in chapters 68 and 69), Melville deploys a rhetoric of sublime description whose sources include Kant, Hegel, and Mary and Percy Bysshe Shelley. The enigmatic gaze of the whale is tantamount to a sphinx's riddle. Melville's sublimation of the whale has also encompassed Egyptian references connecting this creature to the ancient culture appropriated by U.S. ideology as a talisman for its secularity, its orientation to principles predating Judeo-Christianity and resistant to the linkage between church and state. The skin-markings on the sperm whale are "hieroglyphical; that is, if you call those mysterious cyphers on the walls of pyramids hieroglyphics" (*MD,* 68: 306). The decapitated forehead of the sperm whale thus incorporates a multifaceted sublimity that speaks to Kantian horizons and limits, a specific negativity that Hegel isolates in Egyptian culture and art and that Derrida relocates as a radical crypt in the space of representation. The sublimity of the whale's gaze plays Scotland to England's relative cultivation and measure. The whale's high forehead recalls the busts of two modern masters: Melancthon, the pseudonym of Philipp Schwartzerd (1497–1560), a founding father and early ideologue of Protestantism, and the Bard. As in the cases of Captains Peleg and Bildad, the narrative places Protestant theology and modern genius in parallel. The issue of "original genius" becomes the crowning point to sperm whale sublimity. The narrative assigns this consummate human capacity, according to Kant, to the prey of the chase. Through the projective displacement involved in the Lacanian dynamic of the gaze, a human "original genius" emerges, as I am arguing, at a moment when systematic thought endowed with a pre–artificial intelligence capacity for self-expansion is projected onto the object of the hunt and the putative occasion for the meditation. The Whale (whether sperm, albino, or both is not material) becomes a simulacrum for the celebrated/feared human potentials that emerge from the moment. Sublimity is for Melville not merely a conceptual term for this immensity; it furnishes an aesthetic, a style, an accompaniment, and a "surround" for the issues of knowledge, freedom, authority, and power with which Melville is contending—and he is not alone in this contention. Melville thus "pushes" a certain sublimity, above all of a naturalistic, externalized nature, but also of a psychological one, throughout the narrative, as we can see in the following example:

> Is it that by its indefiniteness it shadows forth the heartless voids and immensities of the universe, and thus stabs us from behind with the thought of annihilation, when beholding the white depths of the milky way? Or is it, that as in essence whiteness is not so much a color as the visible absence of color, and at the same time the concrete of all colors; is it for these reasons that there is such a dumb blankness, full of meaning, in a wide landscape of snows—a colorless, all-color of atheism from which we shrink? And when we consider that other theory of the natural philosophers, that all other earthly hues—every stately or lovely emblazoning—the sweet tinges of sunset skies and woods; yea, and the gilded velvets of butterflies, and the butterfly cheeks of young girls; all these are but subtle deceits, not actually inherent in substances, but only laid on from without; so that all deified Nature absolutely paints like the harlot, whose allurements cover nothing but the charnel-house within; and when we proceed further, and consider that the mystical cosmetic which produces every one of her hues, the great principle of light, for ever remains white or colorless in itself, and if operating without medium on matter, would touch all objects, even tulips and roses, with its own blank tinge—pondering all this, the palsied universe lies before us a leper; and like wilful travellers in Lapland, who refuse to wear colored and coloring glasses upon their eyes, so that the wretched infidel gazes himself blind at the monumental white shroud that wraps all the prospect around him. And of all these things the Albino whale was the symbol. Wonder ye then at the fiery hunt? (*MD*, 42: 195)

Reminiscent of the sublimity that Kant attaches to Judaism in the absence and unrepresentability of its deity, the whiteness of Moby-Dick is at once vast, enigmatic, uncanny, uncontainable, morbid, monstrous, mystical, nonspecific, and *vaguely* threatening. Melville makes a splendid case here for whiteness as a de facto envelope for marginality, the exceptionality of Derridean writing itself. Whiteness somehow straddles the Transcendental and the empirical while being precisely of neither; refuses to succumb to (an ultimately Christian) reconciliation with specificity, specifically with the particularity of color, thus betraying the ministrations of "Nature"; places itself in league with uncanny blanknesses and absences. Even the pied "harlotry" of Nature, a certain variety of Derridean writing, is preferable to the treachery of invisible (white) ink. The nonsympathy of this whiteness links it to polar inclemency and death; by association, Moby-Dick's home becomes the arctic flanks of P. B. Shelley's "Mont Blanc" and the North Pole and alpine wastes in Mary Shelley's *Frankenstein*.[5] At the level of a rhetorical symbol, Moby-Dick becomes as systematic as both the whaling enterprise and the body of cetology that frame and delimit this creature. As a comprehensive symbol or cypher, Moby-Dick encompasses an incongruity, violence, and uncanniness extending from the *absences* of writing to the indifferent monstrosities at play in Nature itself.

While Kant's *Critique of Pure Reason* does not address art as specifically as certain of his subsequent works, it does, in a most telling and significant way, establish the terrain for an investigator who wanders beyond the relative containment of the empirical in a quest for the Transcendental (or its underlying architecture), and who is ultimately repelled homeward by the Transcendental's uncanny gaze. (We have begun to explore this dynamic in Chapter 5.) The implicit philosophical subject of the first Critique becomes a prototype for an investigative protagonist in Romantico-modern fiction with an insistence and popularity far beyond anything Kant could have imagined. Melville makes sure to endow the moving force behind the hunt for Moby-Dick, Ahab, with all the personal monstrosity and uncanniness that would befit a Kantian original genius and the expedition leader in a B-grade monster movie in which the primary investigator is invariably sent packing by the threatening and deficient Object of which she or he has been in monomaniacal quest. The design of *Moby-Dick* requires that a high degree of detail go into the image of Ahab:

> Reality outran apprehension: Captain Ahab stood upon his quarter-deck.
> There seemed no sign of commonly bodily illness about him, nor of the recovery from any. He looked like a man cut away from the stake, when the fire has overrunningly wasted all the limbs without consuming them, or taking away one particle from their compacted aged robustness. His whole high, broad form, seemed made of solid bronze, and shaped in an unalterable mould, like Cellini's cast Perseus. Threading its way out from among his grey hairs, and continuing right down one side of his tawny scorched face and neck, till it disappeared in his clothing, you saw a slender rod-like mark, lividly whitish. It resembled that perpendicular seam sometimes made in the straight, lofty trunk of a great tree, when the upper lightning tearingly darts down it, and without wrenching a single twig, peels and grooves out the bark from top to bottom, ere running off into the soil, leaving the tree still greenly alive, but branded. Whether that mark was born with him or whether it was the scar left by some desperate wound, no one could certainly say. By some tacit consent, throughout the voyage little or no allusion was made to it, especially by the mates. . . . So that no white sailor seriously contradicted him when he said that if ever Captain Ahab should be tranquilly laid out—which

might hardly come to pass, so he muttered—then, whoever should do that last office for the dead, would find a birth-mark on him from crown to sole.

So powerfully did the whole grim aspect of Ahab affect me, and the livid brand which streaked it, that for the first few moments I hardly noted that not a little overbearing grimness was owing to the barbaric white leg upon which he partly stood. (*MD*, 28: 123–24)

In this passage, Ahab enters the prevailing aesthetic contract of European Romanticism. A fitting partner to the White Whale's systematic uncanniness, which includes hieroglyphic markings on the outer skin, Ahab has been marked, inscribed, by the grandiosity of his quest and by the forces he encounters and unleashes. Brother to Kant's original genius, Ahab has been lightning-struck by the flash of apprehension and inspiration through which, in the philosopher's system, the underlying Laws of the universe are disclosed, but only to the selectest few. The relentlessness of Ahab's quest has caused him to be marked by a scar, a mark of Cain, which in a Romantic context inscribes the danger of excessive intimacy with the Transcendental domain. From the viewpoint of contemporary object-relations theory, it is unclear whether the wound, described specifically as a lightning slash upon a tree, is the result of the quest, its inspiration, or both. Melville marks Ahab in this passage as the bearer of a wound. The wound is part of Ahab's overall, general strikingness, uncanniness, and captivation. He inspires the same awe as do Benvenuto Cellini's most memorable Florentine sculptures; he bespeaks the miraculousness attached to the burning bush of Exodus, in which Moses makes his most direct (empirical) approach to God: like that bush, Ahab has been burned but not consumed. Like other monstrous characters in Romantic literature, including Poe's Hop-Frog and E. T. A. Hoffmann's René Cardillac,[6] Ahab is physically powerful at the same time as he is wasted, disfigured. It takes such a creature of uncanniness to be a worthy adversary to the White Whale.

Ahab declares himself to be the transcendental horizon of the whaling hunt. From the perspective of Judeo-Christian theology, this is a gesture of usurpation, an act of sacrilege. This *hubris* is not only in the tradition of the Miltonic Satan, but also in keeping with the "experience" of other compelling Romantic surrogates, including Coleridge's Ancient Mariner and Mary Shelley's "Modern Prometheus," Victor Frankenstein. Ahab's act of transcendental usurpation involves precisely his declaration of his own vision, his own gaze, to mark the parameters of reality for the ship and its voyage:

Before this equatorial coin, Ahab, not unobserved by others, was now pausing.

"There's something ever egotistical in mountain-tops and towers, and all other grand and lofty things; look here,—three peaks as proud as Lucifer.

The firm tower, that is Ahab; the volcano, that is Ahab; the courageous, the undaunted, and victorious fowl, that, too, is Ahab; all are Ahab; and this round globe is but the image of the rounder globe, which, like a magician's glass, to each and every man in turn but mirrors back his own mysterious self." (*MD,* 99: 431)

Ahab's vision is folded, englobed upon itself. The narrative seeks out images of roundness for a narcissistic imaginary with global pretensions. Melville anticipates the twentieth-century theory of object relations, which will link self-centeredness to fundamental narcissistic wounds and projective fantasies. In the above passage, the "I" of Ahab, which in a Lacanian sense demarcates both an "eye" and a surrogate subjectivity, appropriates and swallows up all potential markers and inhabitants of a world that might otherwise claim some (relative) "objectivity": a tower, a volcano, birds. Melville's global image anticipates a similar one in Virginia Woolf's *The Waves*: an imaginary shape for a creative self always in a state of (depressive) dispersion and disintegration.[7] Ahab has offered a coin as reward for the first sighting of the White Whale. The disk of a coin shares the curvature of a globe, but with one dimension of roundness less. A coin is a Kantian mediator within the numismatic and economic spheres; it inscribes value upon a signifier and bearer of material exchange. Ahab has declared his Ecuadorian doubloon a charm for the successful culmination of the chase (*MD,* 99: 430–31). The coin brings on board, and in miniature form, the full magical and metaphysical *compass* of the quest for the White Whale.

Melville appropriates the Bible and Shakespeare as sourcebooks for a language of sublime inspiration and possible madness. This is the language in which Ahab issues forth in his ejaculations, in a narrative that at several junctures breaks off from its discursive specifications and enters the genre of dramatic dialogue (as do, for example, chapters 36–40, 120–22). It is as if Melville designates the Bible, the canonical text of Judeo-Christianity, and Shakespeare, producer of the single most-cited artifacts of the broader modernity, as works achieving transcendental status in their centrality. Within the overall economy of *Moby-Dick,* the Bible and Shakespearean drama attain the status of Barthesian mythology: a language of transcendental vision and pitch achieving focus and fixity amid the turbulence of the sea and the empirical flux the sea embodies. As the speaker in biblical and Shakespearean language, Ahab attains the status of a late-Enlightenment-Romantic prophet, with all of the marginality, opposition to the political status quo, overarching vision, and immediate insight that coincide in biblical prophets, Rousseauan lawgivers, and Kantian artists. It is a highly distinctive language of transcendental overview and grandiose pretension that Melville assigns to Ahab:

That inscrutable thing is chiefly what I hate; and be the white whale agent, or be the white whale principal, I will wreak that hate upon him. Talk not to me of blasphemy, man; I'd strike the sun if it insulted me. For could the sun do that, then I could do the other. . . . Who's over me? Truth hath no confines. Take off thine eye! more intolerable than fiends' glarings is a doltish stare. So, so; thou reddenest and palest; my heat has melted thee to anger-glow. But look ye, Starbuck, what is said in heat, that thing unsays itself. . . . The crew, man, the crew! Are they not one and all with Ahab, in this matter of the whale? See Stubb! he laughs! See yonder Chilian! he snorts to think of it. Stand up amid the general hurricane, thy one tost sapling cannot, Starbuck! (*MD,* 36: 164)

The poetry of Ahab's discourse would have him a force of nature, one of lesser magnitude but greater articulation than the White Whale itself. Ahab would strike out against the sun. He, not Starbuck, would "Stand up amid the general hurricane," not unlike Lear at the peak of his crisis.

The dramatis personae of *Moby-Dick* does not involve itself with your homegrown variety of "normal" characters, with the possible exception of Ishmael, the novel's lens or shifter. It takes uncanny characters to join and at least temporarily survive a world of animated sublimity, a world in a state of perpetual expansion evoking exuberance and terror on the part of its human inhabitants. As in the case of the implied philosophical subject of Hegel's *Phenomenology of Spirit,* relentless expansion-around-one defines the very nature of experience. Yet it is the epistemological specification of the age that this expansion does not transpire haphazardly; it is systematic. The expansion in human knowledge, technology, communications, and administrative compass must assume the form of a system. A system is growing at a frightening speed and with no predictable outcome *around* the citizens of this epoch. One feels this in Poe's *Eureka* as well. The ultimate nightmare implied by this phenomenon is the loss of all measures, parameters, and bearings. Melville figures this eventuality as Pip's terminal agoraphobia. But before he brings us to this point (or rather vaccuum), the narrative tags a number of interrelated systems implicated by whales and their industry. We would have before us a much abbreviated *Moby-Dick,* and one much more in keeping with earlier sea novels such as *Omoo* and *Typee,* if Melville did not insist on the *systematic* logic and dimensions of a vertiginous world in a state of perpetual expansion.

Philosophy, with its regimen of logic and its atmosphere of conceptuality, is one of the primary models to which Melville appeals in his opening of a systematic frame and backdrop to the whale adventure. It is in this context that the *Pequod,* straining under the burden of a sperm whale's and a right whale's heads at the same time, finds itself poised, respectively, between the heads of Locke and Kant: "So, when on one side you hoist in Locke's head, you go over that way; but now, on the other side, hoist in Kant's and you come back again; but in very poor plight. Thus, some minds for ever keep trimming boat" (*MD,* 73: 327). The philosophical theater of the novel's systematic dimension hovers between Locke and Kant, between empirical observation and transcendental speculation, between, as we would say today, "Anglo-American and continental philosophy." Once established, this dialogue between talking (and thinking) heads is food for endless irony and displacement: "But mark the other head's expression. See that amazing lower lip. . . . Does not this whole head seem to speak of an enormous practical resolution in facing death? This Right Whale I take to have been a Stoic; the Sperm Whale, a Platonian, who might have taken up Spinoza in his latter years" (*MD,* 75: 335).

The whale fishery itself surely plays a pivotal role in establishing the novel's systematic dimension, a scale that is put to ironic as well as dramatic use. For one, the fishery determines the *economic* framework within which men encounter the sublimity of whales:

> As for the residue of the Pequod's company, be it said, that at the present day not one in two of the many thousand men before the mast employed in the American whale fishery, are Americans born, though pretty nearly all the officers are. Herein it is the same with the American whale fishery as with the American army and military and merchant navies. . . . in all these cases the native American liberally provides the brains, the rest of the world as generously supply the muscles. . . . They were nearly all Islanders in the Pequod, *Isolatoes* too, I call such, not acknowledging the common continent of men, but each *Isolato* living on a separate continent of his own. Yet now, federated along one keel, what a list these Isolatoes were! An Anacharsis Clootz deputation from all the isles of the sea, and all the ends of the earth, accompanying Old Ahab in the Pequod to lay the world's grievances before that bar from which not very many of them ever come back. Black Little Pip—he never did! Poor Alabama boy! On the grim Pequod's forecastle, ye shall ere long see him, beating his tambourine; prelusive of the eternal time. (*MD,* 27: 121)

This passage foreshadows Pip's uniquely late-Enlightenment-Romantic martyrdom at the same time that it introduces us to the "American whale fishery" and above all, to its men. The scenario that the narrative sets for the fishery is that of a democracy of loners, of proto-writers. In the context of chapter 1, "Loomings," and this passage, it is no accident that our immediate surrogate in the text, Ishmael, has arrived here. Ishmael specifies that, on the whole, the men aboard ship are Isolatoes, islands unto themselves. Deploying a metaphor that the narrative repeats in describing the cast of characters aboard the *Fidèle* in *The Confidence-Man,* Ishmael describes the ship as an Anacharsis Clootz congress of Isolatoes, that is, as a ragtag collection of eccentrics whose basic relations to each other, in terms of the teamwork of whaling, need to be egalitarian. The democracy of the ship is in sharp contradistinction to the grandiosity of Ahab's monomaniacal mission.

The ship's crew is a subset of the American whaling industry, which in turn is a global system. Within this system, the United States serves as the conceptual command post; foreigners are the body producing the physical labor (MD, 121). In its democratic aspect, the crew-as-deputation will address all "the world's grievances." Ishmael compares the whaling industry, in its expansive, far-reaching, imperial dimension, to the engineers constructing the U.S. canal system and railroads.

A global enterprise based on and in search of a sublime quarry necessarily demands the highest sort of conceptual systematization. The narrative, even at the expense of diverting, delaying, and otherwise impeding the exciting adventure of the chase, lays bare the systems of classification, literary allusion, pictoral representation surrounding the signifier "whale." It is central to my epochal observations here that the *quality of the novel's "internalized" systems is as pivotal a character in the overall economy as Ahab, Queequeg, and Moby-Dick.* These systems, which are supposedly a life-preserver thrown to the reader during the effort of containing and framing a certain literary monstrosity, are themselves gigantic, awesome, and disorienting. The very systems that modern culture has generated in order to delimit the uncontainable have taken on the disequilibrating qualities of the sublime, the uncanny, and the Real. "Cetology," for example, is a chapter introducing a discourse of logical classification that might be applied to whales and their environment with some profit. Not long into the chapter, logical classificatory categories become hopelessly intertwined with the literary dimensions of printed volumes: with quartos, octavos, and the like, to humorous effect. The chapter nonetheless begins to dramatize the vicissitudes of logical systematization stretched to unprecedented dimensions of human physical and organizational capability:

> Now the various species of whales need some sort of popular comprehensive classification, if only an easy outline one for the present, hereafter to be filled in all its departments by subsequent laborers. As no better man advances to take this matter in hand, I hereupon offer my own poor endeavors. I promise nothing complete: because any human thing supposed to be complete, must for that very reason infallibly be faulty. I shall not pretend to a minute anatomical description of the various species, or—in this place at least—to much of any description. My object here is simply to project the draught of a systematization of cetology. I am the architect, not the builder.
>
> But it is a ponderous task; no ordinary letter-sorter in the Post-office is

equal to it. To grope down into the bottom of the sea after them; to have one's hands among the unspeakable foundations, ribs, and very pelvis of the world; this is a fearful thing. What am I that I should essay to hook the nose of this leviathan! (*MD*, 23: 136)

The systematization of whales and whaling is no neat task: it is to quake amid "unspeakable foundations," to sully one's hands on the "ribs" and "very pelvis of the world" (*MD*, 136). Like the Hegelian bondsman, the cetologist will "tremble in every fibre of [his] being" (*PS*, 117). Humdrum Bartlebys are not up to the demands of cetology. The narrator may, in his modesty, renounce the "minute anatomical description of the species" in favor of the more realizable (and literary) "draught of a systematization of cetology" (*MD*, 136). Yet even this humble draft has been conditioned by the tremors within a system stretched to the limits of an uncannily expanding field.

Even when the effort at systematization displaces itself from whales and their environment to pictorial representations of whales, the result is a deranged and misshapen encyclopaedia:

I shall ere long paint to you as well as one can without canvas, something like the true form of the whale as he actually appears to the eye of the whaleman. . . . It may be worth while, therefore, previously to advert to those curious imaginary portraits of him which even down to the present day confidently challenge the faith of the landsman. It is time to set the world right in this matter, by proving such pictures of the whale all wrong.

It may be that the primal source of those pictorial delusions will be found among the oldest Hindoo, Egyptian, and Grecian sculptures. . . .

But go to the old Galleries, and look now at a great Christian painter's portrait of this fish; for he succeeds no better than the antediluvian Hindoo. . . .

But quitting all these unprofessional attempts, let us glance at those pictures of leviathans purporting to be sober, scientific delineations, by those who know. In old Harris's collection of voyages there are some plates of whales extracted from a Dutch book of voyages, A.D. 1671, entitled "A Whaling Voyage to Spitzbergen in the ship Jonas in the Whale, Peter Peterson of Friesland, master." In one of those plates the whales, like great rafts of logs, are represented lying among ice-isles, with white bears running over their living backs. . . .

But the placing of the cap-sheaf to all this blundering business was reserved for the scientific Frederick Cuvier, brother to the famous Baron. (*MD*, 55: 260–62)

The hypothetical catalogue to the Universal Exhibition of Whale Pictures is itself "an indeterminate heap of contradictory drafts."[8] Having already dramatized the appeal to systems as a foundation of stability and objectivity in an endlessly evolving and self-displacing world, the narrative invokes sci-

ence, the system of systems, as an agency capable of putting to rest the plethora of the whale's imaginary representations. Yet the sea of representations is
as chaotic and potentially maddening as the ocean. The delusional plate from
A Whaling Voyage to Spitzbergen that the narrative cites, with polar bears dis-
porting over a living raft of whales among ice floes, is an artifact of sublime
Romantic painting reminiscent of Friedrich, Turner, and Courbet.

The whale has thus been earmarked as a vast and enigmatic subject for its
times. The disciplines and faculties that might contain and rationalize the
whale have themselves taken on sublimity, awe, and chaos. It comes as no
surprise in such a treatise that the writing of the whale—writing, the notation of the alterity and alienation that the sublime is all "about"—itself becomes discombobulation and disorientation. Writing is itself a character in
Moby-Dick, a bunk and soulmate to Ahab and the White Whale:

> One often hears of writers that rise and swell with their subject, though it
> may seem but an ordinary one. How, then, with me, writing of this Levia-
> than? Unconsciously my chirography expands into placard capitals. Give me
> a condor's quill! Give me Vesuvius' crater for an inkstand! Friends, hold my
> arms! For in the mere act of penning my thoughts of this Leviathan, they
> weary me, and make me faint with their outreaching comprehensiveness of
> sweep, as if to include the whole circle of the sciences, and all the generations
> of whales, and men, and mastodons, past, present, and to come, with all the
> revolving panoramas of empire on earth, and throughout the whole universe,
> not excluding its suburbs. Such, and so magnifying, is the virtue of a large
> and liberal theme! We expand to its bulk. To produce a mighty book, you
> must choose a mighty theme. No great and enduring volume can be ever
> written on the flea, though many there be who have tried it.
> Ere entering on the subject of Fossil Whales, I present my credentials as
> a geologist, by stating that in my miscellaneous time I have been a stone-
> mason, and also a great digger of ditches, canals, and wells, wine-vaults, cel-
> lars, and cisterns of all sorts. Likewise, by way of preliminary, I desire to re-
> mind the reader, that while in the earlier geological strata there are found the
> fossils of monsters now almost completely extinct; the subsequent relics dis-
> covered in what are called the Tertiary formations seem the connecting, or
> at any rate intercepted links, between the antechronical creatures, and those
> whose remote posterity are said to have entered the Ark; all the Fossil Whales
> hitherto discovered belong to the Tertiary period, which is the last preceding
> the superficial formations. (*MD,* 104: 456)

As a prelude, in this passage, to invoking yet another science, geology, in
ironic "grasp" of a thoroughly untenable "subject" (or is that "object"?), the
narrative addresses the effect that writing the whale has on the writer. At this
moment, *Moby-Dick* joins the philosophy of writing, the discourse that ren-

ders an accounting of the impact of writing's intransigence, resistance, delusions, solitudes, manias, depressions, and obsessions upon Those who Write. In the first paragraph of the above extract, the writer rises and swells with his subject. The grandiosity of the enterprise, reminiscent of certain "experiences" of Swift's Gulliver and Carroll's Alice, is visited upon the narrator of *Moby-Dick,* Ishmael or whatever we call him. "To produce a mighty book, you must choose a mighty theme!"

With a condor's feather as a quill and Vesuvius's crater as an inkstand, the "writer" of *Moby-Dick,* as much a fictive character as Herman Melville, "himself" undergoes the relentless expansion taking place in the systems "around" him. The writer is "himself" enlarged by the inebriating moment and scene of conquest, discovery, and a vast increase in trade and production. Within this heady if not delirious atmosphere, the writer's writing itself might be proffered as a measure, a guardrail hastily erected against ensuing chaos. Yet as Melville demonstrates on several occasions, the inscription of the whale is as oceanic as the whale's aquatic home.

The writer's potentially disorienting expansion places him in league with Ahab. Hunting the whale, as Ahab does, is tantamount to writing it: in both cases, the sublimity of the "object" (or is that "subject"?) places the agent on intimate terms with a grandiosity spanning both "outside" and "inside" frames of reference. The whale hunter and the writer have both accepted a dare: to penetrate the sublime and still somehow return to tell the story. Ahab and Ishmael are thus facets of the same double character: Ishmael succeeds where Ahab fails. Ahab and the entire crew of the Pequod save Ishmael are ultimately engulfed by the immensity and sublimity of their enterprise. By virtue of the logic discussed so well by John Irwin, Ishmael, the "internal" scribe in the novel, must return home to tell his tale.[9] But narrative script requires a high degree of sanity; there is only a certain extent to which the presumed communicator of experiences, even of disquieting ones, can be deranged by those events and remain an effective communicator. For this reason, the persona of agency in *Moby-Dick* splits yet another time. A new element becomes necessary for the dyad in which whale hunter and whale writer are placed in tandem. There must be someone who is affected, moved, deranged, and disoriented by the expanding panorama of systematicity, and who remains an ongoing mark of this epistemological as well as subjective experience. This character is Pip, whose blackness, diminution, and crippling constitute a deconstructive counter to the duality of Ahab-Ishmael and the ideological parameters they together explore. The open-endedness of a world at large, a Western expansionism in economy, technology, imperialism, and in systematic dimensions themselves, is ultimately registered upon the body as well as the mind of Pip. It falls to Pip to register the grave threats constituted by this expansion that may otherwise seem so delirious to its beneficiaries. On different wavelengths, Rousseau has also been swept up in this world at large.

Eternal vigilance is the price of this particular liberty. More than ever, an unwavering sense of identity and sharply defined, polarized values will be necessary defenses, preventive measures against the impact of this unprece-dented opening. When the narrative inscribes the lasting effects of Pip's abandonment at sea, it is not merely culminating an episode: it is furnishing the *motive* for a set of vivid personal and cultural defenses that will character-ize the conditions of subjectivity and aesthetic transcendence for the dura-tion of modernity:

> But it so happened, that those boats, without seeing Pip, suddenly spying whales close to them on one side, turned, and gave chase; and Stubb's boat was now so far away, and he and all his crew so intent upon his fish, that Pip's ringed horizon began to expand upon him miserably. By the merest chance the ship itself at last rescued him; but from that hour the little negro went about the deck an idiot; such, at least, they said he was. The sea had jeeringly kept his body up, but drowned the infinite of his soul. Not drowned entirely, though. Rather carried down alive to wondrous depths, where strange shapes of the unwarped primal world glided to and fro before his passive eyes; and the miser-merman, Wisdom, revealed his hoarded heaps; and among the joyous, heartless, ever-juvenile eternities, Pip saw the multitudinous, God-omnipresent, coral insects, that out of the firmament of the waters heaved the colossal orbs. He saw God's foot upon the treadle of the loom, and spoke it; therefore his shipmates called him mad. So man's insanity is heaven's sense; and wandering from all mortal reason, man comes at last to celestial thought, which, to reason, is absurd and frantic; and weal or woe, feels then uncom-promised, indifferent as his God. (*MD*, 93: 414)

> He could not stay in his chamber: the house contracted to a nut-shell around him; the walls smote his forehead; bare-headed he rushed from the place, and only in the infinite air, found scope for that boundless expansion of his life. (*P*, 66) [10]

> On the third night following the arrival of the party in the city, Pierre sat at twilight by a lofty window in the rear building of the Apostles'. The chamber was meager even to meanness. No carpet on the floor, no picture on the wall; nothing but a low, long, and very curious-looking single bedstead, that might possibly serve for an indigent bachelor's pallet, a large, blue, chintz-covered chest, a rickety, rheumatic, and most ancient mahogany chair, and a wide

board of the toughest live-oak, about six feet long, laid upon two upright empty flour-barrels, and loaded with a large bottle of ink, an unfastened bundle of quills, a pen-knife, a folder, and a still unbound ream of foolscap paper, significantly stamped, "Ruled; Blue." (*P*, 270)

It is no accident, in terms of the reading of Rousseau and Melville that we have pursued so far, that the entrance of the title character Pierre into the ultimate, and ultimately fatal, *dark* phase of his life should be formulated as the contraction of a "nut-shell" replacing the "boundless expansion of his life" (*P*, 270). Our second paragraph immediately above lists the somber, almost morbid trappings of an unsanctioned artistic existence. Contraction summarizes the terrible punishment visited upon a distinctively American creation, and writer, Pierre Glendinning, in response to his repudiation of his birthright and destiny; his (at least symbolically) adulterous domestic arrangement with two women, one of whom is possibly a long-lost sister; and his grandeur as a poet *manqué*. It falls to Pierre to suffer the limitation and enclosure of the expansive freedom celebrated so deliriously in *Moby-Dick*. As has been suggested above, this turn of events comprises not so much the substitution of (feminine) domesticity for (masculine) sublimity as the opening up of a domestic, "interior" sublime, figured as genealogical and sexual uncertainty, as a counterweight to the sublimity of spatial expanses and monstrosities.

As figured in *Pierre,* the underside or netherworld to American manifest destiny is a Manhattan of horribly confined spaces, degraded architecture, random social violence, and intellectual charlatans and eccentrics. The title character arrives at this hellhole through the repudiation of his own familial destiny and the resignation of his symbolic sexual roles as the son-husband of his widowed, socially potent, and still attractive mother and as the fiancé of the blonde and socially acceptable Lucy Tartan. Melville places Pierre between two confinements: the position of American social eminence that is his for the asking by virtue of his family's patriotic past (his great-grandfather was a hero at the Revolutionary War battle of Saratoga) and the marginality and destitution he chooses by abandoning this inherited post and pursuing the aspirations of a writer. Pierre's sanctioned fate is limited by its predetermination and social conventionality; his chosen path by its pretensions to Kantian original genius and its social deviance. Pierre suffers for his artistic predilections. His fate is both a lament for the struggle of the American artist of the epoch and an admonition against an excessive *jouissance* of the creative sublime. Within the body of Melville's works, the warning inherent to *Pierre* may be read as a literary defense against the grandeur that may otherwise seem attainable in *Moby-Dick*.

The trajectory described by *Pierre* begins in an idyllic merging with a maternal estate and nature, and with a mother, and ends in the travesty contained in Pierre's final surroundings. The atmosphere with which the novel begins, surrounding Pierre's interactions with his mother and his fiancée, is heady and expansive, flavored by the intimate witticisms that prevail between a favored (only) son and his adoring mother:

> Pierre had more than once, with a playful malice, openly sworn, that the man—gray-beard or beardless—who should dare propose marriage to his mother, that man would by some peremptory unrevealed agency immediately disappear from the earth.
>
> This romantic filial love of Pierre seemed fully returned by the triumphant maternal pride of the widow, who in the clear-cut lineaments and noble air of the son, saw her own graces strangely translated into the opposite sex. There was a striking personal resemblance between them; and as the mother seemed to have long stood still in her beauty, heedless of the passing years; so Pierre seemed to meet her half-way, and by a splendid precocity of form and feature, almost advanced himself to that mature stand-point in Time, where his pedestaled mother so long had stood. In the playfulness of their unclouded love, and with that strange license which a perfect confidence and mutual understanding at all points, had long bred between them, they were wont to call each other brother and sister. . . . Thus freely and lightsomely for mother and son flowed on the pure joined current of life.
>
> An excellent English author of these times enumerating the prime advantages of his natal lot, cites foremost, that he first saw the rural light. So with Pierre. It had been his choice fate to have been born and nurtured in the country. . . . On the meadows which sloped away from the shaded rear of the manorial mansion, far to the winding river, an Indian battle had been fought, in the earlier days of the colony, and in that battle the paternal great-grandfather of Pierre, mortally wounded, had sat unhorsed on his saddle in the grass, with his dying voice, still cheering his men in the fray. This was Saddle Meadows, a name likewise extended to the mansion and the village. (*P,* 5–6)

In this passage, Pierre's patrimonial estate; his historical heritage and destiny; his uniquely intimate rapport to his mother, one of whose aspects is a pronounced "twinning"; and his recognizable status as a Romantic protagonist coincide. The composition of these statuses is, however, not coincidental: the character "Pierre" is an aggregate of qualities and interests, several of which would put him on the sociopolitical, metaphysical, and creative margin of his times. Pierre evolves in the course of the novel into the *bête noir* and martyr of his composite marginal statuses.

For one, there is the uncanny aura surrounding his relationship to his mother: an "unclouded love," a "strange license," and a "perfect confidence" between these characters. The elder's traits have been "strangely translated" to the younger, producing an uncanny transsexual resemblance. On the father's side, there is the patrimony itself, an estate, Saddle Meadows, steeped in reminiscences of the nation's native and bellicose origins. And there is the cultural surround to Pierre's vicissitudes furnished by the Romantic mass culture rising to a pitch during Pierre's youth. Indeed, there may be chance elements at work in Pierre's status: an oedipally involved, precocious son-master, belonging to a privileged class and owning a special property marked by the history and mythology of American origins, in the heyday of Romantic mass culture, with its Rousseauan and Wordsworthian pronouncements on the beneficence of nature and urban evil. But the narrative, I think, makes a case for the *parallelism* of Pierre's attributes: the joy of a unique rapport with a still-beautiful mother is *like* being a proud, unencumbered Rousseauan subject—is *like* being the citizen of a yet-young radical nation with strong links to the American Revolution—is *like* owning a choice piece of real estate in a sheltering but free country, and so on. The character Pierre, then, is not only an idiosyncratic fictional surrogate. "He" is an exemplar of a certain national, historical, class-linked, and epistemological (Romantic) status. This status, at least at the outset of the novel, incorporates newness, virginity, naivete, expansiveness, and purity in the sense of being unmarked, unsullied by the involutions of writing as well as of sexual knowledge. The story of "Pierre" details the vicissitudes of all these statuses.

Which is why, then, the narrative allows itself to go so far afield as to furnish commentary on issues like the rapport between Old and New Worlds, the contrast between monarchies and democracies:

> The monarchical world very generally imagines, that in demagoguical America the sacred Past hath no fixed statues erected to it, but all things irreverently seethe and boil in the vulgar caldron of an everlasting uncrystalizing Present. This conceit would seem peculiarly applicable to the social condition. With no chartered aristocracy, and no law of entail, how can any family in America imposingly perpetuate itself? Certainly that common saying among us, which declares, that be a family as conspicuous as it may, a single half-century shall see it abased; that maxim undoubtedly holds true with the commonality. In our cities families rise and burst like bubbles in a vat. For indeed the democratic element operates as a subtile acid among us; forever producing new things by corroding the old; as in the south of France verdigris, the primitive material of one kind of green paint, is produced by grape-vinegar poured upon copper plates. Now in general nothing can be more significant of decay than the idea of corrosion; yet on the other hand, nothing can more vividly suggest luxuriance of life, than the idea of green as a color; for green is the peculiar signet of all-fertile Nature herself. Herein by apt

analogy we behold the marked anomalousness of America; whose character
abroad, we need not be surprised, is misconceived, when we consider how
strangely she contradicts all prior notions of human things; and how wonder-
fully to her, Death itself becomes transmuted into Life. So that political institutions, which in other lands seem above all things intensely artificial,
with America seem to possess the divine virtue of a natural law; for the most
mighty of nature's laws is this, that out of Death she brings Life. (*P,* 8–9)

The "hinge" of this passage is the connection between two shades of
green: a cupric one arising from the chemical reaction of acid on metal and
hence associated with engraving and the democracy of a free press; and the
pastoral green irradiating the Romantic, American countryside. U.S. culture
may suffer from a certain absence of markings, traditions, and directions, but
this lack is more than compensated for by the dynamism of a vibrant if im-
pure ferment. No "chartered aristocracy" exists to predicate where things
stand. This is a society, specifies the narrative, that thrives in the countryside
rather than in towns or cities. Cities are, like monarchy and the European
past in general, arbitrary, predetermined, and inert in their orders and divisions. In the passage below, the narrative finds itself in league with a Europe
that situates (and dissembles) its power in the countryside. "Pierre" is a citizen of the countryside; this exurban frontier also forms part of his—and his
culture's—preexistent patrimony:

> Too often the American that himself makes his fortune, builds him a great
> metropolitan house, in the most metropolitan street of the most metropolitan
> town. Whereas a European of the same sort would thereupon migrate into
> the country. That therein the European hath the better of it, no poet, no phi-
> losopher, and no aristocrat will deny. For the country is not only the most
> poetical and philosophical, but it is the most aristocratic part of this earth, for
> it is the most venerable, and numerous bards have ennobled it by many fine
> titles. Whereas the town is the more plebeian portion: which, besides many
> fine things, is plainly evinced by the dirty unwashed face perpetually worn
> by the town; but the country, like any Queen, is ever attended by scrupulous
> lady's maids in the guise of the seasons, and the town hath but one dress of
> brick turned up with stone; but the country hath a brave dress for every
> week in the year; sometimes she changes her dress twenty-four times in the
> twenty-four hours; and the country weareth her sun by day as a diamond on
> a Queen's brow; and the stars by night as necklaces of gold beads; whereas the
> town's sun is smoky paste, and not diamond, and the town's stars are pinch-
> beck and not gold. (*P,* 13)

As it seeds the fictive conditions that will make Pierre's fate plausible, the
narrative specifies one additional element of his heritage: his readiness for a
permanent romantic attachment; his vulnerability to Love. Though it can be

argued that the history of romance exceeds the boundaries of Romanticism's epoch, there is nonetheless a privileged rapport between these two categories, especially at a moment when the laws of society emanate from an immanent, human source and when relations of fraternity have replaced those of patriarchy as the basis of authority. (This in a society where the blush of freedom offers an understated erotic tinge.) In addition to a mother, an estate, and an utterly predetermined (if pleasant) fate, Pierre has love to contend with. The narrative characterizes love as a pervasive sublime dimension whose underlying violence undermines a superficial allure.

> Love was first begot by Mirth and Peace, in Eden, when the world was young. . . . So, as youth, for the most part, has no cares, and knows no gloom, therefore, ever since time did begin, youth belongs to love. Love may end in grief and age, and pain and need, and all other modes of human mournfulness; but love begins in joy. Love's first sigh is never breathed, till after love hath laughed. Love laughs first, and then sighs after. Love has not hands, but cymbals; Love's mouth is chambered like a bugle, and the instinctive breathings of his life breathe jubilee notes of joy! (*P*, 33)

> No Cornwall miner ever sunk so deep a shaft beneath the sea, as Love will sink beneath the floatings of the eyes. Love sees ten thousand fathoms down, till dazzled by the floor of pearls. The eye is Love's own magic glass, where all things that are not of earth, glide in supernatural light. There are not so many fishes in the sea, as there are sweet images in lovers' eyes. In those miraculous translucencies swim the strange-eye fish with wings, that sometimes leap out, instinct with joy; moist fish-wings wet the lover's cheek. . . .
>   Endless is the account of Love. Time and space cannot contain Love's story. All things that are sweet to see, or taste, or feel, or hear, all these things were made by Love; and none other things were made by Love. Love made not the Arctic zones, but Love is ever reclaiming them. (*P*, 33–34)

These two passages precede the sublime disruption to Pierre's complacent fate through the invasion of the taboo "dark" woman Isabel into his existence. In the first extract immediately above, the narrative humanizes and personifies Love. Love is a character with a certain lifespan. It begins and ends; it speaks. Love may be an oddball; there may be anomalies in its temporality; but it is basically a familiar fellow of the mortal human being. By the second segment of the extract Love has become a phenomenon of sublime proportions, no linger a "he" or "she," but an It. It resides in the immensities of the subterranean and submarine deep; its complexities dwarf the immensities of Time and Space themselves. Love's gaze is the Uncanny itself. Love's operation redefines the conditions of subjectivity pertaining to those mythical and mythologized individuals under its thrall; it makes them other-than-human, both more and less.

Pierre's characterization of love is itself uncanny, fusing the recognizability of a subjective love model with the impersonality and seeming indifference of the sublime. An already uncanny love sets the stage for a split in Pierre's affections. This split may seem to be between the blond Lucy and dark Isabel; between sanctioned romance and its adulterous supplement; between altruism and incest. Indeed, the novel involves all these countereconomies. But the split in Pierre's affections derives from a more ancient lineage than the plot propositions of this particular novel; we recognize it as a precondition of knowledge and subjectivity pertaining to the broader modernity itself. Consciousness is itself split as the hypothetical but still pained subject is beset with regulating him- or herself in an age of disconcerting freedom decorated by a surround of morally dire consequences. Language is the network that articulates and inscribes the polymorphic splits characterizing subjectivity. It is in relation to language as an aesthetic medium that the splitting of modernity plays itself out.

In *Pierre,* Melville, at the same time that he purportedly penetrates a female reading audience, elaborates the domestic supplement to the "outside" sublime, the one set and depicted in some external landscape. Everything in Melville's poetics and in his delineation of the conditions prevailing in the aesthetic contracts under which he writes and "produces art" demands that this domestic sublime be every bit as disruptive and overwhelming to "normative" (male? white? ruling class? U.S.?) subjectivity as the sublime assuming the form of monsters unearthed in polar (and other out-of-the-way) locations. It falls to the character known as Isabel to be so fantastic, sublime, uncanny, and disconcerting as to wreak the havoc within the domestic, matrimonial, and patrimonial spheres that the White Whale visits upon the *Pequod.* Isabel is the instrument of disruption to "Pierre's" existence that the Kantian sublime is to scale, order, comfort, and everyday reason. In the wake of Isabel's overall disruptiveness and re-scaling there will prevail, as in the case of the *Pequod,* only demoralization and death; Melville's sublime fictions cannot furnish the salutary reassurance offered by the Kantian model, that of an ongoing existence (Winnicottian "continuity of being"?) [11] periodically shaken but then restored by the outbreak of sublimity.

It will take quite a woman to initiate all this disruption.

> The girl sits steadily sewing; neither she nor her two companions speak. Her eyes are mostly upon her work; but now and then a close observer would notice that she furtively lifts them, and moves them sideways and timidly toward Pierre; and then, still more furtively and timidly toward his lady mother, further off. All the while, her preternatural calmness sometimes seems only made to cover the intensest struggle in her bosom. Her un-

adorned and modest dress is black; fitting close up to her neck, and clasping it
with a plain, velvet border. To a nice perception, that velvet shows elastically;
contracting and expanding, as though some choked, violent thing were risen
up there from within the teeming region of her heart. But her dark, olive
cheek is without a blush, or sign of any disquietude. So far as this girl lies
upon the common surface, ineffable composure steeps her. But still, she side-
ways steals the furtive, timid glance. Anon, as yielding to the irresistible cli-
max of her concealed emotion, whatever that might be, she lifts her whole
marvelous countenance into the radiant candlelight, and for one swift instant,
the face of supernaturalness unreservedly meets Pierre's. Now, wonderful love-
liness, and a still more wonderful loneliness, have with inexplicable implor-
ings, looked up to him from that henceforth immemorial face. There, too, he
seemed to see the fair ground where Anguish had contended with Beauty, and
neither being conquerer, both had laid down on the field. (*P*, 46–47)

Like the sea itself, Isabel initially presents a calm surface under which the
most jarring repercussions may be taking place. A "preternatural calmness"
hovers over her. Her gaze moves "furtively and timidly." Isabel is a creature
of the Freudian Uncanny: within the terms of this economy, she is modest
yet threatening; passive yet immeasurably strong. Her most powerful weapons may be "inexplicable longings" and "Anguish," but these exert a force
over Pierre far in excess of their initially modest and passive appearance. The
narrative has Isabel, in her first apparition, as a dark American Lucy Gray:
a passion-arousing image of passivity, awaiting, even demanding appropriation, penetration, projection, whether corporeal or intellectual, by he who
apprehends her. That "the other woman," the dark foil to Pierre's otherwise
glowing prospects, could be a Lucy-figure posed against Lucy Tartan, is an
irony not lost to the narrative.

Isabel has evolved, and not evolved, by the moment when she and Pierre
possess each other, the instance closest to a seduction the narrative describes.
She is not entirely above physical contact, yet she retains an aura of self-
containedness, passivity, and even death. In Isabel, the supplement to his personal manifest destiny, who replaces marriage, domesticity, and the access to
patrimony with the sublimities of adultery and incest, Pierre opts for his own
symbolic death:

> He felt a faint struggling within his clasp; her head drooped against him; his
> whole form was bathed in the flowing glossiness of her long and unimpris-
> oned hair. Brushing the locks aside, he now gazed upon the deathlike beauty
> of the face, and caught immortal sadness from it. She seemed as dead; as suf-
> focated,—the death that leaves most unimpaired the latent tranquillities and
> sweetnesses of the human countenance. . . . Tenderly he leads her to a bench
> within the double casement; and sits beside her; and waits in silence, till the

first shock of this encounter shall have left her more composed and more prepared to hold communion with him. (*P,* 112)

Here and elsewhere, Isabel's allure is her dark, textually involuted tresses.
The narrative frames this scene of Pierre and Isabel's mutual surrender in a
Romantic casement (as in Keats's "The Eve of St. Agnes," XXIV–XXV),
but it is precisely as a counter to the stable enclosure of the Romantic image
that Melville elaborates the lurid coupling of Isabel and Pierre. In a pre-
emptive twist to the Freud of *Beyond the Pleasure Principle,* sexuality is the
road to death in *Pierre,* a death whose stately morbidity contrasts with the
awesome dynamism of death in *Moby-Dick.* The death drive is not an add-
on to the pleasure principle: here the perverse pleasure of unsanctioned, un-
domesticated sex is the royal road to death itself.

The instrument of this seduction and punishment is Isabel, whose name
is a variant of the biblical temptress Jezebel. Everything the narrative tells us
about this character, other than her various allures, concerns her being an
intuitive artist, specifically a musician. Isabel's passion and intuition fit her
out as a musical original genius, a musician by sympathy and predilection
rather than by training:

> One day there came to this house a pedler. In his wagon he had a guitar, an
> old guitar, yet a very pretty one, but with broken strings. He had got it slyly
> in part exchange from the servants of a grand house some distance off. Spite
> of the broken strings, the thing looked very graceful and beautiful to me; and
> I knew there was melodiousness lurking in the thing, though I had never
> seen a guitar before, nor heard of one; but there was a strange humming in
> my heart that seemed to prophesy of the hummings of the guitar. Intuitively,
> I knew that the strings were not as they should be. I said to the man—I will
> buy of thee the thing thou callest a guitar. But thou must put new strings to
> it. . . . Straightway I took it to my little chamber in the gable, and softly laid
> it on my bed. Then I murmured; sung and murmured to it; very lowly, very
> softly; I could hardly hear myself. And I changed the modulations of my
> singings and my murmurings; and still sung, and murmured, lowly, softly,—
> more and more; and presently I heard a sudden sound; sweet and low beyond
> all telling was the sweet and sudden sound. I clapt my hands; the guitar was
> speaking to me; the dear guitar was singing to me, the guitar. Then I sung
> and murmured to it with a still different modulation; and once more it an-
> swered me from a different string; and once more it murmured to me, and it
> answered me with a different string. The guitar was human; the guitar taught
> me the secret of the guitar; the guitar learned me to play on the guitar. No
> music-master have I ever had but the guitar. I made a loving friend of it; a
> heart friend of it. It sings to me as I to it. . . . All the wonders that are un-

imaginable and unspeakable; all these wonders are translated in the mysterious melodiousness of the guitar. It knows all my past history. (*P,* 125)

The epistemology of *Pierre* pivots around foreknowledge, not afterthought. Foreknowledge is to the sphere of characterology what intuition is to the domain of knowledge. Sight unseen, Isabel knows what a guitar is, and how to play music on it. The above passage reverberates with Isabel's inherent sympathies and immediate recognitions. With Pierre, in a literary instance of *folie à deux,* she *knows* that she is a long-lost half-sister, the issue of an adulterous liaison on the part of Glendinning *père.* A considerable portion of *Pierre's* narrative is devoted to tracing the implications of such misrecognitions and foregone conclusions. The narrative will even deign, as we shall see, to cast doubt on the very inferences that by its own connivance have motivated these characters.

In the passage immediately above, there is an uncanny sympathy between Isabel and her guitar. She is mysteriously drawn to this object. The dynamic between Isabel and her instrument, which becomes the instrument of Pierre's perdition and death, is one of intuitive sympathetic vibration. Her increasingly sublime murmurings are *already* music. Isabel's relation to the guitar is one of immediate recognition and appropriation. She knows that the strings aren't right and that she can play it. There is a "touch of the artist" about Isabel as there is about Ahab; she is an intuitive American artist. When the scene of the encounter with the sublime shifts indoors, music, no longer whaling, becomes the activity with transcendental implications. Music, in the West, is one of the longstanding womanly arts.

The guitar, in return, speaks to Isabel in a human voice; becomes a human friend. There is a peculiar poignancy in the alienation and solitude that force Isabel to find human sympathy and immediacy in a wooden object, even if it is a guitar. The guitar is an object that speaks with a human voice. It is not only human, but a human agent; it teaches Isabel: "It knows all [her] past history" (*P,* 125). In this sense, it is a magical object indeed; it is a thing, an old and broken-down one at that, that has metamorphosed itself into a loving human caregiver (a teacher).

Isabel may not be an intellectual, but what she knows she knows with the finality of intuition. She, and her uncanny knowledge, live in the paradoxical time warp of predictive finality. The moment of an inevitable conclusion that has been predicted is the present, the absolute present. The force of Isabel's art and attraction in some measure derive from the presentness of her situation and bearing. Isabelle's bizarre presentation is magnetic. Music and

magnets exert an attraction that is ongoing, uniform, and undeniable. It is
not far from this magnetism to the allure of sexuality itself:

> I am called woman, and thou, man, Pierre; but there is neither man nor
> woman about it. Why should I not speak out to thee? There is no sex in our
> immaculateness. Pierre, the secret name in the guitar even now thrills me
> through and through. Pierre, think! think! Oh, canst thou not comprehend?
> see it? The secret name in the guitar thrills me, thrills me, thrills me, whirls
> me, whirls me; so secret, wholly hidden, yet constantly carried about in it;
> unseen, unsuspected, always vibrating to the hidden heart-strings—broken
> heart-strings; oh, my mother, my mother, my mother! (*P,* 149)

> Now this first night was Pierre made aware of what, in the superstitiousness
> of his rapt enthusiasm, he could not help believing was an extraordinary
> physical magnetism in Isabel. And—as it were derived from this marvelous
> quality thus imputed to her—he now first became vaguely sensible of a cer-
> tain still more marvelous power in the girl over herself and his most interior
> thoughts and motions;—a power so hovering upon the confines of the invis-
> ible world, that it seemed more inclined that way than this;—a power which
> not only seemed irresistibly to draw him toward Isabel, but to draw him away
> from another quarter—wantonly as it were, and yet quite ignorantly and
> unintendingly. . . . For over all these things, and interfusing itself with the
> sparkling electricity in which she seemed to swim, was an ever-creeping and
> condensing haze of ambiguities. Often, in after-times with her, did he recall
> this first magnetic night, and would seem to see that she then had bound him
> to her by an extraordinary atmospheric spell—both physical and spiritual—
> which henceforth it had become impossible for him to break, but whose full
> potency he never realized till long after he had become habituated to its sway.
> This spell seemed one with that Pantheistic master-spell, which eternally
> locks in mystery and in muteness the universal subject world, and the physical
> electricalness of Isabel seemed reciprocal with the heat-lightnings and the
> ground-lightnings nigh to which it had first become revealed to Pierre. She
> seemed molded from fire and air. (*P,* 151)

In these passages Isabel consummates her own brand of sublimity, inhering to herself, the allure of sexuality, the register of textuality, and "original genius," the modern raison d'être of artists and artistry.[12] Isabel has transformed herself from an uncanny, Romantic, sublime "unmoved mover" to
someone only too susceptible to vibrations, too caught up in the whirling
that both deranges and is the mark of derangement of more than one Romantic character (I think of Hoffmann's Nathanael at the end of "The Sandman").[13] In the first passage above, Isabel, introjectively addressing and conjuring up the mother who was by her own account denied her, dramatizes
how musically, sexually, and possibly delusionally attuned she is. The music
of the guitar strings becomes conflated with that of heartstrings: the experi-

ence of music serves as an accompaniment to an intense, near-superhuman sensitivity allowing Isabel to conjure up and symbolically merge with her absent mother. Isabel protests the chastity of her rapport with Pierre; her receptivity to thrilling and vibrations nonetheless interpolates a potent aura of sensuality into communicating with her mother. Isabel's precipitating herself into the domain of sexuality is tantamount to her initiating this communication, symbolically accessing her mother within herself.

Isabel has metamorphosed herself from an uncannily quiescent female character into an electric personage. Electricity is the physical manifestation incorporating the s-curve of the musical and sexual vibrations that have become Isabel's signature.[14] The character Isabel encompasses both "the sparkling electricity in which she seemed to swim" and the murkiness of "an ever-creeping and condensing haze of ambiguities" (*P*, 151). Within the novel's dramaturgy of characters, or subject-surrogates, Isabel is a polymorphic source of power as well as light. Within the work's allegory of reading, she is a source of textual complexity, here called "ambiguities," the novel's subtitle. Isabel is deadly both as a femme fatale and as a textual creature. Her engagement with Pierre compromises him definitively within his fictive network of conventional social relations. In light of the fact that the narrative describes him artistically as a hit-and-miss lightweight poet, his engagement with her destroys him intellectually; the ambiguities she condenses and sets into play are too much for him. Socially, that is, interpersonally, and aesthetically, Pierre is no match for Isabel.

Isabel's electricity is reminiscent of certain elements in the landscape, or rather seascape, surrounding Moby-Dick, notably the preternatural glow issuing from the masts and Ahab's harpoon (*MD*, 36: 162–66; 119: 505–8). A characteristic Melvillian ambiguity is the fact that "internal" and "external" ambiguities cannot strictly keep to their places. Isabel achieves her full measure of mystery, uncanniness, and genius only projected outward as a phenomenon of nature, as a textual electric eel of unbridled power and seduction:

> There is a dark, mad mystery in some human hearts, which, sometimes, during the tyranny of a usurper mood, leads them to be all eagerness to cast off the most intense beloved bond, as a hindrance to the attainment of whatever transcendental object that usurper mood so tyrannically suggests. Then the beloved bond seems to hold us to no essential good; lifted to exalted mounts, we can dispense with all the vale; endearments we spurn; kisses are blisters to us; and forsaking the palpitating forms of mortal love, we emptily embrace the boundless and the unbodied air. We think we are not human; we become as immortal bachelors and gods; but again, like the Greek gods themselves,

prone we descend to earth; glad to be uxorious once more; glad to hide these
god-like heads within the bosoms made of too-seducing clay.

Weary with the invariable earth, the restless sailor breaks from every en-
folding arm, and puts to sea in height of tempest that blows off shore. But
in long night-watches at the antipodes, how heavily that ocean gloom lies
in vast bales on the deck; thinking that that very moment in his deserted
hamlet-home the household sun is high, and many a sun-eyed maiden me-
ridian as the sun. He curses Fate; himself he curses; his senseless madness,
which is himself. For whoso once has known this sweet knowledge, and then
fled it; in absence, to him the avenging dream will come.

Pierre was now this vulnerable god; this self-upbraiding sailor; this dreamer
of the avenging dream. Though in some things he had unjuggled himself, and
forced himself to eye the prospect as it was; yet, so far as Lucy was concerned,
he was at bottom still a juggler. True, in his extraordinary scheme, Lucy was
so intimately interwoven, that it seemed impossible for him at all to cast his
future without some way having that heart's love in view. But ignorant of its
quantity as yet, or fearful of ascertaining it; like an algebraist, for the real Lucy
he, in his scheming thoughts, had substituted but a sign—some empty x—
and in the ultimate solution of the problem, that empty x still figured; not the
real Lucy. . . . Now finally, to top all, there suddenly slid into his inmost heart
the living and breathing form of Lucy. His lungs collapsed; his eyeballs glared;
for the sweet imagined form, so long buried alive in him, seemed now as
gliding on him from the grave; and her light hair swept far adown her shroud.
(*P,* 180–81)

Pierre struggles here with his grandiosity. The narrative frames his meditations as the conflict in some general "we" over maintaining constancy in
our bonds of love. The hypothetical subject, in such deliberations, "experiences" itself as weighing its options, as if in total control over the situation.
The narrative compares this narcissistic deliberation to the ruminations of a
sailor's night watch. If Isabel has become a creature of sublime ambiguity and
electricity projected into the outside world, in this passage Pierre appears as
the sailor, and the narrative reinforces its implicit parallelism between marine
and domestic sublimities.

With Isabel a demonic seductress and Pierre a sailor of lofty night-
deliberations, the role of Lucy Tartan, as of conventionality, has been subjected to a dramatic reduction in scope. Lucy's familial name intimates the
Cartesian rectangularity and domestic comfort of a plaid design. Through his
own waverings, Pierre has "ruined" the fate of a young woman of considerable stature, legitimacy, and plaidlike "squareness." It is upon her fate that
Pierre presumes to deliberate in the detachment described in the above passage. The narrative here characterizes the "fallen" Pierre, not unlike Jean-
Jacques Rousseau, as part mathematician, part spasmodic adventurer in the
sublime.[15] The narrative suggests that at this stage of the travesty, Pierre, hav-

ing adopted Isabel and abandoned Lucy to her own devices, is not so much an "identity" selecting female essences as a dabbler in algebra. The narrative downplays the drama of Pierre's selection in favor of intimating a certain substitutability within the domestic sublime. Lucy is not so different from Isabel after all. The sublimity of Woman in General is an irreducible component in Pierre's "experience." In the end, it is not so crucial whether the occasion for the domestic sublime is called "Lucy" or "Isabel." The indeterminacy of the x in an equation is what grants it its sublimity. At this point in Pierre's trajectory, when it has turned decidedly downward, the narrative intimates that it was the indeterminacy—in Melville's terms, the ambiguity—of the quest for Woman, and not Pierre's specific turnabout, that predicated his actions and their consequences.

The narrative associates Pierre's ambiguities with the Shakespearean character Hamlet. We have seen that Hamlet stands at the head of the Western subjective conditions—and the status that art and language maintain in determining and possibly releasing them—prevailing over an epoch still extending into our most recent modernism (c. 1890–1945). Pierre's appeal to Hamlet is in the spirit of Michael Kohlhaas's to Luther, and of Benjamin's to Shakespeare and German baroque tragedy—to the purported origin of such painful personal rumination, and the role that art might play in an apotheosis and escape:

> If among the deeper significances of its pervading indefiniteness, which significances are wisely hidden from all but the rarest adepts, the pregnant tragedy of Hamlet convey any one particular moral at all fitted to the ordinary uses of man, it is this;—that all meditation is worthless, unless it prompt to action; that it is not for man to stand shillyshallying. . . .
>
> Pierre had always been an admiring reader of Hamlet; but neither his age nor his mental experience thus far, had qualified him either to catch initiating glimpses into the hopeless gloom of its interior meaning, or to draw from the general story those superficial and purely incidental lessons, wherein the painstaking moralist so complacently expatiates.
>
> The intensest light of reason and revelation combined, can not shed such blazonings upon the deeper truths in man, as will sometimes proceed from his own profoundest gloom. Utter darkness is then his light, and cat-like he distinctly sees all objects through a medium which is mere blindness to common vision. Where have Gloom and Grief been celebrated of old as the selectest chamberlains to knowledge? Wherefore is it, that not to know Gloom and Grief is not to know aught that an heroic man should learn?
>
> By the light of that gloom, Pierre now turned over the soul of Hamlet in his hand. (*P,* 169)

Pierre here steps into the guise of a modernist, that is, in its broadest sense. In Hamlet he finds a kindred spirit, a fellow traveler through the age pre-

vailing from Luther, Calvin, Descartes, and Shakespeare into our own waning century. Like Benjamin, Pierre appeals to Hamlet as an ur-melancholist.
Pierre, having entered the arc on his trajectory at which he reaps the produce of his unsanctioned love, tantamount, as we have seen, to his thirst for
death—Pierre finds a soulmate in the tragic, unhappy, and immobilized
Hamlet.

Fetchers and carriers of the worst city infamy as many of them are; professionally familiar with the most abandoned haunts; in the heart of misery they
drive one of the most mercenary of all the trades of guilt. Day-dozers and
sluggards on their lazy boxes in the sunlight, and felinely wakeful and cat-
eyed in the dark; most habituated to midnight streets, only trod by sneaking
burglars, wantons, and debauchees; often in actual pandering league with
the most abhorrent sinks; so that they are equally solicitous and suspectful
that every customer they encounter in the dark, will prove a profligate or
knave; this hideous tribe of ogres, and Charon ferry-men to corruption
and death, naturally slide into the most practically Calvinistical view of humanity, and hold every man at bottom a fit subject for the coarsest ribaldry
and jest; only fine coats and full pockets can whip such mangy hoards into
decency. The least impatience, any quickness of temper, a sharp remonstrat-
ing word . . . will be almost sure to provoke, in such cases, their least endur-
able disdain. (*P,* 232)

Pierre's prospects have indeed taken a somber turn. The *dénouement* of
Pierre devotes itself to the underside of the joyous expansion celebrated ec-
statically at times in Rousseau and in *Moby-Dick*. Through "his own" impulses, those of an exemplary individual schooled under a Romantic epistemology of aesthetic transcendence and sensual essentiality, Pierre has arrived
at a definitive impasse represented as a morbid enclosure: within a city, a
madhouse, a prison, a tomb.

At stake here is an entire tradition, not merely an individual literary character. In the figure of Pierre, a secular liberal tradition of human-based ethical standards and solutions to ongoing conceptual and practical problems
finds its limits. These constraints are tantamount to the repressions, the points
of ideological fixity, within the modern predicament. Pierre runs afoul of the
law for reasons he cannot exactly fathom. Is it a gene of perversity he has
inherited from his father? Is Isabel so essentially different from the Lucy who
embodies both his fate and his heritage? Pierre runs afoul of the law for reasons he cannot articulate.[16] His rash actions taken, however, he is at once an

outcast and a prisoner. Indeed, imprisonment, undergoing physical confinement and discretionary *contraction,* is precisely the revenge meted out on such an unknowing outlaw. There is an uncertainty about Pierre's crimes that uncannily anticipates the trespasses of the Kafka protagonists who are in legal trouble from the outset: Joseph K. of *The Trial,* the narrator of "The Knock at the Manor Gate," the prisoner of "In the Penal Colony."

There is something ineradicably repressive about the punishment to which Pierre is ultimately subjected; there is something irreducibly arbitrary in the late-Enlightenment-Romantic ideology whose explicit intent was to delimit the authoritarian, to uproot the arbitrary. Pierre stands on the threshold of Nietzsche's ethical deliberations, because he is the martyr of the anti-system that was to obviate the need for martyrdom. This is why he must be a bad artist, an *artiste-manqué.* He cannot quite enter the martyrdom that Kant designed for the artist. That very liberal aspiration of transcendence, penetration into the Universe's operating system, has turned against him.

Invoking Calvin, the passage at the head of this section assumes a tone of stark moralism in equating the city's corruption with the depravity of its characteristic denizens. Pierre's fellow-travelers in the domain of the American patrimony that he *has* elected are a sorry and disconcerting lot indeed. Pierre's new company is not only lower-class, "fetchers and carriers of the worst city infamy" (*P,* 232). These companions are nocturnal, utterly cynical, physically ugly, and morally perverse (or perhaps better, *inverse*).

In lower Manhattan, Pierre and entourage have come upon a Hegelian topsy-turvy world[17] at the outer limits of whose logic are situated Derridean features of writing (duplicity, insubordination, death).[18] The first of the new urban neighbors on whom Pierre sets eyes dwell in "abandoned haunts"; vacillate between assumed solicitousness and suspicion in their interpersonal interactions; stand ready to treat their fellow human beings with utmost contempt; and apply rigidly Calvinist criteria to the very individuals they intend to attack and betray. The narrative rises to a pitch of sermonizing moralism here: "the worst city infamy"; "day-dozers and sluggards on their lazy boxes"; "the most abhorrent sinks"; "this hideous tribe of ogres, and Charon ferry-men to corruption and death" (*P,* 232). Pierre, in the reduced circumstances he has elected, has not only erred into a New York that Melville has imported from the torments of Dante's Inferno; he has entered an environment more conducive to his writing than the historical romance of Saddle Meadows. Pierre is, unfortunately, not the sort of writer who can rise to this presumably edifying shift. Melville's logocentric setting of a writer-*manqué's* hell depicts Pierre as stifled and defeated in a "prison-house of language" as well as on the wrong side of town.[19]

An urban hell depicted from a logocentric point of view demands a specific architecture, and in *Pierre,* Melville rises in an unprecedented way to the architectural occasion:

> In the lower old-fashioned part of the city, in a narrow street . . . stood at this period a rather singular and ancient edifice, a relic of the more primitive time. The material was a grayish stone, rudely cut and masoned into walls of surprising thickness and strength; along two of which walls—the side ones— were distributed as many rows of arched and stately windows. A capacious, square, and wholly unornamented tower rose in front to twice the height of the body of the church; three sides of this tower were pierced with small and narrow apertures. Thus far, in its external aspect, the building—now more than a century old,—sufficiently attested for what purpose it had originally been founded. In its rear, was a large and lofty plain brick structure, with its front to the rearward street . . . leaving a small, flagged, and quadrangular vacancy between. At the sides of this quadrangle, three stories of homely brick colonnades afforded covered communication between the ancient church, and its less elderly adjunct. A dismantled, rusted, and forlorn old railing of iron fencing in a small courtyard in front of the rearward building, seemed to hint, that the latter had usurped an unoccupied space formerly sacred as the old church's burial inclosure. . . . The old Church of the Apostles had had its days of sanctification and grace; but the tide of change and progress had rolled clean through its broad-aisle and side-aisles, and swept by far the greater part of its congregation two or three miles up town. (*P,* 265–66)

The Church of the Apostles is a wayward house of God, a house of worship transformed into (what the narrator considers to be) a contemporary tower of Babel, a house of trite and fruitless discourse. The architecture of the church is emblematic of Pierre's predicament. It contains a noble past (a "capacious" tower; a "large and lofty" brick structure) brought down to reduced and dubious current circumstances (the "dismantled, rusted, and forlorn old railing"—*P,* 265). The church has lost its "sanctification and grace" (*P,* 266).

The residents of this impacted, circumscribed architecture are empty-headed *poseurs* who issue forth in voluminous but vacant language. The emptiness of their pronouncements is in keeping with the poverty of their circumstances. From Saddle Meadows, in which Pierre could have written the sanctioned and official narrative of his nation's and family's past, he has erred into a purgatory of bombast with no firm (that is, economic) backing. From the perspective of *Pierre,* this is a travesty; in terms of Herman Melville's career, there may be some parallelism between the rhetorics of Pierre's decline and the terms in which the historical author understood his own vocation:

Here they sit and talk like magpies; or descending in quest of improbable dinners, are to be seen drawn up along the curb in front of the eating-houses, like lean rows of broken-hearted pelicans on a bench; their pockets loose, hanging down and flabby, like the pelican's pouches when fish are hard to be caught. But these poor, penniless devils still strive to make ample amends for their physical forlornness, by resolutely reveling in the region of blissful ideals.

They are mostly artists of various sorts; painters, or sculptors, or indigent students, or teachers of languages, or poets, or fugitive French politicians, or German philosophers. Their mental tendencies, however heterodox at times, are still very fine and spiritual upon the whole; since the vacuity of their exchequers leads them to reject the coarse materialism of Hobbes, and incline to the airy exhalations of Berkelyan philosophy. Often groping in vain in their pockets, they can not but give in to the Descartian vortices; while the abundance of leisure in their attics (physical and figurative), unites with the leisure in their stomachs, to fit them in an eminent degree for that undivided attention indispensable to the proper digesting of the sublimated Categories of Kant; especially as Kant (can't) is the one great palpable fact in their pervading impalpable lives. These are the glorious paupers, from whom I learn the profoundest mysteries of things. (*P*, 267)

The narrative here gives ample attention to the discrepancy between the inflation of the Apostles' subjects and interests and the "reality" of their material circumstances. These men would presume to discourse on subjects as grand as the prevailing operating systems of the universe, articulated from empiricist and idealist points of view, yet they can't quite provide for their breakfasts. They elicit a mixture of amusement and contempt, being both "broken-hearted pelicans" and penniless "devils." Their practical shortcomings, their "can'ts," are in direct relation to Kant, the systems-maker and aesthetician whose designs they presumably fathom and attempt to disseminate.

Pierre is the protagonist in two radically diverging counter-stories. The fate he elects, in one, in which he functions as a historical and familial subject, with a certain degree of free will, is a disaster; but the same fate, undergone in an allegory of writing, is a necessity. Contraction, reduction in the social order; architectural confinement: these are the images that the narrative selects for Pierre's withdrawal from the *jouissance* of systematic expansion. Yet while such contraction may be a travesty for Pierre's tale as a "man," it may be utterly indicative for his vocation as a writer.

Writing, it turns out, may well be the only freedom worth anything that survives a shipwrecked age of systematic aspiration and growth. It may be Pierre's fate to die before the end of the novel that is his namesake; but he outlasts Ishmael as the heritor of the writerly vocation. The sublime, whether encountered "externally" in bizarre landscapes and White Whales, or domestically in the intangibilities of love, ultimately persists only in one domain, in the ambiguities of writing. Writing is the always-generative homeland of a sublime that Western culture insists on displacing to the worlds of adventure (or external action) and love.

Writing may be the most authentic freedom in a culture predicated by bipolar values and an open field of activity demanding a high degree of defensive *Angst* and repression; but without the "eternal vigilance" of rigorous theoretical oversight, writing is itself subject to the possibilities for original genius made accessible, in Promethean fashion, by Kant above all. The modern writer is in the position of the being most elect to exit (or at least see the way out of) the defensive system. Yet this privileged post is beset by its own temptations and possible corruptions; above all the temptation to appropriate the privilege inherent to Western modernity's secular (art) religion. The modern writer, of which Melville's Pierre is not the most intelligent example, is predicated by one of the antinomies that did not get included in Kant's *Critique of Pure Reason*: (1) *Writing is the only true liberty.* (2) *In the relaxation of theoretical (as opposed to sublime) tension, writing is at all times susceptible to the baggage of intellectual transcendence and original genius.*

From practical and existential points of view, the sublimity of love, its duplicity and expansiveness, bring Pierre low, bring him to a station of spatial contraction and reduced economic circumstances. But the same set of events, which existence and practicality can represent as loss, comprise an increase of power from a writerly point of view. Indeed, writing, in the epoch of high capitalism that Melville is in part chronicling, is situated at the margin of efficiency, foresight, and profit. The losses that Pierre undergoes are a tax levied upon the individual for severing the association with the system that determines practicality and social value.

Pierre pays the price for detaching himself from a system already in a state of crisis, a system always in crisis, one already facing its built-in limits toward the middle of the nineteenth century. He is too silly a character to be deemed a martyr. And yet Pierre, like Melville, secures an ineradicable bridgehead connecting to the domain of script. He is a writer in a world in which writing constitutes the only enduring freedom and vestige of the sublime.

⁓

All things that think, or move, or lie still, seemed as created to mock and torment him. He seemed gifted with loftiness, merely that it might be dragged down to the mud. Still, the profound willfulness in him would not give up. Against the breaking heart, and the bursting head; against all the dismal lassitude, and deathful faintness and sleeplessness, and whirlingness, and craziness, still he like a demigod bore up. His soul's ship foresaw the inevitable rocks, but resolved to sail on, and make a courageous wreck. Now he gave jeer for jeer, and taunted the apes that jibed him. With the soul of an Atheist, he wrote down the godliest things; with the feeling of misery and death in him, he created forms of gladness and life. For the pangs in his heart, he put down hoots on the paper. . . . For the more and the more that he wrote, and the deeper and the deeper that he dived, Pierre saw the everlasting elusiveness of Truth; the universal lurking insincerity of even the greatest and purest written thoughts. Like knavish cards, the leaves of all great books were covertly packed. He was but packing one set the more. (*P,* 338–39)

A subject under siege, Pierre writes. Under house arrest, his "soul" undergoes the motions of seasickness. (Is Pierre the unwitting model for Kafka's "seasickness on dry land"?)[20] "Dry" and "wet" sublimities "join hands." In keeping with the aspiration for a secular art-religion regulating a liberal-democratic society that prevailed during his fictive epoch, Pierre is an "Atheist" writing down "the godliest things" (*P,* 339). Pierre writes. His writing is both a liberty and a sentence. His writing is not merely a semiological activity but a condition situated toward the open end of his existential range. This is how Flaubert could locate an *artiste-manqué* in every bourgeois.[21] We are all Pierre, in the sense that we are all Madame Bovary.[22]

The conditions that bring Pierre to his dire (and confining) straits in Manhattan are of far less consequence than his particularly modern predicament: a subject whose register of possibility extends from bipolar logic and repressive defensiveness to writerly *jouissance*. As the novel reaches its deliberately tragic conclusion, the narrative renounces the very circumstances that have putatively determined Pierre's actions. Indeed, it is the conditions of imagination and writing that have set Pierre's course, not errant guitars and seductive dark tresses. The narrative's retrospective repudiation of a "circumstantial" basis for Pierre's deeds and their consequences is peculiar indeed:

> How did he know that Isabel was his sister? Setting aside Aunt Dorothea's nebulous legend, to which, in some shadowy points, here and there Isabel's still more nebulous story seemed to fit on,—though but uncertainly enough—and both of which thus blurredly conjoining narrations, regarded in the unscrupulous light of real naked reason, were anything but legitimately conclusive; and setting aside his own dim reminiscences of his wandering father's death-bed. . . . and setting aside all his own manifold and inter-enfolding mystic and transcendental persuasions,—originally born, as he now seemed to feel, purely of an intense procreative enthusiasm . . . setting all these aside,

and coming to the plain, palpable facts,—how did he *know* that Isabel was his sister? The chair-portrait, *that* was the entire sum and substance of all possible, rakable, downright presumptive evidence. . . . Yet here was another portrait of a complete stranger,—a European; a portrait imported from across the seas, and to be sold at public auction, which was just as strong an evidence as the other. Then the original of this second portrait was as much the father of Isabel as the original of the chair-portrait. But perhaps there was no original at all to this second portrait; it might have been a pure fancy piece. (*P,* 353)

The narrative here performs the uncharacteristic action of questioning the very inferences (on the part of Pierre) that it made possible. Perhaps this retraction is a privilege of the romance genre; perhaps it conveys a subliminal message that novels (at least domestic ones) are indeed frivolous. These questions may initiate a vertiginous cycle of doubt in the novel, but the doubt is hardly of the awesome variety. What kind of novel is so silly that it "takes back" the inferences that it orchestrated?

Pierre is ultimately a novel of bad faith, the poise between human awe and triviality conditioning the "subjectivity" of the broader modernity. No better than Hamlet his European predecessor can Pierre serve the dictates of sublimity, the household gods of domestic obligation, and the play of writing. It matters little, in the end, whether his fate terminates in a Manhattan prison or in the pastoral banality of Saddle Meadows. Both are stations in his range of possibility. He can be edified by his own writing, under comfortable "house arrest," or be put to death in a prison. (The mode of his death is itself ambiguous: does he join a mass-suicide, by poisoning, along with his two beloveds? Or has he been smitten in Glen Stanly and Fred Tartan's unsuccessful attempt at revenge?) The expansiveness and contraction of Pierre's modern condition merge at the penpoint where he would presume to set words on paper. Melville has set us on some roller-coaster course, one that terminates at the same Shakespearean tragedy at which the dual novel *Moby-Dick-Pierre* and modernity began:

That sundown, Pierre stood solitary in a low dungeon of the city prison. The cumbersome stone ceiling almost rested on his brow; so that the long tiers of massive cell-galleries seemed partly piled on him. His immortal, immovable bleached cheek was dry; but the stone cheeks of the walls were trickling. The pent twilight of the contracted yard, coming through the barred arrow-slit, fell in dim bars upon the granite floor.

"Here, then, is the untimely, timely end;—Life's last chapter well stitched into the middle! Nor book, nor author of the book, hath any sequel, though each hath its last lettering!—It is ambiguous still. Had I been heartless now, disowned, and spurningly portioned off the girl at Saddle Meadows, then I had been happy through a long life on earth, and perchance through a long eternity in heaven! Now, 'tis merely hell in both worlds. Well, be it hell. I will mold a trumpet of the flames, and, with my breath of flame, breathe back my defiance! But give me first another body! I long and long to die, to be rid of this dishonored cheek. *Hung by the neck till thou be dead.*—Not if I forestall you, though!—Oh now to live is death, and now to die is life; now, to my soul, were a sword my midwife!—Hark!—the hangman?—who comes?" (*P,* 360)

Parting Shots: Final Portraits

If it can be said that Dürer's *Portrait of Hieronymus Holzschuher* initiates a certain era—an era of unprecedented freedom, multiple authority sources, pervasive *Angst,* melancholy, and psychological splitting, in which art both exemplifies and presents itself as a (secular) *salvation* for these conditions; in which writing veers *hors-système* but then is misconstrued as a promise of systematic escape or deliverance—then let us close our study in examining a rogue collation of portraits at the other extreme of the gallery, but not the end. For if the eccentric checks and balances joining repression to freedom and banality to art over the broader modernity teach us anything, it is that there is no definitive closure, no end.

What is the fate of the history I have begun to trace if Egon Schiele's 1910 *Self-Portrait, Nude* is its other extremity? Schiele's self-representation in the portrait is emaciated, suffering. Its limbs have been sheared off. The corporeal mass is surrounded in the rays indicative of psychotic systematization.[1]

What has happened to the sublime confidence in Caspar David Friedrich's 1810 *Self-Portrait*? (For the aesthetic of sublimity is not without its own faiths and assurances: above all in the human subject's ability to *experience* something awesome, magnificent, and possibly life- or sanity-threatening, and in the end *to come through*. A certain bottom line of physical and mental stamina, and of the human will to knowledge, is posited by the theater and aesthetics of the sublime.) For all its shattering of proportion, and the threat to sanity and even life that the sublime entails, it is curiously predicated on vitality and health.

What can be inferred from Schiele's *Self-Portrait, Nude* regarding the his-

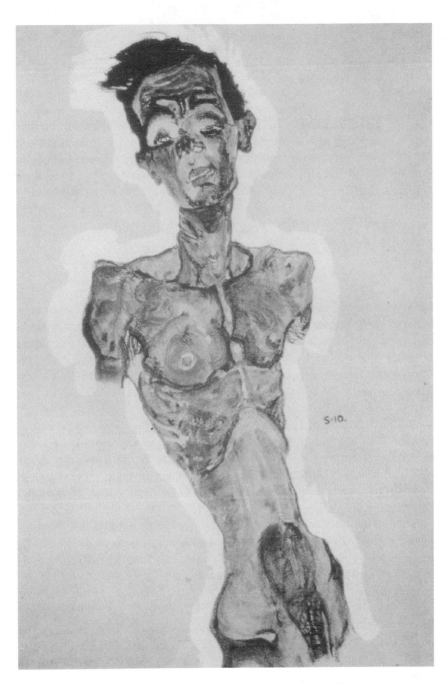

Figure 5.   Egon Schiele, *Self-Portrait, Nude,* 1910. Collection, Viktor Fogarassy, Graz, Austria. Reproduced with his kind permission.

tories of art and subjectivity in which it arises is that the artist's privileged position as the lightning rod of the Transcendental has consumed him. The condition of the modern artist is consumption, starvation, contraction. All art has become Kafka's hunger artistry, an attack upon systematic expansiveness and pretension along the front of minimalism. The artist still has her weapons, as Kafka assures his readers of their own formidableness at the end of his *Diaries*,[2] but these are instruments of measurement, constraint, bounding, not of positivism or assertion. Art and subjectivity have both lost their confidence, their will to power, their drive. What persists in the wake of this depression, this devaluation, is the enervating frail scratching of the writer's pen, the tool that both bounds the messianic body and confirms the psychosis in Schiele's *Self-Portrait, Nude.*

So in what sense can we read abstractions—say, those of Piet Mondrian— as portraits? As suggested in Chapter 6, we might interpret the pristine paintings of Mondrian or Joseph Albers as one turn further along the dimension established by the aesthetic contract of cubism. Cubism's initial disfigurations, in the hands of Braque and Picasso, were referential. We might say that Mondrian and Albers displace the enterprise of cubist visual analysis to a formal and rigorously nonrepresentational sphere.

Within this latter domain, painting encounters the Other of its being-written. Painting entirely renounces its metaphysical and ontological functions of representation and enacts its writerly status. Painting becomes a panorama of writing. Mondrian's "Broadway Boogie Woogie" (1941–42), as merely one example, becomes a map, both of a city and of writing's Otherness.

Writing has usurped the centrality of the subject throughout the history of the portrait. The "I" of the portrait is the mechanisms of language that result in script, architecture, plans, and maps. The portrait's setting is Manhattan, the city that fulfills human desire while effacing personal motives and considerations.

The Manhattan map with which Mondrian furnishes us near the end of his own anguished drama emphasizes primary colors, nearly to the exclusion of all others. The primacy of maps and the writing that inscribes their parameters has usurped the place of the human face, visage, gaze, in the history of the portrait.

The city is the setting of the writing that has passed through the stage of subjectivity and emerged on the other side, as an autonomous mechanism,

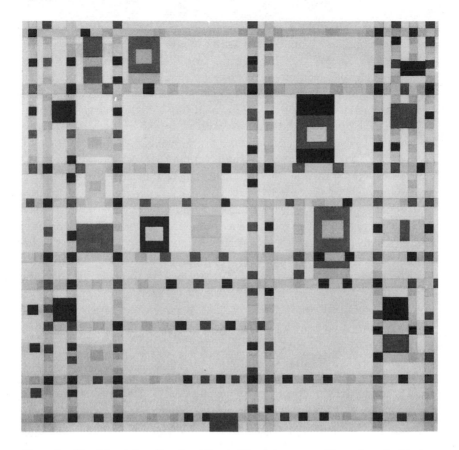

Figure 6. Piet Mondrian, *Broadway Boogie Woogie*, 1941–42. Reproduced with the kind permission of the Museum of Modern Art, New York.

with a dynamics of its own. In the abstract painting of Mondrian, the portraiture of language as the Other of subjective metaphysics gravitates to the city as its "natural" landscape. The city is the place where individual and collective desire receive their translation into the transsubjective. Mondrian, on the way out of his own existence, is one of the abstract artists who most clearly records this displacement.

⁓

Rothko's blobs hover. (You have just witnessed the first truly compressed sentence in a book abounding with examples that barely manage to end.)

The configuration of the blobs is generally vertical, although there are notable exceptions, for example, *Deep Red on Maroon* (1954).

Orange and Yellow (1956) happens to hang in Buffalo, my city. A large, slightly watery and vacuous yellow rectangle with indefinite edges hovers over a mandarin-orange rectangle of the same qualities. Both blobs are entirely contained within the frame of the painting. They are set against a pale-tangerine background that manages to clash with both of them. The tangerine background also shows through the horizontal bar separating the blobs. To the left of the midpoint of this bar, the tangerine-colored background achieves its lightest tone in the entire painting, as if in that spot some background light glimmers through.

In what sense can *Orange and Yellow* be considered a portrait, a "final shot" at the conclusion of the present exercise? The compelling content in Rothko's blob-paintings is the hovering relation that the color masses maintain to each other and, through the painted medium, to the viewer. I would argue that Rothko's quintessential blob-paintings are the ones in which the color masses maintain a vertical configuration.

In these paintings, the Kantian horizon between the empirical and the Transcendental undergoes a postmodern reinscription. Within the parameters of Rothko's frames, these vertical shapes, in which were once read an entire history of idealism, perfectionism, and the subjugation of language to transcendental values, hover indifferently, in relation to each other and the "background," which affirms and denies neither. The artist is no more the representative of the yellow blob than of the orange. Rothko's painting in no way privileges or identifies with the hierarchically superior domain. The blobs hover; the hovering is their essential Being, their relation, and their ultimate message.

Rothko the artist and we the viewers stand at a remove from the transcendental history and drama. We observe this history askance, with detachment and with critical distance. We are not compelled to enter this history, to assume any of its metaphysically mandated roles, whether as inspired artist, ordinary women and men, or discerning viewers. Rothko has endowed this history and drama with indeterminacy and a distance from itself. He has created a place of severance, but not decisive liberation, from this history.

Rothko's blob-paintings constitute a time-out, a disruption within the modern history of the subject and her rapport with language, whenever it "begins." The history is not bounded, limited, ended, merely marked. In this sense, Rothko is performing, in relation to this history, which has had its impact on all of us, what a vibrant discursive criticism can also do. To enter any "postmodernity" following upon the history I have begun to trace in this book is merely to exercise the discretion available to any aware critic, a freedom whose terms include detachment, disruption, placement in reserve. The critical contract underlying any postmodernity that we can imagine is a supplement to the aesthetic contract of the broader modernity, from whose clauses and specifications emerges anything we begin to recognize as an artist.

Reference Matter

Introduction

1. For the distinction between the constative and the performative, see John Austin, *How to Do Things with Words* (Cambridge, Mass.: Harvard University Press, 1975), 3, 6–7, 19–22, 32–33, 45–54, 95–112, 133–50; Paul de Man, *Allegories of Reading* (New Haven: Yale University Press, 1979), 7–8, 12–14, 278–85, 297–301.

2. My reference here is to the process of ossified representations that understanding produces, in the pivotal third chapter of Hegel's *Phenomenology of Spirit,* as the law, modeled at this point on scientific procedure, evolves through a sequence of abstractions and inversions. See G. W. F. Hegel, *The Phenomenology of Spirit,* trans. A. V. Miller (New York: Oxford University Press, 1977), 91–95.

3. Passages from Proust's meganovel derive from Marcel Proust, *Swann's Way,* trans. C. K. Scott Moncrieff and Terence Kilmartin (New York: Vintage, 1989), henceforth abbreviated *SW.*

4. See Albert Einstein, *Relativity: The Special and General Theory* (New York: Crown, 1961), 9–10, 79–86, 108–14.

5. J. Hillis Miller, *Topographies* (Stanford: Stanford University Press, 1995), 1–23. I'll be referring to this broad and integrative work again when my discussion turns to Kleist's "Michael Kohlhaas," in Chapter 4 below.

6. Henry Sussman, *Psyche and Text: The Sublime and the Grandiose in Literature, Psychopathology, and Culture* (Albany: State University of New York Press, 1993).

7. Roy Schafer, *A New Language for Psychoanalysis* (New Haven: Yale University Press, 1976), 9–15, 123–26, 155–78.

8. Margaret S. Mahler, "On Human Symbiosis and the Vicissitudes of Individuation," *Journal of the American Psychoanalytic Association* 15 (1965), 740–63, repr. in *Essential Papers on Object Relations,* ed. Peter Buckley (New York: New York University Press, 1986), 200–221; and "On the First Three Subphases of the Separation-Individuation Process," *Interna-*

tional Journal of Psycho-Analysis 53 (1972), 333–38, repr. in *Essential Papers on Object Relations,* 222–32. Also see Jay R. Greenburg and Stephen A. Mitchell, *Object Relations in Psychoanalytic Theory* (Cambridge, Mass.: Harvard University Press, 1983), 270–303. Roy Schafer questions some of Mahler's rhetoric in *A New Language for Psychoanalysis,* 179–87.

9.   See Jay R. Greenberg and Stephen A. Mitchell, *Object Relations in Psycho-analytic Theory,* 21–49.

10. Heinz Kohut, *The Analysis of the Self* (Madison, Conn.: International Universities Press, 1971), 175–99.

11. Otto Kernberg, *Borderline Conditions and Pathological Narcissism* (New York: Jason Aronson, 1975), 214–15.

12. Ibid., 213–26.

13. Heinz Hartmann, *Essays on Ego Psychology* (New York: International Universities Press, 1964), 142–54.

14. See Kernberg, *Borderline Conditions,* 25–30, 33–39, 41–44; also Kohut, *Analysis of the Self,* 15–21, 25–34, 144–48, 175–85.

15. On parabasis, see Freidrich Schlegel, *Lucinde and the Fragments,* trans. Peter Firchow (Minneapolis: University of Minnesota Press, 1971), 164, 175, 205. I'm suggesting here that in anticipation of the disputations of contemporary critical theory, Romantic theory and poetics offer two scenarios for fragmentation, one psychological and one linguistic, sometimes interrelated and sometimes not. Romantic instances of a shattering or fragmentation apprehended *primarily* as a linguistic proliferation would surely include the spectacles in Poe's tale of the same title and a number of phenomena related to the character Coppelius in E. T. A. Hoffmann's "The Sandman" (the eyeglasses *he* throws on a table in front of Nathanael; the "thousand fragments" into which he breaks Spalanzani's laboratory). Yet some of the same authors, and here Dostoyevsky can be added to Hoffmann and Poe, launch an investigation in subjective terms into the possibilities and values attached to human (or characterological) doubling. See "The Sandman," in *Tales of E. T. A. Hoffman,* trans. Leonard J. Kent and Elizabeth C. Knight (Chicago: University of Chicago Press, 1974), 98, 111–12, 119–20; also see Edgar Allen Poe, "The Spectacles," in *Tales of Mystery and the Imagination* (New York: Dutton, 1976), 333–55. Needless to say, the issue as to whether there *can* be a psychologically determinate mode of fragmentation is a profound one, hardly treatable in passing. But I would argue that the notion of a distinctively modern splitting does have something to offer our understandings of fragmentation.

16. Jacques Derrida, *Glas,* trans. John P. Leavey Jr. and Richard Rand (Lincoln: University of Nebraska Press), 1a, 1b, 2b, 4a, 5a, 11b, 92a–93a, 95a,

99a, 184b–85b. I am not arguing here that Derrida's lines of inquiry in *Glas* are psychological; merely that the elaborate rhetoric of blows, clefts, and divisions does have ramifications for a number of conditions prevailing in the West over the broader modernity, including subjective ones.

17. Joan Copjec, *Read My Desire* (Cambridge, Mass.: MIT Press, 1994), 5–14, 24–26, 30–43, 135–39, 152–79; Slavoj Žižek, *The Sublime Object of Ideology* (London and New York: Verso, 1989), 11–84.

Chapter 1

1. See Fernand Braudel, *Civilization and Capitalism: 15th–18th Century*, trans. Siân Reynolds (Berkeley: University of California Press, 1992), I (*The Structures of Everyday Life*): 187–210, 266–80, 294–99, 308–35; II (*The Wheels of Commerce*): 100–124, 138–60. Indeed, at the end of the second volume of this magnificent material and commercial account of modernity, Braudel refers to a certain House of Holzschuher, perhaps the very family from which the subject of Dürer's painting stems. See Braudel, II, 572.

2. Martin Heidegger, "The Origin of the Work of Art," in *Poetry, Language, Thought*, trans. Albert Hofstadter (New York: Harper & Row, 1971), 21, 32–39.

3. In *Renaissance Self-Fashioning*, a groundbreaking demonstration of the interplay between cultural and subjective conditions, Stephen Greenblatt gives this painting a far fuller treatment than I will. In addition to the painting's synthesis of Catholic and Protestant imagery, Greenblatt notes its proliferation of artificial (nonnatural) tools and apparatuses of knowledge, its confinement to a space itself withdrawn from any external world, and its sensibility of death. Greenblatt takes Holbein's representational project at its word: he identifies its figures as Jean de Dinteville (on the left) and Georges de Selve, "young, successful men," with "impressively wide-ranging interests." Greenblatt's reading of the painting goes on to detail its functioning as an emblem of the Renaissance in manners all relevant to the present study. I focus on the uncanny resemblance between the painted figures merely to demonstrate how, at this moment evocative of strikingly personalized and individualistic portraiture, the issue of identity itself is entirely up for grabs. See Stephen Greenblatt, *Renaissance Self-Fashioning* (Chicago: University of Chicago Press, 1980), 17–27.

4. Natalie Zemon Davis, *The Return of Martin Guerre* (Cambridge, Mass.: Harvard University Press, 1983), 19–24, 30–34, 38–61, 78–93; *Society and Culture in Early Modern France* (Stanford: Stanford University Press, 1975), 68–95, 97–151.

5. This is a term that Martin Heidegger develops in his essay *Identity and Difference. Gestell,* or "framework," serves as an arena in which the cultural activity of appropriation occurs. See Martin Heidegger, *Identity and Difference,* trans. Joan Stambaugh (New York: Harper & Row, 1969), 34–40, 100–105.

6. Ludwig Wittgenstein discusses the notion of family resemblance in an illuminating fashion in *The Blue and Brown Books* (Oxford: Basil Blackwell, 1964), 125–27, 165–67, 180–81; also see his *Philosophical Investigations,* trans. G. E. M. Anscombe (Oxford: Basil Blackwell, 1984), 32e, 35e, 98e, 143e–145e, 177e, 193e–200e, 215e.

7. Morris Bishop, "She Used to Let Her Golden Hair Fly Free," in *Love Rimes of Petrarch,* trans. Morris Bishop and decorated by Alison Mason Kingsbury (Ithaca, N.Y.: The Dragon Press, 1932), repr. in *An Anthology of Medieval Lyrics,* ed. Angel Flores (New York: Modern Library, 1962), 259.

8. Derrida introduces the notion of the guardrail (*garde-fou*) to describe the deployment of historical frameworks to confirm but also to contain certain of the evils traditionally associated with nonrepresentational language. I find the image particularly vivid in characterizing the defenses, within both the "subject" and language, necessitated by the Enlightenment-Romantic ideologies of freedom and individuality. See Jacques Derrida, *Of Grammatology,* trans. Gayatri Chakravorty Spivak (Baltimore: Johns Hopkins University Press, 1976), 179.

Chapter 2

1. Max Weber, *The Protestant Ethic and the Spirit of Capitalism,* trans. Talcott Parsons (London: HarperCollins, 1991), henceforth abbreviated *PESC.*

2. Weber, *Protestant Ethic,* 80–81, 113–14, 151, 180–83.

3. Braudel, *Civilization and Capitalism,* trans. Siân Reynolds (Berkeley: University of California Press, 1992), II: 160. Braudel's progressive construction of the socioeconomic conditions of modernity, beginning with raw materials and progressing through the structures and mechanisms of commerce and industry, is a magnificent introduction to some of the conceptual, epistemological, and textual issues that I am trying to raise.

4. See, for example, Norman F. Cantor, *Medieval History: The Life and Death of a Civilization* (New York: Macmillan, 1965), 18, 502–5, 513–16, 530–31, 545–49; Johann Huizinga, *The Waning of the Middle Ages* (London: Edward Arnold, 1963), 19–22, 28–33, 46–49, 136–43, 182–88, 206–16; William H. McNeill, *A History of the Human Community,* 4th edition (Englewood Cliffs, N.J., 1992), I, 323, 332–43; David Knowles and

Dimitry Obolensky, *The Middle Ages* (New York: McGraw-Hill, 1968), II: 3–6, 246–58, 359–75, 444–56.

5. See, for example, Jean-Luc Nancy, *Ego Sum* (Paris: Flammarion, 1979), 11–38, 63–94; Dalia Judowitz, *Subjectivity and Representation in Descartes* (Cambridge: Cambridge University Press, 1988), 8–60, 137–59, 184– 200; Hiram Caton, *The Origin of Subjectivity* (New Haven: Yale University Press, 1973), 1–20, 30–39, 66–100; Jeffrey Tlumak, "Certainty and Cartesian Method," and Daniel Garber, "Science and Certainty in Descartes," in *Descartes: Critical and Interpretative Essays,* ed. Michael Hooker (Baltimore: Johns Hopkins University Press, 1978), 40–73, 114–51; Charles Larmore, "Descartes' Empirical Epistemology," and John A. Schuster, "Descartes' *Mathesis Universalis, 1619–28,*" in *Descartes: Philosophy, Mathematics, Physics,* ed. Stephen Gaukroger (Totowa, N.J.: Barnes and Noble, 1980), 6–22, 41–96; Raymond E. Fancher, *Pioneers of Psychology* (New York: W. W. Norton, 1990), 23–30.

6. Another major figure of the period in whom the conflictual forces of authority and freedom make themselves evident is Montaigne. For a fascinating study of Montaigne's compulsion to write at the outset of the period whose contours are sketched out in this study, see John O'Neill, *Essaying Montaigne: A Study of the Renaissance Institution of Writing and Reading* (London: Routledge and Kegan Paul, 1982), 1–46, 139–62.

7. James Joyce, *Ulysses,* ed. Hans Walter Gabler (New York: Vintage, 1986), 165, 411.

8. Max Weber, *The Sociology of Religion,* trans. Ephraim Fischoff (Boston: Beacon Press, 1964), 4–16, 20–28.

9. When one applies the *sociological critique* of Western institutions initiated by Weber to the linguistico-infrastructural review of idealism by deconstruction, one observes a striking procedural parallelism between diverse Western institutions, whose underlying operating principles are, precisely, exclusion, fidelity, verification, and the sacrifice of present understandings in the name of some higher forthcoming truth. Western marriage, for example, is itself a wedding to the ideal applied to another person; adherence to Judeo-Christianity and Islam demands the fidelity of Western marriage. The protocols of Roman and post-Roman jurisprudence are strikingly similar to the procedures of precedents, verifiability, and the questioning of present results in the future that will emerge in Western science. There is at the same time a close affinity between philosophical logic and dialectics in the West and the teleology of Western science. The "fingerprint" of Western culture is less the emergence of idealism in one or another sphere of cultural endeavor than the relatively

uniform prevalence of this conceptual-metaphysical mode across the
culture.

10.   All citations of Plato derive from the Bollingen edition: Plato, *Collected
      Dialogues,* ed. Edith Hamilton and Huntington Cairns (Princeton:
      Princeton University Press, 1969), henceforth abbreviated *CD.*

11.   Martin Luther, *Selections from His Writings,* ed. John Dillenberger (New
      York: Doubleday, 1961), henceforth abbreviated *SW.*

12.   The historical differences between societies whose political organization
      was centralized as opposed to confederate surely form an interesting and
      surprising (to me, at least) context for reevaluating the American Civil
      War.

13.   On the question of bipolarity, see Otto Kernberg, "Structural Derivatives
      of Object Relations," *International Journal of Psycho-Analysis* 47 (1966),
      236–53; rpt. in *Essential Papers on Object Relations,* ed. Peter Buckley
      (New York: New York University Press, 1986), 350–84. Also see in this
      volume Melanie Klein, "A Contribution to the Psychogenesis of Manic
      and Depressive States," 47; and W. R. D. Fairbairn, "A Revised Psycho-
      pathology of the Psychoses and Psychoneuroses," 94–95.

14.   For the distinction and interplay between good and bad writing, see
      Jacques Derrida, "Plato's Pharmacy," in *Dissemination,* trans. Barbara
      Johnson (Chicago: University of Chicago Press, 1981), 103, 149, 155.

15.   In the Enlightenment consolidation of Western ontotheology and meta-
      physics performed so brilliantly by Hegel and chronicled so exhaustively
      by Derrida in *Glas,* there are crucial moments at which horizontal figures
      and movements are literally upended to the point at which they structure
      vertical alignments. To my mind, the pivotal Hegelian instance of the
      transformation of horizontal relations into vertical determinations takes
      place in the third chapter of *The Phenomenology of Spirit,* "Force and the
      Understanding." I furnish a gloss on this "event" and its implications in
      *The Hegelian Aftermath: Readings in Hegel, Kierkegaard, Freud, Proust, and
      James* (Baltimore: Johns Hopkins University Press, 1982), 33–49.

16.   All citations from the work of Calvin are from John Calvin, *On the Chris-
      tian Faith: Selections from the Institutes, Commentaries, and Tracts,* ed. John T.
      NcNeill, The Library of Liberal Arts (Indianapolis: Bobbs-Merrill, 1957),
      henceforth abbreviated *OCF.* In my text, I also indicate from which
      texts by Calvin the citations derive.

17.   Max Weber, *The Protestant Ethic and the Spirit of Capitalism,* trans. Talcott
      Parsons (London: HarperCollins, 1991), 110–18.

18.   Louis Marin, *La Critique du discours* (Paris: Minuit, 1975), 51–77, 92–
      100, 134–46, 181–90, 245–50, 327–39. Also see Milad Doueihi, "Traps

of Representation," *Diacritics* 14 (1984), 66–69; and Carol Jacobs, *Telling Time* (Baltimore: Johns Hopkins University Press, 1993), 83, 85–89, 216–18.

19. The inertness of the Jewish spirit is a condition that Derrida, consolidating Hegel's theological speculations, makes abundantly clear in *Glas,* trans. John P. Leavey, Jr. and Richard Rand (Lincoln: University of Nebraska Press), 44–51a.

20. See Chapter 2, note 3.

21. The implied self to be discerned between the lines of Luther's theology is conflicted between sharply drawn moral alternatives and susceptible to pronounced fragmentation and dissociation. It is from this perspective, as suggested in the Introduction above and Chapter 7 below, that the contemporary themes of object relations are germane to the nineteenth- and twentieth-century descendents of this self.

22. Erik H. Erikson, *Young Man Luther* (New York: W. W. Norton, 1962), 23, 34, 38–43, 58–62, 66–67, 101–4, 116–25, 227–50, 254–67.

23. Henry Sussman, *Afterimages of Modernity* (Baltimore: Johns Hopkins University Press, 1990), 199–201.

Chapter 3

1. William Shakespeare, *Hamlet,* The Pelican Shakespeare, ed. Willard Farnham (New York: Penguin, 1970), 39–40.

2. Ibid.,89.

3. Ibid.,113–14.

4. See Henry Sussman, *Psyche and Text: The Sublime and the Grandiose in Literature, Psychopathology, and Culture* (Albany: State University of New York Press, 1993), 51–54, 94–97, 141–45, 150–52, 167–83.

5. For the Derridean notion of logocentrism, see Jacques Derrida, *Of Grammatology,* trans. Gayatri Chakravorty Spivak (Baltimore: Johns Hopkins University Press, 1976), 10–14, 18–26.

6. John Donne, *Poetical Works,* Oxford Standard Authors (London: Oxford University Press, 1966), 14–15.

7. For a reading of another Donne poem, "The Flea," in which the rhetoric and situation of seduction define the possibilities of knowledge, see Roy Roussel, *The Conversation of the Sexes* (New York: Oxford University Press, 1986), 10–36.

8. John Locke, *An Essay Concerning Human Understanding,* Book II, Chapter 1, Proposition 2. The *Essay* as well as the texts I will be quoting by Berkeley and Hume are conveniently reproduced, in abridged form, in *The Empiricists: Locke, Berkeley, Hume* (Garden City, N.Y.: Anchor Books,

1974). Locke's designation of the sources of ideas appears on pp. 10–11 of this edition, which I henceforth abbreviate *E*.

9. Ludwig Wittgenstein, *The Blue and Brown Books* (Oxford: Basil Blackwell, 1964), 91–92.

10. On the method of the early modernity, see Michel Foucault, *The Order of Things* (New York: Vintage, 1973), 138–50, 157.

11. It is Derrida who most clearly and forcefully enunciates the paradox that to think the limits of the (speculative) system is not to secure any definitive break—or exit—from it. Derridean marginality is a play taking place precisely at the limits of the system. See, for example, *Of Grammatology*, trans. Gayatri Chakravorty Spivak (Baltimore: Johns Hopkins University Press, 1976), 30–46, 157–64, 295–316.

Chapter 4

1. Walter Benjamin, *The Origins of German Tragic Drama,* trans. John Osborne (London: New Left Books, 1977), henceforth abbreviated *OGTD*.

2. I think of such characters in *The Confidence-Man* as the agent of the Black Rapids Coal Company, the herb doctor, and the dusk giant, who rail against hypochondriacs as destroyers of public confidence, and of Orchis, destroyer of China Astor, who in the course of his transformation becomes a hypochondriac himself. See Herman Melville, *The Confidence-Man,* ed. H. Bruce Franklin (Indianapolis: Bobbs Merrill, 1969), 68, 119–21, 298, 301–2. Also see Henry Sussman, "The Deconstructor as Politician: Melville's *The Confidence-Man,*" in *High Resolution: Critical Theory and the Problem of Literacy* (New York: Oxford University Press, 1989), 98, 107–8.

3. See Walter Benjamin, "On Some Motifs in Baudelaire," in *Illuminations,* trans. Harry Zohn (New York: Schocken, 1969), 167–70, 176–77, 184, 191.

4. See, for example, Heinz Kohut, *The Analysis of the Self* (Madison, Conn.: International Universities Press, 1971), 16–22, 117–18, 177–83; Otto Kernberg, *Borderline Conditions and Pathological Narcissism* (New York: Jason Aronson, 1975), 18–21, 119–20, 213–23; Alice Miller, *The Drama of the Gifted Child,* trans. Ruth Ward (New York: Basic Books, 1981), 5, 21, 30–37, 42–48, 50–63, 100–113.

5. On the narcissistic wound, see Kohut, *Analysis of the Self,* 45–47, 98–99, 300–301; Kernberg, *Borderline Conditions,* 230–38.

6. Max Weber, *The Protestant Ethic and the Spirit of Capitalism,* 80–81, 86, 160–63, 166, 181–83.

7. See Chapter 2, note 3, above.

8. Michel Foucault, *The Order of Things* (New York: Vintage, 1973), 17–30, 46–56.

9. Hence, Hegel finds in classical Greek tragedy an exemplary artifact to dramatize the symmetrical aspects of the dialectical process that is for him "preinstalled" within Western speculative thought. The heroine Antigone, for example, is situated in the crux between the law of the family, an immediate derivative of the law of nature, and the civil law promulgated and enforced by the state. The tragic situations of Oedipus and Antigone are of course impasses, but they reside within a cognitive-cultural setting in which the dialectical logic of symmetry and continuity predicates the possibility of the individual and collective subject's thinking her way out of the bind. See G. W. F. Hegel, *The Phenomenology of Spirit,* trans. A. V. Miller (New York: Oxford University Press, 1977), 256–62, 266–78.

10. All references to Kleist derive from Heinrich von Kleist, *The Marquise of O—and Other Stories,* trans. David Luke and Nigel Reeves (London: Penguin Books, 1978), henceforth abbreviated *MO.*

11. E. T. A. Hoffmann, "The Sandman," in *Tales of E. T. A. Hoffmann,* trans. Leonard J. Kent and Elizabeth C. Knight (Chicago: University of Chicago Press, 1969), 98, 112–15, 117, 119–25; Edgar Allen Poe, "The Pit and the Pendulum" and "The Spectacles," in *Tales of Mystery and the Imagination* (London: Everyman's Library, 1968), 228–34, 334, 337–40, 352–55.

12. See Carol Jacobs, "The Style of Kleist," in *Uncontainable Romanticism: Shelley, Bronte, Kleist* (Baltimore: Johns Hopkins University Press, 1989), 171–200.

13. Franz Kafka, "A Country Doctor" and "The Knock at the Manor Gate" in *The Complete Stories,* ed. Nahum N. Glatzer (New York: Schocken, 1971), 220–25, 418–19; also *The Castle,* trans. Willa and Edwin Muir (New York: Schocken, 1974), 3–15, 145–52.

14. J. Hillis Miller, *Topographies* (Stanford: Stanford University Press, 1995), 80–104.

15. Ibid., 80–83, 94–95.

16. See Jacques Lacan, *The Four Fundamental Concepts of Psycho-Analysis,* trans. Alan Sheridan (New York: W. W. Norton, 1978), 17–18, 62, 76–77, 83, 103–5, 112–13, 116, 118, 134, 142–43, 145–48, 151, 155, 159, 168, 170, 180, 182, 184–86, 190, 193–94, 196, 198, 206, 209, 214–15, 221, 239, 241–46, 256–59. This volume is also known as *Seminar 11.*

17. On the matter of kinship, see Claude Lévi-Strauss, *The Elementary Structures of Kinship,* trans. James Harle Bell, John Richard von Sturmer, and

Rodney Needham (Boston: Beacon Press, 1969), 29–51, 69–83, 98–118, 134–45; *The Savage Mind* (Chicago: University of Chicago Press, 1966), 109–33, 161–90.

18. "Recognition" is a Lacanian term indicating the inevitable degree of error in perception and insight. For misrecognition (*méconnaissance*), see Lacan, *Four Fundamental Concepts,* xvii, 18, 74, 83.

Chapter 5

1. Jacques Derrida, *Glas,* trans. John P. Leavey and Richard Rand (Lincoln: University of Nebraska Press, 1986), 212.

2. All citations derive from Immanuel Kant, *The Critique of Judgment,* trans. J. H. Bernard (New York: Macmillan, 1951), and *The Critique of Pure Reason,* trans. Norman Kemp Smith (New York: St. Martin's Press, 1965), henceforth abbreviated *CJ* and *CPR.*

3. Oscar Wilde, *The Picture of Dorian Gray* (London: Penguin, 1985), 21–22, 25–36, 45–46, 102, 130–35.

4. Derrida, *Of Grammatology,* 65–73, 265.

5. Jorge Luis Borges, "Death and the Compass," in *Ficciones* (New York: Grove, 1962), 129.

6. Henry Sussman, *Psyche and Text: The Sublime and the Grandiose in Literature, Psychopathology, and Culture* (Albany: State University of New York Press, 1993), 27–43.

7. Jacques Lacan, "Kant with Sade," trans. James B. Swenson, Jr., *October* 51 (1989), 55–75.

8. Ludwig Wittgenstein, *Philosophical Investigations,* trans. G. E. M. Anscombe (Oxford: Basil Blackwell, 1984), 88e–90e, 93e–100e, 113e, 117e, 166e–167e, henceforth abbreviated *PI.* Also see *The Private Language Argument,* ed. O. R. Jones (New York: St. Martins, 1971).

9. The mediatory position of the gifted individual who "receives" the otherwise unintelligible intuitions of the Transcendental at the cost of moral or general social disorientation is a Romantic commonplace that Hollywood learned how to elaborate well. Among notable literary heroes, Goethe's Faust, M. W. Shelley's Victor Frankenstein, E. T. A. Hoffmann's Nathanael, and Melville's Captain Ahab inhabit this position. There will be an analysis of the sublime imagery accruing to Melville's contribution to this corpus in Chapters 8 and 9 below. It could be argued that the Kurtz of Conrad's "Heart of Darkness" continues this tradition within a scenario of colonialist expansion: it is an interesting twist that this mediator is largely invisible.

10. See John R. Anderson, *Cognitive Psychology and its Implications,* 3d edition (New York: W. H. Freeman, 1990), 126–33, 143–44, 344–45, 379–82,

397; Stephen Michael Kosslyn, *Ghosts in the Mind's Machine* (New York: W. W. Norton, 1983), 32–36, 41–47, 99–102, 119–30, 160–71, 175–76, 189, 201–3.

11.   William Butler Yeats, "Sailing to Byzantium," in *The Collected Poems of W. B. Yeats* (New York: Macmillan, 1966), 191.

12.   Ezra Pound, "An Immortality," in *Collected Shorter Poems* (London: Faber and Faber, 1968), 88.

13.   Sigmund Freud, *The Ego and the Id* (New York: W. W. Norton, 1960), 18, 24–29, 38–42, 46, 48.

14.   Otto Kernberg, *Borderline Conditions and Pathological Narcissism* (New York: Jason Aronson, 1975), 213–16.

15.   In the "Wandering Rocks" episode of *Ulysses,* Lenehan says to M'Coy of Bloom: "He's not one of your common or garden . . . you know . . . There's a touch of the artist about old Bloom." James Joyce, *Ulysses,* ed. Hans Walter Gabler (New York: Vintage, 1986), 193.

16.   Søren Kierkegaard, *Either/Or* (Princeton: Princeton University Press, 1971), I, 22, 29–31, 37–38, 40–41, 45–48, 55–59, 61–65, 88–92, 286–93; II, 20–22, 65–89, 110–33. Also see Henry Sussman, "Søren Kierkegaard and the Allure of Paralysis," in *The Hegelian Aftermath: Readings in Hegel, Kierkegaard, Freud, Proust and James* (Baltimore: Johns Hopkins University Press, 1982), 70–93, 105–25, 141–58.

17.   Franz Kafka, *The Complete Stories,* ed. Nahum N. Glatzer (New York: Schocken, 1971), 447.

18.   For this classical phrase from the discourse of social thought, see Robert Michels, *Political Parties: A Sociological Study of the Oligarchical Tendencies of Modern Democracy* (New York: The Free Press, 1962), 46, 50–55, 117–48, 333–56.

19.   For a comprehensive account of this mediocrity and its consequences, see Eugenio Donato, *The Script of Decadence* (New York: Oxford University Press, 1993), 22–23, 48, 64, 200.

Chapter 6

1.   This notion, that photography in general and specifically Civil War photography spelled an end to several basic clauses in the aesthetic contract of Romantic fiction and ushered in the experiments of realism, is merely one of a number of crucial ideas that Neil Schmitz is exploring in current work on the American late nineteenth century. The current working title for the forthcoming project is *Against Ahab, Against Uncle Tom: Unionist Discourse in American Literature.* Also see Linda Nochlin, *The Politics of Vision: Essays on Nineteenth-Century Art and Society* (New York: Harper and Row, 1989).

2.   For a theoretically suggestive account of cubism, see Claude Lévi-Strauss, *The Savage Mind* (Chicago: The University of Chicago Press, 1966), 16–24, 30.

3.   Henry Sussman, *Afterimages of Modernity* (Baltimore: Johns Hopkins University Press, 1990), 10–20.

4.   This point was brought home by two recent art exhibitions at major museums, "Rembrandt / Not Rembrandt," at the Metropolitan Museum of Art in New York, and the epochal Vermeer retrospective at the National Gallery in Washington. Both exhibitions, particularly the former, demonstrated that their "subjects" provided the painterly terms and styles that their colleagues and fellow travelers were able to enter and appropriate. The signatures "Rembrandt" and "Vermeer" thus designate limited sets of artifacts proper to the artist of that name *and* wider, indeterminate bodies of artifacts designed in accordance with the specifications of the aesthetic contracts that art history has attributed to those artists. Indeed, a major focus of the explanatory material furnished with the Rembrandt exhibition was the virtual impossibility of distinguishing certain Rembrandt "takeoffs" from "originals." This is but one of many graphic instances of the aesthetic contract, as I am characterizing it, at work.

5.   G. W. F. Hegel, *The Philosophy of History,* trans. J. Sibree (New York: Dover, 1956), 29–37.

6.   Jean-François Lyotard, *The Postmodern Condition: A Report on Knowledge,* trans. Geoff Bennington and Brian Massumi (Minneapolis: University of Minnesota, 1984), 81.

7.   Jacques Lacan, *The Seminars of Jacques Lacan: Book I: Freud's Papers on Technique 1953–54,* trans. John Forrester (New York: W.W. Norton, 1988), 43, 53, 58, 67, 283, 289n.

8.   Henry Sussman, *Afterimages of Modernity,* 161–75.

9.   M. M. Bakhtin, *The Dialogic Imagination,* trans. Carolyn Emerson and Michael Holquist (Austin: University of Texas Press, 1981), 3–40, 146–224. Moshe Ron, my most gracious host in Israel during Spring 1994, pointed out to me the centrality of such enduring aesthetic subcontracts as Menippean satire and the carnivalesque.

10. Walter Benjamin, "The Image of Proust," in *Illuminations,* trans. Harry Zohn (New York: Schocken, 1969), 201.

11. Sigmund Freud, *Beyond the Pleasure Principle,* trans. James Strachey (New York: Liveright, 1970), 8–11.

Chapter 7

1.   Any semblance of elegance assumed by the following propositions is owing to the extraordinary editing and rewriting performed upon them

by Prof. Richard Macksey of the Johns Hopkins University. I am enormously grateful to him not only for a mid-career refresher course in the
optimal coherence of academic script, but for thirty years of the most
generous support and encouragement imaginable.

2. Charles Taylor, *Sources of the Self: The Making of the Modern Identity* (Cambridge, Mass.: Harvard University Press, 1989), 18–22, 28–36.

3. Jürgen Habermas has productively placed the interstice between the public and the private in the context of the historical emergence of a "bourgeois public sphere." See his *The Structural Transformation of the Public
Sphere,* trans. Thomas Burger (Cambridge, Mass.: MIT Press, 1989), 1–
12, 14–26, 27–36, 43–56, 141–59.

Habermas brings a historical and social-scientific focus to his groundbreaking study that readers will find sadly lacking in my own formulations, with their incursions into psychoanalysis, analytical philosophy,
and even ethics. He explores the precedents to the public sphere in contemporary Western "liberal" societies in the bourgeois society of the European Enlightenment. He goes on, with admirable comprehensiveness,
to explore social structures and political functions within the public
sphere in the course of its "structural transformation." As diffuse as my
own fragments may be, their motivation and source is a series of literary
readings I have done over the years. My readers may well ask: What is the
study of literature coming to if formulations such as these can come out
of it?

4. See Heinz Kohut, *The Analysis of the Self* (Madison, Conn.: International
Universities Press, 1989), 5–17.

5. Learning theory, as developed by the American psychologist Edward L.
Thorndike, is a branch of this discipline accounting for behavior through
the dynamics and mechanics of learning. See Edward L. Thorndike and
R. S. Woodworth, "The Influence of Improvement in One Mental
Function upon the Efficiency of Other Functions," *Psychological Review* 8
(1901), 247–56, rpr. in *A Sourcebook in the History of Psychology,* ed. Richard J. Herrnstein and Edward G. Boring (Cambridge, Mass.: Harvard
University Press, 1968), 557–63. Also see Raymond E. Fancher, *Pioneers
of Psychology,* 2d edition (New York: W. W. Norton, 1990), 269–74.

6. I am indebted for my understanding of the particular "spin" on sexuality
in the novel, as well as of the centrality of Slothrop's conditioning, to
Mark Singer and Takashi Aso, participants in my Spring 1995 graduate
seminar on postmodernism at SUNY/Buffalo.

7. Avital Ronell, *Crack Wars* (Lincoln: University of Nebraska Press, 1992).

8. See Ferdinand de Saussure, *Course in General Linguistics,* trans. Wade Bas-
kin (Indianapolis: Bobbs-Merrill, 1966), 13–14:

Neither is the psychological part of the circuit wholly responsible:
the executive side is missing, for execution is never carried out by
the collectivity. Execution is always individual, and the individual
is always its master: I shall call the executive side *speaking* [*parole*]. . . .
If we could embrace the sum of word-images stored in the minds
of all individuals, we could identify the social bond that constitutes
language. It is a storehouse filled by the members of a given community through their active use of speaking, a grammatical system
that has a potential in each brain.

Also see 71–83, 87–91.

9. Ludwig Wittgenstein, *The Blue and Brown Books* (Oxford: Basil Black-
    well, 1964), 2–3, 14, 20, 23–25, 31, 34–35, 46, 49–53, 55–57, 60–61,
    102, 137–39, 147–49, 155–56, 159; Henry Sussman, *Afterimages of Mo-
    dernity* (Baltimore: Johns Hopkins University Press, 1990), 81–93.

10. Jacques Derrida, *Of Grammatology,* trans. Gayatri Chakravorty Spivak
    (Baltimore: Johns Hopkins University Press, 1976), 29–43, 45–48, 50–
    57, 66, 68–73.

11. In this essay, I am indebted to a certain aspect of empiricism as well, to
    the notion of a progressive evolution and branching of associations ex-
    plored with particular prominence in the writings of Locke and Hume.
    This empiricist model, as well as the notion of a "self-system" to which it
    leads, in no way disqualifies my observation that Wittgenstein's scenario
    for the expression of experience is too body-oriented, or that focusing on
    private language's *possibility* diverts inquiry from the *between* of the spec-
    trum linking privacy to publicity. Please also note that there are obvious
    textual dimensions to a self-system emerging from the historical accretion
    of meanings in a person's life. If there is an empiricist slant to my implicit
    genealogy of private personal meanings, then an important interplay is
    taking place between this particular empiricism and deconstructionist
    (and other) notions of textuality.

    Indeed, the contemporary discipline that studies the empiricism of as-
    sociations is cognitive science. The current debate in cognitive psychol-
    ogy as to whether thoughts are organized in images or propositional net-
    works is a case in point. No enormous cognitive dissonance needs to be
    overcome in order to appreciate the mutual relevance of textuality to
    what the propositionalists call "propositional networks."

    See Stephen Michael Kosslyn, *Ghosts in the Mind's Machine* (New
    York: W. W. Norton, 1983), 1–11, 29–52, 100–102, 120–23, 132, 136,
    160–71, 175, 181–82, 189; Jerry A. Fodor, *Representations: Philosophical*

Essays on the Foundations of Cognitive Science (Cambridge, Mass.: MIT
Press, 1986), 35–62, 100–123, 177–203; Jerome Bruner, *Actual Minds,
Possible Worlds* (Cambridge, Mass.: Harvard University Press, 1986), 11–
43, 70–78, 88, 139–49; Paul Miers, "The Other Side of Representation:
Critical Theory and the New Cognitivism," *MLN* 107 (1992), 950–75;
John R. Anderson, *Cognitive Psychology and Its Implications*, 3d edition
(New York: W. H. Freeman, 1990), 112–45, 160–67, 178–202, 277–87,
340–56.

12. Ludwig Wittgenstein, *Philosophical Investigations,* trans. G. E. M. Anscombe (Oxford: Basil Blackwell, 1984), 88e–89e, henceforth abbreviated
PI.

13. O. R. Jones, ed., *The Private Language Argument* (New York: St. Martins,
1971).

14. With regard to introjections, see Otto Kernberg, "Structural Derivatives
of Object Relationships," in Peter Buckley, ed., *Essential Papers on Object
Relations* (New York: New York University Press, 1986), 355–70.

15. In Paragraph 246 Wittgenstein does, however, place some limits on behaviorism: "Other people cannot be said to learn of my sensations *only*
from my behaviour,—for I cannot be said to learn of them. I *have* them"
(*PI,* 89e). Here the doctrine that language needs to be operational and
communicative takes precedence over the role that Wittgenstein sees for
behaviorism.

16. Henry Sussman, "Kafka and Modern Philosophy: Wittgenstein, Deconstruction, and the Cuisine of the Imaginary," in *Afterimages of Modernity*
(Baltimore: Johns Hopkins University Press, 1990), 58–75, 81–94.

17. Otto Kernberg, *Borderline Conditions and Pathological Narcissism* (New
York: Jason Aronson, 1975), 30–31, 33–39.

18. I describe above the therapist's disinterest; a few lines before this I speak
in terms of some shared "societal commitment" on the part of both
therapeutic parties. How so? I am arguing in this essay that the *social*
function of psychotherapy involves a negotiation of private meanings,
nuances, and memories with the therapist, who, to some extent, represents the public. It is difficult to separate the therapeutic practitioner
from the ideal of social welfare. When this happens, as it does in *The Silence of the Lambs,* whose secondary villain, Hannibal Lecter, is a socio-
pathic psychiatrist, the public's reaction evinces fascinated horror. (The
film won the 1992 Academy Award for, among other things, "Best Picture.") In this essay, I am arguing that the "therapeutic contract" doesn't
get off the ground unless the patient as well as the therapist imputes some
wider social good to the therapeutic process. What is the therapeutic

"disinterest" that could go together with this "societal commitment"? It is the reservation of judgment, not at all alien to social welfare, which throughout the history of psychoanalysis has proven essential to the free play of memory, association, and expression by which the patient "reconstructs," among other things, his personal meanings, tendencies, and essential pains. I would argue that the Hollywood of recent years has been a showcase of borderline psychopathology: *Blue Velvet, Fatal Attraction, Cape Fear* (the 1961 "original" as well as the 1992 remake), and *The Silence of the Lambs* are cases in point. For a reading of this latter film in terms of borderline psychopathology, see my *Psyche and Text: The Sublime and the Grandiose in Literature, Psychopathology, and Culture* (Albany: State University of New York Press, 1993), 163–83.

19. Melanie Klein, "A Contribution to the Psychogenesis of Manic-Depressive States," in *Essential Papers on Object Relations,* ed. Peter Buckley (New York: New York University Press, 1986), 52–55, 57, 66–67, 70. Also see D. W. Winnicott, "The Theory of the Parent-Infant Relationship," in *Essential Papers on Object Relations,* 249–51; and "Transitional Objects and Transitional Phenomena," in *Playing and Reality* (New York: Basic Books, 1971), 11–14, 66, 69, 72. Also see Heinz Kohut, *The Analysis of the Self,* 170–71, 212–14, 224.

20. In the parlance of contemporary object-relations theory, introjections constitute a heavily nuanced internal language regarding the self and other primary "self-objects," often learned or "absorbed" at an early stage of consciousness, corresponding to the Lacanian pre-Oedipal, before the basic apparatus of rationality has been established. In everyday terms, introjections form certain ongoing captions about ourselves and significant others that repeat themselves with remarkable persistence throughout our lives and that carry a distinctive ingrained quality. For an attempt to elaborate the basic psychoanalytical setting and role of introjections, see Otto Kernberg, "Structural Derivatives of Object Relationships," in *Essential Papers on Object Relations,* 350–84.

21. For Heinz Kohut, integration describes both the modality and one of the chief goals of psychoanalysis. See his *The Analysis of the Self,* 10, 171–72, 213–14, 224.

22. This is certainly the case with Flaubert, at least as he has been read by Eugenio Donato. See the latter's *The Script of Decadence* (New York: Oxford University Press, 1993), 19, 22–23, 42, 44–48, 57, 73, 200–202.

23. Søren Kierkegaard, *Either/Or* (Princeton: Princeton University Press, 1971), I, 51–57, 220–22; II, 27–29, 61–63, 174–76, 333–35.

24. Søren Kierkegaard, *The Concept of Irony,* trans. with notes by Lee M.

Capel (Bloomington: Indiana University Press, 1965), 93, 98, 120—24, 134, 151, 163—65, 192, 248, 253, 260, 275, 287—89, 296—98, 328, 330—31, 335, 341.

25. Jorge Luis Borges, *Ficciones* (New York: Grove, 1962), 17—36.

26. Italo Calvino, *t zero*, trans. William Weaver (New York: Harcourt Brace Jovanovich, 1976), 95—127, 137—52.

Chapter 8

1. Where to begin the impossible task of condensing important recent contributions to the field of postcolonial theory in a note? See Edward Said, *Orientalism* (New York: Pantheon, 1978) and *Culture and Imperialism* (New York: Alfred E. Knopf, 1993); Homi K. Bhabha, *The Location of Culture* (London and New York: Routledge, 1994), and his edited collection, *Nation and Narration* (London and New York: Routledge, 1993); Gayatri Chakravorty Spivak, *In Other Worlds* (New York: Methuen, 1987) and *The Post-Colonial Critic* (New York and London: Routledge, 1990); Jenny Sharpe, *Allegories of Empire* (Minneapolis: University of Minnesota Press, 1993); and Sara Suleri, *The Rhetoric of British India* (Chicago: University of Chicago Press, 1992). My colleague Shaun Irlam has done yeoman's work in introducing my university and myself to this literature.

2. For a view of the economic underpinnings of the systematic expansion experienced in Europe during the period of our immediate concern, see Fernand Braudel, *Capitalism and Civilization: 15th—18th Century*, trans. Siân Reynolds (Berkeley: University of California Press, 1992), II, 432—33:

    One's impression then . . . is that there were always sectors in economic life where high profits could be made, *but that these sectors varied.* Every time one of these shifts occurred, under the pressure of economic developments, capital was quick to scent them out, to move into the new sector and prosper. Note that as a rule it had not precipitated such shifts. This differential geography of profit is a key to the short-term fluctuations of capitalism, as it veered between the Levant, America, the East Indies, China, the slave trade, etc., or between trade, banking, industry, or land. (II, 432)

    Let me emphasize the quality that seems to me to be an essential feature of the general history of capitalism: its unlimited flexibility, its capacity for change and *adaptation.* If there is, as I believe, a certain unity in capitalism, from thirteenth-century Italy to the present-day West, it is here above all that such unity must be located and observed. . . . In the so-called merchant or commercial capitalism phase, as in the so-called industrial phase . . . the essential characteristic of capitalism was its capacity to slip at a moment's notice from one form or sector to another, in times of crisis or of pronounced decline in profit rates. (II, 433)

3. For the Derridean guardrail, see Chapter 1, note 8, above.

4. Citations refer to Herman Melville, *Moby-Dick,* Northwestern-Newberry edition, ed. Harrison Hayford, Hershel Parker, G. Thomas Tanselle (Evanston and Chicago: Northwestern University Press and the Newberry Library, 1988), henceforth abbreviated *MD*.

5. For the Lacanian misrecognition, see Chapter 4, note 18, above.

6. We owe to Paul de Man the splendid readings of Rousseau indicating their fundamental rhetorical constitution and complexity. See Paul de Man, *Allegories of Reading* (New Haven: Yale University Press, 1979), 135–301.

7. Translations for these settings in *Faust II* derive from Johann Wolfgang von Goethe, *Faust: A Tragedy,* Norton Critical Edition, trans. Walter Arndt (New York: W. W. Norton, 1976).

8. On the notion of ornamentality in art as an intensification of its secondariness, artificiality, and falseness, see Jacques Derrida, "Parergon," in *The Truth in Painting,* trans. Geoff Bennington and Ian McLeod (Chicago: University of Chicago Press, 1987), 37–46, 55–82, 96–103, 115–18, 144–47.

9. Jean-Jacques Rousseau, *The Social Contract,* trans. Maurice Cranston (London: Penguin, 1968), henceforth abbreviated *SC*.

10. Jacques Derrida, in his bicolumnar account of modernity's extremes in *Glas,* also develops a rhetoric of contraction, in his case to dramatize how Western metaphysics places itself under constraint and to characterize certain images of annularity (and anality) in Genet's perverse counterculture to the metaphysical mainstream. See Jacques Derrida, *Glas,* trans. John P. Leavey and Richard Rand (Lincoln: University of Nebraska Press, 1986), 243a–244a, 246a.

11. George Orwell, *1984* (New York: Signet, 1954), 15, 23, 210.

12. Michel Foucault, *The Order of Things* (New York: Vintage, 1973), henceforth abbreviated *OT*.

13. This is a point that was made brilliantly and compellingly to me in private conversation some twenty years ago by Carol Jacobs. To my knowledge, she has never capitalized on her analysis of the simultaneous synchronicity and diachronicity of hermeneutic models (presented as "ages") in Foucault's *The Order of Things* in her published work.

14. Jacques Derrida, *Of Grammatology,* trans. Gayatri Chakravorty Spivak (Baltimore: Johns Hopkins University Press, 1976), 251, 260–61, 267–68.

15. I do not deploy the term "extreme idealism" haphazardly. It is a position that Jorge Luis Borges establishes in his theoretical short story, "Tlön, Uqbar, Orbis Tertius," where it denotes an idealism (or conceptuality) so powerful that it affects "reality." See Borges, *Ficciones* (New York: Grove, 1962), 24, 28–29, 83.

16. Henry Sussman, "An American History Lesson: Hegel and the Historiography of Superimposition," in *Theorizing American Literature,* ed. Bainard Cowan and Joseph G. Kronick (Baton Rouge: Louisiana State University Press, 1991), 37–52.

17. Citations from the novel derive from Jean-Jacques Rousseau, *Emile,* trans. Allan Bloom (New York: Basic Books, 1979), henceforth abbreviated *E.*

18. Franz Kafka, *The Trial,* trans. Willa and Edwin Muir (New York: Schocken, 1974), 1.

19. Sigmund Freud, *The Ego and the Id* (New York: W. W. Norton, 1960), 16, 25–28, 40, 42–48.

20. Jean-Jacques Rousseau, *The Confessions,* trans. J. M. Cohen (London: Penguin, 1953), henceforth abbreviated *C.*

21. For the notion of secondary gain, see Sigmund Freud, *The Standard Edition of the Complete Psychological Writings of Sigmund Freud* (London: Hogarth Press, 1953–74), VI, 115; XVIII, 158–59.

22. Slavoj Žižek, *For they know not what they do: Enjoyment as a Political Factor* (London: Verso, 1991), 234, 243, 257, 271–73.

23. Paul de Man, "Excuses (*Confessions*)," in *Allegories of Reading* (New Haven: Yale University Press, 1979), 278–301.

24. Melanie Klein, "A Contribution to the Psychogenesis of Manic-Depressive States," in *Essential Papers on Object Relations,* ed. Peter Buckley (New York: New York University Press, 1986), 42–44, 47–48, 51, 58–59, 64–65, 67–70; D. W. Winnicott, *Playing and Reality* (New York: Basic Books, 1971), 10–14.

Chapter 9

1. See Jacques Derrida, "Parergon," in *The Truth in Painting,* 9, 69–82.

2. Herman Melville, *Moby-Dick,* 5, 223, 225, 378, 448–50, 460, 491.

3. The very first readers of the novel, including Evert A. Duyckinck and George Ripley, noted the obstructions to the smooth unrolling of the story brought about by the whaling lore and other nonessential information. Their remarks are reproduced in the Norton Critical Edition of *Moby-Dick,* ed. Harrison Hayford and Hershel Parker (New York: W. W.

Norton, 1967), 613–18. Also see Henry A. Murry, "'In Nomine Diaboli': *Moby-Dick,*" in *Moby-Dick: Modern Critical Interpretations,* ed. Harold Bloom (New York: Chelsea House, 1986), 39–48.

4. Rodolphe Gasché has contributed to the Melville literature a splendid extrapolation of *Moby-Dick*'s speculative and systematic dimensions through a close reading of chapter 32, "Cetology." See his "The Scene of Writing: A Deferred Outset," in *Glyph 1,* ed. Samuel Weber and Henry Sussman (Baltimore: Johns Hopkins University Press, 1977), 150–71.

5. Mary Shelley, *Frankenstein,* ed. Maurice Hindle (London: Penguin, 1987), 59–61, 69–70, 85, 103, 118–19, 137–41, 143, 243, 245–47, 254–57, 261.

6. E. T. A. Hoffmann, "Mademoiselle de Scudéry," in *Tales of E. T. A. Hoffmann,* trans. Leonard J. Kent and Elizabeth C. Knight (Chicago: University of Chicago Press, 1969), 188; Edgar Allen Poe, "Hop-Frog," in *Tales of Mystery and the Imagination* (London: Everyman's Library, 1968), 235–36.

7. Virginia Woolf, *The Waves* (New York: Harcourt Brace Jovanovich, 1978), 145, 251, 256.

8. Jorge Luis Borges, "The Garden of Forking Paths," in *Ficciones* (New York: Grove, 1962), 96.

9. I am referring here to the scenario that Irwin finds pivotal to nineteenth-century American literature in which a fictive protagonist, fulfilling the role of an "internalized" narrator or scribe, undergoes a symbolic death as a prelude to and permission for disclosing his tale. See John T. Irwin, *American Hieroglyphics: The Symbol of the Egyptian Hieroglyphics in the American Renaissance* (New Haven: Yale University Press, 1980), 66–73, 183–95, 284–87, 303–12, 346–49.

10. Herman Melville, *Pierre,* The Northwestern-Newberry Edition, ed. Harrison Hayford, Hershel Parher, and G. Thomas Tanselle (Evanston and Chicago: Northwestern University Press and the Newberry Library, 1971), henceforth abbreviated *P.*

11. D. W. Winnicott, "The Theory of the Parent-Infant Relationship," in *Essential Papers on Object Relations,* 249, 251.

12. For a study of the Kantian sublime in Melville treating the interface between sublimity and gender in *Pierre* more extensively than this one, see Nancy Fredricks, *Melville's Art of Democracy* (Athens: University of Georgia Press, 1995), 14–26, 86–97, 115–31.

13. E. T. A. Hoffmann, *Tales of E. T. A. Hoffmann,* 124–25.

14. My colleague, James H. Bunn, writes compellingly of structures deriving from the physical world that also exert a profound impact on culture, among them the s-curve. This work is forthcoming.

15. Walter Benjamin, in his overview of the dual textual and subjective traumas presiding over twentieth-century culture in "On Some Motifs in Baudelaire," observes the spasmodic behavior, indicative of what he calls shock, that Baudelaire and certain of his contemporaries attributed to each other. See Walter Benjamin, *Illuminations,* trans. Harry Zohn (New York: Schocken, 1969), 162–65.

16. On the belatedness of the subject to comprehend a law he or she is fated to trespass, see Jacques Lacan, *The Four Fundamental Concepts of Psycho-Analysis,* trans. Alan Sheridan (New York: W. W. Norton, 1978), 20, 22, 24–25, 34–36, 45, 130–31, 165, 169, 193, 204.

17. G. W. F. Hegel, *Phenomenology of Spirit,* trans. A. V. Miller (New York: Oxford University Press, 1977), 96–98.

18. Jacques Derrida, "Plato's Pharmacy," in *Dissemination,* trans. Barbara Johnson (Chicago: University of Chicago Press, 1981), 70, 120, 125, 136, 147, 149–52.

19. "Prison-house of language" is a phrase that gave Fredric Jameson the title for an important book. See his *The Prison-House of Language* (Princeton: Princeton University Press, 1972).

20. Franz Kafka, "Description of a Struggle," in *The Complete Stories,* 33.

21. Gustave Flaubert, *Madame Bovary,* trans. Paul de Man, Norton Critical Edition (New York: W. W. Norton, 1965), 211.

22. Flaubert's odd dictum, "Mme. Bovary is myself," is quoted by Henri Troyat in *Flaubert,* trans. Joan Pinkham (New York: Viking, 1992), 139.

Conclusion

1. Jacques Lacan, *The Seminar of Jacques Lacan: Book III: The Psychoses 1955–56,* trans. Russell Grigg (New York: W. W. Norton, 1993), 16–43, 59–101, 117–29; David B. Allison et al., eds., *Psychosis and Identity: Toward a Post-Analytic View of the Schreber Case* (Albany: SUNY Press, 1988), 18–29, 43–60, 102–203; Silvano Arieti, *Interpretation of Schizophrenia* (New York: Basic Books, 1974), 75–78, 93, 101–23, 140–45.

2. Franz Kafka, *Diaries: 1914–23,* ed. Max Brod (New York: Schocken, 1965), 233.

INDEX

In this index an "f" after a number indicates a separate reference on the next page, and an "ff" indicates separate references on the next two pages. A continuous discussion over two or more pages is indicated by a span of page numbers, e.g., "57–59." *Passim* is used for a cluster of references in close but not consecutive sequence.

Adorno, Theodor, 5
Aesthetic contract, 4f, 15, 38, 135, 137, 152, 161f, 165–77, 183, 186, 190, 287; defined, 38, 165f, 174f
Aesthetics, 13f, 80, 101f, 106, 133–40 *passim*, 144, 147, 153, 161, 165–77, 187, 214, 226, 242, 260, 277
Africanus, Constantinus, 105
Albers, Joseph, 172, 284
Alighieri, Dante, 275
Allegory, 5, 30, 101–6 *passim*, 112, 116f, 124, 133, 169, 225, 244, 271, 277
American Revolution, 155, 263f
Antinomics, 143f
Aphorisms, 144, 172
Architecture, 128, 144, 172, 221–22, 261, 276, 284
Aristotle, 64, 101, 103, 105
Artaud, Antonin, 42
Artist, the, 19, 37f, 66, 69f, 135ff, 140, 150, 152, 155f, 159–62, 175, 183, 186, 214, 232, 253, 268–71, 275, 279, 287
Art-religion, secular, 37, 54, 70, 135, 144, 150ff, 236, 278
Augustine, Saint, 64
Austin, John, 291

Bakhtin, Mikhail Mikhailovich, 173, 302
Barnes, Djuna, 169

Barthes, Roland, 4, 169, 172, 225
Baudelaire, Charles, 3, 42
Beauty, 139–41 *passim*, 143–50
Beckett, Samuel, 42, 172, 201
Behaviorism, 180–81, 190, 303
Benjamin, Walter, 1, 3, 25, 42, 57, 68, 74f, 101–12, 122, 129, 132, 169, 174, 178, 228, 273f, 298, 302, 311; "On Some Motifs in Baudelaire," 105; *The Origin of German Tragic Drama*, 74f, 101–12, 129, 132
Berg, Alban, 172
Berkeley, George, Bishop, 1, 70, 82f, 86f, 90, 92–100, 297–98
Bernhard, Thomas, 201
Bhabha, Homi, 307
Bipolarity, 16–18, 33, 48–50, 58, 68–70 *passim*, 74, 84, 89, 94, 98, 104, 123, 176, 190, 204, 212, 216, 245
Bishop, Morris, 32, 294
Blake, William, 217, 225
Blanchot, Maurice, 3, 42, 173, 201, 246
Borderline: psychological, 16, 36, 74, 157f, 172; and creativity, 200; personality, 196–98, 306
Borges, Jorge Luis, 3, 9, 146, 173, 204, 307, 309
Bosch, Hieronymus, 124
Botticelli, Sandro, 30
Braque, Georges, 167, 284

Library of Congress Cataloging-in-Publication Data
Sussman, Henry.
The aesthetic contract : statutes of art and intellectual work in modernity /
Henry Sussman.
p.   cm.
Includes bibliographical references and index.
ISBN 0-8047-2842-9 (cloth : alk. paper). — ISBN 0-8047-2843-7 (pbk. : alk. paper)
I. Aesthetics, Modern.   2. Arts, Modern—Philosophy.   I. Title.
BH151.S97   1997
111'.85—dc21   97-12245
                                                                                  CIP

This book is printed on acid-free, recycled paper.
Original printing 1997
Last figure below indicates year of this printing:

06   05   04   03   02   01   00   99   98   97